D0205873

DIVERGENT
PATHS

DIVERGENT PATHS

THE ACADEMY AND THE JUDICIARY

Richard A. Posner

Harvard University Press

Cambridge, Massachusetts
London, England

2016

Copyright © 2016 by the President and Fellows of Harvard College

ALL RIGHTS RESERVED

Printed in the United States of America

First printing

Library of Congress Cataloging-in-Publication Data

Posner, Richard A., author.

Divergent paths : the academy and the judiciary / Richard A. Posner.

pages cm

Includes index.

ISBN 978-0-674-28603-0 (alk. paper)

1. Judicial process—United States.   2. Judges—Training of—United States.

3. Law—Study and teaching—United States.   I. Title.

KF8775.P67 2016

347.73′5—dc23

2015010906

For Charlene

CONTENTS

PREFACE

When I became a judge of the U.S. Court of Appeals for the Seventh Circuit (the Seventh Circuit's jurisdiction encompasses Illinois, Indiana, and Wisconsin) in December 1981, at the age of forty-two, with no previous judicial experience except for my clerkship for Justice Brennan in the Supreme Court's 1962 term, it didn't occur to me to seek the advice of my new colleagues as to how to be a federal appellate judge. I had my own ideas, some heretical—such as writing all my own judicial opinions and continuing to do as much academic research and writing as I had done as a full-time academic. But I didn't devote a great deal of thought to the practices of other judges or to the federal judiciary as a whole.

My attitude changed, many years later—thirty years later, in fact—when I read, first in draft and later in the published version (for which I wrote the Foreword), David Dorsen's biography of Judge Henry Friendly.[1] I had known Friendly personally and I knew that he was a great judge, but reading about his skills and accomplishments made me want to emulate him, so far as I could. To this end I decided to allocate more of my time to my judicial work and less to academic work than I had been doing. When I did this I discovered that I'd been complacent about the judiciary and specifically about the role and performance of the federal judiciary. I had taken too much for granted. I had missed a certain staleness in the current judicial culture—a tendency of judges to recite propositions of doubtful veracity

---

1. David M. Dorsen, *Henry Friendly: Greatest Judge of His Era* (2012).

just because they had been repeated before; a lack of curiosity and imagination; a lack of clarity and candor; and a weak sense of fact. Exacerbating these deficiencies was the increased technical complexity of many federal cases as a result of the growing role of science and technology in American society.[2] Coping with that complexity has become a major challenge to the judiciary.

Institutions whether public or private don't look the same from the outside as from the inside. To outsiders they present a smooth, untroubled countenance—self-assured, impervious. The insiders, who create the façade, know (many of them) better; for all institutions are troubled to a greater or lesser extent. That is true of the federal judiciary. Judges have had roughly two thousand years of experience in trying, with considerable success, to awe the laity, project a self-congratulatory aura, conceal their failures and inadequacies. As an insider I know how to pull back the curtain, and I think it will actually help the institution for me to do so. I don't intend to go overboard with my criticisms. The federal judiciary has undoubted strengths. For example, with rare exceptions the judges comply with the Aristotelian duty to do "corrective justice," which is often misunderstood to mean a duty to ensure that victims of wrongful acts are compensated but which really means impartiality—in the words of the federal judicial oath, that the judge shall decide cases "without respect to persons" (that is, without regard to the social status or other personal characteristics, attractive or unattractive, of a litigant or lawyer). Judges also deal well with routine litigation. And there have been and are outstanding federal judges who have made substantial contributions to American law.

But there is a dark side. I don't think we judges are as good as we should be at preventing hunch and ideology and personal experiences of various sorts—and resulting intense emotions and deeply felt be-

---

2. A theme of my book *Reflections on Judging* (2013).

liefs—from influencing our decisions unduly. (I say "unduly" because, as I'll be arguing primarily in Chapter 2, elements of human thought and feeling have a legitimate and not merely an inevitable role in judicial decision making.) Troublesome too is the fact that often we judges don't know enough about a case to decide it sensibly because often all we know is what the lawyers tell us, and that can be very little. And when we don't know enough about a case to decide it sensibly we necessarily fall back on how we "feel" about it, and our feelings can lead us astray. We tend also to be overly committed to adversary procedure, excessively passive, enmeshed in outworn traditions, timid about change, and (some of us) self-satisfied.

So there is much to criticize in the judicial profession and therefore much room for improvement. But where is the improvement to come from? A possibility that appeals to me as a former law professor is the law schools. Law professors write a great deal about the judiciary—and mainly the federal judiciary. But there is a question how well informed about, or helpful to, the judiciary that writing is. At present, not very, I have discovered. Not that I'm inclined to apply Brendan Behan's comment about film critics to law professors by comparing the professors (relative to judges) to "eunuchs in a harem; they know how it's done, they've seen it done every day, but they are unable to do it themselves." Some judges might think the comparison apt, however. They would acknowledge that law professors write illuminatingly about legal doctrine but argue that the professors' criticisms of judicial decisions tend to be obtuse, because the professors don't understand the constraints that judges labor under. In particular they don't grasp the implications of the fact that a judge *has* to decide a case presented to him (provided that it's within his jurisdiction) even if he has no clear idea of what the decision should be. He can't wait, as a law professor contemplating writing a law review article can, for inspiration to strike.

Of course this criticism of law professors by judges is to an extent self-serving. But there really is a gulf between these two branches of the legal profession, and the gulf has been growing. My goals in this book are to explain and document the separation, identify the areas in which federal judicial performance is deficient, and explain what the law schools can do to remedy, or more realistically to ameliorate, these deficiencies. I shall thus be both criticizing the judiciary—fundamentally for what I call a "stale judicial culture"—and criticizing the academy for not doing more to try to remedy the judiciary's deficiencies.

This is not an ignored subject but it has not received the sustained attention that it deserves. My hope is that if my own treatment of it is flawed—it is surely incomplete—the book will encourage others to explore it in greater depth. It is incomplete in the further sense that it is limited to the *federal* judiciary, which handles only about 10 percent of the cases filed in American courts, and whose problems are on the whole less serious than those of the state and local courts. And implicitly I limit my attention to the elite law schools and therefore to the elite law students, for they are most likely to become federal law clerks and leading federal practitioners. Just as the problems of the federal courts are less grave than those of other American courts, so the problems of the elite law schools and their students and graduates are less grave than those of the nonelite law schools and their students and graduates; those law schools are shrinking as their graduates find it increasingly difficult to obtain good legal jobs, which has the effect of discouraging enrollment. But I don't know enough about the nonfederal judiciary and the nonelite academy to be able to write authoritatively about them, and, if I did, still it would make the book unwieldy to try to encompass these far larger chunks of the American legal system than those that I examine.

A brief note on the book's structure. The gap between the academy and the judiciary is explained in the Introduction. The deficiencies of the judiciary that I would like to see the academy do more to address—in scholarship, teaching, and continuing judicial education (teaching judges as distinct from teaching law students)—are the subject of Part One. My specific suggestions for what the academy might do to ameliorate those deficiencies are the subject of Part Two.

Although this is not a very long book as books about law go, it covers a lot of ground and I thought it would help the reader if I consigned some of my material to appendices. There are four. Appendix A (to the Introduction) amplifies the data presented in the Introduction concerning the changing composition of law school faculties—the supplanting of law professors who have practical grounding and interests by theoreticians. Appendix B (to Chapter 2) discusses a striking example of judges failing to look outside the briefs and record for clues to understanding a case. Appendix C (also to Chapter 2) examines a related but more serious problem: judges' tendency to remain wedded to manifestly dysfunctional practices that they could change at any time. Appendix D (to Chapter 6, the last chapter of Part Two) is a reminder list of the numerous problems of the federal judiciary identified in Part One and of my suggestions in Part Two for how the legal academy might provide at least partial solutions.

I have debts of gratitude to a large number of persons for helping me with this project. I thank Adam Chilton, Tom Ginsburg, Dennis Hutchinson, Marin Levy, Anne Mullins, Richard Revesz, Geoffrey Stone, Lior Strahilevitz, and Diane Wood for discussing all or parts of the subject matter of this book with me. And for comments on earlier drafts of the manuscript I thank Hutchinson, Levy, Mullins, Strahilevitz, and Stone, together with Michael Aronson, Paul Carrington, Colleen Chien, William Domnarski, Sean Driscoll, Steven Eisman, Lee Epstein, Collins Fitzpatrick, Barry Friedman, Jacob Goldin, Tom Gorman, David Greenwald, Mitu Gulati, Robert Hochman, John Karin, Brian Leiter, Jonathan Masur, Michael McConnell, Larry Piersol, Charlene Posner, Eric Posner, Mary Schnoor, Eric Segall, Steven Winter, and two anonymous readers for Harvard University Press. Professor Strahilevitz's two rounds of extensive and invariably helpful comments on the manuscript deserve a special acknowledgment, as do the extensive and penetrating comments of Professor Stone and the careful reading and helpful comments by Professors Segall and Winter. Finally I thank Rajan Aggarwal, Kali Frampton, Adina Goldstein, Samuel Jahangir, Michael Kenstowicz, Xingxing Li, Max Looper, David Suska, and Patrick Wu for research assistance and cite checking, without which the completion of the book would have been significantly delayed. Ms. Frampton, with assistance from Mr. Wu, is responsible for Appendix A.

DIVERGENT
PATHS

INTRODUCTION:
A TROUBLED RELATIONSHIP

Questo tuo grido farà come vento,
che le più alte cime piu percuote;
e ciò non fa d'onor poco argomento.   —*Paradiso* xvii, ll. 133–135

Two branches of one profession divided by their own insularity

—DENNIS J. HUTCHINSON

RECENTLY I ASKED a lawyer friend of mine—a very successful litigator (Robert Hochman of Sidley Austin LLP, a former law clerk of mine and then of Justice Breyer)—how he would answer a prospective client who said to him: "What are my chances of prevailing in this lawsuit [prospective or actual] that I am asking you to represent me in?" He said he would answer as follows: "The way to approach the question is to set aside all the legal technicalities and ask: if this were a dispute submitted for resolution to a wise man who was not law-trained, but who simply applied his moral intuitions, would he resolve the dispute in your favor or your opponent's? His suggested resolution might be blocked by some legal technicality—statutory language, precedents, what have you—but in all likelihood we would be able to get around such obstacles." (An alternative formulation he suggested was: the lawyer's "position should be the one that would prevail if resort to traditional legal materials were disallowed.")

I think this is the right approach. Most judges evaluate cases in a holistic, intuitive manner, reaching a tentative conclusion that they then subject to technical legal analysis. But do judges realize that this is what they're doing? Do law professors realize that that's what judges are doing? Do the professors try to make their students understand how judges decide cases? Do they equip their students to become judicial law clerks? These are the kind of questions on which I focus in this book.

Three major branches of the legal profession are concerned with, and influence, the operation of the court system. One of course is the judiciary itself. Another consists of lawyers who practice in the courts. A third is the legal academy—the law schools. Their role in legal education and legal research is important to the judiciary, but, I shall argue, not as important as it should be. The professoriate is neglecting the judiciary, with the exception of the Supreme Court—the court least likely to pay attention to academic critique though perhaps most in need of reform, as I'll be suggesting at various points in this book.

Many lawyers outside these three branches of the profession, such as those who serve in or work for legislatures, are also concerned with the courts, but I ignore them in order to keep this book within a manageable length. And I focus primarily on the federal courts of appeals and on the Supreme Court, with only occasional mention of the district courts, which are trial courts. The courts of appeals (the layer between the district courts and the Supreme Court) are the courts I know best—I've been a judge of one of them for thirty-four years, though I also handle litigation at the trial level as a volunteer in district courts from time to time and so have some first-hand familiarity with those courts, as well as the second-hand familiarity with them that one acquires from hearing appeals from their decisions. I have a nodding acquaintance with state courts, largely because of the diversity, bankruptcy, and supplemental jurisdictions of the federal courts, which require federal judges to decide issues of state law; but in this book I do not discuss the state courts themselves.

The academy has both a direct and an indirect influence on courts. Law schools give future judges, and the future lawyers who will appear before them, their initial training in the law—indeed their only formal training in it. The Federal Judicial Center, an arm of the federal judiciary, does some training of judges, mainly district judges. The Center is not an academic institution, but it is enough like one that I discuss its role in research and training (see Chapter 6). The legal academy supplies a few professors to the judiciary: me for example, and four Justices of the current Supreme Court, though all of them had left the academy before their appointment to the Court, Elena Kagan to become Solicitor General and the others to become federal court of appeals judges. (A fifth Justice, Anthony Kennedy, taught part-time at a law school for a number of years before his appointment to the Supreme Court.)

Law professors don't just teach, of course. They're scholars as well as teachers and they analyze, often disagreeing with, judicial decisions. They also attack and defend philosophies of adjudication—originalism and other formalist approaches at one end of the current spectrum, legal pragmatism at the other end—and advocate legal reforms, both substantive and procedural. Increasingly law school faculties cultivate knowledge of fields outside of law but pertinent to it, including economics, psychology, statistics, computer science, history, philosophy, biology, and literature. They make their knowledge available to lawyers and judges, as well as to students, in books and articles and sometimes in programs of continuing legal education, including continuing judicial education. In part because of the increased influence of wealthy donors on law schools as on other institutions of higher learning, the emphasis in extralegal teaching and scholarship in law schools is on fields of social science, such as economics (and a branch of economics—finance—now regarded as virtually a separate field), that bear directly on business. Some graduates of law schools have become wealthy practitioners of corporate law or other fields of business law, and some have become big businessmen in their own right.

The academy supplies the judges with their law clerks, usually just graduated from law school and hired for just one year, though a nontrivial fraction of federal judges have one or more career law clerks, and some judges who hire one-year law clerks take them from practice rather than fresh out of law school. Most judges rely heavily on their clerks not only for research but also for the drafting of the judge's judicial opinions—indeed the number of federal judges who write their own opinions, as distinct from editing (sometimes quite lightly) law clerks' opinion drafts, can probably be numbered on the fingers of two hands. But some judges who mainly work from their clerks' drafts do draft some opinions themselves.

Federal judges don't rely only on *their* law clerks for staff assistance with drafting. Each federal court of appeals has a pool of law clerks, usually called "staff attorneys," hired by administrative personnel of the court rather than by the judges, not assigned (except on an ad hoc basis) to particular judges, and employed mainly in handling motions and pro se appeals (appeals in which the plaintiff is representing himself rather than being represented by a lawyer). They may also handle some counseled cases considered insufficiently difficult or important to warrant oral argument. And in my court and I imagine in other courts of appeals as well, staff attorneys advise judges on the disposition of motions, prepare bench memos that are shared among the judges assigned to a case, and also prepare drafts of dispositive orders based on their bench memos in some cases that though orally argued present only a single issue and that usually a simple one. Some nonargued cases are handled by the judges' law clerks rather than by staff attorneys, however, often cases that had originally been thought difficult or important enough to warrant oral argument but that later had been removed from the oral-argument calendar by a screening panel of judges or by the judges who had been scheduled to hear the case but who upon reading the briefs or a bench memo decided it didn't merit oral argument.

The role that the legal academy plays, albeit indirectly, in the court system is large. It trains the judges' future law clerks. It provides—because law professors are scholars as well as teachers—informed critique of legal doctrines. (I use "critique" in its classic sense as disciplined analysis; nowadays it is commonly used as a synonym for "criticism," which is a waste of the word.) Economic analysis of law, for example—a joint project of law professors and economists but centered in the law schools—has had a transformative effect on a number of fields of law, not just antitrust law and other fields of economic regulation, though the effect has been greatest in those fields.[1] They are the fields to which (with the notable exception of Bentham's late eighteenth-century utilitarian analysis of criminal law and Robert Lee Hale's interesting though largely forgotten applications of economics to a variety of fields of law in the 1920s through 1940s) economics was first applied.

But the role of the academy in relation to the judiciary is smaller than it should be, in part because it is smaller than it used to be, as I pointed out in Chapter 8 ("Judges Are Not Law Professors") of my book *How Judges Think,* published eight years ago. I was not the first to point this out; the credit for that belongs to Judge Harry Edwards.[2] As an indirect consequence of the fact that law faculties have become increasingly interdisciplinary, and the corollary that law professors in-

---

1. On the scope of this subdiscipline, see, for example, *Research Handbook on Economic Models of Law* (Thomas J. Micheli and Matthew J. Baker eds. 2013), and my treatise *Economic Analysis of Law* (9th ed. 2014).
2. See Harry T. Edwards, "The Growing Disjunction between Legal Education and the Legal Profession," 91 *Michigan Law Review* 34, 48–50 (1992). Judge Edwards is a judge of the U.S. Court of Appeals for the District of Columbia Circuit.

creasingly are specialized, professors both as teachers and as scholars are providing less information and fewer insights helpful to judges, and probably conveying less understanding of the judiciary to law students, than used to be the case. The professoriate also is failing fully to recognize and address, whether in teaching or in academic research, the deficiencies of the federal judiciary that I'll be describing in subsequent chapters.

These are not new insights and concerns; what is new in this book is, in Part One, a fuller account of where the judiciary needs help and in Part Two an effort at constructive suggestions for reforms of legal education and scholarship that would give the judiciary some of the help it needs.

Critical analysis of judicial doctrine, though a traditional strength of law schools, is dwindling as a result of the schools' growing interdisciplinary emphasis. Especially being neglected is critical analysis of the personnel who apply doctrine to new cases, which is to say the judges. The tendency of the law schools is to treat judges, with the exception of Supreme Court Justices—who hold a fascination for many law professors that is unrelated to the quality or even importance of the Court—as black boxes. Evidence and argument go in, a decision eventually comes out, but no one seems to know, or to be telling, what happens in between. This may be why most law professors, though not reluctant to criticize judicial decisions, shrink from publicly criticizing living judges and the present-day judicial process more broadly—though another reason may be fear of a judge's retaliation against an academic critic by refusing to hire law clerks from the critic's school, or speak at the school, or judge a moot court there.

It's true that in the classroom, in books and articles, in amicus curiae briefs and increasingly in blogs, law professors are quick to register disagreement with particular judicial decisions, with particular doctrines and methodologies, and sometimes with the judges who habitually produce those decisions or invoke those doctrines. Criticism can be implicit in disagreement, yet is likely to elude notice when the disagreement is between lawyers, or between lawyers and judges, or between judges. The reason is the adversary nature of American law. Disagreement and debate are fundamental to it, just as rivalry is fundamental to professional sports. Neither the members of the general public, nor the politicians (who are interested in the judiciary, though for reasons having much more to do with the politicians' political aims and needs than with the quality of judicial appointments), pay attention to law professors' disagreement with judges.

More surprising, neither do the judges. There are several reasons.[3] One, already noted, is the muted character of professors' criticisms. Another is that most federal judges are generalists, while most legal academics are specialists writing for other specialists—at first for the members of hiring and tenure committees, then for the other academics in their particular field of law, though some write also or instead to be read by practitioners who specialize in that field.[4] It might

---

3. See "Judges Are Not Law Professors," Chapter 8 of my book *How Judges Think* (2008), especially pp. 204–219, and my more recent book *Reflections on Judging* (2013), 337–344, for further discussion of topics covered in this chapter and elsewhere in this book—not only the increased gap between the judicial and professorial outlooks (the subject of this introductory chapter) but also judicial deficiencies and how the legal academy could do more to alleviate them.

4. There are exceptions, primarily bankruptcy judges, judges of the U.S. Tax Court, and judges of the U.S. Court of Appeals for the Federal Circuit. I should add that bankruptcy and tax court judges, along with magistrate judges (who are in effect auxiliary district judges) and administrative law judges and other judicial officers in federal administrative agencies, though they are responsible federal judicial officers, are not appointed pursuant to Article III, the judicial article of the Constitution. Article III requires presidential appointment and Senate confirmation of federal judges and confers lifetime tenure on them. Supreme Court Justices, court of appeals judges (intermediate appellate judges), and district judges (trial judges) are the only judges appointed under Article III.

seem that since any legal case is bound to fall within a specialized area of law (sometimes more than one such area), criticisms by academic specialists would get through to the judges. But not if academics are uninterested in communicating with judges—if they don't think that judges will pay any attention to them and therefore they'll have to find their audience elsewhere—or can't communicate effectively because they don't know how much the judges can understand and absorb. And as legal academia has expanded—between 1998 and 2008 alone the average size of law school faculties increased by 40 percent—law professors have found a large enough audience within their own ranks not to want to spend time trying to communicate with judges without much hope of succeeding.[5] The expansion of law school faculties has also resulted in a greater variety of law school courses and increased faculty specialization, further widening the gap between the academy and the judiciary—between specialists and generalists.

The process is Darwinian. In nature each animal species must find a niche for itself, critically including a food that it can find and eat without encountering destructive competition from another species. In the academy each species of professor must find an academic niche in which he can avoid destructive competition from other professors. The tax professors occupy one niche, the contract professors another, and so on. The "list serve"—a list of email addresses of persons, often

5. "Law School Faculties 40% Larger Than 10 Years Ago," *National Jurist,* March 9, 2010, www.nationaljurist.com/content/law-school-faculties-40-larger-10-years -ago. This may be somewhat misleading, as part of the increase is attributable to giving part-time teaching duties to librarians and other members of the administrative staffs of the law schools. Still, as shown below in Appendix A, the long-term increase in full-time faculty at leading law schools has been very large, greatly exceeding increases in the number of students.

academics, sharing an interest such as, in the case of tax professors, tax law—vastly increases the number and size of communities of legal academics. The subscribers to a list serve become colleagues in cyberspace, forming a substantial academic subgroup that fills a niche in academic ecology. Their need to communicate with persons outside of their niche, such as judges, like the need of a squirrel to learn to eat dandelions as well as nuts, is minimized.

It's not just the increase in the number of law professors that in the ways I've noted has impeded professorial communication with judges. It is also the change—though a change related to the increase in the size of law school faculties—in the background and career goals of the modern law professor. Beginning with the emergence and growth of economic analysis of law in the 1960s and 1970s, and the parallel emergence and growth of other interdisciplinary fields of legal scholarship—such as critical legal studies, law and philosophy, feminist law, critical race theory, law and society, and law and literature—academic law increasingly has attracted refugees from other disciplines. These disciplines include economics, philosophy, psychology, history, literature, race or gender studies, and, increasingly, biology, physics, finance, and electrical engineering (including computer science). All these are fields in which there is intense competition for academic jobs and in which, with the principal exceptions of economics, finance, and engineering, most of the jobs are poorly paid. Whether or not they have advanced degrees, many of these refugees have a natural inclination to base their legal teaching and writing on insights gleaned by them in the disciplines that were their first choice. Often indeed they have little interest in the traditional topics and methods of academic legal inquiry. The law school is thus the safe berth for the philosopher *manqué,* the historian *manqué,* and so on.

The fields that I've mentioned are not new, and so a mystery remains why their acolytes have since the 1960s been moving in force into academic law. I am guessing that the reason is that those fields were advancing rapidly, and academic law, as traditionally practiced, was not. This observation is related to a general theme of this book, which is the tendency of members of all branches of the legal profession to look behind themselves at every step, as if the heads of lawyers and judges faced backward and so their eyes were fixed on what was receding. "Originalism" is just the most extreme manifestation of a belief that every new case is ruled by something done in the past, whether an enactment of some sort or a judicial precedent. Law's lack of progressivity provided a rich field for invasion by practitioners of other disciplines. The invasion in turn fostered insecurity on the part of the traditional law professors and encouraged a law school faculty culture of intellectual pretension. We are seeing the "Ph.Deification" of law school faculties.

As a result of the increased if not always genuine or productive intellectuality of academic law—its love of theory—especially at the elite law schools (of which the practical definition is the law schools that rank highest in *U.S. News & World Report*'s ranking of law schools and as a result draw the best students), many faculty members—often the most illustrious—have little experience in the practice of law. They will have entered law school after postgraduate study in another field and become tenure-track law faculty after a one-year clerkship, or maybe two or even three one-year clerkships, and, following the clerkship(s), two or three years as a research or teaching fellow. As part of a community of scholars with only a weak identification with the practicing legal profession, these "law and" scholars may have difficulty conveying to the students a feel for how the legal system actually operates and producing scholarship accessible by and helpful to the judiciary. And given the common academic failing known as "what I don't know is not knowledge," these theoretical scholars may deride applicants for law school teaching positions who have a rich background of practical experience in law. The hiring committee at one prominent law school is said to have turned down an applicant who had such a background, remarking: "He's ruined for theory."

Professionals—it doesn't matter the profession—love jargon. Some need jargon, in the sense of a specialized vocabulary. Law does not, yet is jargon-ridden to a quite horrible extent. The judges understand law jargon, but much of the jargon employed by interdisciplinary law professors will have come from another field, and this will trip up the judge-reader. Moreover, judges' accessibility even to conventional legal-doctrinal scholarship is impeded by the fact that the student-edited law reviews remain the principal venue of such scholarship. Law review editors are not well equipped to evaluate scholarship, and they have an unfortunate proclivity for accepting overlong articles dense with footnotes—which they are prone to insist that the authors multiply. Authors comply, because they want to be published. Wordiness is a traditional characteristic of lawyers, and law students are methodologically conservative. To them, as neophytes, whatever is commonly done is canonical. If published legal scholarship is verbose, pretentious, obscuranist, the students will consider these badges of eloquence, and most authors will fall in line. But few judges have the patience to wade through long articles clogged with footnotes.

An increasing number of legal academics, it is true, are blogging, and their blogs are more accessible to nonacademics than their scholarly books and articles. But my impression is that judges don't pay much attention to legal blogs. One reason is that many judges are elderly, and uncomfortable with the Internet culture. Also, the law blogs tend to focus on particular cases, and the probability that a given case will relate to a case before a particular judge is small. Having to read a lot of material directly related to their cases, judges don't feel they have time to study judicial opinions, and analyses of those opinions, that will relate to cases of theirs only in the future, if at all. The Internet is a great underutilized resource for the judiciary, but less as a source of legal analysis (though there is plenty of that online as well) than as a source of factual information relating to the activities and institutions that provide the occasions for, and the background of, litigation.

Most law professors used to identify with the legal profession rather than with the academy and believed not without reason that lawyers and judges were a substantial part of their audience. But as law schools have expanded and academic law has become more competitive and more interdisciplinary, the focus has shifted. Some law schools, it is true, make efforts to provide continuing education for judges, often in the form of short seminars (usually just a few days) in a particular field, like antitrust, or economic analysis of law—these seem in fact to be the most popular subjects for such seminars. But the federal judges who attend the seminars, being for the most part generalists, are apt to forget what they learn in them because as generalists they're likely to have only infrequent encounters with the subject matter of a particular seminar that they attended. As a result, for some judges the seminars turn out to be boondoggles or bores rather than serious learning experiences.

As more and more judges fall out of the audience for scholarly books and articles, those books and articles become ever less accessible to judges. Increasingly the scholar's object is to impress other scholars. His field is his world, and it is a world of scholars rather than of legal professionals in general. He teaches students, who are future lawyers, but he does not write for them. Degree-laden intellectuals now dominate current elite law school faculties.

What might seem an antidote to estrangement between the judiciary and the academy is that a number of judges, not all of them former academics, teach part-time in law schools. But I gather from discussion with students who have taken courses at various law schools from judges who had been law professors that most teach the same way they did before they became judges, and, partly because they are part-time, have little interaction with the full-time faculty. This was my experience as a judge teaching part-time in a law school (after having been a full-time law professor), before I began to focus my part-time teaching on judicial behavior.

I come back to the expansion of law faculties as a factor in alienating the judiciary from the academy. The expansion reflects both the increased number of law schools and the increased ratio of faculty to students. Law schools will do almost anything to boost their ranking in *U.S. News & World Report,* which treats faculty-student ratio and number of library books as plus factors in the ranking, though they have little (library books virtually nothing) to do with the quality of legal education.[6]

The increase in the number of law schools has caused a reduction in the average quality of law school graduates and a concomitant reduction in the average quality of the lawyers who practice in the federal courts. And the increased size of law school faculties has resulted in an increased number of the faculty members whom I've termed "refugees" from more competitive or less lucrative fields and who have little interest in the actual judicial process and little ability to contribute to that process or even to the formation of their students as future law clerks and litigators. An essentially mindless expansion in

---

6. See Sam Flanigan and Robert Morse, "Methodology: 2016 Best Law School Rankings—Find Out How U.S. News Ranks Law Schools," March 9, 2015, www.usnews.com/education/best-graduate-schools/top-law-schools/articles/2014/03/10/methodology-2015-best-law-schools-rankings?page=2.

the size of the legal professoriate, though understandable in economic terms—the relentless competitiveness that now characterizes almost all American institutions, including those nominally "not for profit"— is on a collision course with declining law school enrollments as law firm hiring declines.

Another thing complicating the relation between the academy and the judiciary is that federal judges, protected by their secure tenure and by tradition from having to justify their authority, are more secretive than most other officials except those in national security jobs.[7] They are secretive, for example, about what goes on in the post-argument conferences in which they discuss and vote (tentatively, though they rarely change their vote) on the outcome of the cases they've just heard. (Law clerks and other staff are not allowed to attend the conferences, though judges sometimes reveal conference deliberations, and not just the conference's decisions, to their clerks.) This is in sharp contrast to nominally private, even secret, presidential conferences, where midlevel members of the White House staff, and not just high officials, often are present and frequently are willing, even eager, to leak the contents of the conference to influential journalists, such as Bob Woodward.

Mystery is a standard defensive measure of professionals; they don't want to be transparent to the persons or institutions to whom they minister. This is true of physicians and practicing lawyers, but even truer of judges because they don't hustle for clients—they don't *have* clients. Although judicial opinions are public, nowadays most of the opinions at all levels of the federal judiciary are as I've said written

---

7. With some notable exceptions, such as Judge Coffin of the First Circuit, see Frank M. Coffin, *On Appeal: Courts, Lawyering, and Judging* 213–217 (1994), and Judge Goodwin of the Ninth. See Stephen L. Wasby, "Goodwin on Judging," 93 *Oregon Law Review Online* 1 (2014). Coffin is dead and Goodwin retired.

by law clerks, and so function as a screen between the judge and the public. Whoever writes them, the opinions are rhetorical statements rather than efforts at transparent communication, and both analysis and result may involve compromise among the judges of the appellate panel or even of the entire court, resulting in a blurring of focus. Readers of an appellate opinion, including law professors, may therefore have difficulty figuring out what the nominal author of the opinion was thinking—what moved him or her, what the real nub of the case is. Judges very rarely talk about their judicial opinions publicly and almost all of them swear their law clerks to eternal secrecy (upon penalty of professional demise) concerning any information, internal to the judiciary, that the clerks obtain during their clerkship. ("What happens in chambers stays in chambers.")

The judges' particular fear is that because the grounds of their decisions are difficult for the laity to understand, because for want of powerful analytical or empirical tools a judge often must rely on hunch or even prejudice to determine his judicial vote, and because there is an inherent tendency to rivalry among the different branches of government, judges may be thought to be wielding power irresponsibly. The response of the English judiciary to this concern was to forbid judges to deliberate, or to have staff, or even a library; everything they did in their judicial role had to be done in public. This was the rule of "orality." The American response is the opposite, and breeds mistrust.

Not that judicial opinions, or judges' verbal comments during their confirmation hearings, provide the only information obtainable about judges. A substantial academic literature, both theoretical and empirical, drawn mainly from economics, political science, and cognitive psychology, analyzes judicial behavior. The focus is on incentives and constraints, ideology and cognition, and other factors that motivate and channel such behavior.[8] There are also judicial biographies. And judges sometimes talk about themselves in print and most are willing to sit for interviews.

A notable recent contribution to the judicial-interview literature is *Blindfolds Off,* a volume of interviews of thirteen federal district judges, designed to explore influences on their decisions.[9] The editor of the volume is a skillful interviewer and the reader does learn a good deal about judging. But among the things he learns is that he's not going to learn everything: "Judges, even when in the hands as it were of a skillful and persistent and unawed interviewer, are very reluctant to acknowledge a personal element in judging even in the most atypical and challenging case" (for it was cases of that character

8. The literature is extensive; it dates back to at least Cardozo's *The Nature of the Judicial Process* (1921), was a preoccupation of the legal realists and later of the critical legal studies movement, and has continued to command scholarly attention, with emphasis on the political or ideological beliefs that influence judicial behavior. See, for a tiny smattering of this literature, Lawrence Baum, *Judges and Their Audiences: A Perspective on Judicial Behavior* (2006); Frank B. Cross, "Decisionmaking in the U.S. Circuit Courts of Appeals," 91 *California Law Review* 1459 (2003); Frank B. Cross and Emerson H. Tiller, "Judicial Partisanship and Obedience to Legal Doctrine: Whistleblowing on the Federal Courts of Appeals," 107 *Yale Law Journal* 2155 (1998); Tracey E. George, "Developing a Positive Theory of Decisionmaking on U.S. Courts of Appeals," 58 *Ohio State Law Journal* 1635 (1997); Pablo T. Spiller and Rafael Gely, "Congressional Control of Judicial Independence: The Determinants of U.S. Supreme Court Labor-Relations Decision, 1949–1988," 23 *RAND Journal of Economics* 463 (1992). The fullest summary of the literature is in Chapter 2 of Lee Epstein, William M. Landes, and Richard A. Posner, *The Behavior of Federal Judges: A Theoretical and Empirical Study of Rational Choice* (2013). A literature on judges' influence within the judiciary, as proxied by the number of case citations to a given judge's judicial opinions, is illustrated by William M. Landes, Lawrence Lessig, and Michael E. Solimine, "Judicial Influence: A Citation Analysis of Federal Courts of Appeals Judges," 27 *Journal of Legal Studies* 271 (1998).

9. Joel Cohen, *Blindfolds Off: Judges on How They Decide* (2014).

about which the author interviewed his thirteen judges).[10] He goes on to say that "the judges are guarded, and that is one limitation of the interview method of piercing the veil. But another is the problem of self-knowledge. There is no inconsistency in saying that Judge X is utterly sincere in disclaiming any personal element in his decisions yet some of his decisions cannot be explained in formalistic, but only in personal, terms."[11]

The problem to which the interviewer was alluding was that of unconscious priors, which will concern me throughout this book. A prior is a belief or inclination, conscious or (frequently) unconscious, that one brings to an issue before obtaining any evidence concerning it.[12] Remember what one of King Lear's bad daughters perceptively observed about her father: "He hath ever but slenderly known himself." That's not an isolated case; there's nothing unusual about deficiencies of self-knowledge. It is priors, conscious and unconscious, that generate the "moral intuitions" that in the Preface I suggested often determine the outcome of cases not clearly ruled by legal doctrines. The tendency in the literature on judicial behavior has been to emphasize political and ideological priors (these are similar but not identical, as the former could include loyalty to a political party based on habit, nostalgia, or ambition rather than a liberal, conservative, religious, or other ideology) to the virtual exclusion of others. But other

10. Id. at xvii.
11. Id.
12. Bayes's Theorem systematizes the role of priors in decision making. See, for an explanation and legal applications, my book *Frontiers of Legal Theory* 343–386 passim (2001). For an interesting discussion of unconscious ideological priors in federal appellate judging, see Dan Kahan, "'Ideology in' or 'Cultural Cognition of' Judging: What Difference Does It Make?" 92 *Marquette Law Review* 413 (2009). See also Richard A. Posner, *How Judges Think* 67–68 (2006); Jason R. Bent, "Hidden Priors: Toward a Unifying Theory of Systemic Disparate Treatment Law," 91 *Denver University Law Review* 807 (2014).

types of prior, such as temperament, class, race, ethnicity, and personal experience, also influence judicial decisions.

A top-down approach to studying judicial behavior involves developing a model of how judges, given the incentives and constraints created by their jobs, are likely to perform, and testing the predictions of the model with empirical data. That was the approach of the book on judicial behavior that I coauthored with Lee Epstein and William Landes.[13] My approach in the present book is bottom-up rather than top-down. I will give a number of examples of judicial deficiencies, but rather than trying to derive them from a model of judicial behavior I will ask what if anything the law schools might do to help cure them. I see the deficiencies as deriving in the first instance from the American legal culture, which for example reverences adversary procedure, but I shall not attempt to explain the origins of the culture or its hold on judges. I'll generally take the deficiencies for granted and ask not how they could be swept away at a stroke by some dramatic change in the judiciary's fundamental outlook but how they might be lessened by specific measures taken by law schools.

The famously impious artist Marcel Duchamp (he of the "ready-made" sculpture—a Parisian urinal—that he titled "Fountain") said that "art has absolutely no existence as veracity, as truth. People speak of it with great, religious reverence, but I don't see why it is to be so much revered. I'm afraid I'm an agnostic when it comes to art. I don't believe in it with all the mystical trimmings."[14] Replace "art" with "law" in the quotation and one has legal realism in a nutshell: law without mystical trimmings, verbosity, pretense, obscurantism. Most judges are realists, at least to a degree, but don't want to admit it. That law is a rigorous discipline, that it deserves reverence and comes with mystical trimmings, is the conception promoted by the judiciary and

13. See note 8 above.
14. Leonard Shlain, *Leonardo's Brain: Understanding Da Vinci's Creative Genius* 73 (2014).

self-flatteringly believed by many judges. But it is false, and by making the judiciary opaque to the academy creates a barrier between these two branches of the legal profession. It is a barrier that judges don't want law professors to overcome—they don't want to be transparent to professors—and that most law professors are reluctant to try to overcome, lest they cause trouble for their students both by instilling in them a premature, professionally unhelpful cynicism and by undermining the students' chances of landing judicial clerkships, valued as stepping stones to a successful career in legal practice or academia.

A further but minor barrier is that some judges, though I think only a few, don't like modern legal academics a great deal as a class, now that federal judges are paid a good deal less than senior law professors at the elite law schools and have many fewer opportunities than law professors for supplementing their salaries, because of the low cap that federal law imposes on federal judges' nonjudicial earned income (the cap is slightly below thirty thousand dollars a year—but senior judges are exempt from the cap, so far as academic income is concerned). They think law professors have it easy, though in fairness it must be noted that many law professors work harder than many federal judges.

Some judges feel underappreciated, undervalued, under pressure—feel even a little sorry for themselves.[15] They like to think they're doing their best in difficult circumstances, given heavy caseloads, resulting time pressures, the inherent uncertainty of American law, reluctance to respond publicly to criticism, occasional hate mail

---

15. Even the great Holmes succumbed to self-pity when he wrote: "It is very painful, when one spends all the energies of one's soul in trying to do good work, with no thought but that of solving a problem according to the rules by which one is bound, to know that many see sinister motives and would be glad of evidence that one was consciously bad." "Law and the Court," February 15, 1913, in *The Essential Holmes: Selections from the Letter, Speeches, Judicial Opinions, and Other Writings of Oliver Wendell Holmes, Jr.* 145 (Richard A. Posner ed. 1992).

and even threats, and the limited help they get from most of the lawyers who practice before them. The lawyers don't *want* to help the judge—they want to win their case, and if obfuscation will help them do that they'll obfuscate. Judges, if they think about academics at all, tend to feel that, not laboring under the pressures that assail and constraints that bind a judge—enjoying instead leisure, sabbaticals, lucrative consulting opportunities, and specialized knowledge denied to a federal judge—academics are taking cheap shots in criticizing judicial decisions. Judges believe that academics often don't realize what generated, and the judge thinks vindicates, a judicial decision and are unaware of or unsympathetic to the limitations of knowledge that a generalist judge labors under. It's ironic that judges should complain about not being understood by academics, when the judges' secretiveness is one of the causes of that lack of understanding. But complain they do, though usually *sotto voce.*

Judges have carried secretiveness to a remarkable extreme by insisting that their judicial papers (notes of conferences, written communications with colleagues, law clerks' memos, and presumably emails as well) are their private property, which they are free to destroy, winnow, keep in a locked vault, or, if they wish, publish in whole or in part.[16] The idea that judges own their work product (other than

---

16. See, for description and criticism, Kathryn A. Watts, "Judges and Their Papers," 88 *NewYork University Law Review* 1665 (2013). I should have known all this before coming across Professor Watts's article, but I did not. I had assumed that all my judicial papers, including emails, were government property. I think they should be. Not that conversations between judges should be recorded and the tapes made available to the public; that would make judges too guarded in their conversations because it is so easy to be embarrassed by one's oral remarks. But I see no persuasive objection to making public their written (including electronic) judicial communications, memoranda, and the like, maybe with a short lag (certainly until the case to which the judicial records in question pertain is finally resolved). I don't think there would be a significant negative effect on candor, because judges usually are quite guarded anyway in their written com-

their published judicial output) strikes me as absurd. The judges write their notes, the law clerks their memos and draft opinions, using paper and computer screens and files (and often the computers themselves, plus cell phones) supplied free of charge by the government. I have always thought that what is produced in a government job, including my government job, especially when using government resources to produce it, belongs to the government.

One can gain further insight into the tension between the academy and the judiciary by considering the tension between poets, novelists, and other creative writers on the one hand and literary critics, including book reviewers, on the other hand. Creative writers tend to regard critics and reviewers as parasites, utterly dependent on the creative writers for the subject matter of literary criticism yet ungrateful, censorious, hypercritical, frequently nasty. That is not to say that the critics are without influence on the creative writers, but it is indirect. The critics' audience consists of readers, and the critics can and often do affect readers' demand for particular books—the market in other words—which may in turn influence the writers. And likewise law professors can influence judges, even judges who don't read academic books or articles, if the books and articles are read by law clerks and practicing lawyers, who extract insights and arguments that they then feed to the judges. But if the professors don't understand judges well, what is fed to the judges may not be what judges need and want, or at least not all they need and want. Moreover, if the professorial books or articles are aimed at professors, lawyers and law clerks may not understand them well enough to convey their insights to the judges; more precisely, they may not have time to master the wordy

---

munications with other judges and with staff. The present practice—every judge the owner of his papers—is chaotic, and entirely unsatisfactory, as explained by Watts. See also Jill Lepore, "The Great Paper Caper: Someone Swiped Justice Frankfurter's Papers. What Else Has Gone Missing?" *New Yorker,* December 1, 2014, www.newyorker.com/magazine/2014/12/01/great-paper-caper.

and esoteric discourse of today's academic scholarship. (I give an example later.)

But at least judges don't feel the sort of antagonism toward professors that creative writers do toward literary critics. The professors do after all supply the judges with law clerks and also produce scholarly work of value to the judiciary, and they tend to treat judges with kid gloves even when criticizing them. Nevertheless federal judges do think they're the players and the academics are the kibitzers. There are some eighteen thousand law professors in the United States, about half tenured, and fewer than one thousand Article IIII judges, of whom very few were once full-time academics. The judges have been entrusted with real power over people, as academics have not, and this feeds the judicial ego. Fewer federal judges would exchange their job for a professorship than law professors would exchange their job for a federal judgeship, but the probability of an academic's being appointed a federal judge is generally very low.

A related tension between these branches of the profession arises from the fact that academics tackle questions they think they can answer—in other words they choose their targets—while judges perforce make decisions in cases that come at them randomly. The paramount judicial duty is to decide, even if the judge has no idea what the correct decision in a particular case might be. In cases in the "open area"—cases in which the guideposts to deciding (a governing precedent, a clear statutory or constitutional provision) are absent—judges perforce fall back on their priors. Those priors (to extend my previous list of them) derive from politics and ideology, religious upbringing and belief, ambition (for example, for promotion, or for posthumous fame), race and gender, temperament (authoritarian or empathetic), collegiality, personal history, career experiences, and strategic considerations, as in *Bush v. Gore:* the Supreme Court had to decide who had won the 2000 presidential election, and the identity of the winner would affect appointments to the Supreme Court should there be vacancies during the new President's tenure—and there were, and the Justices appointed had very different priors from those of the Justices that a President Gore would have appointed.

Reliance on priors is something academics strive to avoid; judges can't avoid them. They have to decide most of the cases within their jurisdiction (though some they can avoid by one or another doctrine of abstention, or by discretionary control of their docket, as in the Supreme Court), and often they have no persuasive guides to deciding except for their priors.

Another cause of the coolness that some judges feel toward academics is that judges resent criticism (though from any source, not just from law professors). They resent it not just as a personal affront but also as weakening the judiciary vis-à-vis competing branches of government—as fouling the nest occupied by lawyers and law professors as well as by judges. Some judges think, self-servingly to be sure, that any criticism of a judge undermines respect for law. For obvious reasons practicing lawyers hesitate to criticize judges openly; they prefer to fawn. Judges value the deference (insincere though it very often is) that they receive from lawyers, and don't see why law professors—not to mention student authors of law review notes—should criticize judges. The fact that the principal vehicles for academic commentary on the judiciary are the student-run law reviews is another source of judicial irritation with academic criticism. Judges think it an impertinence that what is published about them should be decided, edited, and even written by law students. Of course many law professors also resent student control of the major publication outlets for legal scholarship.

Judges sense that law professors consider themselves superior to judges. Literary critics generally feel inferior to the authors whose works they analyze, but academic critics of judicial opinions feel superior to the opinions' authors. And this for several reasons. One is that the professoriate is more meritocratic than the judiciary—federal judges, after all, are nominated by a politician (the President) and confirmed by other politicians (Senators). Another reason is that the average law professor was a better law student than the average judge had been. And relative intellect to one side, the professoriate is more specialized than the federal judiciary—a law professor will usually teach and write in just one or two fields of law. As a result there are bound to be professors who know more about the issues in any case than the judges assigned to hear and decide it. It's shooting fish in a barrel for a professor to pick a decision that he can criticize persuasively, even if the judge who wrote it is a very good judge.

Neil Duxbury, an English law professor, has done the most thorough analysis of the relations between academy and judiciary in the United States that I know of. He finds that until late in the twentieth century American judges were lavish in their praise of the value to them of academic scholarship.[17] Wisely, he is uncertain how sincere that praise was.[18] Sincerity, candor, are not outstanding characteristics of any branch of the legal profession. But what is certain is that such praise has diminished, to the point where some judges openly regard much academic legal scholarship as navel-gazing.

Duxbury identifies as a watershed event in this shift Judge Edwards's 1992 article that I cited earlier.[19] Returning to the attack two years later Edwards wrote that

> in legal education, the principal problem that I see nowadays is the lack of a healthy *balance* between "impractical" and "practical" teaching and scholarship. By "practical," I mean teaching and scholarship that is both *prescriptive,* in the sense

17. Neil Duxbury, *Jurists and Judges: An Essay on Influence,* ch. 3 (2001).

18. Id. at 29.

19. See note 2 above; and Duxbury, note 17 above, at 43–45. I criticized Judge Edwards's article in my book *Overcoming Law,* 91–100 (1995). But that was twenty years ago and in that interval the academy has changed in ways that have vindicated many of his criticisms.

that it instructs lawyers, judges, and other legal decisionmakers on how to resolve legal issues, and also *doctrinal,* in the sense that it gives due weight to the various constraining sources of law, namely precedents, statutes, and constitutions. The paradigm example of "practical scholarship" is the law treatise. In contrast to the "practical" theory employed by the "practical" scholar, the "impractical" scholar's scholarship consists of "abstract" theory divorced from legal doctrine— that is, divorced from the authoritative sources of law that necessarily constrain the arguments available to a legal professional.[20]

20. "Another 'Postscript' to 'The Growing Disjunction between Legal Education and the Legal Profession,'" 69 *Washington Law Review* 561, 564 (1994) (emphases in original). See also Edwards, "A New Vision for the Legal Profession [Speech]," 72 *New York University Law Review* 567 (1997). In the "Growing Disjunction" article, at pp. 568–569, Edwards lists what he views as the ten worst results from the imbalance he observes between practical and impractical teaching and scholarship in law schools (italics omitted):

    1. Law school hiring favoring "'impractical' scholars";

    2. A dramatic change in course offerings;

    3. Clinical training and ethics receiving "too little attention in time and money";

    4. A "refus[al] to do any real 'cost-benefit' analysis of what is useful in legal education. So we continue to indulge the personal preferences of law teachers as to what to teach. I suspect that if we ever seriously assessed our course offerings, more high quality clinical courses would be taught, and a large number of esoteric 'seminars' would disappear" [the economic travail in legal education is causing such an assessment at many law schools];

    5. That many law professors "hold the profession in disdain, and a number of such professors are assigned to teach basic law courses in which students likely are most impressionable";

    6. The view of some law professors that "what practitioners and judges do [is] 'mundane' and 'dull,' while the obscure work of a new breed of law scholars is viewed as 'richer and more complex.' This attitude is communicated to students, implicitly and explicitly";

Other judges chimed in. For example, the chief judge of New York's highest court wrote that

despite a challenging, important array of issues, despite the mass of material the law reviews generate, and despite diligent searching, I am disappointed not to find more in the law reviews that is of value and pertinence to our cases. Invariably the treatises are better source material, though they have neither the purpose nor the potential of law review articles. Another noticeable change in law reviews is that fewer contributions today are made by judges and practitioners. Most articles are written by full-time academics.[21]

One of Judge Edwards's colleagues on the D.C. Circuit, Laurence Silberman, has remarked that "many of our law reviews are dominated by rather exotic offerings of increasingly out-of-touch faculty members."[22]

Judge Edwards has returned to the fray in a recent article, arguing that

intensely theoretical, philosophical, and empirical scholarship, which is very much in vogue in the legal academy these days, is rarely of interest or use to wide audiences. It is too abstract.

---

7. That "legal scholarship often does not aim to serve the profession";
8. That "'advocacy' seen by judges sometimes is horrendous";
9. The "growing inattention" paid to the "disadvantaged" in society;
10. That "the law schools do not really heed the views of practitioners."

21. Judith S. Kaye, "One Judge's View of Academic Law Review Writing," 39 *Journal of Legal Education* 313, 320 (1989). See also Kaye, "Changing Courts in Changing Times: The Need for a Fresh Look at How Courts are Run," 48 *Hastings Law Journal* 851–853, 866 (1997); Thomas L. Ambro, "Citing Legal Articles in Judicial Opinions: A Sympathetic Antipathy," 80 *American Bankruptcy Law Journal* 547, 549 (2006); Patricia M. Wald, "Teaching the Trade: An Appellate Judge's View of Practice-Oriented Legal Education," 36 *Journal of Legal Education* 35, 42 (1986).
22. *United States v. $639,558*, 955 F.2d 712, 722 (1992) (concurring opinion).

Indeed, it does not even purport to address concrete issues relating to legal practice, procedure, doctrine, legislation, regulation, or enforcement. Yet, many young legal scholars report that they are under pressure to write articles of this sort, and law reviews readily accept their offerings for publication . . . In order for law reviews to be relevant outside the legal academy, they should *balance* abstract articles with scholarly works that are of interest and use to lawyers, legislators, judges and regulators who serve society through legal arguments, decision making, regulatory initiatives, and enforcement actions.[23]

Law professor Pierre Schlag has written that "the academic practice of writing for judges increasingly appears as a degraded art-form used to communicate with persons who are not listening in order to achieve nothing very much whatsoever,"[24] and that "by and large, neither judges nor any other bureaucratic decision makers are listening to academic advice that they are not already prepared to believe."[25]

Against such skeptics Neil Duxbury argues that "the fact that judges quite regularly cite academics indicates (even accounting for the role played by law clerks) that academics must be doing something right, that their work is having an impact."[26] That's not true. A judicial opinion is a rhetorical exercise. The primary aim is to convince other judges, the bar, and indirectly the public (which rarely reads a judicial decision) that the decision is sound, and also to reassure legislators that the judge-author isn't legislating but is merely

23. Harry T. Edwards, "Another Look at Professor Rodell's *Goodbye to Law Reviews*," 100 *Virginia Law Review* 1483, 1484 (2014) (emphasis in original).
24. Schlag, "Writing for Judges," 63 *University of Colorado Law Review* 419, 422 (1992).
25. Schlag, *Laying Down the Law: Mysticism, Fetishism, and the American Legal Mind* 70 (1996).
26. Duxbury, note 17 above, at 45.

applying settled doctrine, using reliable methods of interpretation. Lawyers kowtow to judges, and judges to legislators. Citations, especially to cases, are intended to show that the judge is not innovating; that he is applying law rather than making it; that he is self-restrained rather than "activist." Citations to academic writings are tendered as additional evidence of soundness. As with any rhetorical exercise the reader shouldn't assume that how a conclusion is expressed reveals how it was reached. Nor should he take for granted that a judge has examined and taken to heart and acknowledged reputable sources of evidence that conflict with his view of the case. Remember that almost all judicial opinions are drafted by law clerks nowadays. A clerk is unlikely to write an opinion that casts even slight doubt on the validity of the decision that he's been ordered to defend.

Studies of legal-academic influence on judges most commonly take the form of counting citations in judicial opinions to academic books and articles by law professors (and sometimes by law review editors). But it should be obvious from the preceding paragraph that that's not a meaningful test of academic influence. What is needed (but won't be attempted in this book) is deep study of academic citations in judicial opinions, attempting to determine which of those citations is to a book or article or other academic work that can fairly be inferred to have influenced the judicial decision. As pungently remarked in a recent article, "Law professors should stop trying to write articles that they imagine judges or justices will use to inform a decision in a case . . . Analyses in opinions . . . usually do not rely on the logic or reasoning of cited legal scholarship. More typically, when legal scholarship is used in an opinion, its use is not substantively important to the opinion's legal analysis."[27]

---

27. Derek Simpson and Lee Petherbridge, "An Empirical Study of the Use of Legal Scholarship in Supreme Court Trademark Jurisprudence," 35 *Cardozo Law Review* 931, 972 (2014). Petherbridge, together with another law professor, David Schwartz, has written two long articles on what the authors call the "use" of

A particular object of current judicial disdain of academic writing is constitutional theory, an area of academic study and writing that some judges consider a gossamer covering of the academics' political ideologies, stifling in its abundance, its pretentious obscurantism, its inconclusiveness, its unhelpfulness, its occasional frivolousness. Not that judges, whatever they say, are free from the tug of ideology. Their claim to be free from it is one of the devices by which they try to defend themselves from encroachments by other branches of government: they disingenuously deny being engaged in political competition with those branches.

There's a lot of wheel spinning in constitutional theorizing. Think of the enormous amount of ink that's been spilled in the law reviews over the right to abortion—all wasted. More than forty years after *Roe v. Wade* was decided in an embarrassingly bad opinion by Justice Blackmun, doctrine and reasoning about abortion rights are approximately where they were then. Some judges think abortion is murder,

---

academic scholarship by courts. See Lee Petherbridge and David L. Schwartz, "An Empirical Assessment of the Supreme Court's Use of Legal Scholarship," 106 *Northwestern University Law Review* 995 (2012), and David L. Schwartz and Lee Petherbridge, "The Use of Legal Scholarship by the Federal Courts of Appeals: An Empirical Study," 96 *Cornell Law Review* 1345 (2011). But by "use of" they mean citation to; they do not attempt to measure influence. No doubt, as they suggest, citing academic scholarship must have some "value" to judges or they wouldn't do it or let their clerks do it. But sources of value unrelated to acknowledgment of an intellectual debt are easily imagined. A judge might want to show that he was learned, an intellectual, respectful of the academy, and that the position he was taking in his judicial opinion was supported by academic scholarship. Yet he might not have been influenced, so far as his analysis and conclusion in the case was concerned, by any of the cited academic materials. Chief Judge Diane P. Wood of the Seventh Circuit, in her article "Legal Scholarship for Judges," 124 *Yale Law Journal* 2592 (2015), finds "that the results of legal scholarship seldom appear in judicial opinions," and "that the articles that are cited are those that fall at the lower end of the prestige scale that is tacitly accepted in elite law schools."

others that first-term abortions, at least (plus later abortions in special circumstances), are a fundamental right of pregnant women. There are no analytical methods for closing the gap, because the antagonists argue not from shared premises but from incommensurable political, moral, or (in the abortion case) religious beliefs (or lack thereof), wasting their time telling judges what to think.

I am struck by a recent statement by the well-known constitutional scholar Laurence Tribe. Replying to the question "Why did you pick constitutional law?" he said: "I mean, come on. Who, with a real opportunity to dig into a subject of law would not want that to be constitutional law? It has everything. It has history. It has moral philosophy. The meaning of liberty, of equality, of dignity. It has legal technicalities galore. It has precedent. It involves strategy, dealing with complicated human situations and the people who are affected by law, and the human dynamics of complicated institutions like the U.S. Supreme Court."[28] It has, in fact, too much. It is a gallimaufry. And Tribe left out a key ingredient: politics—which is what makes the academic preoccupation with constitutional law not only excessive but largely futile. In important constitutional cases Justices vote "their own personal policy preferences."[29] What else could they do?

---

28. SCOTUSblog on Camera: Laurence H. Tribe (Part two), www.scotusblog.com/media/scotusblog-on-camera-laurence-h-tribe-part-two/.

29. Geoffrey R. Stone, "The Behavior of Supreme Court Justices When Their Behavior Counts the Most: An Informal Study," *Judicature*, September/October 2013, 82, 89. Professor Stone so characterizes only the Justices whom he describes as "very conservative." He thinks the moderatively conservative, and especially the moderately liberal, Justices (he does not regard any of the current liberal Justices as "very" liberal), are less political. I would call them differently political. Judges can be ideological without occupying a position at either end of the ideological spectrum. Libertarians, for example, tend to be socially liberal but fiscally conservative. They support same-sex marriage and the decriminalization of marijuana but also abolition of the income tax, of minimum wage laws, of zoning laws, and of welfare laws. I return to Stone's article in Chapter 5.

The constitutional provisions that generate litigation are for the most part not only very old, and sometimes obsolete, but also very vague; and as I keep reminding the reader, deciding cases is the judge's primary duty even if he must decide without external guideposts. When Justices do hold back from voting their political preferences, it is mainly, I believe, because of strategic considerations rather than legal analysis: not wanting to seem extreme, not wanting to roil the political waters, not wanting to offend colleagues unnecessarily, not wanting to attract too much criticism or be thought political. So they may sometimes adhere to precedents that they disagree with, being especially reluctant to overrule a precedent that the public strongly supports or that has been widely relied upon. Yet at the same time they may chip away at the precedent, narrowing its reach in preparation for eventually overruling it—that is, for killing it when it is already nearly dead.

Politicization of law is a two-way street: judges and Justices suspect, not without reason, that a good deal of legal scholarship reflects the politics of the scholars. A recent study finds a strong correlation between the political party to which a law professor makes donations and the political character of the professor's scholarship. Scholars who donate to Republican candidates tend to write articles and books that have a conservative slant, while those who donate to Democratic candidates tend to produce scholarship that has the opposite slant.[30] The correlations are strongest in constitutional law, the most politicized field of law.[31] The implication is that a significant amount of le-

---

30. Adam S. Chilton and Eric A. Posner, "An Empirical Study of Political Bias in Legal Scholarship" (University of Chicago Coase-Sandor Institute for Law & Economics, Research Paper No. 696, August 11, 2014). See also Eric Posner, "Do Republican Law Professors Strategically Conceal Their Views?" (August 29, 2014), http://ericposner.com/do-conservative-law-professors-strategically-conceal-their-views/.

31. Chilton and Posner, note 30 above, at 22.

gal scholarship consists of dressing up the scholar's political views in legal language. And sometimes their religious views, which could, and doubtless often do, influence judges' votes in such areas as abortion rights, contraception, and homosexual marriage.

Against this it can be argued that since academics choose their topics and cannot write about everything, it is natural that they should write books and articles that support the positions they care about, but as long as they limit their choices to positions that they can defend on neutral analytical grounds their academic work will not be infected by their ideological predilections. This would be a good argument in a different field. Suppose a biologist is a biblical literalist. He would like the theory of evolution to be disproved, but knows it cannot be, and so he doesn't bother to write an article denying the truth of the theory. But biology is a science, and law isn't. There are few even remotely plausible positions in law that cannot be supported by arguments that at least some law professors will consider respectable.

The study I just mentioned notes the extreme imbalance in modern law faculties in favor of liberals. Roughly half the current federal judges are appointees of Republican Presidents, and therefore mostly conservative. They can't be happy that most articles and books by law professors that have a political slant have a liberal one. But they're not too unhappy, because they can and usually do ignore scholarship that has a political slant they don't like.

Political preferences to one side, judges tend to be skeptical about legal scholarship other than the type, best represented by legal treatises, that many law professors in the leading law schools have since the 1970s considered pedestrian because of the treatises' narrow focus on technical fields such as tax, antitrust, insurance, pension, and commercial law, on procedure and evidence, and on common law fields, and because treatises are largely descriptive and where prescriptive tend to be limited to proposing modest, incremental reforms, which may be sound and useful but are not intellectually exciting. The current legal academic career tends to focus on publishing severely academic, often interdisciplinary, sometimes pie-in-the-sky scholarship of limited interest—sometimes limited intelligibility—to most judges and to the lawyers who appear before them. The aim is to surprise, to demonstrate ingenuity and learning, to draw attention to the author. Feasibility, practicality, are not these academics' forte. Some of their "scholarship" would strike most judges as frivolous, even narcissistic.[32]

Economic analysis of law largely escapes the criticisms leveled at other intellectually ambitious modern legal scholarship because its value in illuminating difficult economic issues in federal cases and sparking legal reform to resolve them is acknowledged. And likewise the newer field of behavioral economics, a cross between economics and psychology.[33] Its practitioners study the psychology of economic behavior broadly understood to embrace a wide range of nonmarket behavior.[34]

Another cause of the estrangement of the academic and judicial subprofessions is the intellectual conservatism of judges, their dislike of legal innovation, their pride. And still another is that judges of courts that have heavy caseloads must, if conscientious, read a great deal of material that is more directly related to their work than academic scholarship is—briefs of course but also motions, issued and

---

32. See, for example, Leo Katz, *Why the Law Is So Perverse* (2011); Laurence H. Tribe, *The Invisible Constitution* (2008).

33. See the massive new treatise *The Oxford Handbook of Behavioral Economics and the Law* (Eyal Zamir and Doron Teichman eds. 2014).

34. See, for example, Doron Teichman, "The Hindsight Bias and the Law in Hindsight," in id. at 354; Russell Covey, "Behavioral Economics and Plea Bargaining," in id. at 643.

circulated opinions, memos and draft opinions by law clerks, parts of trial records. Given those burdens, the difficulty and verbosity (encouraged by law reviews, which as I repeat favor long articles) of much current academic writing make the incremental cost of reading legal scholarship seem excessive to many judges.

The current estrangement between the legal academy and the judiciary is strikingly shown in a recent review, by the distinguished Harvard Law School professor Adrian Vermeule, of the first biography of Judge Henry Friendly. A judge of the Second Circuit between 1959 and his death in 1986, Friendly is generally considered the most distinguished federal court of appeals judge—quite possibly the most distinguished American judge, period—since the death of Learned Hand two years after Friendly's appointment to the same court. Yet about Friendly, Vermeule writes: "It is actually a bit difficult to say what Friendly stood for, or what ideas of general and lasting significance he contributed to law and legal theory . . . The reputations of judges such as Friendly generally have a shorter half-life than the reputations of judges who offer fertile theoretical ideas that can be distilled into formulas, theorems, and pithy aphorisms."[35] Who are those judicial theorists? Vermeule doesn't say. I can't think of a judge of any court in the era since Friendly's appointment to the Second Circuit who would be considered his equal as a judge (he also wrote a number of highly influential articles).

It's been remarked astutely that if Vermeule is right about Friendly, "It may well be because of the peculiar preoccupations of the legal academy, where theoretical sophistication, even in judges, is more

---

35. Adrian Vermeule, "Local Wisdom," in The *Book: An Online Review at the New Republic,* March 22, 2012, www.tnr.com/book/review/henry-friendly-supreme-court-david-dorsen. Cf. Erwin Chemerinsky, "The Inescapability of Constitutional Theory," 80 *University of Chicago Law Review* 935, 937 (2013) ("There is simply no way to avoid a constitutional theory in deciding, or having views on, constitutional issues").

highly valued than good judgment."[36] In other words, a good judge is a professor *manqué*. That isn't true. Friendly's opinions have been called "the gold standard in American appellate judging . . . Friendly's way of judging has a timeless attraction: the predicate mastery of precedent and record; a care alike for doctrine and for equity and for social need; the reasoned and candid explanation of the result; and an awareness always of the comparative competencies and limits of judges."[37]

I had thought when I began this book that another cause of the estrangement between the academy and the judiciary was that the preacademic legal careers of today's law professors were being truncated. Aspirants to a law professorship are expected to have demonstrated an ability and commitment to produce high-quality legal scholarship *before* being considered for a tenure-track appointment— an expectation connected to the increased intellectual ambition of law professors that is associated with the rise of "law and" scholarship. I had concluded that the limited preacademic legal experience of so many modern-day law professors had widened the gap between the judges, whose engagement with the law is practical rather than academic, and the academics. I thought it therefore no surprise that despite the growth in the quantity of published legal scholarship, such scholarship is said to be cited less frequently in judicial opinions than before academic law was as academic as it has become.[38] Or that

36. Marc P. DiGirolami and Kevin C. Walsh, "Judge Posner, Judge Wilkinson, and Judicial Critique of Constitutional Theory," 90 *Notre Dame Law Review* 633, 687–688 (2014).

37. Michael Boudin, "Judge Henry Friendly and the Craft of Judging," 159 *University of Pennsylvania Law Review* 1, 2, 14 (2010).

38. See Brent E. Newton, "Law Review Scholarship in the Eyes of the Twenty-First-Century Supreme Court Justices: An Empirical Analysis," 4 *Drexel Law Review* 399, 416 (2012); Richard Brust, "The High Bench vs. the Ivory Tower: More Law Reviews Give Professors Places to Publish, but Judges Stick up Their Noses at Elite and Useless Articles," *American Bar Association Journal,* February 2012, 50,

judges and academics tend to cite different types of law review articles.[39] Or that academic participation in activities regarded as services to the judiciary, such as the projects of the American Law Institute, has declined among the professorial elite.

Speaking of the American Law Institute, which deserves my attention in this book because it is regarded as a high-status quasi-academic institution, I note that in recent years it's been criticized for being "too [methodologically] conservative—frozen in time in the late 1800s or early 1900s—and fail[ing] to incorporate the best contemporary practices in the study of law . . . [It] faces steady criticism regarding its membership, its mission and goals, its perceived insularity, its conservatism in the face of proposed reform, its philosophy of law,

---

54; Adam Liptak, "When Rendering Decisions, Judges Are Finding Law Reviews Irrelevant," *New York Times,* March 19, 2007, A8; Michael D. McClintock, "The Declining Use of Legal Scholarship By Courts: An Empirical Study," 51 *Oklahoma Law Review* 659, 660, 684 (1998); Deborah L. Rhode, "Legal Scholarship," 115 *Harvard Law Review* 1327, 1342 (2002); see also David Hricik and Victoria S. Salzmann, "Why There Should Be Fewer Articles Like This One: Law Professors Should Write More for Legal Decision-Makers and Less for Themselves," 38 *Suffolk University Law Review* 761, 763 (2005). But Petherbridge and Schwartz, in the two articles by them that I cite in note 27 above, find, to the contrary, that published opinions of the federal courts of appeals cite academic scholarship increasingly. Unsurprisingly, judges who are former academics are the most likely to cite academic writings in their opinions. Petherbridge and Schwartz, "The Use of Legal Scholarship by the Federal Courts of Appeals: An Empirical Study," note 27 above, 96 *Cornell Law Review* at 1370.

39. See Deborah J. Merritt and Melanie Putnam, "Judges and Scholars: Do Courts and Scholarly Journals Cite the Same Law Review Articles?" 71 *Chicago-Kent Law Review* 871 (1996). Their study compares most-cited articles in judicial opinions with most-cited articles in academic journals in order to "assay the nature of any divide between courts and the academy." Id. at 873. The authors find that "more than two-thirds of the articles most cited in scholarly journals have received no more than a single judicial citation. Conversely, two of the articles most frequently cited by courts have received no scholarly citations." Id. at 880.

and its level of utility as a resource for practitioners and judges."[40] The institute has been said to have strayed from its stated purpose of simplifying and clarifying the law, and that it "understandably vest[s] immeasurable, unfettered, unchecked, and unaccountable quasi-judicial and quasi-legislative power in the hands of the very few elitist people who control [it]," that the institute consists only of lawyers and that lawyers don't have enough of the right answers to issues of social policy and administration, and that the need for interdisciplinary scholarship has been ignored, while "special interests lobby the institute as if it were a lawmaking body, and . . . members respond to such efforts, and, in some instances, act as partisans . . . [Also] the ALI eschews empirical or field research in favor of library research to the detriment of its product."[41]

The Institute used to be a major site of interaction between leading judges, such as Benjamin Cardozo and Learned Hand, and leading law professors and leading members of the bar. But the protracted process involved in producing Restatements of the law (still the principal output of the ALI) does not commend itself to the modern social-science oriented law professor, and online legal research tools

40. Kristen David Adams, "Blaming the Mirror: The Restatements and the Common Law," 40 *Indiana Law Review* 205, 206, 207 (2007) (citations omitted); see also her earlier article, "The Folly of Uniformity: Lessons from the Restatement Movement," 33 *Hofstra Law Review* 423 (2004).
41. Alex Elson, "The Case for an In-Depth Study of the American Law Institute," 23 *Law and Social Inquiry* 625, 626 (1998) (citations omitted). For other criticisms, see, for example, Elizabeth Laposata, Richard Barnes, and Stanton Glantz, "Tobacco Industry Influence on the American Law Institute's Restatements of Torts and Implications for Its Conflict of Interest Policies," 98 *Iowa Law Review* 1 (2012); Juliet M. Moringiello and William L. Reynolds, "What's Software Got To Do with It? The ALI *Principles of the Law of Software Contracts*," 84 *Tulane Law Review* 1541, 1542, 1547, 1555–1556 (2010); Robin Fretwell Wilson, "Trusting Mothers: A Critique of the American Law Institute's Treatment of De Facto Parents," 38 *Hofstra Law Review* 1103, 1110, 1111 (2010).

have made the Restatements less valuable to judges and practicing lawyers as summaries of case law. With more than four thousand members, many elderly—there is no retirement age—and all eligible to vote at the annual meeting, and a Senate-like "Council" of more than fifty members, the American Law Institute has some of the character of an honorific legislature, like the House of Lords.

I am troubled by the ALI's heavy emphasis—natural though it is given the Institute's composition—on legal doctrine. Doctrine, especially common law doctrine, which has been evolving for centuries, is something that judges and law professors (especially law professors who write treatises) tend to formulate, explain, apply, and criticize pretty well. There isn't a great need for institutional participation. The various Restatements (of torts, contracts, conflict of laws, and the like) are valuable, but their contribution to improving the legal system in general and the federal judiciary in particular has dwindled, because they mainly "restate" bodies of common law and today the common law is the least problematic domain of American law. As I argue in subsequent chapters, the problems of the judiciary are administrative, operational, structural, attitudinal, and cultural, and the solutions do not include ever greater refinement of legal doctrine by deployment of traditional tools of legal analysis. A greater challenge is how to apply doctrine sensibly to particular cases against a background of rapid technological and scientific (including social-scientific) change that is colliding with antiquated methods of determining facts. To contribute meaningfully to reform of the legal system the American Law Institute requires a different focus, a different structure (more compact, streamlined), and a smaller, younger, and more diverse membership.

Although a number of judges belong to it, the Institute is unlikely to bridge the current gap between the academy and the judiciary. Indeed the gap may continue to grow if law professors' interest and experience in legal practice continue to decline. The Institute does bring judges and professors together to an extent, but I wonder how many judges get much out of belonging to it—and I suspect that those who do are mainly state judges and so outside the scope of this book. Since most common law is state law and the ALI's traditional emphasis has been on common law, it is natural and appropriate that its most active judge participants should be state rather than federal judges, but that does diminish the relevance of the ALI to my concerns in this book.

The Institute's current director (since May 2014), Richard Revesz, former dean of New York University School of Law, may prove an effective force for change. He is an experienced administrator, is conscious of the weaknesses of the ALI, and in the short time that he's been the Institute's director has already engineered some significant reforms designed to streamline the organization, broaden the scope of its activities, and lower the average age of its members and the Council's members. So there is hope.

But I think the Institute has less potential to become a major force in reform of the federal judiciary than the law schools do. Just as I was finishing this book I was invited to become an "Adviser" to an ALI project of creating a new Restatement in an important area of law and one that it happens I'm quite interested in. (Although I have been a member of the Institute for more than thirty years, I had never before been invited to participate in any of its projects—which, as I think about it, is a little surprising.) Included with an invitation was a list of other participants. The list included a Reporter (who would lead the drafting of the Restatement and indeed be in charge of the entire project), four Associate Reporters, and forty-three Advisers, consisting of academics, judges, and practicing lawyers. And after the Restatement was drafted it would have to be submitted first to the fifty-five or so members of the Institute's Council and then to the four thousand members of the Institute. I declined the invitation to become another Adviser to the project. The waste of manpower struck me as appalling. How could one expect a first-rate product to emerge from so large a crowd? One would think that the project would be assigned to one person, who would of course consult with experts in the field and whose draft Restatement would be submitted to a review process conducted by a board far smaller than fifty-five members, let alone four thousand.

Having flailed at the American Law Institute for a few pages, let me get back on track by noting that I had expected the decline in the practical orientation of academic scholarship to manifest itself in a truncation of the preacademic legal careers of law professors at top-tier law schools. I was therefore surprised to discover that, at least if the University of Chicago Law School is representative of those schools, law professors' preacademic legal careers are only trivially shorter today than they were in the 1968–1969 school year, the last year before I joined the University of Chicago faculty. The decrease is too small to explain the growing estrangement between the law schools and the judiciary. The average preacademic legal career of University of Chicago law professors was 3.64 years then; it was 3.50 years in the most recent (2013–2014) school year for which there are statistics. But the University of Chicago Law School may not be representative; for in the same span of time the average preacademic legal career of Columbia Law School faculty fell from 6.85 years to 4.97 years.

More important in explaining changes in the legal professoriate than the reduction in years of practical experience, though probably positively correlated with it, is the change in law professors' postcollegiate pre-law intellectual backgrounds. The change is shown for ten leading law schools in Table I.1. The table compares for each school, and for both the 1968–1969 and 2013–2014 academic years, the percentage of the faculty that had an advanced degree and the percentage that had an advanced degree other than in law—the latter being the more germane degree category. The changes are striking. In the 1968–1969 academic year an average of 43 percent of faculty had advanced degrees legal or nonlegal but only 22 percent had nonlegal advanced degrees. By 2013–2014 these figures had increased to 56 percent (all

Table I.1. Advanced Degrees, Nonlegal or Any, Law School Faculties, 1968–1969, 2013–2014

School	1968–1969		2013–2014	
	% Nonlegal	*% Any*	*% Nonlegal*	*% Any*
Columbia University	25	43	37	52
Georgetown University	24	62	36	50
Harvard University	22	38	30	58
Northwestern University	23	50	61	64
Stanford University	29	42	47	51
University of California, Los Angeles	15	35	49	56
University of Chicago	29	43	60	63
University of Virginia	18	28	43	49
Washington University in St. Louis	6	50	43	57
Yale University	28	42	54	61
Average	22	43	46	56

advanced degrees) and 46 percent (nonlegal advanced degrees). In contrast, the number of federal judges with advanced degrees has always been and remains very small.[42]

Although my sample is too small to be statistically significant, I would be surprised if the trends at other law schools were greatly different. For of all new tenure-track hires by American law schools in 2014, 84 percent had had a post–law school fellowship, 60 percent a clerkship, and 51 percent an advanced degree, half of the advanced degrees being PhDs.[43]

These trends must flatten at some point (100 percent!) but seem unlikely to be reversed, because as a practical matter existing faculty controls future appointments. Of course just as the old-line law professors were unable to withstand the tide that has produced the cur-

42. For amplification of this analysis of the trend in law professors' acquisition of advanced degrees, see Appendix A, below.

43. PrawfsBlawg, "Spring Self-Reported Entry Level Hiring Report 2014," May 2, 2014, http://prawfsblawg.blogs.com/prawfsblawg/2014/05/spring-self -reported-entry-level-hiring-report-2014.html.

rent highly intellectualized, degree-laden, practice-alienated law faculties, so these faculties may fail to withstand some future tide in legal culture. But the old guard's inability to hold its ground was a consequence of the political turbulence of the sixties and the rise in the application of the social sciences to law, and nothing comparable to those forces for change is on the horizon today. There is, it is true, as we'll see in Chapter 5, a movement afoot for greater "skills training" of law students, reflecting pressure from law firms, which are operating in a much more competitive environment than they were decades ago. That will lead to greater recruitment of law professors who have a more practical orientation. But it is unlikely to change the character of the elite law schools, which feel little pressure to change.

To see how legal scholarship has changed, consider the career of Richard Fallon, a leading professor at the Harvard Law School. He has never practiced law. Besides his college and law degrees he has a bachelor's degree from Oxford (where he was a Rhodes Scholar) in Philosophy, Politics, and Economics. I chanced recently on an article by him on statutory interpretation, obviously an important subject for appellate judges. I quote the last paragraph of the conclusion (minus the first two sentences, which are peripheral to the point he makes in the paragraph):

The experience of partly value-based interpretive dissonance often supplies the trigger for appeals to theories of statutory interpretation, including both textualist and purposivist theories. And within both textualist and purposivist theories, the ultimate outcome will frequently depend on the breadth or narrowness with which the relevant context for a statute's interpretation is specified. To put the point only slightly more strongly, the specification of an interpretive context—which is irreducibly value driven at least in part—may frequently matter as much, in practice, as the seemingly more consequential decision whether to adopt a textualist or a purposivist theory in the first place. Debates about theories of statutory interpretation will remain misleadingly incomplete until they reckon adequately with this insight.[44]

Judges will not understand this paragraph even if (an important qualification, because a passage taken out of context may become lucid when the context is restored) they read carefully the forty-eight pages of Professor Fallon's article that precede it—for they won't understand those pages either. Nor will their law clerks understand it, nor law students, nor practicing lawyers. The paragraph I have quoted, and the entire article of which it is an excerpt, are of a complexity, and pitched at a level of abstraction, that only law professors will understand, unsurprisingly because they are the intended audience. And this is typical of modern legal scholarship, especially that produced by the smartest law professors at the best law schools.

I do not mean to criticize Professor Fallon. Nowhere is it written that all legal academic books and articles must be readable by judges or for that matter by anyone other than a law professor. Most judges are too busy, or think they're too busy, to pay attention to academic scholarship anyway. But the resulting gap in communication between the academy and the judiciary is lamentable, given the judiciary's problems.

What one is seeing in Fallon's article, and in much other elite legal scholarship as well, is academic law becoming esoteric. We've seen this in other fields, such as literary criticism and philosophy. These were fields once inhabited by academics and nonacademics, such as F. R. Leavis and T. S. Eliot in literary criticism and William James and John

---

44. Richard H. Fallon, Jr., "Three Symmetries between Textualist and Purposivist Theories of Statutory Interpretation—and the Irreducible Roles of Values and Judgment within Both," 99 *Cornell Law Review* 685, 734 (2014).

Stuart Mill in philosophy, the first of each pair being the academic and the second the nonacademic. Moreover, whether academic or nonacademic, most literary criticism and most philosophical writing were accessible to and widely read by persons in other fields and indeed by many members of the general public. The analogy was to academic legal scholarship read—and sometimes written—by judges. At present, literary criticism and especially philosophy are for the most part jargon-ridden, technical, and inaccessible to persons in other fields. And at present, increasingly, academic legal scholarship, especially that published in the elite law journals, is inaccessible to outsiders, including I fear most judges.

Such obscurantism in legal scholarship is gratuitous. It would not be asking too much of Professor Fallon that he try writing more simply; I'm sure he'd be able to do so. I happen to think, as I'll explain in Chapter 2, that professors and judges alike tend to exaggerate the complexity of statutory interpretation (the subject of his article), which I believe actually quite simple both in theory and in practice, and not at all as described by Fallon. But my present point is about style. The paragraph I quoted—and, to repeat, it is representative—is needlessly convoluted. I suspect that the style of his article reflects the fact that the author is content or perhaps even desires to reach only a small, very select audience and that he places precision, requiring constant picky qualification of his claims, above clarity.

I don't mean to be insinuating that academic scholarship has no impact on the courts. However little of it the judges read, some filters through to them in their law clerks' bench memos and opinion drafts, in the lawyers' briefs and arguments, in testimony by expert witnesses, and in the occasional amicus curiae brief authored by a professor. Yet the lawyer and law clerk intermediaries will have great trouble understanding abstract theory pitched at the level that Fallon pitched his article, and so translating that theory into language that a judge can understand.

Fortunately, practical as distinct from theoretical legal scholarship continues to be produced and to be cited by judges even if deemed pedestrian by many professors at leading law schools (but so what?—judges don't care). But because of the estrangement of judiciary from academy that I've been describing, critique of the judiciary itself (as distinct from specific judicial decisions), as it is currently practiced in the legal academy, tends to be denigrated or (more commonly) ignored by many judges. They do not want to be studied by a professional group from which they feel alienated. To some of them the principal value of law professors is as recommenders of law clerks. If advanced modern legal academics such as Professor Fallon want to get through to judges, either directly or through their students who become law clerks and litigators, they'll have to learn to simplify rather than complexify law. They'll have to dim their lights. I'm not optimistic that they will.

Some legal scholarship falls flat from the judicial perspective not because of problems of expression but because of sheer impracticality. So consider a recent article by Professor Bijal Shah entitled "Uncovering Interrelated Interagency Adjudication."[45] An article seventy-eight pages in length, it addresses coordination among federal agencies with overlapping regulatory responsibilities. Shah shows convincingly that there are serious problems of coordination. His proposed solution is to vest coordinating authority in an executive branch agency,[46] such as the Office of Information and Regulatory Affairs,[47] a White House staff agency. A large number of federal agencies are involved in litigation of one sort or another and often their litigation-related activities overlap. They work out arrangements with each other for cooperation and for avoidance of conflict. The arrangements are imperfect, as Shah

---

45. 128 *Harvard Law Review* 805 (2015).
46. Id. at 867–875.
47. Id. at 871.

points out. But what would paralyze federal regulation would be for White House staff to attempt to regulate the relations among the agencies. It would be a bureaucratic disaster.

For many years now the Federal Trade Commission and the Justice Department's Antitrust Division, which have overlapping antitrust jurisdiction, have amicably divided the federal government's antitrust enforcement activities between themselves. Shah might argue that a coordinating agency would leave well enough alone and thus not disturb the relation between the FTC and the Antitrust Division. But to expect that would be to misunderstand bureaucracy. Bureaucrats need to justify their existence by imposing their authority on subordinate bodies. Someone in the coordinating agency would be bound to take a role in parceling out work between the FTC and the Antitrust Division. The result would be to slow down enforcement and foment bickering. Bureaucrats would be locking horns with the Attorney General and the chairman of the FTC. Higher officials in the immense White House staff would be called in to arbitrate the disputes.

Shah's proposal is unrealistic. If adopted it would make things worse. Any judge who reads, or more likely was told about, the article (for its length and density would deter most judges from actually attempting to read it) would think it confirmation of judicial skepticism of "advanced" scholarship in marquee law journals such as the *Harvard Law Review*.

Another sign of the widening gap between the academy and the judiciary is the decline of the legal treatise. No longer is it common for law professors at leading law schools to write treatises. One reason is that such treatises do not resemble the scholarly output of social scientists, which so many leading legal academics have become. A related reason is that a major function of treatises was and is to gather and sort cases, something that judges and their law clerks can now do themselves more or less effortlessly by means of online legal search services such as WestlawNext. The best treatises did more—were at once analytical and synthesizing—but remained closely tied to case law; and deriving legal principles from cases has ceased to seem a challenging form of legal scholarship, in addition to being tedious.

When I think back over the conversations I've had with my judicial colleagues over the past thirty-four years I can't remember any mention, whether approving or disapproving, of law professors. Few judges have much interest in or contact with law professors. As for professors' lack of interest in judicial behavior, consider the May/June 2014 issue of *The Bencher: The Magazine of the American Inns of Court*. Entitled "The State of Legal Education in America," the issue contains interesting articles criticizing current legal education and suggesting reforms. But none of the articles suggests that legal education may be falling short by failing to give students a realistic understanding of judges.

A subtler reason for law professors' lack of interest in judges is what I'll term the problem of the authorless text, which creates a gap of understanding between these two branches of the profession. We venerate as we should the *Iliad* and the *Odyssey* as supreme literary achievements. But nothing is known of their author or authors. We don't know whether there was anyone named Homer, when the "Homeric" epics were composed, whether there was one author of both epics (which seems unlikely, however, given linguistic differences between the two), or one author of each; or whether there were multiple authors, though perhaps two persons—one for each epic—produced a written version of what theretofore had been a body of traditional oral poetry, thereby creating the *Iliad* and the *Odyssey* as we know them. With so little understood about the authorship of the two epic works, the focus in evaluation and interpretation has had to be on the texts themselves. The parallel to the modern judicial opinion is that most judicial opinions of both federal and state judges are written by law clerks rather than by the judges who are the nominal authors of the opinions, as "Homer" is the nominal author of the *Iliad* and the *Odyssey.* Law students, moreover, encounter judicial opinions mainly in casebooks, and the editors of casebooks edit severely the opinions that they include, thus placing the judge "author" at an even farther remove from the student reader. The judge might as well be anonymous.

It's true that many law professors were themselves judicial law clerks; and one might think they'd be eager to impart to the judiciary insights into the judicial process that they had gleaned from that experience. But many judges are guarded with—formal, even distant from—their law clerks. More important, almost all judges, as I said earlier, expect and require their law clerks to reveal nothing about the work of the judge and the clerks to outsiders. It is remarkable how rarely clerks violate this variant of *omertà,* though it has happened, famously in *The Brethren,* the exposé of the Warren Court. Ex-clerks are grateful for the clerkship, and seek by their silence to protect their judge from criticism and themselves from accusations of being disloyal or indiscreet. Indeed it's in the career interest of former law clerks to hype their judge, because to have been hired and worked for an outstanding judge casts reflected glory on the former clerk.

We thus have a problem of "dueling opacities." Academic jargon creates one screen between professors and judges; judicial secretiveness creates another.

The estrangement between academy and judiciary that I have been discussing has the further unfortunate consequence of reducing the pool of law professors eligible for judicial appointments. A number of distinguished federal judges have been former law professors and some of these judges, past and present—such as Stephen Breyer, Guido Calabresi, William Fletcher, Felix Frankfurter, Douglas

Ginsburg, Calvert Magruder, Michael McConnell, Kenneth Ripple, J. Harvie Wilkinson III, and Ralph Winter—had only limited experience in the practice of law before becoming law professors and then judges.[48] But all of them had as academics taught and written about practical problems. The more remote the law professoriate becomes from the concerns of practicing lawyers, the fewer will be the professors appointed to federal judgeships, and the judiciary will be poorer as a result. Which is not to say that professors should dominate the pool from which federal judges are selected. But able academics, unless so theoretical in outlook that they cannot adjust to the practical world of judging, bring a valuable perspective to the judiciary, just as would experienced politicians—who surely deserve representation on the Supreme Court, if only to keep the Court from making political waves gratuitously, as it did in refusing in *Clinton v. Jones* to grant President Clinton immunity until the end of his presidential term from having to defend a sex suit—and also private and government lawyers.[49]

A final observation: There are many more law professors today than there were half a century ago, when I was a law student; and one supposes that there would be more "great" law professors today because they would be a constant percentage of a growing number. But there are fewer. The number of great law professors at Harvard when I

48. Judge Frank Easterbrook of my court is an example of a law professor turned judge who had extensive experience, consisting of five years as an assistant to the Solicitor General of the United States, before becoming a professor. And likewise his boss, Robert Bork, who was Solicitor General before his appointment to the D.C. Circuit and also had practiced law for several years before becoming a law professor.

49. 520 U.S. 681 (1997). For criticism of the Court's decision, see my book *An Affair of State: The Investigation, Impeachment, and Trial of President Clinton* 225–230 (1999). Clinton's testimony in the Paula Jones case precipitated his impeachment and Senate trial, roiling American politics to no purpose at all.

was a student was legion—Henry Hart, Abram Chayes, Austin Scott, Derek Bok, Donald Turner, John Dawson, Paul Freund: I could go on and on. And earlier there had been such giants of the legal academy as Langdell, Ames, Pound, and Frankfurter. All those I've named were at just one law school, Harvard. But Yale Law School had such notables as Alexander Bickel and Eugene Rostow. And Columbia and the University of Chicago and Penn and other schools had great law professors as well (think for example of Karl Llewellyn at Columbia and later at Chicago, Edward Levi and Harry Kalven at Chicago, and William Prosser at Berkeley). And soon other notables, young when I was a law student, emerged, such as Paul Bator, Robert Bork, Ronald Dworkin, Duncan Kennedy, Guido Calabresi, Catharine MacKinnon, and Anthony Amsterdam. And again there are a number of others whom I could name.

There are many very able law professors today—indeed I would guess that on average today's law professors are abler than those of a half-century ago—yet few stand out in the way the ones whom I've named stood out. The reason may simply be the growth of specialization, as a result of which, with few exceptions, even the brightest law professors are confined to niches. The growth in the number of professors made specialization inevitable; for as a field becomes more crowded, individuals become specialized in order to minimize the competition they face. The drop in the number of recognizably "great" law professors, whatever its cause, may explain some of the estrangement between the academy and the judiciary today: there aren't many academics that judges look up to any more.

The emphasis that the elite law schools are placing on preappointment demonstration of scholarly commitment and quality by acquisition of a PhD or by undergoing a two- or three-year post–law school fellowship may actually foster the disappearance of great law professors. Most of the best law students do not have PhDs, and have no desire after clerking (for two years, if they are lucky enough to land a Supreme Court clerkship, since almost all Supreme Court clerks have completed a court of appeals clerkship) to attend graduate school or undergo a two- or three-year clerkship as a preclude to a teaching career. They would rather plunge into a lucrative and exciting career in one of the nation's premier law firms.

APPENDIX A

THEN AND NOW—THE ACADEMY'S CHANGING FACE

Amplifying my brief discussion of changes in law schools over approximately the last half-century, this appendix provides more detailed data on professors at the ten U.S. law schools analyzed in Table I.1—Columbia University, Georgetown University, Harvard University, Northwestern University, Stanford University, the University of California, Los Angeles, the University of Chicago, the University of Virginia, Washington University in St. Louis, and Yale University—in a comparison of the 1968–1969 and 2014–2015 academic years. The data consist of numbers of advanced degrees, broken down by whether they are advanced degrees in law, mainly the LLM and JSD, or in nonlaw-related fields (mainly MA and PhD). The faculty samples are limited to regular, full-time, tenure-track faculty and thus exclude visiting professors, professors emeriti, and lecturers. Clinical professors are also excluded. The number of faculty included in the data, for each school and each of the periods compared, is indicated by "n" in the left-most column of the table.

The principal data sources are the law schools' annual announcements and bulletins, faculty webpages, and curricula vitae, and the Directories of Law Teachers published by the Association of American Law Schools.

The analysis begins with statistics concerning the advanced degrees, and notes the sample size of the 1968–1969 and 2014–2015 samples and the percentages of professors from each school who had one advanced degree, two or more advanced degrees, and any number of advanced degrees, and the percentage who had one advanced nonlaw degree, two or more advanced nonlaw degrees, and any number of advanced nonlaw degrees.

A Welch's t-test was used to determine whether the average number of advanced degrees held by faculty in the 1968–1969 sample was the same as the average number in the 2014–2015 sample. The analysis was then repeated for just the nonlaw advanced degrees. The reasons for using Welch's t-tests were that the 1968–1969 academic faculty sample size was not the same as the 2014–2015 sample size and that the two samples had unequal variances.

The results of the basic analysis are reported in Table A.1, and of the Welch's tests in Tables A.2 and A.3.

Most schools had between one and four professors in both samples ("repeat professors"). The University of Chicago had one repeat professor, Columbia two, Georgetown two, Harvard three, Northwestern one, Stanford two, UCLA none, Virginia four, Washington University one, Yale one.

Normally, t-tests are conducted on two independent samples. The presence of the repeat professors in both samples (1968–1969 and 2013–2014) violated independence. However, regressing the number of advanced degrees (and, separately, the number of advanced nonlaw degrees) on year and number of repeat professors revealed that the existence of those professors had an insignificant effect on the number of advanced degrees. So the repeat professors are excluded from the Welch's t-tests.

In Tables A.2 and A.3 the values are t-statistics and the numbers in parentheses are the p-values. A p-value with one asterisk is smaller than 0.05 (that is, 5 percent); a p-value with two asterisks is smaller than 0.01 (1 percent). The lower the p-value, the smaller the likelihood that the number of advanced degrees held by members of each faculty in both periods is actually the same, and the variations shown in Table A.1 therefore spurious.

Table A.2 reports the results of two-sided Welch's t-tests, which test whether the average number of advanced degrees and of advanced nonlaw degrees were the same in the 1968–1969 and 2014–2015 samples of law faculty. The table reveals that at all schools except Georgetown the average number of advanced nonlaw degrees differed in the two periods.

Finally, Table A.3 reports the results of one-sided Welch's t-tests, which determine whether the average number of advanced degrees and the average number of advanced nonlaw degrees were lower (rather than just different) in the 1968–1969 sample compared to the corresponding average numbers in the later sample. A positive t-statistic signifies that the average numbers were lower in the earlier sample; a negative t-statistic indicates the opposite. The table reveals that the average numbers were indeed lower in the earlier sample and thus that they increased between the two periods, though with the partial exception of Georgetown. The total number of advanced degrees of faculty decreased but the number of advanced nonlaw degrees increased.

Table A.1. Advanced Degrees and Advanced Nonlaw Degrees

Year	Advanced degrees	Advanced, nonlaw degrees
Columbia University		
1968–1969	One: 30.00%	One: 22.50%
(n = 40)	Two or more: 7.50%	Two or more: 2.50%
	Any number: 37.50%	Any number: 25.00%
2014–2015	One: 31.65%	One: 25.32%
(n = 79)	Two or more: 21.52%	Two or more: 13.92%
	Any number: 53.16%	Any number: 39.24%
Georgetown University		
1968–1969	One: 43.24%	One: 16.22%
(n = 37)	Two or more: 18.92%	Two or more: 5.41%
	Any number: 62.16%	Any number: 21.62%
2014–2015	One: 33.90%	One: 24.58%
(n = 118)	Two or more: 16.10%	Two or more: 11.86%
	Any number: 50.00%	Any number: 36.44%
Harvard University		
1968–1969	One: 29.09%	One: 20.00%
(n = 55)	Two or more: 9.09%	Two or more: 3.64%
	Any number: 38.18%	Any number: 23.64%
2014–2015	One: 31.96%	One: 29.90%
(n = 97)	Two or more: 25.77%	Two or more: 20.62%
	Any number: 57.73%	Any number: 50.52%
Northwestern University		
1968–1969	One: 33.33%	One: 16.67%
(n = 30)	Two or more: 13.33%	Two or more: 6.67%
	Any number: 46.67%	Any number: 23.33%
2014–2015	One: 46.43%	One: 46.43%
(n = 56)	Two or more: 17.86%	Two or more: 14.29%
	Any number: 64.29%	Any number: 60.71%
Stanford University		
1968–1969	One: 29.03%	One: 22.58%
(n = 31)	Two or more: 12.90%	Two or more: 6.45%
	Any number: 41.94%	Any number: 29.03%
2014–2015	One: 28.57%	One: 27.14%
(n = 70)	Two or more: 22.86%	Two or more: 20.00%
	Any number: 51.43%	Any number: 47.14%
University of California, Los Angeles		
1968–1969	One: 11.76%	One: 14.71%
(n = 34)	Two or more: 23.53%	Two or more: 2.94%
	Any number: 35.29%	Any number: 17.65%

Year	Advanced degrees	Advanced, nonlaw degrees
2014–2015	One: 26.47%	One: 19.12%
(n = 68)	Two or more: 29.41%	Two or more: 29.41%
	Any number: 55.88%	Any number: 48.53%
University of Chicago		
1968–1969	One: 28.57%	One: 25.00%
(n = 28)	Two or more: 7.14%	Two or more: 0%
	Any number: 35.71%	Any number: 25.00%
2014–2015	One: 42.50%	One: 42.50%
(n = 40)	Two or more: 20.00%	Two or more: 17.50%
	Any number: 62.50%	Any number: 60.00%
University of Virginia		
1968–1969	One: 20.00%	One: 15.00%
(n = 40)	Two or more: 7.50%	Two or more: 2.50%
	Any number: 27.50%	Any number: 17.50%
2014–2015	One: 31.76%	One: 29.41%
(n = 85)	Two or more: 17.65%	Two or more: 11.76%
	Any number: 49.41%	Any number: 41.18%
Washington University in St. Louis		
1968–1969	One: 27.78%	One: 5.56%
(n = 18)	Two or more: 22.22%	Two or more: 0%
	Any number: 50%	Any number: 0%
2014–2015	One: 39.62%	One: 33.96%
(n = 53)	Two or more: 16.98%	Two or more: 9.43%
	Any number: 56.60%	Any number: 43.40%
Yale University		
1968–1969	One: 25.58%	One: 20.93%
(n = 43)	Two or more: 16.28%	Two or more: 6.98%
	Any number: 41.86%	Any number: 27.91%
2014–2015	One: 38.89%	One: 35.19%
(n = 54)	Two or more: 22.22%	Two or more: 18.52%
	Any number: 61.11%	Any number: 53.70%

Table A.2. Two-Sided Welch's T-Tests

School	Advanced degrees	Advanced nonlaw degrees
Columbia University	−2.2549 (0.0263★)	−2.0525 (0.0427★)
Georgetown University	1.0645 (0.2919)	−1.9205 (0.0585)
Harvard University	−2.5787 (0.0110★)	−3.6253 (0.0004★★)
Northwestern University	−1.5261 (0.1318)	−3.2677 (0.0016★)
Stanford University	−0.9676 (0.3374)	−2.1323 (0.0364★)
University of California, Los Angeles	−1.6653 (0.1001)	−4.3329 (0.0000★★)
University of Chicago	−2.4028 (0.0195★)	−3.6852 (0.0005★★)
University of Virginia	−2.5439 (0.0128★)	−3.1510 (0.0021★★)
Washington University in St. Louis	−0.1892 (0.8513)	−4.2816 (0.0001★★)
Yale University	−1.4104 (0.1620)	−2.6726 (0.0089★★)

Table A.3. One-Sided Welch's T-Tests

School	Advanced degrees	Advanced nonlaw degrees
Columbia University	−2.2549 (0.0132★)	−2.0525 (0.0213★)
Georgetown University	1.0645 (0.8540)	−1.9205 (0.0292★)
Harvard University	−2.5787 (0.0055★★)	−3.6253 (0.0002★★)
Northwestern University	−1.5261 (0.0659)	−3.2677 (0.0008★★)
Stanford University	−0.9676 (0.1687)	−2.1323 (0.0182★)
University of California, Los Angeles	−1.6653 (0.0501)	−4.3329 (0.0000★★)
University of Chicago	−2.4028 (0.0096★★)	−3.6852 (0.0002★★)
University of Virginia	−2.5439 (0.0064★★)	−3.1510 (0.0011★★)
Washington University in St. Louis	−0.1892 (0.4257)	−4.2816 (0.0000★★)
Yale University	−1.4104 (0.0810)	−2.6726 (0.0044★★)

I | PROBLEMS OF THE MODERN FEDERAL JUDICIARY

1 | STRUCTURAL DEFORMATIONS

THE CHASM BETWEEN the academy and the judiciary described in the Introduction would be of little consequence were there no room for constructive critique of the judiciary—if the judiciary couldn't be improved (an absurd suggestion) or if law schools could do nothing to improve it except import scholars from other disciplines (wrong again, though not as wrong). The judiciary has many problems to which law schools might be able to offer at least partial solutions, or at least might be able to illuminate, leaving others to solve the problems (maybe the judges themselves). I discuss these problems in this and the following two chapters.[1] In places I note the neglect and even aggravation of the judiciary's deficiencies by the academy, but later (in Part Two of the book) I try to show how the academy can play a constructive role in alleviating those deficiencies.

Not all the problems of the judiciary are amenable to solution by the academy, yet a discussion of the insoluble ones belongs in this book because their existence underscores the importance of solving the soluble problem, and thus enlarges the potential role of the academy in their solution.

The stubbornest problems, which are the ones addressed in this chapter, I call "structural"; they are the uneven quality of federal judicial appointments at all levels, excessive delay in filling federal judicial

1. For fuller discussions of a number of the problems, see Lee Epstein, William M. Landes, and Richard A. Posner, *The Behavior of Federal Judges: A Theoretical and Empirical Study of Rational Choice,* ch. 1 (2013); Richard A. Posner, *How Judges Think,* pt. 1 (2008), and *Reflections on Judging,* chs. 3–9 (2013).

vacancies (because of the requirement of senatorial confirmation of the President's judicial appointees), the poor draftsmanship of so many federal statutes, the indeterminacy of much American law (including but not limited to the Constitution), certain salary anomalies, and excessive expenditures on federal courthouses.[2] The last two problems are the least serious.

The uneven quality of the federal judiciary is a result of two structural features that undoubtedly will not be changed in the foreseeable future, and maybe shouldn't be, because there don't appear to be superior alternatives. The appointment of federal judges by the President subject to confirmation by the Senate not only results in significant variance in quality across federal judges but also tends to make the judiciary more political than it would be were the judges not appointed by politicians. Politicians tend to favor judicial candidates who can be expected to advance, or at least not impede, the politicians' goals. What else could one expect? And those goals are largely political.

The requirement of Senate confirmation of judicial nominees

2. The requirement of senatorial confirmation of the President's judicial appointees is a particularly serious problem in the federal district courts, because of a great increase in the number of federal prison inmates (and hence in prisoner civil rights cases) and the reluctance of Congress to act on nominees promptly or to create needed new district court judgeships in crowded circuits. See Joe Palazzolo, "Record Backlog Jams [Federal District] Courts," *Wall St. Journal,* April 8, 2015, A1. The article points out that the federal prison population has increased by 55 percent since 1999. Id. at A8. I disagree, however, with William M. Richman and William L. Reynolds, who in *Injustice on Appeal: The United States Court of Appeals in Crisis* (2013), while pointing to real problems of the appellate courts, many of which I'll be discussing in this book (such as judicial delegation of opinion writing, the proliferation of unpublished—that is, non-precedential—opinions, and the like), urge a doubling of the number of federal court of appeals judges and underestimate the difficulty of coordination were there so many more judges.

makes the problem worse than it would be if the President had carte blanche to appoint federal judges. A President has some incentive to appoint good judges, because he's blamed for the poor appointments he makes even when he has delegated the appointing power to Senators, as is common in the case of district judge appointments. But the President doesn't have a free hand, because he needs the Senate to confirm his nominees. And in deciding whether to support or oppose a judicial candidate a Senator is more likely than the President to give free rein to political considerations, for his constituents are unlikely to blame him for voting to confirm a mediocre candidate or voting not to confirm a superior one. The requirement of senatorial confirmation is also an impediment to prompt filling of judicial vacancies, as individual Senators are unlikely to be blamed by their constituents for delay between a judge's nomination and confirmation.[3]

Senatorial confirmation has another and more serious drawback: it results in federal judges invariably being local—the federal district judge is a resident of the district in which he lives, the court of appeals judge a resident not just of the circuit to which he is appointed but of the state (in the circuit) to which the judgeship has been allocated. So although the big cities contain a larger pool of excellent lawyers and law professors than small cities and rural areas contain, the members of the big-city pool are not considered for appointment elsewhere than where they live. Since federal law is national rather than regional, there is no reason other than the politics of confirmation to limit the appointment pool to the appointees' stamping ground.

I don't want to leave the impression that were it not for the requirement of senatorial confirmation Presidents would always or

---

3. For a comprehensive analysis of the confirmation process, see Geoffrey R. Stone, "Understanding Supreme Court Confirmations," *Supreme Court Review* 381 (2010).

even often appoint the *most* qualified candidates. Presidents are as political as Senators. Especially when filling a vacancy on the Supreme Court—an appointment bound to receive a good deal of media attention—a President wants not the best qualified candidate but the candidate most likely to cast his or her judicial votes consistently for the government in cases important to the appointing President, or to increase the President's standing with influential interest groups or with the media and other sources or transmitters of public opinion and therefore of political influence. He will not be indifferent to a candidate's quality, but that is unlikely to be his paramount consideration in choosing among candidates. And though he is unlikely to support an incompetent—and an incompetent would in any event be unlikely to be confirmed—"competent" is not a symptom for "best" or for "most independent—least political."

President Jimmy Carter, who appointed more federal judges in his single term of office than any other President has ever appointed in one term, established "nominating commissions" to recommend appointments with emphasis on minority and female candidates, and this resulted in a number of high-quality appointments.[4] But the experiment was not continued by his successors.

Judges like to say that upon being appointed they laid their political preferences to one side and in judging became political neuters. That is true of some judges; also some appointees have lacked strong political views going in. But there is abundant evidence that the liberal versus conservative character of a judge's judicial votes tends to be positively correlated with the Democratic versus Republican identity of the appointing President and to a lesser extent the Democratic-Republican balance in the Senate at the time the appointee was con-

---

4. See Carl Tobias, "Rethinking Federal Judicial Selection," *Brigham Young Law Review* 1257, 1259–1264 (1993).

firmed.[5] The reason, to which I'll return several times in subsequent chapters, is that in many cases, and those usually the most important, the orthodox sources of law, such as constitutional or statutory provisions and authoritative precedents, do not dictate the outcome. Unavoidably in such cases the judges fall back on their priors—the impulses, dispositions, attitudes, beliefs, and so on that they bring to a case before they engage with the briefs, argument, lower court decision, and trial record. Those priors are likely to include political beliefs or leanings that can influence decision in cases that have political implications.

The emphasis placed nowadays on "diversity" as a plus factor in a judicial nominee has the paradoxical effect of reducing *relevant* diversity. The diversity that politicians favor in federal judicial nominees is generally of race and sex. Yet it is very difficult to see how the only current African-American member of the Supreme Court, Justice Thomas, differs by virtue of his race from the other conservatives, or how the three liberal women differ by virtue of their sex from the liberal man, Justice Breyer, or how the Hispanic woman (Justice Sotomayor) differs by virtue of her ethnicity from the non-Hispanic liberal women or the non-Hispanic liberal man. Justice O'Connor, a woman, differed little from Justice Kennedy, a man, in her judicial voting, though she was somewhat less conservative.[6] The diversity that the Supreme Court and the lower federal courts need is diversity in political and other pertinent vocational experience besides just law.

5. See Epstein, Landes, and Posner, note 1 above, chs. 2–4 and studies cited in those chapters.
6. See Adam Liptak, "Court under Roberts Is Most Conservative in Decades," *New York Times,* July 24, 2010, A1, together with graphic: "Measuring the Conservatism of the Roberts Court: Under Chief Justice John G. Roberts Jr., the Supreme Court Has Moved to the Right," *New York Times,* July 24, 2010, www.nytimes.com/interactive/2010/07/25/us/20100725-roberts-graphic.html.

Few federal judges are former elected politicians, or former high-ranking government officials such as Attorneys General, or former businessmen, or have significant scientific or other technical knowledge. No current member of the Supreme Court was ever a legislator or ever held a senior executive branch position. Sandra Day O'Connor was the last Supreme Court Justice who had a legislative background. The only current member of the Court with significant administrative experience is Elena Kagan, who before being appointed to the Court had been Deputy Director of the White House Domestic Council during the Clinton Administration, then Dean of the Harvard Law School, and then Solicitor General of the United States. The contrast, in point of diverse professional background, between the current Justices and those of, say, half a century ago, is striking (more on this in Chapter 3).

The current Supreme Court Justices all have a humanities rather than a science or even social science background. Few have a rich cultural background either, as did such judges of yore as Holmes, Hand, and Cardozo.

Curiosity, which is related to receptivity, deserves weight in the selection of judges, yet is given none and as a result is an uncommon judicial trait because most judges don't think it relevant to their job. Lack of curiosity is a corollary of the umpireal conception of adjudication, an influential conception that I shall be criticizing throughout this book. Diversity in priors (religious, ideological, and so forth) would also be worth considering in choosing federal judges, but no President wants *that* diversity; he wants to appoint as Justices and judges persons who share *his* priors.

The quality of the federal judiciary is uneven mainly because politicians look beyond quality in deciding whom to appoint—to any position. If it's a senior position in the executive branch they figure the civil servants will keep the appointee out of trouble and anyway that everything of consequence will be controlled by the White House staff, now grown to enormous size. If it's a judgeship they figure the law clerks and the bar will keep the judge out of trouble. Quality is a floor; excellence a ceiling that the appointing authorities cannot be expected, most of the time, to aim for.

Another structural feature that undermines the quality of the federal judiciary is the lifetime tenure of federal judges. Article III of the Constitution (the judicial article) doesn't say "lifetime tenure," but only that federal judges "shall hold their Offices during Good Behaviour," and it can be argued that a judge who is senile is incapable of good judicial behavior. True, the only provision of the Constitution concerning the removal of federal judges is Article II, section 4, which provides that "all civil Officers of the United States, shall be removed from Office on Impeachment for, and Conviction of, Treason, Bribery, or other high Crimes and Misdemeanors."[7] Senility doesn't seem to be a high crime or misdemeanor. But "during good Behaviour" need not be equated with not being a criminal, and so it's been argued that federal judges can be removed for good cause, if not from the office then from exercising judicial powers, without impeachment.[8]

Congress could enact standards of good behavior to flesh out the "good Behaviour" clause. But there is no likelihood that it will do

7. Article II, § 2, cl. 2, makes clear that federal judges are "Officers of the United States."

8. See Saikrishna Prakash and Steven Douglas Smith, "How to Remove a Federal Judge," 116 *Yale Law Journal* 72 (2006). As an aside I note that a judge who takes senior status (amounting for most judges to semi-retirement) can be barred from hearing cases by his circuit's judicial council (in other words, can be forced to retire), but cannot be forced to take senior status in the first place. If, however, a judge is found to be disabled yet refuses to retire, an additional judge can be appointed to his court without Congress's having to authorize another judgeship. See Judicial Conduct and Disability Act, 28 U.S.C. § 372(b).

that in the foreseeable future, even though secure lifetime tenure adversely affects the work ethic of some judges and induces others to remain in office despite failing powers attributable to illness or old age. These are consequences of lifetime tenure in any calling, not just the judicial—except that federal judicial tenure is more secure than any other form of tenure that I'm aware of and therefore a greater drag on needed turnover. And chief judges of the courts of appeals and the district courts have little incentive, and severely limited ability, to force elderly incompetent judges off the bench, as by enlisting family members of a judge to persuade him that he should retire in order to protect his reputation.

With the increased longevity of Americans, the downside of secure lifetime tenure has become more pronounced, and not only because more judges are threatened with senility. In a society increasingly in flux as a result of a variety of largely technological challenges, an elderly judiciary even if *compos mentis* may lose touch and become an impediment to needed reforms, as happened in the 1930s. Yet there is an upside to lifetime tenure: it mitigates, to a degree, the politicization of the judiciary. It prevents Presidents from correcting their mistakes, which may not be mistakes from a public-interest standpoint. Examples are the appointments of Justices Brennan and Souter by Republican Presidents who may not have realized (this is clearer in Souter's case than in Brennan's) that the two were liberals. Once they were confirmed, the appointing President and his successors were stuck with them. Tenure frees the judge from control by the President who appointed him, enabling a judge to drift ideologically. Secure lifetime judicial tenure thus tends to promote ideological diversity, which is a good thing given the influence of ideology on the decision of closely balanced cases. Had Justice Kennedy not drifted, at least slightly, to the left since his appointment, the Supreme Court would be significantly more conservative than it is today—and it is more conservative today than it has been since the 1930s.

It's odd that while Presidents are allowed to serve for only eight years, there's no limit on the tenure of Supreme Court Justices, even though the Supreme Court is largely a political court because of how the Justices are selected, the absence of a court empowered to reverse it, and the political significance of so many of the Court's decisions. But there doesn't seem to be a satisfactory solution to the tenure problem, even assuming as I do that Congress could define "good Behaviour" in a way that would allow forced retirement of judges no longer able to do their job. One concern with setting limits on judicial tenure (especially tight limits, such as the nonrenewable ten-year terms that are common in foreign constitutional courts) is that in deciding cases under such a regime judges may be thinking about how their decisions might affect their future employment opportunities, which could influence the decisions. For depending on age and length of term they might well be too young to be comfortable retiring when their term expires. There might in other words be a "revolving door" problem.

Another concern is that the shorter the term of judicial office the greater the frequency of appointments; that would be a problem in the case of the Supreme Court because of the controversy that appointments to the Court frequently engender. Against these considerations, however, must be set the increase in the longevity of Americans, which increases the danger that life-tenured judges will serve beyond their sell-by date. A solution—not without its own problems, however—would be to require elderly judges to take a battery of physical and mental tests every couple of years, with forced retirement the consequence of failing to achieve a predetermined score on the tests. But there is no realistic possibility of such a reform.

The federal judicial appointment process has become more politicized of late and given us a more polarized Supreme Court, in the sense of a Court with fewer moderates.[9] Paradoxically the politicization of judicial appointments has been encouraged by notable increases in the size and quality of judicial staffs (consisting primarily of law clerks), because the stronger those staffs the less the appointing authorities need worry that a weak but politically attractive appointee will be an embarrassment to the President who appointed him and the Senate that confirmed him. Federal appellate judges, who once had only one law clerk, can now have five law clerks, though if the judge has five they'll have to divide up secretarial duties among themselves because there won't *be* a secretary—the judge's staff is limited to five. (As a result, most of the judges have a secretary and four clerks.) And the average quality of law clerks has improved because the overall quality of law students at the law schools from which most law clerks to federal judges are hired has improved. Also, clerkships have become a more coveted first law job. At this writing, federal law clerks who go to work for a major law firm after their clerkship can expect a $50,000 signing bonus (more if they clerked for more than a year); for law clerks to Supreme Court Justices the signing bonus is now $300,000.[10] The understanding, which I believe is a gentlemen's agreement rather

9. See Adam Liptak, "The Polarized Court: The Perception That Politics Has Infected the Process May Damage the Justices' Prestige," *New York Times,* May 11, 2014, Sunday Review, 1. Not that politicization leads inevitably to polarization. A Court consisting of nine right-wingers or nine left-wingers would be politicized but not polarized.

10. See, for example, Cravath, Swaine & Moore LLP, "Benefits," summer 2014, www.cravath.com/benefits/; Debra Cassens Weiss, "New High Is Reached for Supreme Court Clerkship Bonuses," *ABA Journal,* August 16, 2013, www.abajournal.com/news/article/new_high_is_reached_for_supreme_court _clerkship_bonuses.

than a contract, is that the former clerk commits to working a minimum of two years for the firm to earn his signing bonus, although because it is a *signing* bonus it's paid when he starts working for the firm.[11]

The problem of senatorial delay in the confirmation of judicial nominees is symptomatic of a general lack of discipline in Congress— a defect in the governmental structure (with its bicameralism, its separation of the legislative and executive branches, the President's veto power) created by the Constitution. One consequence is the poor drafting of so many federal statutes—often so poor that their meaning can't be discerned, making statutory "interpretation" in such cases a misnomer (a problem I discuss in the next chapter). And statutory opacity is only one illustration of the indeterminacy of so many of the legal questions that federal courts, especially appellate courts and above all the U.S. Supreme Court, are called upon to answer. A court asked to determine the applicability of a constitutional, statutory, regulatory, or contractual provision, or a judicial decision that is entitled to weight as a precedent, to a situation that the promulgators of the

---

11. The reason for the extravagant signing bonus for Supreme Court law clerks appears to be the emergence of firms that specialize in Supreme Court litigation. The Court hears few cases, yet receives an enormous number of petitions for certiorari, some filed by large companies. Law firms believe that having former Supreme Court law clerks in their employ helps them to obtain Supreme Court business. True, even with all those cert. petitions there isn't that much Supreme Court work to go around, but that doesn't matter; a law firm that becomes known for being hired to litigate before the Supreme Court will attract clients having cases in lower courts. One not very reputable reason that it will attract them is that a corporation's or other organization's general counsel wants to be able to tell his boss, in case he loses a case, that it's not his (that is, the general counsel's) fault—he hired the best: an elite law firm, staffed with former Supreme Court clerks. So blame the court, not the law firm or the general counsel that hired it, for the adverse judgment.

statute, precedent, and so forth, had not foreseen, can appeal to a variety of "interpretive" techniques—linguistic, consequentialist, purposive, pragmatic, and so on. But there is no neutral, objective basis for choosing among the techniques.[12] In indeterminate decisional settings judges, like other people, are as I keep saying forced back on their priors, which are likely to determine the choice of technique, and that choice is likely in turn to determine the outcome.

A pair of structural deformations of the federal judiciary, fortunately not so consequential as the ones I've discussed so far, concern salary. I'm not going to echo Chief Justices, who are constantly clamoring for raises for federal judges (a painless way for a Chief Justice to curry favor with his subordinates)—the current salaries ($201,000 for district judges, $213,000 for court of appeals judges, and $246,000 for Supreme Court Justices except that the Chief Justice's salary is $258,000) should be adequate to recruit and hold able judges, especially when nonmonetary compensation is factored in—the secure lifetime tenure, generous retirement and health benefits, prestige, power, intrinsic job satisfactions, autonomy, and brilliant law clerks. The problems that concern me are, first, the salary differential between court of appeals judges and district judges. It's not very large ($12,000) but it causes some district judges who are both happier as and better suited to be district judges to accept and sometimes angle for "promotion" to the court of appeals. They seek both to increase their income and to acquire the additional prestige, slight though it is, conferred by a salary increase, implying that the recipient has indeed been promoted and not just shifted to a different job. There is also the fact that court of appeals judges can't be reversed by district judges but that district judges can be and not infrequently are reversed by the

12. See, with reference to constitutional law, Philip C. Bobbitt, *Constitutional Interpretation* xii–xvii (1991); André LeDuc, "The Relationship of Constitutional Law to Philosophy: Five Lessons from the Originalism Debate," 12 *Georgetown Journal of Law and Public Policy* 99, 154–156 (2014).

court of appeals for their circuit. No one likes to be reversed, especially when the reversal is accompanied by a remand to the reversed judge, requiring him or her to do more work on the case.

The higher salaries of Supreme Court Justices have no function except to enhance their prestige, an enhancement they don't need. Were they paid the same as federal court of appeals judges, there would be no effect on the quality of the Supreme Court; it is inconceivable that someone who wanted to be appointed to the Supreme Court would refuse the appointment if his salary would be a mere $213,000.

A more serious problem with federal judicial salaries is the absence of a cost of living differential for federal judges. The cost of living varies widely across the United States. In Manhattan it is 135 percent higher than in Jackson, Mississippi. It is 45 percent higher in Boston than it is in Boise, Idaho. A judicial salary that would be considered adequate for residents of New York City would be overly generous in much of the United States, while a judicial salary that would be adequate for residents in the less pricey parts of the nation would be inadequate for residents of New York City and other expensive cities, such as San Francisco, where the cost of living is 76 percent higher than it is in Boise.[13] The geographical uniformity of federal judicial salaries is an unsatisfactory as well as an unnecessary compromise: just right in some parts of the country, too high in others, too low in still others. But even if there were a political will to introduce a cost of living differential, without a constitutional amendment it would be impossible to lower the salaries of judges who are overpaid because a uniform salary overpays the judges in the low cost-of-living parts of the country while underpaying the other judges. The cost-of-living differential would have to take the form of raising judges' salaries in

---

13. These figures are from Bankrate, "Cost of Living Calculator," www.bankrate.com/calculators/savings/moving-cost-of-living-calculator.aspx.

the most expensive areas in the country while leaving other judges' salaries unchanged. Those other judges would squawk loudly.

Another financial issue is the wasteful use of space by the federal judiciary. It is important that courthouses have a certain dignity, even majesty, and that courtrooms be impressive. These features serve to impress the lay persons who find themselves in these facilities—as litigants, litigants' family members, witnesses, jurors, and observers—with the seriousness of the occasion. What is not important is that judges have large, expensively furnished offices, as most of them do, or that every district judge have his own courtroom, as he does, even if he's likely to use it only a few days a month—the situation in many federal judicial districts. Extravagant courthouses are popular with Congressmen—it enhances a Congressman's prestige to have "brought" an impressive building to his district—and with the building industry, which donates to Congressmen. Only a budget crunch brings efforts to curtail wasteful spending on judicial edifices, furniture, and libraries (the last being largely superfluous in the Internet era). At this writing there is a federal budget squeeze and some efforts to bring about a federal judicial "space reduction."[14] Specifically, the federal judiciary has embarked recently on a five-year plan to reduce judicial building space—by just 3 percent.[15] Surely more could be done along that line. Waste in government is pervasive, and the judiciary is not exempt.

The issue of use of space to one side, the problems discussed in this chapter all bear on the quality of federal judges. But I don't think the

14. See Memorandum of Judge D. Brooks Smith, Chairman of the Judicial Conference Committee on Space and Facilities, "Judicial Conference Policies on Space Reduction," July 21, 2014.
15. "First Year of Space-Cutting Initiative Yields Major Successes," January 8, 2015, *United States Courts,* http://news.uscourts.gov/first-year-space-cutting-initiative-yields-major-successes.

innate quality or competence of federal judges is the major problem of the federal judiciary. With different methods of judicial appointment, a different compensation structure, and so forth, the average quality of the judiciary would be somewhat higher. Yet almost all federal judges today are competent, motivated, and diligent—they are good enough, one might say. The problems of the federal judiciary have less to do with raw ability or potential than with a legal culture too little attuned to current needs, too backward looking. That legal culture, which I refer to sometimes as our "stale legal culture," is the subject of the next chapter—by far the longest in the book—and of Chapter 3 as well, though the focus of that chapter is on managerial problems of the federal judiciary rather than on decision making. The problems, both decisional and managerial, that a stale legal culture gives rise to, though they are problems that unlike those discussed in this chapter should be readily soluble—and by the judges themselves—are proving resistant to solution. Judges tend to cling to the old ways even as the rise of technological and broader societal complexity renders the old ways ever more dysfunctional. The legal academy ought to be able to play a role in breaking the logjam.

2 | PROCESS DEFICIENCIES

Law, says the judge as he looks down his nose
Speaking clearly and most severely,
Law as I've told you before,
Law is as you know I suppose,
Law is but let me explain it once more,
Law is The Law   —W. H. AUDEN

I CONFESS TO BEING outspoken for a judge, and the remarks I made in Chapter 1 about structural deformations of the federal judiciary, and the more extensive remarks in this and the next chapter about judicial deficiencies, should dispel any doubts on that score.[1] To put these remarks in perspective I need to remind the reader that no human institution is flawless—whether a government agency, a successful business, a great university, or for that matter a family. If you want a flawless institution go visit a beehive or an anthill. I am proud to be a federal judge, participating therefore in the governance of the country (albeit in a minor way) and striving to make the legal system more accurate, efficient, humane, and, in a word, just. The federal judiciary is among the better professional bodies in the United States. But like every human institution, including almost every government instrumentality, it

1. See, for example, Ronald K.L. Collins, "Posner on Posner," December 2014, http://concurringopinions.com/archives/category/posner-on-posner; Joel Cohen, "An Interview with Judge Richard A. Posner," *ABA Journal,* July 1, 2014, www.abajournal.com/magazine/article/an_interview_with_judge_richard_a._posner/.

has flaws. And they are serious. The question I ask in Part Two of this book is whether the law schools can do more than they're doing to help eliminate some of those flaws, or, more realistically, to minimize them. But first I must explain the flaws in detail.

To maintain perspective requires recognizing that at this writing the United States exhibits an unprecedented array of failed social systems. The political system is in disarray—Congress is a mess, the executive branch poorly managed. The Supreme Court bears some of the responsibility for congressional malfunction because of its refusal to allow reasonable limitations on campaign expenditures and its refusal to outlaw, as a denial of equal protection of the laws, political gerrymandering. Likewise in disarray is the medical industry (as in matters of cost and coverage, preventive medicine, and care of the elderly and the poor); also education (other than in the elite private and public high schools and the elite colleges and universities), public pensions, immigration, federal taxation, and the nation's transportation infrastructure. Our prison systems and our criminal laws (especially sentencing) are an international disgrace, and the judges, including federal judges, are complicit. A number of state and local governments are seriously underfinanced. Our foreign and national security policies are pervaded by a degree of indecision unseen since the 1930s. Although admired by most Americans, our armed forces are plagued by serious cost, competence, and leadership problems. Economic inequality has reached a dangerous level. There are too many guns in private hands. Conflict between religious and secular views on issues of public policy such as abortion, contraception, same-sex marriage, and the teaching of evolution is increasingly bitter. The government cannot get a handle on global warming or environmental regulation generally. There are sectional tensions, racial and ethnic tensions along with sexual and religious ones, regulatory failures everywhere, bureaucratic incompetence, widespread corruption and fraud both public and private, and a weakening of family structure as reflected in the greatly increased prevalence of single-parent households. One can hardly expect the federal judiciary to be completely immune from so pervasive a national malaise, and it isn't.

The judicial deficiencies that I discuss in this chapter are neither structural (the subject of the preceding chapter) nor managerial (the subject of the next). Rather they are deficiencies in how federal judges decide cases and justify their decisions in judicial opinions. I begin with—

1. *Legal formalism,* still the dominant style of judicial opinions although the extent to which it is merely decorative rather than an actual decision driver is unclear. The formalist premise (or pretense) is that cases can be responsibly decided only by a two-step process. The first step is interpretation—guided by dictionaries and by interpretive principles special to law (such as "canons of construction")—of authoritative legal materials. The second step is the application to the facts of the case of a legal rule or standard derived by interpretation. By teaching that an objective meaning can always be extracted from authoritative sources of law (consisting largely of statutes, constitutional provisions, binding precedents, and valid rules and regulations), and often just by consulting a dictionary, and that once extracted such meanings can be seen to resolve all legal disputes, formalism engenders an exaggerated belief in the existence of objectively correct answers to all legal questions and the possibility that ideology, intuition, experience, policy, consequences, and emotion need play no role in the judicial process, any more than they play a role in deciding what the sum of two plus two is. I don't suppose that any intelligent judge takes formalism to this extreme, but some take it very far, or at least pretend to.

Formalism is backward-looking. Instead of the judge's asking: here is a novel issue—how should it be resolved?—he asks: here is a novel issue—what resolution is dictated by existing legal materials, the product of decisions (by legislatures, judges, regulatory agencies, and the like) made in the past, often long in the past? This method of seeking answers to current legal questions is comparable to seeking answers to current ethical questions in the Bible or the Talmud (which of course many people do, though seemingly without much success). It's saying: let the past control the present and the future, or as Nietzsche put it sarcastically, "Let the dead bury the living."[2] It's a habit of thought exemplified by Blackstone's belief that the origins of the common law of England were Saxon and that the common law would reach perfection only when its original Saxon character was restored. That kind of golden-age thinking, inherited from Greek mythology, persists in many law-trained people. Exaggerating the prescience of the nation's founders—treating them as seers, as geniuses—lawyers and judges search the meager text of an eighteenth-century document for answers to twenty-first century questions of public policy.

I do not mean to denigrate the historical sense, so richly displayed for example in Holmes's *The Common Law* (1881). But equally timely is T. S. Eliot's reminder that "the historical sense involves a perception not only of the pastness of the past, but of its presence . . . It is not preposterous that the past should be altered by the present as much as the present is directed by the past."[3]

Judges have things backward when, as is common, they start their analysis of a new case with a consideration of precedents—related cases decided earlier. By definition a precedent was created in a differ-

---

2. "On the Uses and Disadvantages of History for Life," in Friedrich Nietzsche, *Untimely Meditations* 57, 72 (R. J. Holldingdale trans. 1983). Every "originalist" should be made to read Nietzsche's brilliant essay.

3. "Tradition and the Individual Talent," in T. S. Eliot, *The Sacred Wood: Essays on Poetry and Criticism* 47, 49, 50 (1920).

ent setting from the present, often a different era, a different world really. The proper way to approach a new case is to ask, without reference to the past as such (I say "as such" in recognition of the fact that clues to a sensible answer may be found in past cases; but extracting wisdom from them is not the same as treating them as "authorities"), what would be a sensible answer as a matter of policy. One does need then to look at precedent, statutory language, and other sources of legal meaning to decide whether the sensible answer is blocked by one of those sources. But if the new case is truly novel, then by definition it isn't blocked.

I'm not denying the importance of continuity in law, and in particular the need to place the interest in continuity in balance with the interest in creativity in order to give reasonable reliance interests deserved protection, a kind of insurance. Abrupt changes even if sound and even if made prospective in order to avoid too sudden an impact can frustrate planning and investment. That's why changing the law retroactively is disapproved—or rather it's the only good reason for hesitancy in overruling precedents. A bad reason, which may however be responsible for most of that hesitancy, is to avoid acknowledging that judges make frequent mistakes, as they—as we—undoubtedly do. I'm denying merely the formalist premise that there is no such thing as a novel case—that every case can be decided by reference to some earlier decision or some otherwise authoritative document. I'm denying that all that there is or should be or can be to legal analysis is interpretation. The formalist is a 100 percent interpretivist. For him nothing is new. He just asks how the authors of a statutory or constitutional provision or other past ukase would have applied it to a case they could not have foreseen though it's within the provision's semantic scope. But since the authors can't be asked what they meant, what is called interpretation is actually creation.

And the realist? Legal realism as a distinct school of judges and law professors flourished most outspokenly in the 1920s and 1930s, but there were realists before and realists after, and there are realists today. Many of today's realists eschew the label as suggestive of cynicism, but some do not.[4] By a realist I mean a judge or a law professor who, perceiving the inadequacies of formalism, wants law, and specifically judicial decision making, to be understood as a practical rather than a theoretical activity. A realist judge pays attention to precedent and the other formal sources of law, but to much else besides, and can be regarded as a political actor though less so than a legislator or an executive branch official.

Realism is equivalent to pragmatism in the lay, not the philosophical, sense of the word; it is decision making guided by practical considerations rather than by theory. It is what I have sometimes called "everyday pragmatism" to distinguish it from philosophical pragmatism, which is multifaceted and abstruse.[5] Everyday pragmatism is concerned primarily with the consequences of a given action. It is an important component of legal realism, and though not the entirety of it has been the component emphasized in many of my previous writings, such as the book I just cited.

My emphasis has invited the observation by Professor Frank Cross, reviewing my book *How Judges Think,* that "one central critique of pragmatism is instability. Although Judge Posner repeatedly emphasizes the pragmatic importance of considering system effects, this consideration is left to the individual judge, and critics question the efficacy of that structure. How is a litigant to know how a particular judge will weight adherence to established precedent?"[6]

---

4. See "New Legal Realism," *Wikipedia,* http://en.wikipedia.org/wiki/New _legal_realism.
5. The distinction between the two concepts of pragmatism is explored at length in my book *Law, Pragmatism, and Democracy* (2003), especially Chapters 1 and 2.
6. Frank B. Cross, "What Do Judges Want?" 87 *Texas Law Review* 183, 218 (2008).

Cross answers his question at the end of his review with a ringing endorsement of judicial pragmatism:

> The question is therefore one of how much we wish to liberate judges to openly pursue their inclination of reaching "good decisions," or how much they can be trusted, as opposed to how much we strive to render judges more legalistic. The answer to this question is still indefinite, but there is certainly reason to believe that open judicial pragmatism is a wise decision-making approach. It is commonly argued that reliance on conventional legalism is the key to good judicial decision making, but there is very little evidence to support this claim. There are plenty of reasons to believe that a general rule of law is very beneficial, economically and otherwise. These reasons cannot support conventional legalism, though, because the research suggests that common law decision making, with its allowance for pragmatic judicial discretion, is typically superior to constrained civil law decision making, which is far more legalistic. And the research also suggests that alternative grand theories of judicial decision making are no better at producing a determinate rule of law. The simple prescription that judges should do the "good" thing is enormously aggravating to legal theorists. As a rule, it seems to have no power to direct or cabin judicial decision making. Yet that is precisely its value. It does not artificially compel "bad" decisions. It places trust in the judiciary, deciding case by case, to assess the facts and law and policy of cases and—drawing upon their diverse individual backgrounds and ideologies— to ultimately reach a "good" legal rule. Judge Posner has previously characterized judges as a council of "wise elders" with good judgment who may be entrusted with "responsibility

for deciding cases in a way that will produce the best results in the circumstances." Judges are ideologically influenced in reaching their decisions, but they are far from pure ideologues. Judges certainly attend to the law, but they are not simply legalistic. Instead, they are balancers of various immediate and systemic interests at stake in litigation. Under the judicial model of pragmatism, numerous "wrong" decisions will surely issue, but the body of the law will adapt and evolve away from them and toward the better opinions—if one trusts the corporate judicial body. While the system, like all human systems, is imperfect, there is evidence of its effectiveness. In *How Judges Think,* Judge Posner places his trust in judges to direct the evolution of the law in a manner that benefits society. If anything, I believe he may be too faint in this trust. Even as individual judges make pragmatic errors in their decisions, the broad systemic effects of the approach can be generally beneficial. This book explains how this is possible and how it has already occurred to some degree, according to empirical research on the nature of judicial decision making.[7]

I don't see any significant difference between legal pragmatism so understood and the more familiar concept of legal realism—and let me stay with that. The realist, as I have explained, asks what is a sensible result in a case—in light of common sense but also of likely consequences and the general legal culture—and is it blocked by an authoritative piece of constitutional or statutory text, or by a precedential decision that even if questionable as an original matter has been relied on so extensively that overruling it would cause more

7. Id. at 232–233 (footnotes omitted).

harm than good (or it might be a precedent that had been established by a higher court and was therefore beyond the authority of a lower court to overrule). The realist appreciates the importance of protecting reliance interests, though he doesn't consider them the only or necessarily the paramount interests to be considered in deciding a case. If the sensible result, all things considered (including reliance on previous decisions), is not blocked by an authoritative enactment or binding precedent, the realist says: go with it!

Judging as understood by realists is a *natural* activity in the sense that a judge (I have in mind an appellate judge) who reads the briefs in a case and does some background research and discusses the case with his law clerks and hears oral argument and afterward discusses the case with the other judges on the panel that heard the case will have a pretty good sense of what the best outcome would be—the best balance of often warring considerations. Among them reliance interests figure but also other social values, caseload considerations, administrability, respect for expertise, moral intuitions, and much else besides. Interpretation of past settlements, such as statutes and precedents, when such interpretation is feasible, figures as well, again as a natural human activity (rather than as a formalized methodology) because we are constantly interpreting.[8] Other such activities engaged

---

8. "The fact that interpretation does not admit to some mechanical procedure of validation is not a fatal objection to the concept of interpretation; a profoundly significant and successful network of intellectual and linguistic practices enables us to try to understand each other's meaning, to enter into each other's purposes, and to understand, interpret, apply, and follow rules, all with no (or only infrequent) resort to mechanical deduction." Paul M. Bator, "The Judicial Universe of Judge Richard Posner," 52 *University of Chicago Law Review* 1146, 1163 (1985). Or as Learned Hand put it, "At times one is more likely to reach the truth by an unanalyzed and intuitive conclusion from the text as a whole, than by following, step by step, the accredited guides." *Van Vranken v. Helvering*, 115 F.2d 709, 711 (2d Cir. 1940).

in by judges include determining the scope of precedents, finding useful ideas in opinions, academic writings, or other sources (including the Internet), and putting all these things together, influenced inevitably by priors of which a judge may be unconscious. Out of the gallimaufry the judge extracts what he considers a sensible result and tries to defend it in an opinion that one hopes is clearly written, balances tact and candor skillfully, and carefully analyzes the likely consequences of a decision one way or the other.

Another way to describe legal realism is as blurring the distinction between form and substance, which is to say between doctrine and fact. The formalist views fact through the lens of doctrine, which is primary to him. The realist forms a preliminary estimate of the best decision in a case by an assessment of the facts (including institutional or systemic facts, such as the possible impact of the decision one way or another on legal uncertainty or on the amount of litigation), and the values and policies promoted or retarded by the facts, and then asks whether the case can be decided on the basis of that assessment without undue violence to legal doctrine.

I don't think there's much more to judging than what I've been describing as legal realism, and if this is correct then judges ought to be able to write opinions that are simple enough to be readable by nonlawyers. Not that many nonlawyers can be expected to read judicial opinions. But writing an opinion that *could* be read by nonlawyers will give the judge earned confidence that his decision and the analysis informing it make practical sense—and indeed that *he* understands the opinion.

The realist opinion will be recognized by how many things *don't* appear in it. No multifactor tests, except to be ridiculed. No standards of review: the ruling of a lower court or of an agency earns the deference it deserves by the quality of its analysis or its greater knowledge of the issues than the appellate court has or can obtain. This I realize is arch heresy. Standards of review are thought by most lawyers and judges to constitute a distinct technical field of law, comparable to civil procedure. A compact and lucid treatise describes the field in exhaustive detail.[9] I don't think the treatise could be improved upon. But essentially it just summarizes what the courts, particularly the Supreme Court, have said about appellate review of trial courts and agencies. And as in the case of statutory interpretation, what the courts have said has tended to muddy the waters. At one point the authors remark that "functional considerations" play a significant role when standards of review are vague.[10] By that they mean, essentially, common sense. My view—more radical than theirs—is that common sense can't be bettered as a guide to appellate review, provided that the judgment or ruling sought to be overturned is reviewable by the appellate court and that the judges apply their common sense to as rich a body of fact as the case can be forced to reveal. If the issue is purely one of law the appellate court can't defer to the trial court, because then the law would differ across trial judges in the same jurisdiction. If the issue is factual, the appellate court will reverse if convinced that the trial court or agency was wrong, and affirm if, even if it harbors doubt, it thinks it quite possible that the trial court or agency, knowing more about the subject and having spent more time analyzing it, got it right. In short, review of purely legal findings is plenary, and of factual findings (and application of law to fact) deferential in the sense of giving respectful consideration to the determination by the lower court or the administrative agency. There is a little more to standards of review, but not much.

9. Harry T. Edwards, Linda A. Elliott, and Marin K. Levy, *Federal Standards of Review: Review of District Court Decisions and Agency Actions* (2d ed. 2013).

10. Id. at 12–16.

Simplification and sense are the hallmarks of a realist judicial opinion. No exaggeration about jurors' abilities will be found in such an opinion, and a bare minimum of legal jargon—and nothing the judge doesn't actually believe, except that in the spirit of compromise he may decide to incorporate a point suggested by another judge on the panel that the writing judge may be doubtful about but considers at least plausible—a common feeling because of the uncertainty of American law.

A realist opinion tends to differ from a formalist one structurally. The formalist will usually begin his opinion with a brief statement of the issue or issues to be decided and a lengthy statement of facts. Then will come a lengthy recital of applicable legal doctrine, whether found in precedent or in a statute or constitutional provision. The judge will then seek in the law as thus expounded a directive to affirm or reverse. He may bolster the conclusion reached by application of "the law" to the facts by referring to the positive effects of his decision on policy or other practical concerns.

This is a standard opinion format, though pedestrian and tending to loquacity, and is often used by realists as well. But the authentic realist opinion is different. It begins with a brief recital of the jurisdictional and procedural context and of the minimum number of facts necessary to set the scene, so that the reader knows what the case is about. Then comes a brief statement of the issue to be resolved (sometimes the sequence of scene-setting and issue-stating will be reversed), followed by the judge's proposal of the resolution that in light of the general legal framework, the lawyers' arguments, and all relevant facts, whether record or extrarecord facts, seems the most reasonable in light of consequences and other relevant considerations. Last the judge will check to make sure that the reasonable solution isn't blocked by some controlling legal rule or principle invoked by the party that the court is leaning against—always bearing in mind, however, that the meaning of a rule or principle will usually be found in its purpose.

The basic difference between the two opinion formats lies in what might be called the "order of thought." The formalist's is strict: a complete factual picture (though drawn entirely from the record) followed by a search of conventional legal materials for a rule or principle that will prescribe the legal consequences of the facts, concluded maybe by intimations of positive practical or human consequences of the decision. The realist's ideal opinion begins with a fact- and values-based quest for a reasonable solution to the issue presented, followed by a check of orthodox legal materials to make sure the reasonable solution is not blocked by binding precedent or other indubitable legal authority.

Realist and formalist opinions are likely to differ most conspicuously in regard to precedent. To the full-blooded formalist nothing is new, and the most abundant body of old authoritative statements to which the formalist judge faced with having to decide a new case can look for guidance consists not of statutory or constitutional provisions but of judicial decisions. Knowing this, lawyers fill their briefs with citations to decisions. But it is rare that such citations should carry the day for a litigant; usually all they'll show is that a court once said something that supports an argument for one party to a case rather than another, and the question should be whether what it said was sensible and is pertinent to the present case. The fact that a *court* said it in a case not materially identical—not therefore "controlling" authority—does not contribute to the intrinsic merit or lack of merit of the statement. The court in the later case might cite the earlier one to indicate agreement with it, but the fact that a *party* agrees with a statement in a case means nothing.

Legal realism in approximately the form in which I embrace and defend it was a highly influential judicial philosophy not just in the

1920s and 1930s but in the entire period that began with the publication of Holmes's *The Common Law* in 1881 and ended with the end of the Carter Presidency a century later.[11] Reagan's election, his conservative appointments to the federal courts of appeals and the Supreme Court, and the more or less simultaneous creation of the Federalist Society, began to shift the federal judicial balance back toward formalism, giving rise to "originalism" and "textualism" and increased resort to dictionaries ("literalism") as sources of statutory meaning—all backward-looking sources of judicial guidance. These touchstones took the place of "judicial self-restraint," which had been set against "judicial activism" as a solemn injunction to judges to "apply" the law rather than to create new law unless they were common law judges. The new vocabulary of "originalism" and "textualism" had the rhetorical advantage over "judicial self-restraint" of enabling ideological change to be represented as methodological progress—the law working itself pure rather than being reshaped by conservative ideology. Overlooked was the tension between originalism and abiding by precedent. If a precedent was not consistent with the original meaning of the Constitution, for example, originalism implied that it should be overruled—unless the Constitution was believed to have

11. All of legal realism is in a sentence on the first page of *The Common Law*—"The life of the law has not been logic: it has been experience"—helpfully amplified on pages 35 to 36: "The very considerations which judges most rarely mention, and always with an apology are the secret root from which the law draws all the juices of life. I mean, of course, considerations of what is expedient for the community concerned. Every important principle which is developed by litigation is in fact and at bottom the result of more or less definitely understood views of public policy . . . The law is administered by able and experienced men, who know too much to sacrifice good sense to a syllogism." Holmes was of course talking about the common law, but much of statutory and most of constitutional law is made by judges. Although they call what they're doing "interpretation," realistically it's common law elaboration of the contents of vague, incoherent, or outmoded texts.

assumed or implied that judges should adhere to a precedent even if based on a misreading of the Constitution, at least if overruling it would destroy important reliance interests.

Yet even after the reversion to premodern ways of thinking (or pretending to think, or feeling one was thinking) about the judicial process that was entailed by originalism and formalism, the leading realists of yore continue to be venerated—and really is there much to add (besides some modern psychology and economics) to Cardozo's *The Nature of the Judicial Process,* published in 1921, as a handbook of judicial realism?

The modern formalists seem oblivious to the fact that *none* of the judges who are still reckoned to have been "great" was a formalist— not John Marshall,[12] not Joseph Story, not Lemuel Shaw, not Holmes, not Brandeis, not Cardozo, not Charles Evans Hughes,[13] not Learned Hand, not Robert Jackson, not Roger Traynor, not Henry Friendly.[14] They were all realists, although some, such as Story and Shaw, had a strong formalist streak (and Holmes a weak such streak).

12. Holmes expressed gratitude that by appointing John Marshall Chief Justice, President Adams "gave it to a Federalist *and loose constructionist* to start the working of the Constitution." Oliver Wendell Holmes, Jr., "John Marshall," February 4, 1901, in *The Essential Holmes: Selections from the Letters, Speeches, Judicial Opinions, and Other Writings of Oliver Wendell Holmes, Jr.* 206, 207 (Richard A. Posner ed. 1992) (emphasis added).

13. Who memorably remarked: "We are under a Constitution, but the Constitution is what the judges say it is, and the judiciary is the safeguard of our liberty and of our property under the Constitution." "Speech before Elmira Chamber of Commerce," May 3, 1907, in *Addresses and Papers of Charles Evans Hughes, Governor of New York, 1906–1908* 133, 139 (1908).

14. Edmund Ursin, "How *Great* Judges Think: Judges Richard Posner, Henry Friendly, and Roger Traynor on Judicial Lawmaking," 57 *Buffalo Law Review* 1268 (2009) (emphasis in original), traces a realist tradition from Shaw and Holmes in the nineteenth century to judges of recent and current times. I am embarrassed by the title and disclaim the adjective "great" applied to me, but the article presents an accurate genealogy of realism and an interesting discussion of the difference between legal realism and the "legal process" school of Henry

To which list I'm inclined to add William Murray, Lord Mansfield, Great Britain's greatest judge, who died in 1793 after a long career as Chief Justice of England. His judicial opinions strongly influenced American law in a variety of fields, not only commercial law, for which he was most noted, but also admiralty law, criminal law, copyright law, the law of slavery, and other fields. He was immensely learned, and his learning was not limited to law; he knew a great deal about mercantile customs, and about other practices and institutions and activities that give rise to litigation. In insisting on understanding the factual context of his cases, and in other respects as well, he was notably realistic. For example, he thought a precedent "valuable only if it is based on a principle," and contended that it was the principle (if sound), not the precedent, that should control future decisions. It has been observed that "he combined his astute understanding of human nature with a vigorous aspiration to achieve justice. To him, morals were an essential element of law." (Shades of "moral intuitions," the key term in the Introduction to this book.) "His rulings were solidly grounded on his encyclopedic knowledge of the law, his understanding of human nature, his diligence in ascertaining the facts of a dispute, his sound common sense, and his overriding instinct for justice."[15] It's hard to improve on this.

Lord Mansfield is the earliest in my list of unquestionably great realist judges, Judge Friendly the latest, and here is a capsule summary

---

Hart and Herbert Wechsler and their epigones. A subsequent article by Professor Ursin, "Holmes, Cardozo, and the Legal Realists: Early Incarnations of Legal Pragmatism and Enterprise Liability," 50 *San Diego Law Review* 537, 550–551 (2013), notes the affinities between Holmes and Shaw, the latter currently rather a neglected figure in the legal-realist pantheon. Notice finally that of the eleven great judges whom I list in the text, only two—Story and Traynor—had been law professors for an extended period. Holmes and Hughes had been law professors for a short time, the others not at all.

15. These quotations are from Norman S. Poser, *Lord Mansfield: Justice in the Age of Reason* 401–402 (2013).

of *his* greatness, from my foreword to David Dorsen's biography of him:

> Friendly's photographic memory combined with his analytical power, energy, speed, and work ethic to make him the most powerful legal reasoner in American legal history. And so one might suppose that he was a formalist judge par excellence, deploying text and precedent to produce decisions that satisfied the legal profession's longing for formal correctness and objective validity. But that was not the kind of judge he was. He tempered academic brilliance with massive common sense. He was less mercurial, more matter of fact, than any of the other great judges . . . He saw cases not as intellectual puzzles to be solved but as practical disputes to be resolved sensibly and humanely. He bent his powerful legal intelligence to the service of shaping legal doctrine to the enablement of sensible results in individual cases. His 31 years as a practicing lawyer enriched his academic brilliance with practical knowledge and seasoned judgment. The aim was to improve the law . . . without unduly perturbing the doctrinal and institutional framework that provides necessary stability and continuity. Like all creative judges, Friendly did not feel himself bound by the issues as framed by the lawyers, and at times . . . was surprisingly casual about waived or forfeited arguments . . . He didn't just decide interesting cases; he made interesting cases.[16]

I don't see much difference between him and Mansfield.

16. Foreword, in David M. Dorsen, *Henry Friendly: Greatest Judge of His Era* ix, xiii (2012). (The sentence "His 31 years as a practicing lawyer enriched his academic brilliance with practical knowledge and seasoned judgment" was definitely part of my statement, but was accidentally omitted from the published version of the

I don't mean to suggest that the absence of formalists from the roster of great judges is conclusive of the relative merits of formalism and realism. The current formalism did not get its jump start until the early 1980s, with Reagan's appointment (his White House Counsel, Edwin Meese, was the moving force) to the federal courts of appeals of Robert Bork, Antonin Scalia, Frank Easterbrook, Ralph Winter, and other conservatives (me for example, though today I am a moderate rather than a conservative). Bork's service as a judge of the U.S. Court of Appeals for the District of Columbia Circuit, though distinguished, was too brief (1982–1988) to earn him recognition as a great judge; he confessed that the job had bored him.[17] Scalia and Easterbrook are influential and widely admired (though Scalia is a target of a good deal of criticism), but they are still serving and maybe a judge has to die before he can be pronounced a "great" judge (though there have been exceptions, including a number of the great realist judges whom I listed). That makes some sense, as it's difficult to reckon a person's achievements great until those achievements have passed the test of time.

A notable characteristic of the great American realist judges whom I listed is that a majority were political moderates (I exclude the conservative Story and Shaw and the liberal Brandeis and Traynor). The common belief that legal realists invariably are liberal is based on the self-characterization of many of the legal realists (most of them not judges) of the 1920s and 1930s.

Oddly, these realist judges, with the exception of Judge Traynor, are admired by conservative judges and Justices, while the formalist

---

Dorsen book.) The greatest maker of interesting cases was Cardozo, who in his opinions took some liberties with the facts. See my *Cardozo: A Study in Reputation,* ch. 3 (1990).

17. David Lauter and Ronald J. Ostrow, "Bork Resigns as Judge So He Can 'Speak Out,'" *Los Angeles Times,* January 15, 1988, http://articles.latimes.com/1988 -01-15/news/mn-24234_1_resignation-letter.

judges of yore generally are not admired by anyone. And many notable realist opinions, such as *Brown v. Board of Education,* are accepted unreservedly by conservative judges and Justices. This makes me doubt whether any American judge is entirely immune to realism, or in other words to the tug of prudence and common sense and those omnipresent priors (though I acknowledge the possibility that some judges are so fixated on precedent that they will abide by past decisions however unsound they consider them to be). Do we think ill of Chief Justice Hughes for having executed the "switch in time that saved nine" by "leaning" (as he seems to have done, though it is not certain) on Justice Owen Roberts to abandon the judicial campaign against the New Deal?[18] Was it wrong for the Supreme Court in *Roe v. Wade* to hold that a court retains jurisdiction to issue a judgment in a case about the right to an abortion, even after the birth of the baby sought to be aborted moots the case, as often happens owing to the fact that gestation is faster than litigation? Even arch-formalist judges think the Supreme Court was correct in *Brown v. Board of Education* to interpret the equal protection clause of the Fourteenth Amendment to outlaw racial segregation by public schools, although the decision appears to have flouted the original understanding of the clause.

The honest formalist is deceived about the nature of interpretation and legal analysis. But for many judges formalism appears to be a fig leaf covering politically motivated conservative decision, whether or not the judges have sufficient self-awareness to be conscious of their motivations. The most conservative judges deny that they exercise any discretion in deciding cases. The least political judges acknowledge that they do. There have been some liberal judges who hid behind formalist rhetoric, and a few notable judges, such as Holmes and Jackson, whose opinions seem totally candid.

18. Jeff Shesol, *Supreme Power: Franklin Roosevelt vs. the Supreme Court,* ch. 24 (2010).

2. *The rearview mirror syndrome.* Formalism is one of the keys to understanding the judiciary's second serious deficiency, which I'll call the rearview mirror syndrome. As I noted earlier, judges are forever looking behind them for the answers to current issues—backward to our eighteenth-century Constitution for example. Or at least they pretend to be doing so. Most realists as well as all formalists claim to be "interpreting" constitutional and statutory provisions when really they're extracting a meaning that they themselves had inserted in these often opaque documents. Other professions pride themselves on their originality. Not law, as when the economic approach to law is derided on the ground that it "take[s] an inherited cultural rhetoric that to a certain extent is already ethically integrated and subject[s] it to the disintegrative pressures of radical market theory."[19] The proper question to ask about economic analysis of law is whether it can increase the contribution of law to human welfare rather than whether it challenges a traditional rhetoric.

It's right, as I've said, for judges to try to protect reliance interests; sudden, unexpected changes in the law can upset settled expectations and by doing so create unforeseen costs and debilitating uncertainty. That is one reason behind the principle that like cases should be treated alike. But that formula should be understood as shorthand for: like cases should be treated alike if decided at more or less the same time. Even then they should not be treated alike if there is a compelling reason not to do so; it's just that there is less likely to be such a reason the closer in time to each other the cases are decided. As society changes, so must law—and indeed judges, especially if they are the Justices of the U.S. Supreme Court, are constantly making new law

19. Peter Read Teachout, "Worlds Beyond Theory: Toward the Expression of an Integrative Ethics for Self and Culture," 83 *Michigan Law Review* 849, 881 (1985). I confess to not understanding the quoted sentence, because I don't know what either "cultural rhetoric" or "ethically integrated" means.

while pretending merely to be discovering what was there all along but overlooked. They pretend not to be policymakers but instead historians, archaeologists, and philologists.

It's difficult enough to figure out what the framers and ratifiers of the Constitution really thought about the problems *they* faced. It is impossible to project their thinking into the twenty-first century and make their words speak to issues they couldn't possibly have had in mind—a process that yields such absurdities as that the framers of the Constitution, since they didn't think that flogging or the stocks were cruel and unusual punishments, wouldn't think so today, and so the judges' hands would be tied if a state legislature or Congress reintroduced flogging as a punishment for crime.[20]

What is called "constitutional law" is for the most part not in the Constitution itself. Compare the text of the Constitution and the understanding of it by its framers and ratifiers with the current body of constitutional law and you'll see that what the judges have done and are continuing to do is to treat the document as having authorized

20. According to Justice Scalia, "If a state enacted a law permitting flogging, it is immensely stupid, but it is not unconstitutional. A lot of stuff that's stupid is not unconstitutional. I gave a talk once where I said they ought to pass out to all federal judges a stamp, and the stamp says—*Whack!* [*Pounds his fist.*]—STUPID BUT CONSTITUTIONAL. *Whack!*" Quoted in Jennifer Senior, "In Conversation: Antonin Scalia," *New York Magazine,* October 6, 2013, http://nymag .com/news/features/antonin-scalia-2013-10/. I wonder why he thinks it's stupid. Maybe he doesn't really. There is quite a lot of evidence that the originalism of conservative Justices is a mask for "result oriented" decisions. See, for example, Eric J. Segall, "The Constitution according to Justices Scalia and Thomas: Alive and Kickin'," 91 *Washington University Law Review* 1663 (2014). In another piece—"Originalist Defenses of Overturning Same-Sex Marriage Ban," February 9, 2015, in *Dorf on Law,* www.dorfonlaw.org/2015/02/originalist-defenses-of -overturning.html—Professor Segall points out the absurdity of liberals' attempt to ground a constitutional right to same-sex marriage in the original meaning of the equal protection clause of the Fourteenth Amendment, ratified in 1868.

courts to create a body of constitutional law related only in the most general sense to the original understanding. The original Constitution did not even create a democratic government. The only federal officials elected by popular vote were the members of the House of Representatives. And the states (which determined who could vote in federal as well as state elections) were left free to impose racial, gender, and property restrictions on voter eligibility. In fact the Constitution was closely modeled on the nondemocratic government of Great Britain—the federal judiciary on the royal courts, the President on the British monarch, the Senate on the House of Lords, and the House of Representatives on the House of Commons.[21] The most important provisions of the original Constitution may have been Article I, section 9, prohibiting the federal government from granting titles of nobility, and Article VI, prohibiting religious tests for federal office.

The *faux* originalism that finds answers to modern questions in the Constitution (though mainly in the Bill of Rights rather than in the original Constitution, ratified two years earlier) obscures the policy judgments that generate constitutional law—sometimes obscures them, it seems, from the Justices themselves.[22] No one doubts that

21. See Eric Nelson, *The Royalist Revolution: Monarchy and the American Founding* (2014). The monarchical character of the Supreme Court, and indeed of the federal judiciary as a whole, with its secure lifetime tenure, is also illustrated by such little things as the fact that in the Supreme Court's postargument conferences the Chief Justice speaks first, and the others in order of seniority, with the result that the most junior Justice speaks last.

22. Well illustrated by Professor Baude's recent statement that "it's terribly important that judges pretend to find law rather than making it (what else could justify its retroactive application to the parties?) and that judges acknowledge the umpire ideal. These ideals may well be exaggerations and imperfectly realized, but they are key to judicial legitimacy." "Originalism: A Debate [between] Will Baude and Eric Posner, *University of Chicago Law School Record,* Spring 2015, 24, 30. Three important considerations are ignored: the unseemliness and indeed dishonesty of judicial false pretense; the fact that the common law is judge-made

common law is pragmatic and policy-oriented—that it is legislative in character, the judges being the legislators of the common law. Professor David Strauss is half right when he says that constitutional law (not all of it, but the parts most often involved in litigation, precisely because they are the parts expressed in the Constitution in language that is vague, ambiguous, or archaic) is a body of common law, thus changing as the society changes, albeit with a lag if there are substantial reliance interests at stake.[23] We are seeing this kind of change today in the area of abortion rights: a gradual whittling away, having nothing to do with a more accurate understanding of the Constitution, of a constitutional doctrine having only the most tenuous constitutional roots.

The reason Strauss is only half right is that common law in its strict sense differs critically from constitutional law in being much less political. Common law refers to judge-made legal doctrines governing private disputes in such fields as torts, contracts, and property. There is general satisfaction with these doctrines, in part because state legislatures can revise state common law and Congress can revise federal common law, whereas amending the federal Constitution is immensely difficult. Common law, whether state or federal, is not a current focus of political controversy. Constitutional law relates primarily to rights against government, is highly controversial, indeed highly politicized. Its only resemblance to common law is that it, too, is judge-made; it does not follow that it is as sound, as authentic, as politically neutral a body of law as common law—it isn't. Constitutional law is the Supreme Court's practice of forbidding whatever a majority of the Justices consider egregious invasions of rights that those Justices think people in the United States should have.

law with no pretense that the judges are merely applying law coming from legislation or the Constitution; and the absurdity of thinking that an eighteenth-century constitution can guide judicial decision making in the twenty-first century.

23. David Strauss, "Common Law Constitutional Interpretation," 63 *University of Chicago Law Review* 877 (1996).

Linda Greenhouse, the long-serving (though now retired) Supreme Court reporter for the *New York Times,* stated recently that "in decades of court-watching, I have struggled—sometimes it has seemed against all odds—to maintain the belief that the Supreme Court really is a court and not just a collection of politicians in robes. This past week, I've found myself struggling against the impulse to say two words: I surrender."[24]

There is a tendency, however, which the passage I just quoted illustrates, to exaggerate the difference between the Supreme Court (a collection of politicians) and a "real" court. In a recent piece entitled "Supreme Court Justices Are Not Really Judges: They Don't Take the Law Seriously Enough," Professor Eric Segall says that it's "important to recognize the [Supreme] court for the purely political institution it is, and to acknowledge that it is not a court of law . . . I do not claim the court always acts like Republicans or Democrats. I do claim the justices don't act like judges bound by prior law, precedent, interpretive canons, or constitutional theory."[25] It's true that courts are political institutions; they are government agencies. And it's true that Supreme Court Justices don't much act as if they really were bound by prior law, precedent (which is prior law), interpretive canons, or constitutional theory. But what appellate judges in the American system *are* bound by such things? Courts are bound by precedents of a higher court, but not by their own precedents or precedents of courts to which their decisions can't be appealed. The interpretive canons are worthless, as I'm about to argue; and constitutional theory as I said is not anchored in the Constitution but is the creation of judges.

24. Linda Greenhouse, "Law in the Raw," The Opinion Pages, *New York Times,* November 12, 2014, www.nytimes.com/2014/11/13/opinion/law-in-the-raw .html?_r=0.

25. *Slate,* November 14, 2013, www.slate.com/articles/news_and_politics/jurispru dence2014/11/supreme_court_justices_are_not_judges_they_rule_on_values _and_politics_not.html.

The principal difference between the Supreme Court and the other federal courts is that there is no court above it. That's an important difference but it does not distinguish a "real" court from a political institution. Like other American courts, the Supreme Court is both.

Professor Segall is unusual because very few law professors will acknowledge publicly the absence of persuasive evidence that American judges typically conform to idealized versions of the judge as the embodiment of thoughtful, disinterested analysis within a framework of accepted doctrines. I think that he exaggerates the difference between Supreme Court Justices and other judges (especially other appellate judges) but that he gets closer to the truth than his critics.

Against this it will be argued, by reference to H. L. A. Hart's distinction between the "internal" and the "external" point of view regarding rules of law, that whereas an ordinary person obeys legal rules out of concern for the consequences if he disobeys them, judges enforce those rules because they consider them to be valid. "They must regard these [rules] as common standards of official behaviour and appraise critically their own and each other's deviations as lapses."[26] I don't get the "must." Rules that are drawn into litigation, whether they are statutory, regulatory, or constitutional rules, often are vague, obsolete, inconsistent with other rules, offensive to current values and beliefs, and on one or more of these grounds vulnerable to invalidation or "creative" interpretation. But no one has a clear idea of the actual thinking processes of judges asked to enforce, reject, or modify such rules; the critical thinking may in fact be unconscious.

3. Naïveté about interpretation of statutes and precedents is inseparable

---

26. Hart, *The Concept of Law* 117 (1994 ed.—differing from the original 1961 edition only in the addition of a postscript responding to Hart's principal critics). The passage I quote in the text is from the original edition, not the postscript. Hart's book is revered; I wish I knew why.

from the first two deficiencies noted in this chapter. It is (so far as relates to statutes) the result of ignorance of or indifference to how people actually interpret words and sentences, to how the legislative drafting process actually works,[27] and to what the function and proper use of dictionaries are.[28] It is also the result of a desire (often uncon-

27. An ignorance exposed in important articles by Abbe R. Gluck and Lisa Schultz Bressman, "Statutory Interpretation from the Inside—An Empirical Study of Congressional Drafting, Delegation, and the Canons: Part I," 65 *Stanford Law Review* 901 (2013); Part II [same title], 66 *Stanford Law Review* 725 (2014). See also Robert A. Katzmann, *Judging Statutes,* ch. 4 (2014); Jarrod Shobe, "Intertemporal Statutory Interpretation and the Evolution of Legislative Drafting," 114 *Columbia Law Review* 807 (2014). So when John F. Manning, in his article "The Means of Constitutional Power," 128 *Harvard Law Review* 1, 67, 68 (2014), says that "a textualist approach that focuses on social and linguistic usage enables Congress to use its words to draw" lines, and that "the Court's new textualism . . . tries to give Congress the tools it needs to draw lines . . . The institutional goal . . . of the [Supreme] Court's new textualism is to enable Congress to speak with precision," he neglects to add that Congress doesn't want to "speak with precision"—a curious neglect since he appears to accept the Gluck–Bressman analysis of how congressional statutes actually are drafted. Id. at 76–77.

28. "'Plain meaning' as a way to understand language is silly. In interesting cases, meaning is not 'plain'; it must be imputed; and the choice among meanings must have a footing more solid than a dictionary—which is a museum of words, an historical catalog rather than a means to decode the work of legislatures." Frank H. Easterbrook, "Text, History, and Structure in Statutory Interpretation," 17 *Harvard Journal of Law and Public Policy* 61, 67 (1994). See also A. Raymond Randolph, "Dictionaries, Plain Meaning, and Context in Statutory Interpretation." Id. at 71, 72. "It is one of the surest indexes of a mature and developed jurisprudence not to make a fortress out of the dictionary; but to remember that statutes always have some purpose or object to accomplish, whose sympathetic and imaginative discovery is the surest guide to their meaning." *Cabell v. Markham,* 148 F.2d 737, 739 (2d Cir. 1945) (L. Hand, J.). The Supreme Court appears to be the worst offender in misusing dictionaries for statutory interpretation. "The Court's tendency to rely on one or at most two dictionaries per case, the wide variation in dictionary brand preferences among the justices, the fact that even justices with 'preferred' dictionaries are far from consistent in usage across individual cases, and the absence of a coherent approach to the time period distinction between statutory enactment and lawsuit filing, combine to suggest that

scious) to exercise broad discretion in interpreting statutes, regulations, and the Constitution without acknowledging that the exercise of judicial discretion in interpretation equates to policymaking. Dictionaries are many, meaning is fluid ("obviously, 'son of a bitch' is a phrase used all the time to mean anything except what it says, anything from 'you're terrific' to "how about that!'"), and by disparaging legislative history as a guide to statutory meaning the formalist judge enlarges his own interpretive role by reducing that of the legislators.[29] Legislative history certainly can mislead, but doesn't always.[30] The ma-

---

this comparatively novel interpretive resource is being applied in strikingly subjective ways . . . In the Rehnquist and Roberts eras, dictionaries have become a principal resource for determining the meaning of statutes . . . Throughout this period of dramatically higher usage, the Court has failed to engage with interested legal audiences who have expressed skepticism regarding the Justices' subjective, standardless, and seemingly impulsive dictionary practices. The Justices also have not engaged with one another on the increased role played by dictionaries." James J. Brudney and Lawrence Baum, "Oasis or Mirage: The Supreme Court's Thirst for Dictionaries in the Rehnquist and Roberts Eras," 55 *William and Mary Law Review* 483, 490–491, 578 (2013).

29. Richard Poirier, *Poetry and Pragmatism* 141–142 (1992). Yet it must be acknowledged that literalism in statutory interpretation can be at once both absurd and correct—on practical grounds, as in *United States v. Black,* 773 F.3d 1113 (10th Cir. 2014), interpreting a statute that states that "an offense involving consensual contact is not a sex offense . . . if the victim . . . was at least 13 years old and the offender was not more than 4 years older than the victim." 42 U.S. § 16911(5)(c). The defendant was eighteen and the victim fourteen, and thus four years younger. But when years are measured in days, weeks, or months, she was more than four years younger, for he was four years and seven months older than she. The court held that he was "more than 4 years older than the victim," within the meaning of the statute. The same logic would compel that result if he were four years and one day older than the victim, which is in a sense absurd. But if age in years were the governing metric, than the defendant would have been off the hook had he been one day short of his nineteenth birthday. The literal approach is preferable, because otherwise the statute would contain a big loophole.

30. See, for example, Andrei Marmor, *Interpretation and Legal Theory* 138 (2d ed. 2005).

terials that judges purport to use to interpret documents are putty in their hands.

The claim that judicial interpretation is a rigorous analytical process, comparable to syllogistic deduction, or at least to skilled translation of technical materials from a foreign language, and so really does generate demonstrably correct answers to even the most difficult-seeming questions that arise in litigation, is fatuous. Yet it is the centerpiece both of modern formalism and (closely related) of judicial denial that adjudication has anything to do with creating rather than merely finding and applying law. The massive treatise on statutory interpretation by Justice Scalia and Bryan Garner (and almost a hundred assistants), with its fifty-seven approved and eighteen disdained "canons of statutory construction,"[31] is to statutory interpretation what the 511-page *Bluebook: A Uniform System of Citation*[32] is to legal-citation form: it is what biologists and anthropologists call "hypertrophy" and

31. Antonin Scalia and Bryan A. Garner, *Reading Law: The Interpretation of Legal Texts* (2012), discussed critically in my book *Reflections on Judging* 179–219 (2013). For a recent devastating critique of canons of construction (ranging even more broadly than the title suggests and containing many useful references), see Joseph Kimble, "The Doctrine of the Last Antecedent, the Example in *Barnhart,* Why Both Are Weak, and How Textualism Postures," 16 *Scribes Journal of Legal Writing* 5 (2014–2015).

32. See my jeremiad (fallen on deaf ears), "The Bluebook Blues" (review of *The Bluebook: A Uniform System of Citation* [19th ed. 2010]), 120 *Yale Law Journal* 850 (2011). And for sharper criticism of the *Bluebook* than mine, see James Kwak, *The Baseline Scenario,* "Richard Posner Is My New Hero," February 11, 2011, http://baselinescenario.com/2011/02/11/richard-posner-is-my-new-hero/. He characterizes my explanation for the existence of the *Bluebook* accurately, as follows: "The *Bluebook* exists because lawyers want to demonstrate that they have rigorous methods; but because their core method, legal reasoning, is uncomfortably close to careful reading, to rhetoric, and to common sense, the profession has instead sought rigor in citation formatting." He offers a different though related explanation: "Lawyers are a cult, citations are our rites, and the *Bluebook* is, not our Bible, but our prayer manual. It is a tradition in the true sense of that word: something we do because we have done it for as long as we can remem-

anthropologists illustrate by the Egyptian pyramids, those grotesquely oversized mausoleums.

The invocation of the "canons" reflects a twofold failure of understanding. The Scalia-Garner treatise treats them as rules of a specialized language shared by legislators, who write the statutes, and judges, who interpret them. In fact the legislators (I am thinking of the members of Congress) don't write the statutes and often don't read them; the original authors are either staff of federal agencies or lobbyists. Legislative staff (including the influential Office of Legislative Council) participates in statutory drafting, revises proposed legislation, doesn't know all the canons that appear in judicial opinions, rejects some they have heard of, and is influenced, in choosing words to convey meaning, by canons of statutory construction of their own devising.[33]

Interpretation is a natural, intuitive, fundamental human capacity that everyone employs many times a day—any time one reads, writes, hears, or utters words—without any awareness of using rules. Literary critics wrestle with texts more opaque, antiquated, and obscure than most statutes or constitutional provisions, yet for the most part without recourse to explicit rules of interpretation. The only sensible canons of statutory construction are, first, intuitive interpretive principles relabeled in legal jargon. An example—I had thought—is *eiusdem generis,* the rule that when a string of words having specific meanings ends with a word of general meaning, that word should be assumed to be of the same kind as the other words—the ones with specific meanings—in the string. So in the string of "stocks, bonds, cash, and other

ber, and not for any other reason (even though people come up with justifications for it all the time). And traditions perpetuate themselves." All true.

33. These are findings of the Gluck-Bressman articles cited in note 27 above. An interesting subject of further study would be the legislative drafters in federal agencies and in lobbyist firms.

things of value," "other things of value" should not be understood to include spouses, pets, or religious observances. I had thought this was obvious, and I was puzzled therefore to discover that judges and professors think there's a need for a formal rule, and in Latin no less.

Would that the rule were just a fossil remnant; for it turns out that its application is fraught with uncertainty and a subject of intense though inconclusive controversy among *soi-disant* experts in statutory interpretation.[34] When courts invoke it, it is either obvious or, as in such cases as *Holy Angels Academy v. Hartford Insurance Group,* wrong.[35] That was a suit under a liability insurance policy for costs that the plaintiff had incurred when its school and convent buildings were damaged by extensive cracking and separation of walls and ceilings caused by blasting and "dewatering" of earth beneath the property caused by the construction of a subway. The policy had an exclusion for "earth movement, including but not limited to earthquake, landslide, mudflow, earth sinking, earth rising or shifting." That's a pretty accurate description of the effects of the subway construction on the plaintiff's property, but the court held without explanation that the exclusion was limited to "natural" perturbations of the earth. The court was construing a contract rather than a statute, but *eiusdem generis* is applicable to both. It does useful work in neither.

Canons of statutory construction such as *eiusdem generis* and plain meaning are known as "linguistic" canons, as they are tools for finding out what the statute at issue means. Other canons, known as "substantive," are not interpretive at all; they are judge-made substantive law imposed on legislation. The commonest is the "rule of lenity," the rule that an ambiguous criminal statute is to be construed in favor of the

---

34. For apt criticisms, see Joseph Kimble, "*Ejusdem Generis:* What Is It Good for?" (unpublished draft by Professor Kimble, Thomas M. Cooley Law School, Lansing, Michigan). The answer is "nothing."

35. 487 N.Y.S.2d 1005 (N.Y. Sup. Ct. 1985).

criminal defendant. The rule has nothing to do with statutory language or presumed legislative intent, for if asked whether an ambiguity in a criminal statute should be interpreted in favor of or against the criminal defendant most legislators, state and federal, would say against the defendant, as criminal defendants are extremely unpopular. The source of the rule is not some interpretive notion but a combination of due process concerns and the requirement that the guilt of a criminal defendant be proved beyond a reasonable doubt.

The problem that statutes create for judges is less difficulty of interpretation than difficulty of application. A vague statute may encompass as a linguistic matter an activity remote from the concerns of the legislators who voted for the statute, or simply overlooked by them, and often the question whether the statute should be thought to govern that activity or institution will perforce devolve into one of policy. The older a statute or a constitutional provision, the poorer the fit that it's likely to make with the needs of a modern society. Much of the Constitution of 1789 and many of the amendments, beginning with the Bill of Rights of 1791, don't fit modern conditions, and the judicial response has been as I said to use the Constitution as a warrant for creating a body of what is in essence common law. An alternative would have been for the Supreme Court to have ruled that vague or archaic provisions of the Constitution are not justiciable.

If a statutory or constitutional provision is unclear or its application will have seriously adverse consequences, the judges are at large. The best they can do is "interpret" the statute in a way that will avoid the adverse consequences. But what a judge is actually doing in "interpreting" a vague or ambiguous text is to *impose* an interpretation, one that the judge thinks has good, or at least avoids bad, consequences. It's what the Supreme Court has done to the Second, Fourth, Sixth, and Eleventh Amendments: rewritten them, ignoring clear text—imposing rather than discerning meaning: completing the meaning of an incomplete text, plugging a hole, not interpreting. To interpret, as I would prefer to see the word used, is to derive meaning, not to impose it on a defenseless text.

An excellent Second Circuit judge, Robert Katzmann (currently the circuit's chief judge), would disagree. He is the author of a recent book on statutory interpretation that is both sensible and eclectic, and deserves careful attention.[36] But like so much legal analysis it makes something that is simple seem complex.

United States v. Gayle,[37] one of three opinions by Judge Katzmann that he discusses in his book, involved a federal law that makes possession of a gun by someone who has been convicted "in any court" of a crime that is punishable by a prison term of more than a year (that is, a felony) a federal crime.[38] The defendant had received such a punishment—but in a Canadian court. The question for Judge Katzmann's court was whether "any court" includes a foreign court. He describes this as a "difficult" question.[39] He says that reading "any court" literally could be defended as something Congress might "reasonably" have intended, but on the other hand that Congress might have been "troubled by whether the prohibition" should apply to persons convicted by procedures and methods alien to our criminal justice system. "The complete silence of the statute on such questions further contributed to our sense that its meaning was not clear."[40] (No kidding!) The court was also troubled by the statute's exemption of persons whose only previous felony was a federal or state antitrust offense, but not persons who had been convicted of foreign such offenses; it was anomalous that the only antitrust offenses that would give rise to the prohibition on possessing a gun would be foreign.

The Senate committee that had recommended enactment of the

36. Cited in note 27 above.
37. 342 F.3d 89 (2d Cir. 2003).
38. 18 U.S.C. § 922(g)(1).
39. Katzmann, note 27 above, at 70, 81.
40. Id. at 73.

statute had mentioned only federal and state crimes. And the conference report (the report of a committee of members of both Houses of Congress) did not mention the reference to federal and state crimes in the Senate committee report—though to infer from that silence that the conference committee thought the law would exclude foreign crimes would be a stretch. The court, saying "we only choose not to write into a statute a meaning that seems contrary to what Congress intended," decided that "any court" meant "any American court."[41]

This is an obstacle-strewn path to an obvious result. It is *ridiculous* to think that a conviction in one of the world's 194 countries—a club with so many dubious members, such as North Korea—of a crime punishable by imprisonment for more than a year would make it a crime to possess a gun in the United States without regard to which country had convicted the person of what crime. Depending on the country, the crime might be insulting a dictator, might be sorcery, might be apostasy, might be advocating vaccination, might be adultery, might be blasphemy, might be refusing to commit a crime against humanity. Can one say with a straight face that confronted with these examples Congress would have said tough luck, a crime is a crime, and therefore Solzhenitsyn, who spent eight years in the Gulag followed by three years in internal exile, for writing a postcard that made fun of Stalin, and later lived in exile in the United States for a number of years, would have been a felon had he bought a gun to kill moles during his sojourn in Vermont?

The point is not that Congress thought about convictions in foreign courts and decided that a foreign court was not within the scope of the statutory term "any court" but forgot to say so. The point is that the judges had to complete the statute so that it would deal sensibly with an issue that the legislators and their staffs had not foreseen.

This was not how Judge Katzmann reasoned in his opinion in

41. Id. at 76, quoting 342 F.3d at 96.

Gayle, however; he said that to interpret "any court" literally would be contrary to legislative intent. That is, had Congress thought about the anomalies that a literal interpretation could have produced, it would have inserted "American" between "any" and "court." But that is far from obvious. Congress is not an individual, but a collection of adversaries operating under complex rules that make statutory enactment difficult. An attempt to insert "American" might have derailed the bill. Speculation about what Congress would have done had it thought about something is—speculative. The candid approach for the judge and his colleagues to have taken would have been to say that Congress had left a hole in the statute for the court to fill.

I imagine that Judge Katzmann realizes all this but thinks it would have been impolitic to acknowledge that in adding "American" the court was legislating. But judges are constantly legislating. They created and continue creating common law. They created constitutional law from a putty made of what is little better than clues planted in the Constitution by the framers of the 1789 and 1791 texts and the post–Civil War amendments, and they are continually altering that law. They made antitrust law out of the cryptic antiquated language of the Sherman Act, enacted in 1890, as later supplemented by the equally cryptic Clayton Act. They created "levels of scrutiny" and "canons of statutory construction" to shape constitutional meaning. Yet especially but not only at their confirmation hearings, federal judges trip over each other claiming merely to apply law, not make it—that is for Congress, they say, and they swear never to step on the members' corns. What modern judge would dare to quote Holmes's characteristically candid statement that "I recognize without hesitation that judges do and must legislate, but they can do so only interstitially; they are confined from molar to molecular motions"?[42] Interstitial is the key. The statute, the regulation, the Constitution, the contract may

42. *Southern Pacific Co. v. Jensen,* 344 U.S. 205, 221 (1917) (dissenting opinion).

have a hole; if so, the judges fill it. When they do so, they are legislating.

What made Judge Katzmann struggle at such length with the interpretive issue in *Gayle* and the other cases was, I am guessing, the
view, which he shares with most judges, that statutory interpretation
is an effort to determine what Congress intended with reference to
the interpretive issue that has arisen.[43] That is the orthodox view. It is
unsound. In most cases in which a statutory issue is uncertain enough
to be the subject of an appeal, Congress intended nothing, because (as
doubtless the case with the gun-possession statute) it did not foresee
an issue that arose after the statute was enacted. Legislators are busy
people who have short horizons because of their limited terms of office. As I mentioned, they do not draft the statutes they vote for and
often they don't read them before voting on them. Often all they understand is the statute's central thrust. Important modern statutes tend
to be unreadable because of length; the Affordable Care Act is 2,700
pages long. It would be unrealistic to suppose that members of Congress often cogitate about disputes, over the meaning of a statute they
vote for, that may not arise for many years if ever. The *Gayle* case was
decided by Judge Katzmann's court thirty-seven years after the enactment of the gun-possession statute (the Gun Control Act of 1968)
that contained the provision to be interpreted. Sufficient unto the day
is the evil thereof would be an apt congressional motto.[44]

43. Including myself—once upon a time: "The judge should try to think his way as
best he can into the minds of the enacting legislators and imagine how they
would have wanted the statute applied to the case at bar." Richard A. Posner,
"Statutory Interpretation—in the Classroom and in the Courtroom," 50 *University of Chicago Law Review* 800, 817 (1983). Very wrong was I; judges are not mind
readers.

44. The other two cases that Judge Katzmann discusses also received from him a
more labored analysis than I would consider necessary.

    1. The Federal Tort Claims Act waives the federal government's immunity
      to suit for claims "for injury or loss of property or personal injury or

death" caused by the negligence of a government employee acting within the scope of his employment. 28 U.S.C. § 1346(b)(1). Obviously that would give someone run over by a carelessly driven Post Office truck, or his survivors, a right to sue. But the Act is explicit that there is no waiver for claims "arising out of the loss, miscarriage, or negligent transmission of letters or postal matter." In Judge Katzmann's case, *Raila v. United States*, 355 F.3d 118 (2d Cir. 2004), the plaintiff hurt herself when she slipped on a package that a postal worker had left just below her front door step. The question was whether this was a "negligent transmission." The court's answer was no. The accident fit the waiver itself, allowing suits for personal injuries; the question was whether it was within the waiver's exception for "loss, miscarriage, or negligent transmission." Again I would have thought the answer obvious—obviously no. The purpose of the exemption was to shield the government from being sued when a piece of mail goes astray, whether lost, delivered to the wrong address, or delayed for a substantial time. The government would be besieged by suits (the U.S. Postal Service delivers more than 60 billion items of mail a year, and it is estimated that 3 to 5 percent of them go astray—a small percentage but a huge number). And the suits would often be very difficult to resolve correctly, because it's so difficult to determine whether someone who says an important letter or package was lost by the Post Office is telling the truth. In contrast, being struck by a postal truck is not a different kind of accident from being hit by any other federal vehicle.

2. Judge Katzmann's third case, *Murphy v. Arlington Central School District*, 402 F.3d 332 (2d Cir. 2005), was reversed by the Supreme Court. 548 U.S. 291 (2006). The Individuals with Disabilities Act, under which the suit was brought, entitles a court to award the parents of a disabled child, if they prevail in their suit, "reasonable attorneys' fees as part of the costs." The term "costs" in reference to litigation expenses usually refers to filing fees, certain printing costs, and other usually modest expenses. But the plaintiffs in the *Murphy* case wanted the costs they had expended on expert witnesses and consultants who had helped them win their case. That was an unconventional request. Judge Katzmann and his colleagues thought it should be granted because otherwise plaintiffs in these parents' position might be unable to afford expenditures essential to their prevailing in a meritorious case. He relied also on a statement in the conference committee report that "the conferees intend that the term 'attorneys' fees as part of the 'costs' include reasonable expenses and fees of expert witnesses

Judge Katzmann has remarked in the course of discussing *Gayle* that "if the plain text [of a statute] is unambiguous, our work usually ends there."[45] That isn't correct. It overlooks the distinction, familiar in contract law, between patent and latent ambiguity. Sometimes a piece of text is ambiguous on its face because it is confusingly written. But often it's clear as a matter of semantics but ambiguous when one considers the activity to which it is sought to be applied: that is, when one moves from semantics to context, from the dictionary to the world. The phrase "in any court" is unambiguous semantically but ambiguous in a law punishing someone for possessing a gun if he's ever been convicted of a crime "in any court"—a context in which reading "any court" literally is an option, not a compulsion. Statutes often fail to define the context of their intended application.

We mustn't forget Holmes's dictum that "the life of the law has not been logic: it has been experience. The felt necessities of the time,

---

and the reasonable costs of any test or evaluation which is found to be necessary for the preparation of the . . . case." Judge Katzmann's position was undermined, however, by three things. First, "costs" is a defined term in the federal judicial code, and the definition does not include the expert and consultant fees that the parents were seeking. 28 U.S.C. § 2412(a)(1). Second, to equate "costs" to any expense reasonably incurred by a litigant would work a dramatic change in the allocation of expenses of litigation between winning and losing parties. And third the statement in the conference report that the conferees "intend[ed]" a broad interpretation of the costs provision in the Act is not a statement of what the provision meant, let alone an enactment. It is the expression of a hope—by legislators unable to enact a provision defining costs to include the kind of expenditures the plaintiffs in the *Ralia* case had made—that a sympathetic court would stretch the statutory language. The Supreme Court was understandably reluctant to enter uncharted waters by allowing prevailing plaintiffs to recover litigation expenditures in the absence of a statutory definition of which expenditures, and how limited in amount, could be recovered.

45. Katzmann, note 27 above, at 72.

the prevalent moral and political theories, intuitions of public policy, avowed or unconscious, even the prejudices which judges share with their fellow-men, have had a good deal more to do than the syllogism in determining the rules by which men should be governed."[46] He was talking about the common law (explicitly judge-made law—of course much statutory and more constitutional law really is judge-made too) but his words apply also to statutory and constitutional interpretation. Often there is no way to determine what the law is (what for example a statute means when it is applied to a particular set of facts), and then the judge is on his own, as in *Gayle*.

Judge Katzmann's approach to that case, and to the other two cases that he discusses, is discordant with other parts of his book, in which for example he makes pungent and unanswerable criticisms of the canons of statutory construction and describes the chaotic process that is statutory drafting and enactment in the modern-day U.S. Congress. I should have thought his observations would have led him to doubt that statutory interpretation in difficult cases is "interpretive" in a useful sense. But he won't embrace that heresy, in part I think out of *politesse* and in part out of *Realpolitik*. Judges tend, at the rhetorical level at least, to treat Congress with kid gloves, in recognition I suppose that Congress has significant power over the federal judiciary. When Judge Katzmann says as he does—all on one page—that "the fundamental task for the judge is to determine what Congress was trying to do in passing the law," "that legislating is a purposive act, and judges should construe statutes to execute that legislative purpose," that "legislation is the product of a deliberate and informed process," that "statutes in this conception have purposes or objectives that are discernible," that "the task of the judge is to make sense of legislation in a way that is faithful to Congress's purposes," and that "when the text is ambiguous, a court is to provide the meaning that the legisla-

---

46. O. W. Holmes, Jr., *The Common Law* 1 (1881).

tion intended," he is flattering Congress rather than describing reality.[47] The process of enactment is rarely deliberative and informed. The purposes motivating it often cannot be recovered. A sensible reading of a statute can't be "faithful to Congress's purposes" if those purposes are unknowable or, relative to an issue in litigation, nonexistent.

When statutes are clearly aligned with evident legislative purposes, interpretation is a lark; often such statutes don't end up in litigation at all. But judges have been given the thankless task of "interpreting" statutes that can't be interpreted in many of the cases to which the statutes apply. Often there is no discernible legislative intent regarding potential cases within the statute's semantic reach, no legislative consensus. The legislators who voted for the proposed statute may have disagreed about its application to some issue that later arose in litigation, with no position on its application having commanded the support of a majority of the legislators who voted for enactment. The consequence is a breakdown in communication between legislature and court.[48]

The sensible way to think about such cases is to conceive of the judges not as interpreters of legislation but as partners of the legislators. If the legislators did not foresee an issue arising under their statute that has become a subject of litigation, there isn't anything to interpret; the judges face hieroglyphs without a Rosetta Stone. Interpretation is recovery of meaning, and there is no meaning to recover in such cases. The judges' role is then the active, not passive, one of

---

47. Katzmann, note 27 above, at 31.

48. There is nothing simple about communication. "Strict transference of or participation in identical experiences does not occur . . . In general, long and varied acquaintanceship, close familiarity, lives whose circumstances have often corresponded, in short an exceptional fund of common experience is needed, if people, in the absence of special communicative gifts, active and receptive, are to communicate." I. A. Richards, *Principles of Literary Criticism* 176, 178 (1925).

completing a statutory project that the legislature began but failed to carry to completion, thus leaving holes for judges to fill.[49]

This is a simpler way of deciding statutory cases than judges and treatise writers and practicing lawyers will acknowledge. But almost the most difficult thing in law is to understand how simple it has to be if it's to make sense, achieve some consistency, and be administrable. To quote Holmes again (this time from a letter he wrote to his English friend Frederick Pollock): "I long have said there is no such thing as a hard case. I am frightened weekly but always when you walk up to the lion and lay hold the hide comes off and the same old donkey of a question of law is underneath."[50]

If my analysis of statutory interpretation by judges is correct, the

49. This is not a new idea; it was well expressed more than half a century ago by Karl Llewellyn, who said that

> on the other hand—and increasingly as a statute gains in age—its language is called upon to deal with circumstances utterly uncontemplated at the time of its passage. Here the quest is not properly for the sense originally intended by the statute, for the sense sought originally to be *put into it,* but rather for the sense which *can be quarried out of it* in the light of the new situation. Broad purposes can indeed reach far beyond details known or knowable at the time of drafting. A "dangerous weapon" statute of 1840 can include tommy guns, tear gas or atomic bombs. "Vehicle," in a statute of 1840, can properly be read, when sense so suggests, to include an automobile, or a hydroplane that lacks wheels. But for all that, the sound quest does not run primarily in terms of historical intent. It runs in terms of what the words can be made to bear, in making sense in the light of the unforeseen. Karl N. Llewellyn, "Remarks on the Theory of Appellate Decision and the Rules or Canons about How Statutes Are to Be Construed," 3 *Vanderbilt Law Review* 395, 400–401 (1949) (emphases in original).

50. Letter of Holmes to Pollock, December 11, 1909, in *Holmes-Pollock Letters: The Correspondence of Mr Justice Holmes and Sir Frederick Pollock, 1874–1932,* 155–156 (Mark DeWolfe Howe ed. 1941). Holmes's use of "hard" to mean "difficult" in this passage strikes me as uncharacteristic. For he was intimately familiar with

enormous academic literature on such interpretation has little utility for or effect on the judicial process.[51] The rhetoric of the judicial opinion undoubtedly has been deeply influenced by the "originalist" and "formalist" tags, but the driving force of the opinions that embrace the tags is political, social, economic, or religious conservatism on the part of some judges, and on the part of others, such as Judge Katzmann, reluctance to acknowledge the ad hoc, untheorized character of interpretation of legal texts. In Chapter 4 I'll be describing briefly an ongoing interview study, conducted by Professor Abbe Gluck of Yale Law School and me, of how federal court of appeals judges decide statutory cases. We find that many judges feel compelled to approach statutory interpretation as if they were applying a multi-factor test. I express my dissatisfaction with such tests later in this chapter. Suffice it to say that they tend to be open-ended (the judge can add factors if he wants) and the factors unweighted, and this is a combination that unavoidably vests considerable discretion in every judge who applies the test. In the case of statutory interpretation, possible factors to consider include ambiguity (alternative possible meanings), vagueness (unclear what the alternative possible meanings are), dictionary definitions, legislative history (anathema to some judges), and the "canons of construction" (some semantic or grammatical, some policy-oriented, such as the rule of lenity)—with different judges often embracing or rejecting different canons. Additional factors are apparent or sensible-seeming statutory purpose, "plain meaning" (se-

---

the expression "hard cases make bad law," where "hard" means not "difficult" but tugging at the heart strings—a "hard case" is one in which the party that has the humanly more attractive case must lose for compelling, albeit hard-hearted, legal reasons.

51. See, for example, the lists of books and articles in Katzmann, note 27 above, at 107–115, 121–159. Exemplifying the formidable length and detail of the major contributions to this literature are William N. Eskridge, Jr., *Dynamic Statutory Interpretation* (1994), and John F. Manning and Matthew C. Stephenson, *Legislation and Regulation: Cases and Materials* (2d ed. 2013).

mantic definiteness), a sense of how legislatures operate, and the practical consequences of alternative interpretations. It's not clear how one sums factors that have no weights, or how one chooses to include or exclude factors of debatable relevance. So it's likely, indeed inevitable, that often judges will consciously or unconsciously have recourse to other, unacknowledged considerations to break the logjam. And so, contrary to the dreams of formalists, different judges, trying in good faith to interpret the same statute—even if they have the same interpretive philosophy—may often fail to agree on its meaning.[52]

Some judges may complain that by emphasizing the ad hoc character of statutory interpretation I am casting judges in a legislative role. I am. If there is no discernible meaning to a statutory provision applicable to a particular case, the judge who decides the case will be importing meaning into it and by doing so becoming a legislator himself. But of course judges *are* legislators, in part, not only as the creators of the common law but also as the creators of constitutional law, the details of which owe little to the constitutional text.

The interpretation of precedents raises the same issue. Often the opinion in the first case in a series of similar cases will lay down a rule to determine the outcome of the case, and will state the rule broadly. Years later a case may arise that is within the rule's semantic scope yet because of changes in technological or other circumstances could not have been foreseen by the court when it declared the rule. Should the court nevertheless apply the rule in the later case, this will be an act not of interpretation but of legislation. The court will be amending the rule rather than just applying it.

I end this section of the chapter with a depressing recent example of the process, not the result in the specific case, of statutory interpretation in the Supreme Court. The Court's decision in *Yates v.*

---

52. See, for example, Jason J. Czarnezki and William K. Ford, "The Phantom Philosophy: An Empirical Investigation of Legal Interpretation," 65 *Maryland Law Review* 841 (2006).

United States exemplifies distended, canons-riddled statutory interpretation.[53]

A federal agent found undersized red grouper on a commercial fishing vessel and told the captain to keep the fish separate from the rest of his catch until the vessel returned to port. Instead the captain tossed them overboard. He was convicted of having violated 18 U.S.C. § 1519, which provides that "whoever knowingly alters, destroys, mutilates, conceals, covers up, falsifies, or makes a false entry in any record, document, or tangible object with the intent to impede, obstruct, or influence the investigation or proper administration of any matter within the jurisdiction of any department or agency of the United States . . . shall be fined under this title, imprisoned not more than 20 years, or both." The question was whether the defendant had "destroyed" or "concealed" a "tangible object," namely the undersized fish, within the meaning of the statute. The Supreme Court held by a divided vote that the defendant had not violated the statute. The Court's three opinions sprawl over forty-three pages. They are larded with canons of construction, all in search of what Congress intended. Of course no one knows what Congress intended; probably Congress didn't anticipate such a case. What is known is that section 1519 was passed as part of the Sarbanes-Oxley Act of 2002, which was stimulated by the collapse of Enron and concerned the protection of investors. To that end, section 1519 makes it a crime to destroy or falsify (or create fictitious) financial records, which nowadays are often found in tangible objects, such as computers. The defendant's fish were tangible objects but had nothing to do with financial records. What the defendant in the *Yates* case had done was to tamper with evidence, which is punished by a separate statute (which Yates was also convicted of violating). Given that statute, there was no need to give "tangible object"

53. 135 S. Ct. 1074 (2015).

a literal interpretation; there was no gap in law to fill. Furthermore, when it is uncertain whether a defendant's conduct is within the scope of the statute that he's being prosecuted for having violated, he's not supposed to be convicted. This is the "rule of lenity," a judicial creation that as I noted earlier sensibly shores up the requirement of proof beyond a reasonable doubt.

So the result in *Yates* was sound. My point is only that an opinion explaining the decision did not have to discuss any canons of construction—which as usual led nowhere, but merely provoked a three-way disagreement over the meaning and applicability of various canons—and need not have exceeded three or four pages.

4. Multifactor tests—and the excesses of legal doctrine. A common pretense of analytical rigor in adjudication is the judiciary's embrace of open-ended multifactor tests as aids to decision making. (Oddly, despite his endorsement of fifty-seven canons of statutory construction, Justice Scalia—to his credit—is critical of multifactor tests, and not only in statutory cases.)[54] These are lists of considerations for the judge to weigh and compare in deciding for example whether to award attorneys' fees to a prevailing party in a copyright case when the rule or statute authorizing such an award leaves the decision to judicial discretion without placing meaningful bounds on the exercise of that discretion. Not only is the list of factors usually open-ended and therefore incomplete, but the factors are rarely given weights, and so unless all line up on one side of the dispute no decision can be derived from them; they are window dressing. The factors that *U.S. News & World Report* uses to rank law schools are also multiple, so if they weren't explicitly weighted by the publisher, as they are, it would be impossible to derive a ranking of law schools from them. One can

---

54. See, for example, *Lexmark International, Inc. v. Static Control Components, Inc.,* 134 S. Ct. 1377, 1391–1393 (2014).

quarrel with the weights the magazine uses and the factors it has chosen; my point is only that weights are needed in order to enable guidance to be obtained from a multifactor test.

Often such a test will be triply open-ended because the factors
will be not only partial and multiple but also vague. The *reductio ad
absurdum* is the fifteen-factor *Georgia-Pacific* test for calculating damages for patent infringement. Invented by a district judge almost half
a century ago, the test is accorded a degree of judicial deference usually reserved for Supreme Court decisions.[55] Fifteen vague factors,

---

55. *Georgia-Pacific Corp. v. United States Plywood Corp.*, 318 F. Supp. 1116, 1120
(S.D.N.Y. 1970):

> A comprehensive list of evidentiary facts relevant, in general, to the
> determination of the amount of a reasonable royalty for a patent li-
> cense may be drawn from a conspectus of the leading cases. The fol-
> lowing are some of the factors *mutatis mutandis* seemingly more perti-
> nent to the issue herein:
>
> 1. The royalties received by the patentee for the licensing of the patent
>   in suit, proving or tending to prove an established royalty.
> 2. The rates paid by the licensee for the use of other patents compara-
>   ble to the patent in suit.
> 3. The nature and scope of the license, as exclusive or non-exclusive; or
>   as restricted or non-restricted in terms of territory or with respect to
>   whom the manufactured product may be sold.
> 4. The licensor's established policy and marketing program to maintain
>   his patent monopoly by not licensing others to use the invention or
>   by granting licenses under special conditions designed to preserve
>   that monopoly.
> 5. The commercial relationship between the licensor and licensee, such
>   as, whether they are competitors in the same territory in the same
>   line of business; or whether they are inventor and promoter.
> 6. The effect of selling the patented specialty in promoting sales of
>   other products of the licensee; the existing value of the invention to
>   the licensor as a generator of sales of his non-patented items; and the
>   extent of such derivative or convoyed sales.
> 7. The duration of the patent and the term of the license.

8. The established profitability of the product made under the patent; its commercial success; and its current popularity.
9. The utility and advantages of the patent property over the old modes or devices, if any, that had been used for working out similar results.
10. The nature of the patented invention; the character of the commercial embodiment of it as owned and produced by the licensor; and the benefits to those who have used the invention.
11. The extent to which the infringer has made use of the invention; and any evidence probative of the value of that use.
12. The portion of the profit or of the selling price that may be customary in the particular business or in comparable businesses to allow for the use of the invention or analogous inventions.
13. The portion of the realizable profit that should be credited to the invention as distinguished from non-patented elements, the manufacturing process, business risks, or significant features or improvements added by the infringer.
14. The opinion testimony of qualified experts.
15. The amount that a licensor (such as the patentee) and a licensee (such as the infringer) would have agreed upon (at the time the infringement began) if both had been reasonably and voluntarily trying to reach an agreement; that is, the amount which a prudent licensee—who desired, as a business proposition, to obtain a license to manufacture and sell a particular article embodying the patented invention—would have been willing to pay as a royalty and yet be able to make a reasonable profit and which amount would have been acceptable by a prudent patentee who was willing to grant a license.

The "some" in the second sentence is particularly rich—how many additional factors may be lurking somewhere? And could a judge or a jury really balance fifteen factors (or more—the fifteen are only "some" of the factors to consider) and come up with anything resembling an objective assessment? Of course not. Yet though just a district court opinion, *Georgia-Pacific* has been adopted by the appellate courts as an authoritative guide to determining damages in patent cases.

For criticism of the *Georgia-Pacific* and other multifactor tests, see, for example, Thomas F. Cotter, "Four Principles for Calculating Reasonable Royalties in Patent Infringement Litigation," 27 *Santa Clara Computer and High Technology Law Journal* 725, 730–731 (2011); Kevin Blum et al., "Consistency of Confusion? A Fifteen-Year Revisiting of Barton Beebe's Empirical Analysis of Multifactor

unweighted, and the judge invited to add his own factors—an analytical nightmare! Judges who think such a test provides guidance to them are fooling themselves. They should forget the test and simply explain in each case, as best they can, what moved them to exercise their discretion in the way they did.

Multifactor tests have a formulaic air, and formulas an air of rigor. But judges should not forget Holmes's dictum that "to rest upon a formula is a slumber that, prolonged, means death."[56] Not that he derided formulas in principle, for he went on to say on the same page that the "formulas of the law" have two implicit postulates: "that such and such a condition or result is desirable and that such and such means are appropriate to bring it about."[57] This is realism—a fact-centered, an empirical, conception of law. Implicitly it is cost-benefit analysis: the benefit of the desired result weighed against the cost of attaining it. It is a conception that collides with the judicial (and professorial) preoccupation with legal doctrine.

Though indeterminate, multifactor tests are used or approved by most judges because the tests disguise factual inference as doctrinal analysis—and judges love doctrine (most law professors too). Think of the elaborate doctrinal edifice that the Supreme Court has erected on the helpless body that is the equal protection clause of the Fourteenth Amendment. One might suppose that if the issue were, for example, whether forbidding same-sex marriage is a denial of the equal protection of the laws (at this writing a hot issue), judges would weigh on the one hand the harm from the prohibition, which depends on such

---

Tests for Trademark Infringement," 2010 *Stanford Technology Law Review* 3, 36 (2010); Christopher B. Seaman, "Reconsidering the *Georgia-Pacific* Standard for Reasonable Royalty Patent Damages," 2010 *Brigham Young University Law Review* 1661 (2010); Barton Beebe, "An Empirical Study of the Multifactor Tests for Trademark Infringement," 94 *California Law Review* 1581 (2006).

56. Oliver Wendell Holmes, "Ideals and Doubts" (1915), in *The Essential Holmes*, note 12 above, at 117, 119.

57. Id.

factors as the impact on the adopted children of homosexual couples of denying such couples the social status and concrete benefits of marriage, the nature of homosexual orientation, and the history and consequences of discrimination against homosexuals and the parallels of that history and those consequences to other and now thoroughly discredited forms of discrimination, such as racial prejudice; and on the other hand the possible adverse social consequences of recognizing same-sex marriages. And maybe that is how the issue will be resolved, although a possible monkey wrench is the religion-based hostility of some judges and Justices to homosexuality. But whatever the Supreme Court's resolution of the issue, it will doubtless be cloaked in an elaborate body of doctrine, opaque and undirective and unmanageable though it is bound to be—a smokescreen of nebulous concepts such as "heightened scrutiny," "strict scrutiny," "intermediate scrutiny," "overinclusiveness," "underinclusiveness," "narrow tailoring," "immutable characteristics," and "suspect class." These terms can be translated, more or less, into facts that can be incorporated into a cost-benefit analysis, which is the character of Holmes's formulation of the postulates that underlie legal formulas. But why bother? The doctrinal surround of equal protection is not a window that, opening into the judicial process, yields a decision. It is not a window at all; it is window dressing.

5. *The fetishism of words.* A fetish is an object believed to have supernatural powers. Judges, along with lawyers, law students, and law professors, fetishize words. The choice of the words to fetishize is based not on utility or charm, but, as so commonly in law, on tradition and obscurity. In countless judicial opinions the reader will encounter a superfluity of legal jargon,[58] numbing de-

---

58. For examples, also of other defects of judicial opinion writing, see *Reflections on Judging,* note 31 above, ch. 8, esp. 250–254. A common example is for the court to say, when as is usual there is more than one argument made by the parties, "We address the parties' arguments in turn." *Laskar v. Peterson,* 771 F.3d 1291,

tail,[59] overstatement, superfluous footnotes, throat clearing, repetition, irrelevance, excessive citations, and needless section headings. Brevity seems alien to the legal mind. Not for lawyers and judges Polonius's insistence that "since brevity is the soul of wit,/And tediousness its outward limbs and flourishes,/ I will be brief."[60] Most judges don't value simplicity either. In both respects judicial opinions are inconsiderate of their readers. What I have enumerated in this paragraph are failures of form and structure, as well as of language—in fact of communication in the broadest sense of the word.

Wordiness and verbal complexity may seem venial sins. Not so. The federal courts of appeals issue more than thirty thousand opinions a year on the merits after briefing and oral argument or after just

---

1296 (11th Cir. 2013). What else could the court do? Another horror is the incessantly invoked "totality of the circumstances standard." *United States v. Thompson,* 772 F.3d 752, 760 (3d Cir. 2014). What work could that possibly do? Obviously a responsible judge will consider all the circumstances relevant to deciding a case. And consider finally a proposition found in many cases since 1946, most recently *Hollybrook Cottonseed Processing, L.L.C. v. American Guarantee & Liability Insurance Co.,* 772 F.3d 1031, 1034 (5th Cir. 2014): faced with a motion for a mistrial based on the submission of prejudicial information to the jury, the district court must decide whether the error is harmless by assessing if "the error did not influence the jury, *or had but very slight effect.*" The phrase I've italicized is baffling. What could it mean for the prejudicial information to have a "slight effect" on the jury? Invariably when a court finds only a "slight effect," it does not disturb the jury's verdict. *O'Rear v. Fruehauf Corp.,* 554 F.2d 1304, 1308 (5th Cir. 1977): "If, when all is said and done, the [trial judge's] conviction is sure that the error did not influence the jury, or had but very slight effect, the verdict and the judgment should stand." But that is to equate "slight effect" to "no effect," since what is a "slight effect" that does not alter the verdict?

59. A notable example is *Gregory v. City of Louisville,* 444 F.3d 725, 747–751 (6th Cir. 2006).

60. In Chapter 8 of *Reflections on Judging,* note 31 above, I rewrote a representative opinion by a distinguished judge of the D.C. Circuit. Her opinion was 3,237 words; my version was 602 words. I don't think I cut anything that was muscle rather than fat.

briefing. Those opinions are read by lawyers, who bill their time to clients. The longer an opinion, the denser its citations, and the more complex its prose, the more billable time lawyers will spend reading it. The cost of lawyer time caused by the excessive length and unnecessary complexity of judicial opinions is a social waste.

The continued use of Latinisms in American judicial opinions is a further tipoff to the staleness of legal language. I am not complaining about foreign words and phrases, including Latin ones, that have become part of the English language, as so many foreign words have. "Rendezvous" is an example from French, "pyjama" from Hindu, and I've already mentioned from Latin "reductio ad absurdum." Such Latin words and terms as "dictum" and "ex post facto" are not common in ordinary discourse but are securely a part of the legal lexicon (hence usually no longer italicized), while "caveat emptor" is an example of a Latin term shared by the legal lexicon and ordinary speech. So far, so good. But why should a judge use *"arguendo"* in an opinion instead of "for the sake of argument"; or *"contra proferentem"* instead of "[construing a document] against the author"; or *"eiusdem generis"* (usually given its medieval Latin spelling *"ejusdem generis"*—in law that counts for being up to date) rather than its English translation, which is "of the same kind"? Why should judges use "instant case" instead of "this case" or "present case," or use "case of first impression" instead of "novel case" or "first case of its kind"? And if judges are to continue using the Latin phrase *"de minimis non curat lex"* rather than the English ("the law doesn't care about trifles"), please would they learn not to misspell *"minimis"* as *"minimus,"* as so many do.

Wikipedia offers a partial list of Latin terms used in law—I counted to two hundred and gave up; I don't think I was more than halfway through the list.[61] The list is ripe for deletion.

61. "List of Legal Latin Terms," http://en.wikipedia.org/wiki/List_of_legal_Latin _terms.

And why do judges continue to refer to the federal courts of appeals and district courts as "inferior courts"? True, that's the term in Article III ("The judicial power of the United States, shall be vested in one Supreme Court, and in such inferior courts as the Congress may from time to time ordain and establish"). But in the eighteenth century "inferior" meant lower as well as worse—indeed that appears to have been its primary meaning and is the meaning that the word bears in our eighteenth-century Constitution.[62] Article III ordains one federal court but authorizes Congress to create federal courts below the ordained court. One can still find that meaning of "inferior" in a dictionary, but the word as used in speech and writing today invariably means "worse." By employing an obsolete usage the courts contribute to the opacity, the staleness, of legal discourse.

The jargon in which judicial opinions abound may be mostly a product of habit but I think it also wells up from an unconscious desire to convince readers that there is a lot more to legal analysis than common sense or the term I used in the introduction—"moral intuition" (there is a little more, I admit). In that respect judges' use of jargon resembles their use of multifactor tests, in statutory interpretation "canons of construction," in constitutional cases the doctrinal intricacies that I mentioned earlier. It resembles the pretentious writing found in other intellectually weak but self-important fields.

---

62. Under "Inferior," *The Oxford English Dictionary*, vol. 1, p. 1428 (compact ed. 1971), quotes from an English law book in 1754: "Inferior courts are those whose sentences are subject to the review of the supreme courts." In Samuel Johnson's great dictionary, published a year later, three of the four meanings given for "inferiour" (his spelling of "inferior") relate to rank rather than quality: "lower in place," "lower in station or rank of life," and "subordinate." The fourth is "lower in value or excellency." *A Dictionary of the English Language* (1979 facsimile ed., no page numbers).

Lately I've been struck by the proliferation of headings and sub-headings in federal court of appeals opinions, another example of judicial superfluity. In *United States v. Campbell,* a recent First Circuit opinion, appears the following sequence of headings and subheadings:[63]

I Background
    A. Facts
    B. District Court Proceedings
II Discussion
    A. Stop and Search of the Vehicle
        1. The Vehicle Stop
        2. The Vehicle Search
    B. Uncounseled Questioning at the Scene of the Vehicle Stop
    C. Mr. Campbell's Sentence
    Conclusion

I don't see how these headings help the reader. I am also struck by the contents of the last section, "Conclusion": "The judgment of the district court is affirmed. **AFFIRMED.**" What work does "The judgment of the district court is affirmed" do, given the word that follows it?

In another recent case, one encounters the following sequence of headings and subheadings:[64]

Background
Discussion
    A. Standard of Review

---

63. 741 F.3d 251 (1st Cir. 2013).
64. *Williams v. Commissioner of Internal Revenue,* 718 F.3d 89 (2d Cir. 2013).

B. Determination Without Face-to-Face CDP Hearing

1. Applicable Law

2. Application

Conclusion

This is more economical, but then the opinion is only four pages long, and there was no need for *any* headings or subheadings. But what is particularly striking, and a better illustration of senseless redundancy than anything in the *Campbell* opinion, is the "Conclusion": "For the foregoing reasons, the Order and Decision of the tax court is **AFFIRMED.**" Why say "For the foregoing reasons"? What other reasons could be in play? Was the court concerned that in the absence of "For the foregoing reasons" the reader might think: "Oh, the court affirmed without any reasons," or "Oh, the court will tell us at some future time what the reasons for the affirmance were"?

Let us (if only we could) banish headings from opinions, and while we're at it banish the *Bluebook* (official title: *The Bluebook: A Uniform System of Citation*), which in its present, distended form is the unwelcome contribution of student law review editors to the quixotic project of making legal writing, including judicial opinions (many judges require their law clerks to "Bluebook" their opinions), appear to be a quasi-scientific, or at least an esoteric, discourse.

Bad as the *Bluebook* is, worse—the acme of absurdity in legal expression—is the growing concern among law review editors and judges' law clerks with improper italicization of the period. Readers may wonder why I would mention such ridiculousness. The reason is that it so wonderfully exemplifies the fetishization of legal language. A period, though securely a part of language, is not even a word. It is a language fragment so tiny that only the keenest eye can discern whether a given period is in roman or italic typeface. Often if a sentence ends with an italicized word (it might be the name of a case), in italicizing the word the writer will inadvertently have italicized the period. This is "wrong." Increasingly, law review editors, and judicial law clerks as well, are correcting, if necessary with the aid of a magnifying glass, this formatting "error"—and another, even more esoteric such error: the boldfaced space. If you boldface a string of words, the spaces between the words will be slightly enlarged. Law review editors are offended by such a solecism. Here one feels law merging with scientific preoccupation with invisible entities—one might be talking about the vast space, empty of matter yet alive with dark energy, between stars. No reader will notice, or care about, the minute enlargement of the spaces between words that is brought about by bold-facing.

What is maddening about the *Bluebook* is that, though it is at once superfluous (because the only proper concern of citation formatting is to enable a reader to find the cited items, and formatting that will achieve this modest goal is easy to devise—it doesn't require 511 pages, the length of the *Bluebook*'s current edition), cancerous (its growth is purposeless and unhealthy), and time-consuming to master and to use, there is no effective opposition to it.[65] Fulminations against it by me and a few others fall on deaf ears. One is put in mind of the horror movie *Invasion of the Body Snatchers* (1956). Extraterrestrials secretly invade a small town in California. From seed pods that they grow they create exact physical duplicates of the townspeople, and at night, while the townspeople are asleep, replace their bodies with the duplicates. Eventually almost the entire population of the town has been converted to zombie-like "pod people." When the local doctor—the hero of the movie—who has figured out what is happening, discovers that even his girlfriend has become a pod person and is shouting for the "pod people" to pursue and transform him, he flees and finds himself on a crowded highway, where he screams ineffectually to the indifferent passing motorists (doubtless pod people) "They're here already!

---

65. Two pages should be plenty. See note 1 in Chapter 5.

You're next! You're next!" That's how I feel about the *Bluebook*. The law review editors who enforce its mindless dictates are pod people. Its relentless growth threatens to lobotomize the legal profession. I can but scream ineffectually.

Citation-format anxiety (which should be listed in *The Diagnostic and Statistical Manual of Mental Disorders*), in all its absurdity, underscores a besetting anxiety of the legal profession, not excluding judges and law professors as well as law students. The anxiety is that law really is not a rigorous field (which is true) but a field dominated by hunch and priors and rough balancing of competing considerations given only subjective weights, and by often inaccurate facts and lying or muddled witnesses and sly lawyers and confused or disingenuous judges. These embarrassing realities induce a call for rigor, and since rigor cannot be achieved in law the call is answered by *faux* rigor, illustrated by obsession with citation format.

Law is not alone in being a field remote from science and math and saturated in rhetoric. Other such fields include philosophy, fiction, and literary criticism. Until deconstruction came along no one thought that literary criticism had to be badly written in order to be authoritative. Until Mallarmé's poetry and James Joyce's *Finnegans Wake* no one thought unintelligibility a marker of serious modern literature. Most historians at least try to write clearly, albeit not always succeeding. But the law is one of those weak fields of intellectual endeavor that proudly embraces bad writing attributed to an indispensable technical vocabulary, ignoring books hopelessly seeking to improve the writerly quality of judicial opinions and lawyers' briefs.[66] The ineffectuality of such books is attributable at least in part to the

---

66. See, for example, William Domnarski, *In the Opinion of the Court* (1996), and my *Law and Literature,* ch. 9 (3d ed. 2009). An impressively comprehensive manual of legal writing contains excellent instruction on writing a judicial opinion. See Stephen V. Armstrong and Timothy P. Terrell, *Thinking Like a Writer: A Lawyer's Guide to Effective Writing and Editing* 358–377 (3d ed. 2009).

fact that most judicial opinions are written by law clerks, and few law clerks read such books. One reason they don't read them is that the inclination of law clerks is to imitate the style, vocabulary, structure, and so forth of their judge, features likely to reflect the efforts of the judge's previous law clerks to follow the same well-trodden path.

There used to be excellent American judicial writers—candid, graceful, cultured—beginning with John Marshall and continuing with Holmes, Brandeis, Cardozo, Hand, Hughes, and Jackson, to name only the brightest stars in that particular firmament. If the line has not quite ended, yet it seems fated to. Will American philistinism eventually do in all art and culture? Are law clerks Sirens luring judges and Justices to rhetorical destruction?

6. *Ignorance of or indifference to context.* Indifference to the full factual context of cases is common in judicial decisions, as is ignorance of fields of knowledge outside law, such as economics, criminology, and psychology, that may illuminate those contexts. Many federal judges know little about foreign countries, even though such knowledge is important to intelligent judicial review of immigration decisions and to cases—increasingly common—that involve foreign law, foreign business practices, or foreign customs. Many judges know little about mental illness, knowledge of which is essential to intelligent judicial review of social security disability determinations, to understanding the behavior, treatment, and discipline of prison inmates, and to rational criminal sentencing. Indeed many judges have only a nodding acquaintance with criminology. A great many lack a feel for science, engineering, medicine, and statistics.

Judges act as if—some doubtless believe that—the adversary process generates all the information, other than perhaps niceties of legal doctrine, that is required to decide a case correctly—that a judge doesn't have to know anything in the realm of fact but just has to listen carefully to the lawyers and the witnesses. That is rarely true. The focus of adversary process is on the facts, specific to the case at hand, on which the parties disagree. Those facts are likely to be only a part of the factual context required to decide the case sensibly. The judges are assumed to know the rest of the factual surround. The assumption is often incorrect, and, when it is, the judges are left guessing and may be led into error.

Much of what judges need to know that the adversary process is unlikely to tell them is readily available on the Internet—in the case of mental illness, for example, on the websites of the major hospitals and medical research centers. About 250 million websites, containing 15 billion pages altogether, are accessible through Google. In my experience it is rare to find nothing in a Google search that is helpful in preparing for oral argument in a case or writing a judicial opinion. One must be careful about accuracy, and though that is of course also true of findings based on evidence presented in trials and other evidentiary hearings, there may be a need for some additions to the rules of evidence to regulate evidence obtained in Internet searches.[67]

Many judges are elderly and some of them shun the Internet. As do many younger judges. This will change. In the meantime the consequence of a meager judicial knowledge base is a hobbled judicial ability to understand many of the disputes, and the quirks and ailments and transactions and commercial practices underlying the disputes, that give rise to federal litigation. It is lamentable how often lawyers fail, because of poor habits of research, or haste, or failure to grasp the limitations of judicial understanding, to provide the judges with the information they need in order to be able to make sensible decisions. Fortunately much of that information is available online. Unfortunately most judges are reluctant to look for it there—and so are most lawyers. The law clerks do not shun the Internet, and that is fortunate, but judges must be careful not to allow law clerks

67. See, for example, Jeffrey Bellin and Andrew Guthrie Ferguson, "Trial by Google: Judicial Notice in an Information Age," 108 *Northwestern University Law Review* 1137 (2014).

to fill opinions with technical matter that the judges do not understand.

7. *Passivity.* Here I have in mind among other things a judge's tendency to conceive of himself as an umpire, and the lawyers as players, in the game of law. That outlook reflects an unthinking commitment to adversary procedure and invites both excessive tolerance of lawyers' shortcomings and excessive delegation of judicial work, especially case preparation and opinion drafting, to law clerks.[68] In this conception of the judicial function the judge is the umpire and makes the call; a law clerk writes it up. Some judges believe, or act as if they believe, that their essential role is limited to determining the outcome of the case (affirm or reverse), that the determination is based on inarticulable but reliable intuition, and that explaining the reasons for the outcome in a judicial opinion is peripheral and so can safely be left to law clerks.

Baseball umpires call balls and strikes, or make other "rulings," without articulating any justification for their actions. Judges who think of themselves in umpireal terms might therefore welcome the advice of Lord Chief Justice Mansfield to a newly appointed military governor whose office required him to perform judicial duties but who had no legal experience: "Tut, man. Decide promptly, but never give any reasons for your decisions. Your decisions may be right, but your reasons are sure to be wrong."[69] This is an extreme version of the "moral intuition" theory of adjudication noted in the Introduction.

The passive tendency is a significant factor in the inordinate delay

---

68. "Most often, judges appear to take for granted what lawyers do, and perhaps they do so when briefs and argument are within a (rather large) zone of acceptability." Stephen L. Wasby, "As Seen from behind the Bench: Judges' Commentary on Lawyers' Competence," 38 *Journal of the Legal Profession* 47 (2013).

69. Quoted in John Cordy Jeaffreson, *A Book About Lawyers,* vol. 1, p. 85 (1867). The paragraph from which the quotation is taken is amusing, and I quote it in full:

The story goes that a general officer of the army, on being appointed governor of a West Indian island, addressed Lord Mansfield in a voice of

common in the resolution of complex cases in federal district courts. Whatever the opposing lawyers agree to, the judge may go along with; the motto of such complaisant judges might be the biblical slogan "sufficient unto the day is the evil thereof." Often what the lawyers will agree to is protracted pretrial discovery, which each lawyer is likely to find attractive as a way of persuading the client that the lawyer is leaving no stone unturned in preparation for trial, of jacking up the fees charged the client, and of setting the stage for a settlement of the case.[70] Most lawyers prefer to settle cases, because then there is no loser—and a lawyer doesn't want to have to tell a client that he lost the client's case. In a case litigated to judgment there is a loser. Some judges, recognizing the questionable motives behind lawyers' agreements to conduct protracted discovery, set tight deadlines for completion of discovery. All should do so.

great concern, "What am I to do, my lord? The governor is commander-in-chief of the troops, and must he preside in the Local Court of Chancery? I can command soldiers, but I know nothing of law." "Tut, man, decide promptly, but never give any reasons for your decisions. Your decisions may be right, but your reasons are sure to be wrong." Acting on this rule, the military Chancellor pushed on well enough; but in an evil hour, forgetting the precept, he gave his first good decision and it was immediately appealed against. Recounting the story to his grandson, Lord Mansfield said, "I was two or three years afterwards sitting at the Cockpit on Plantation Appeals, when there was one called from my friend and pupil the general, which the losing party had been induced to bring on account of the ludicrously absurd reasons given for the judgment, which, indeed, were so absurd that he incurred some suspicion of corruption, and there was a clamour for his recall. Upon examining it I found that the judgment itself was perfectly sound and correct. Regretting that my advice had been forgotten, I was told that the general[,] acquiring reputation by following it, began to suppose himself a great lawyer, and that this case brought before us was the first in which he had given his reasons, and was the first appealed against."

70. I say "often," but wish to emphasize that often is not always. One side's case (rarely both sides' cases) will sometimes not depend significantly on information

The passive tendency plays a malign role in the judicial knowledge base, and specifically in the attitude of judges toward the acquisition of broad background knowledge about their cases. It is another reason for their reluctance to do Internet research, or to appoint their own expert witnesses though authorized to do so by Rule 706 of the Federal Rules of Evidence.[71] The conventional record on which a judicial decision is based is created by the lawyers. That is the defining characteristic of an adversarial legal system, as opposed to the inquisitorial system that prevails in most of Europe and indeed most of the world. Commitment to the adversarial system is one reason for judges' reluctance to appoint their own expert witnesses; for a judge to appoint a witness is felt as inconsistent with—in fact *is* inconsistent with (but so what?)—a wholehearted commitment to adversary procedure.[72] To a considerable extent, therefore, what I am calling judicial

---

in the private possession of the other side, and the side that doesn't depend on such information will have little incentive to incur discovery costs.

71. By "Internet research" I mean not only searching for information that appears only on the Internet, but also searching for information found in books and articles and other documents (including judicial opinions) but often more easily accessed via the Internet than in a search for or in the original hard copy. For a comprehensive analysis of the general weakness of the judiciary in determining facts by the conventional methods of judicial fact-finding, see James L. Robertson, "Variations on a Theme by Posner: Facing the Factual Component of the Reliability Imperative in the Process of Adjudication," 84 *Mississippi Law Journal* 471 (2015).

72. See Joe S. Cecil and Thomas E. Willging, *Court-Appointed Experts: Defining the Role of Experts Appointed under Federal Rule of Evidence 706*, at 20–21 (Federal Judicial Center 1993); Samuel R. Gross, "Expert Evidence," 1991 *Wisconsin Law Review* 1113, 1197–1201 (1991). Another reason for the reluctance of judges to appoint their own (i.e., neutral) expert witnesses is that it means more work for the judge. A judge's witness, unlike parties' witnesses, is not shepherded by any of the lawyers in the case; the judge has to do the shepherding. For example, when a party's expert is deposed, the party's lawyer attends the deposition to protect him from the lawyer for the other party, who will be doing the deposing. No judge is present. In the case of a judge's expert, the judge presides (or should

passivity could be renamed unwavering commitment to the adversary system.

It could be argued that the proper response of judges to the shortcomings of such procedure is simply to make the lawyers work harder (thus incidentally increasing the demand for lawyers' services)—so if in an appeal the lawyers fail to provide information that the judges want, the judges should direct the filing of supplemental briefs. This is sometimes the proper course, but not always. For it is time-consuming, as is the alternative of a limited remand to the district court to fill in whatever gaps in the record are troubling the appellate court.

The judge's proper role is to render just decisions rather than to decide which lawyer is better. But a judge who thinks of himself as an umpire will often be in fact deciding a case on the basis of which lawyer is better, because the better lawyer will do a better job of advocacy, dig deeper for the facts that support his position, find more support in the case law and academic commentary. The judge should lean in favor of the weaker lawyer, tell the lawyers what evidence he (or the jury) needs in order to render a just decision, produce his own evidence as by appointing a neutral expert or conducting his own research.

Against this it will be argued not only that judges don't have time for this—which I doubt, for the existing tendency is to allow the lawyers to produce masses of evidence often of doubtful relevance to a

---

preside—that at least is my practice) at the expert's deposition; otherwise the expert might decide he should hire his own lawyer to attend. Another reason that appointing a neutral expert might make for more work for the judge is that the judge has to find and evaluate the expert before appointing him. But I have found that most of this chore can be delegated to the parties by requesting that they ask their expert witnesses to agree on two or three neutral experts for the judge to choose among. That both sides agree is a guarantee that the neutrals they suggest will indeed be neutral as between the parties. I have found that the party experts have no problem agreeing on well-qualified neutrals. The approach thus solves the problem "that the court-appointed expert may turn out

just result but requiring a great deal of time by the judge and his clerks to sort through and evaluate—but also that the umpireal approach will improve the legal profession by rewarding better lawyers with more wins, enabling them to attract clients away from the worst lawyers. But this Darwinian theory ignores disparity in resources between clients, which will tend to price the best lawyers out of reach of the clients who do not have a deep pocket.

A recent study finds that sixty-six lawyers—fewer than one half of one percent of the lawyers who filed petitions for certiorari in the Supreme Court over the past nine years—handled 43 percent of the cases in which the Court granted the petition and went on to hear and decide the case.[73] Of the sixty-six, fifty-two (77 percent) work for law firms that mainly represent large corporations or other big-business interests. These highly paid lawyers often are extremely able and outclass the humbler lawyers whom their less affluent adversaries can afford to hire. The study quotes Justice Ginsburg as accepting this disparity in quality of representation as an unalterable fact of life, and Justice Scalia as having "voted against what would be a marginally granted petition when it was not well presented . . . where the petition demonstrates that the lawyer is not going to argue it well." That is the wrong attitude, though consistent with an exaggerated confidence in the adversary system. The Justices and their clerks can repair the defects in a weak lawyer's presentation, and should do so at least when it can be inferred that the client could not pay the fee that a first-rate lawyer would have charged.

A recent case of mine, *Browning v. Colvin,* illustrates the limita-

---

to have unanticipated bias for one side." Douglas N. Walton, *Appeal to Expert Opinion: Arguments from Authority* 193 (1997).

73. Joan Biskupic, Janet Roberts, and John Shiffman, "At America's Court of Last Resort, A Handful of Lawyers Now Dominates the Docket," *Reuters, The Echo Chamber,* December 8, 2014, www.reuters.com/investigates/special-report/scotus/.

tions of the adversary system.[74] The Social Security Administration had denied disability benefits, ruling that despite limitations (mental retardation, obesity, and the continuing effects of a childhood disease that had impaired the applicant's use of one of her legs), there were many jobs that she was physically and mentally capable of doing. As is customary in such cases, the Administration's adjudicator had described the applicant's limitations to a "vocational expert," whose job is to provide statistics on the number of jobs the applicant is physically and mentally capable of doing; if there are no, or an insignificant number of, such jobs in the economy, the applicant is deemed disabled. Recently I became curious about the source of the statistics that vocational experts trot out in social security disability hearings. I discovered to my surprise that there is no reliable source of such statistics—in fact, as explained in my opinion, vocational experts' estimates of the number of jobs of different types in different parts of the country appear to be made out of whole cloth.[75]

---

74. 766 F.3d 702 (7th Cir. 2014).
75. For additional evidence of this, see *Herrmann v. Social Security Administration*, 772 F.3d 1110 (7th Cir 2014); *Brault v. Social Security Administration*, 683 F.3d 443, 446–447 (2d Cir. 2012) (per curiam); *Guiton v. Colvin*, 546 Fed. App'x 137, 143–145 (4th Cir. 2013) (concurring opinion); *Coppernoll v. Astrue*, 2009 WL 1773132, at *8 (W.D. Wis. June 23, 2009); Jon C. Dubin, "Overcoming Gridlock: *Campbell* After a Quarter-Century and Bureaucratically Rational Gap-Filling in Mass Justice Adjudication in the Social Security Administration's Disability Programs," 62 *Administrative Law Review* 937, 964–971 (2010); Peter J. Lemoine, "Crisis of Confidence: The Inadequacies of Vocational Evidence Presented at Social Security Disability Hearings (Part II)," *Social Security Forum*, September 2012, 1. The problem is that the only reliable statistics are census data of broad categories of jobs, rather than data on the number of jobs in the narrower categories of jobs that the applicant for benefits could actually perform. Typically, it appears, the vocational expert simply divides the census data on number of jobs in the broad category that includes the narrow category of jobs that the applicant can perform by the total number of narrow categories in the broad category, thus assuming that each narrow category has the same number of jobs—a preposterous assumption.

I have written many opinions in social security disability cases in my thirty-four years as a federal court of appeals judge. (All are cases in which the Social Security Administration had denied benefits. Grants are not appealable.) Statistics purporting to reveal the number of jobs the applicant can perform appear (I believe) in all of them. I am embarrassed to confess that I had never questioned the accuracy of the statistics offered by the vocational expert. The reason is that, as far as I can recall, no lawyer had ever questioned them. I assumed (without conscious thought about the matter) that since the lawyers implicitly were conceding their accuracy, it was not an issue for the court. That was a dumb assumption, but a natural one in an adversary system, where the factual record is generated by the lawyers rather than by the judge. Actually, social security disability proceedings (as distinct from the appeals) are not formally adversary; the only lawyer at the disability hearing, apart from the administrative law judge, is the applicant's lawyer. But the administrative law judge invariably relies on the vocational expert's—ungrounded—estimate of the jobs that the applicant could perform.

I don't know why applicants' lawyers don't question the statistics, but they don't.[76] Part of the answer may be that social security disability practice is not lucrative and so doesn't attract the best lawyers or justify the lawyers' conducting deep research. And in an adversary system, when the lawyers do not raise an issue the judges usually ignore it, though they are required to address some matters, such as issues of subject-matter jurisdiction and settlements in class action cases, even if the parties agree about them or ignore them. In fact, as I'll note, some judges appear to shirk their duty to scrutinize settlements in class action cases carefully. This is understandable although unforgivable. Busy judges couldn't handle their caseload unless most of their

---

76. The principal exception appears to be Peter Lemoine. See id.

cases settled rather than having to be litigated to judgment; but as a result they are predisposed to approve *all* settlements.

It's important to understand that there is nothing to *prevent* a judge from addressing an issue in a case before him that the lawyers have ignored, and either directing the lawyers to address it in supplemental briefs or resolving it without further briefing if the correct resolution is clear, as we believed it was in the *Browning* case. It goes against the grain, however, for the judge to supplement the record or even ask the lawyers to do so—such is the grip that the adversary mindset has on the judicial mind.

That's a shame. The Internet is a vast repository of information relevant to the just resolution of legal disputes. In fact it's an extraordinary treasure of knowledge. There are inaccuracies—but there are inaccuracies in conventional legal evidence. The Internet is greatly underutilized by judges, and one reason is that it is greatly underutilized by lawyers, and in an adversary system of justice what the lawyers don't feed the judges, the judges don't eat. I am distressed to discover, in an otherwise entirely sensible article on how to write a good brief, that the author does not mention Internet research.[77]

Yale law professor John Langbein is one of the few American jurists to want to replace the adversary system with the unfortunately named "inquisitorial" system that prevails in Europe (outside the United Kingdom) and indeed in most of the world outside the United States and other former British possessions. Langbein's argument is capsulized in the following excerpt (reproduced here with his permission) from his side of a recent correspondence between us:

The core adversary system blunder is privatization of fact-gathering and fact presentation . . . The core fallacy in adver-

---

77. Douglas E. Abrams, "One Judge's 'Ten Tips for Effective Brief Writing' (Part II)," 8 *Precedent* 15 (2014).

sary theory is the idea that the truth will emerge when no one is incentivized to seek it. Counsel's incentive is to win, and hence to conceal or submerge relevant evidence, to coach witnesses, to advance biased expertise, and to distort the truth by means of abusive cross-examination. Expressed in modern economic terms, the core insight of the European nonadversarial tradition in civil and criminal procedure is that the investigation of fact in contested disputes is best re-garded as a public good. In European civil procedure, the liti-gants play a role in nominating proofs, that is, in telling the court what they think should be investigated, but the main role in investigating fact is assigned to the court, that is to judges, whose job is not to win, but to seek the truth. In criminal procedure, we Americans have developed over the past two centuries a crude version of state-conducted investi-gation, but we made the blunder of assigning it to politically-engaged prosecutors, in contrast to the European systems, in which the prosecutor is a judge-like officer whose job is to operate a state investigation service that is equally responsible for investigating.

The grip of the adversary system on the American legal mentality contributes to the irascibility of some judges toward the lawyers who appear before them—a consequence sometimes of irritability and im-patience, sometimes of ill temper, sometimes of conceit or arrogance, but more often of lawyers' deficiencies of preparation and presenta-tion.[78] Those deficiencies, which reflect the enormous variance in the

---

78. Producing what William Domnarski calls "black robe-itis," in his book *Swim-ming in Deep Water: Lawyers, Judges, and Our Troubled Legal Profession* 27–28, 107–108 (2014).

quality of lawyers who argue cases in the federal courts, frustrate the judges because of their felt dependence on the lawyers to present the information that judges need in order to be able to decide a case sensibly. Criticizing lawyers doesn't do much good, though. Lawyers don't want to do a bad job. Sometimes they're incapable of doing a good one and sometimes they have the ability but not the time or resources. The solution, if there is one, is for the judges to play a more active role in adjudication—and bury the umpireal analogy.

More serious than any of the examples I have given so far is the irresponsible attitude of a great many federal judges, the Congress, prosecutors and defense lawyers, and the U.S. Sentencing Commission, toward what is called "supervised release," which since 1987 has been an integral component of federal sentencing. But I reserve discussion of the grave defects in the conception and administration of supervised release for Appendix C, at the end of this chapter.

8. Conservatism, not in the political sense but in the sense of reluctance to change, is almost a defining characteristic of American judges. It is related to the rearview mirror syndrome, and to the passivity that I have just been discussing. But it is also its own kind of thing, as when manifested in judicial resolution of factual disputes. Many judges, in part because they don't realize how difficult cases have become and in part because their instinct is to go on doing what they've always been doing without realizing that the times they are a-changin', have an exaggerated regard for the cognitive competence of jurors. As a result they do little to enable jurors to understand a case. Because they don't understand jurors' needs and limitations, notably in patent and other technical cases and in cases involving complex financial transactions— all being types of case that are growing in difficulty and importance— they are reluctant to allow jurors to take notes or ask questions, reluctant to forbid lawyers and witnesses to use jargon, reluctant to insist on brevity and intelligibility in jury instructions, reluctant to limit documentary evidence to what jurors can reasonably be expected to absorb, reluctant to limit the length of trials.[79]

Judges seem sometimes to be veritable prisoners of anachronism, such as the nineteenth-century forensic psychology that insists against modern understanding that the truthfulness of a witness's testimony can be determined by the witness's "demeanor"—his body language, tone of voice, and other misleading signals of veracity.[80] According to Viktoras Justickis, "The law has its own set of psychological principles and concepts that permeate all its activities. By keeping these independent of 'basic legal psychology' its statements are protected from any criticism from scientific psychology. Therefore, the law can regard

79. There is a rich literature on jurors' needs and limitations that would be an eye-opener for judges if they read any of it. See, for example, Pamela Casey, Kevin Burke, and Steve Leben, "Minding the Court: Enhancing the Decision-Making Process," 49 *Court Review* 76 (2012); Guri Bollingmo et al., "The Effect of Biased and Non-Biased Information on Judgments of Witness Credibility," 15 *Psychology, Crime & Law* 61 (2009); Wendy P. Heath, Bruce D. Grannemann, and Michelle A. Peacock, "How the Defendant's Emotion Level Affects Mock Jurors' Decisions When Presentation Mode and Evidence Strength Are Varied," 34 *Journal of Applied Social Psychology* 624 (2004); Aldert Vrij, "Why Professionals Fail to Catch Liars and How They Can Improve," 9 *Legal and Criminological Psychology* 159, 165, 172, 173 (2004); Amina Memon, Aldert Vrij, and Ray Bull, *Psychology and Law: Truthfulness, Accuracy, and Credibility* 147–167, 174, 178 (2d ed. 2003); Dennis J. Devine et al., "Jury Decision Making: 45 Years of Empirical Research on Deliberating Groups," 7 *Psychology, Public Policy, and Law* 622 (2001); Lawrence S. Wrightsman, Judicial *Decision Making: Is Psychology Relevant?* (1999); Alan Reifman, Spencer M. Gusick, and Phoebe C. Ellsworth, "Real Jurors' Understanding of the Law in Real Cases," 16 *Law and Human Behavior* 539 (1992).

80. I discuss these and other problems with jury trials in *Reflections on Judging,* note 31 above, at 301–312. An exemplary study is Devine et al., cited in the preceding footnote.

its basic psychological statements as valid even if scientific verification qualifies them as invalid."[81]

I happened in a recent case to stumble on two anachronistic Federal Rules of Evidence.[82] One, Rule 803(1), captioned "present sense impression," allows into evidence an out-of-court statement, which would ordinarily be inadmissible hearsay if offered for its truth, "describing or explaining an event or condition, made while or immediately after the [out of court] declarant perceived it." The other rule—the "excited utterance" hearsay exception, found in Rule 803(2)—allows into evidence "a statement relating to a startling event or condition, made while the declarant was under the stress of excitement that it caused."

The rationale of the hearsay exception for a "present sense impression" is that if the event described and the statement describing it are near each other in time, this (in the words of the committee that drafts federal rules of evidence and explains them in accompanying notes) "negate[s] the likelihood of deliberate or conscious misrepresentation." Not true. Immediacy is no guarantor of truthfulness. It's untrue that people can't make up a lie in a short period of time—in

81. Viktoras Justickis, "Does the Law Use Even a Small Proportion of What Legal Psychology Has to Offer?" in *Psychology and Law: Bridging the Gap* 223 (David Canter and Rita Žukauskienė eds. 2008). For an excellent book-length treatment of the implications of scientific psychology for trials, with particular reference to evidence concerning jury decisions, see Memon, Vrij, and Bull, note 79 above. And on the psychology of judges' decision making, see Wrightsman, note 79 above. Academic criticism of jury fact-finding is widespread. See, for example, Bollingmo et al., and also Reifman et al., both cited in note 79. But I don't think psychology receives much attention from judges or lawyers, or for that matter from law professors who teach evidence and trial advocacy.

82. What follows is an abbreviated version of my concurring opinion in *United States v. Boyce*, 742 F.3d 792, 799–802 (7th Cir. 2014).

fact most lies are spontaneous.[83] Lying is an instinctive human mechanism of both defense and aggression.

The committee provides no more convincing a justification for the "excited utterance" rule, saying "that circumstances *may* produce a condition of excitement which temporarily stills the capacity of reflection and produces utterances free of *conscious* fabrication." The two words I've italicized drain the attempted justification of any content. As they should (though that's a reason for abolishing the rule). If a person is so excited by something that he loses the capacity for reflection (which does happen), how can one be confident that his unreflective utterance, provoked by excitement, is reliable? As pointed out eighty-eight years ago, "One need not be a psychologist to distrust an observation made under emotional stress; everybody accepts such statements with mental reservation."[84]

The committee remarks that while the excited-utterance exception to the hearsay rule indeed has been criticized, "it finds support in cases without number." That is less than reassuring. Like the exception for present-sense impressions, the exception for excited utterances

---

83. See Monica T. Whitty et al., "Not All Lies Are Spontaneous: An Examination of Deception across Different Modes of Communication," 63 *Journal of the American Society of Information Science & Technology* 208, 208–209, 214 (2012); Jeffrey Bellin, "Facebook, Twitter, and the Uncertain Future of Present Sense Impressions," 160 *University of Pennsylvania Law Review* 331, 362–366 (2012); Douglas D. McFarland, "Present Sense Impressions Cannot Live in the Past," 28 *Florida State University Law Review* 907, 916–917 (2001); Daniel Stewart, Jr., "Perception, Memory, and Hearsay: A Criticism of Present Law and the Proposed Federal Rules of Evidence," 1970 *Utah Law Review* 1, 27–29; *Lust v. Sealy, Inc.,* 383 F.3d 580, 588 (7th Cir. 2004).

84. Robert M. Hutchins and Donald Schlesinger, "Some Observations on the Law of Evidence: Spontaneous Exclamations," 28 *Columbia Law Review* 432, 437 (1928). See also 2 *McCormick on Evidence* § 272, p. 366 (7th ed. 2013).

rests on no firmer ground than judicial habit, in turn reflecting judicial incuriosity and reluctance to reconsider ancient dogmas and the general backward-looking character of legal thought that I remarked on earlier.[85]

All that can be said in favor of these two hearsay exceptions is that they allow the admission of more hearsay evidence in trials, which is often a good thing, though obviously not if it's unreliable hearsay evidence. I said in the opinion I've been paraphrasing that I didn't "want to reduce the amount of hearsay evidence admissible in federal trials." I added that the "'hearsay rule' is too complex, as well as being archaic. Trials would go better with a simpler rule, the core of which would be the proposition (essentially a simplification of Rule 807 [of the Federal Rules of Evidence]) that hearsay evidence should be admissible when it is reliable, when the jury can understand its strengths and limitations, and when it will materially enhance the likelihood of a correct outcome."[86]

85. Both hearsay exceptions that I've been discussing are powerfully criticized in Melissa Hamilton, "The Reliability of Assault Victims' Immediate Accounts: Evidence from Trauma Studies," 26 *Stanford Law and Policy Review* (forthcoming in 2015). As the author observes in the Abstract at the beginning of her paper, "Evidence law is often intransigent in its reliance upon folk psychological assumptions about human behavior." Amen!

86. *United States v. Boyce,* note 82 above, 742 F.3d at 802. Another, no less dubious, hearsay exception is the "dying declaration": "In a prosecution for homicide or in a civil case, a statement that the declarant, while believing the declarant's death to be imminent, made about its cause or circumstances." Fed. R. Evid. 804(b)(2). The rationale is religious—that someone believing himself about to die would not dare tell a lie lest doing so send him straight to hell. Not only have such beliefs weakened a good deal (and would a court allow the parties to present evidence concerning the dying declarant's religious beliefs and sincerity?), but also "no empirical studies are available as to the psychological effect that the knowledge of imminent, certain death has on a human being. There are several other factors which tend to weaken the argument that dying declarations

Another example of the law's archaic attitude toward hearsay was brought to my attention recently by J. Gregory Sidak, a distinguished lawyer-economist who has testified frequently as an expert witness in patent and other complex cases. He notes the anomaly that an expert's report, which is required to be submitted before the expert is allowed to testify, typically is not itself admissible in evidence, because it is an out-of-court statement offered to prove the truth of the assertions in it and is therefore hearsay. Yet an expert witness is allowed to base his expert opinion on hearsay and to testify to that expert opinion at trial. Were the expert's report admissible there would at least be complete documentation of the hearsay upon which he'd relied—or a conspicuous absence of such documentation, which would suggest that the expert lacked a sound basis for his opinion. In the absence of the report an expert may be able to get away with making very general statements about what might be the consequence if certain facts asserted were true and then tell the jurors that it's for them to decide whether a particular conjecture is plausible. With the expert's report excluded from the trial, his effectiveness as a witness may depend more on his congeniality as a storyteller than on the accuracy of his analysis.

Lack of realism about the trial process is a particular problem for appellate judges who have never been trial judges or trial lawyers, but who of course have to evaluate trials as part of their appellate duties.

---

are inherently trustworthy. First, the declarant, being in pain and agony as a result of the wounds that he received, may have a defective memory. Second, the declarant, surrounded by his family and friends, is apt to state only his side of the affair. Third, the dying declaration is apt to be distracting and confusing to the witness to whom it is related. Fourth, those about the declarant do not usually seek to elicit qualifying facts unfavorable to the declarant." Comment, "The Admissibility of Dying Declaration," 38 *Fordham Law Review* 509, 514 (1970) (footnotes omitted).

But there is a solution: volunteering to handle trials in the local federal district court. I had no trial experience when I became a federal appellate judge, but I accepted the advice of one of the judges of my court to conduct trials in the district courts of the circuit and have been doing so ever since. It's been an eye-opening experience! I consider it invaluable. But my impression is that few appellate judges who could benefit from such experience undergo it. They should be required to. It might even be a good idea to assign every newly appointed federal appellate judge who lacks trial experience to the local district court for the first six months of his judgeship. His inexperience would be a challenge for him, but he could lean to a degree on the district court's experienced judges. At the very least, newly appointed appellate judges should study videotapes of actual trial-court proceedings. How can an appellate judge review a trial when he has never seen one, except perhaps in a movie?

9. *Complacency and overconfidence* are characteristics, found in some judges, that contribute to standpattism in matters of procedure and evidence. A judge may assume that because it's difficult to obtain a federal judicial appointment he *must* be capable of occupying the office with distinction and therefore *is* occupying it with distinction, even if he doesn't put forth much effort but instead relies on a combination of intuition and of delegation to staff to discharge his judicial duties.

A highly experienced judge may exaggerate the substitutability of experience for careful case preparation. Judging is a job in which experience does generate knowledge and can sharpen intuition, and in these ways can go quite a distance toward replacing analytical effort and acuity. But it is easy to exaggerate the value of experience. Judges who have sentenced a great many criminal defendants may believe that as a result of all these encounters they must know what the right sentence is to impose on a given defendant without having to think much about it. Not so. Defendants differ from one another even if they've committed the same crimes, and what is the right sentence for each defendant depends on the characteristics of each defendant and each crime; for those characteristics determine what is the optimal sentence in terms of the likelihood of achieving, by means of the punishment meted out to the defendant, deterrence of future crimes by him or others.

A factor contributing to judicial complacency, particularly of federal court of appeals judges, is the very low rate of review by the Supreme Court. The courts of appeals decide tens of thousands of cases in the course of a year, but the Supreme Court decides only about seventy-five a year and some of these are appeals from state rather than federal courts. The average court of appeals judge is therefore reversed very rarely. (Sometimes a decision is overturned by the judge's court, sitting en banc, but that is rare too.) A high success rate in an endeavor can breed overconfidence, even if the rate is the product of factors extraneous to the successful person.

Judges need to be reminded of Holmes's dictum that

> certitude is not the test of certainty. We have been cocksure of many things that were not so . . . One cannot be wrenched from the rocky crevices into which one has grown for many years without feeling that one is attacked in one's life . . . But while one's experience thus makes certain preferences dogmatic for oneself, recognition of how they came to be so leaves one able to see that others, poor souls, may be equally dogmatic about something else. And this again means skepticism.[87]

So some judges, to whom it does not occur that they may have been "cocksure of many things that were not so," are confident that if they

---

87. O. W. Holmes, "Natural Law" (1918), in *The Essential Holmes,* note 12 above, at 180, 181.

find a witness to be credible he *must* be telling the truth. Some judges impose very long or very short prison sentences confident that their every sentence is of just the right severity, though in fact little is known about optimal sentence lengths. Many judges, however, sensibly repose a degree of confidence in the recommendations of federal probation officers and information in the presentence report that the federal probation service provides in all cases in which the defendant has been convicted and will therefore be sentenced. The probation service is a repository, though fallible and its personnel overworked, of criminological knowledge and experience.[88] Its sentence recommendations deserve and often receive careful consideration by the sentencing judges.

Judicial standpattism is reflected in the judiciary's reluctance to modify the adversary system of evidence production and proof despite the flaws that I and others have discussed, and despite the existence of doctrines such as judicial notice (of incontrovertible facts) and judicial use (without adversary process) of legislative as distinct

88. It's important to distinguish between the probation service, which is part of the federal judiciary (it is lodged within the Administrative Office of the U.S. Courts), and the U.S. Sentencing Commission, which promulgates sentencing guidelines that were mandatory until the Supreme Court in *United States v. Booker*, 543 U.S. 220 (2005) demoted them to advisory status. By doing so the Court made more work for the lower federal courts, especially the district courts, which are the sentencing courts. As expected, greater variance in sentences resulted, but another result was a reduction in average sentence length, because for many years there's been a widespread feeling among judges that the guidelines are too severe. The Sentencing Commission was created by Congress and has doubtless been somewhat responsive to politicians' ferocity toward criminals, a ferocity not shared by probation officers or all judges. There is growing awareness, based partly on soaring prison costs, that the American criminal punishment system is excessively severe across the board. See, for example, Oliver Roeder, Lauren-Brooke Eisen, and Julia Bowling, "What Caused the Crime Decline?" February 12, 2015, www.brennancenter.org/publication/what-caused-crime-decline. One of the most problematic features of current federal sentencing— "supervised release"—is the subject of Appendix C to this chapter. It is a disturbing illustration of judicial standpattism.

from adjudicative facts that provide levers for loosening the traditional hold that adversary procedure has over proving facts, and also despite the transformative potential of the Internet.[89] Gradually we're learning that the traditional passivity of the American judge in the development of the factual basis of decision requires adjustment. It is now understood, for example, that the terms of settlement of a class action must be subject to approval by the presiding judge. Otherwise class counsel, ungoverned as a practical matter by either the named plaintiffs or the other members of the class, will be able to maximize their attorneys' fees at the expense of the class. The defendant cares only about the size of the settlement, not how it's divided between attorneys' fees and compensation for the class. So from the selfish standpoint of class counsel and defendant the optimal settlement is one that is modest in overall amount (which is what the defendant wants) but heavily tilted toward attorneys' fees (what class counsel care most about). It's up to the judge to make sure that the settlement doesn't give class counsel an exorbitant share of the settlement proceeds, thus selling out the class—an endeavor in which the defendant is happy to join. Similarly, in criminal cases judges aren't supposed to rubberstamp the sentence that the prosecutor and the defense have agreed to recommend to the judge, but to make an independent judgment, advised by the probation service as well as by the litigants' lawyers.

American judges, habituated as they are to expect the clash of the adversaries to generate all the information that a judge needs in order to be able to decide the case intelligently, are uncomfortable at having as it were to swing at the pitch rather than just call a ball or a strike. So one encounters judicial language such as the following, oblivious to the serious conflicts of interest inherent in class actions: "Because settlement of a class action, like settlement of any litigation, is basically a bargained exchange between the litigants, the judiciary's role is prop-

89. See, for example, Chapter 5 of *Reflections on Judging,* note 31 above.

erly limited to the minimum necessary to protect the interests of the class and the public. Judges should not substitute their own judgment as to optimal settlement terms for the judgment of the litigants and their counsel."[90] Hence too the reluctance that I mentioned earlier of federal district judges to invoke Federal Rule of Evidence 706, which authorizes judges to appoint their own expert witnesses rather than having to rely, or make the jury rely, entirely on party experts in cases that require expert testimony. Judges tend to be complacent about the adversary system. It's our system. It's one of the rocky crevices we've grown into. And it requires less work by judges than if they took a more active role.

A related form of passivity is excessive appellate deference to trial courts. I will illustrate with one of the cases I cited earlier, in which the judges had questioned the source and accuracy of the statistics that vocational experts trot out in social security disability hearings to inform the administrative law judge of how many jobs in the economy the applicant for disability benefits is capable of doing. The case is *Brault v. Social Security Administration,* and the opinion recognizes, to its credit, the problem of the reliability of vocational experts' estimates of the number of jobs in the economy that a given applicant for social security benefits can perform.[91] The vocational expert had derived his

---

90. *Armstrong v. Board of School Directors of City of Milwaukee,* 616 F.2d 305, 315 (7th Cir. 1980). See also *Isby v. Bayh,* 75 F.3d 1191, 1196–1197 (7th Cir. 1996). The problem of the conflict of interest between class counsel and class members is being alleviated to some extent, however, by the rise of the "objector"—a class member who challenges a proposed settlement as shifting too much of the settlement amount from the class members to the class counsel. If successful, the objector is entitled to compensation for his efforts on behalf of the class. See, for recent examples of class action settlements rejected on the basis of objectors' submissions, *Pearson v. NBTY, Inc.,* 772 F.3d 778 (7th Cir. 2014), and *Redman v. RadioShack Corp.,* 768 F.3d 622 (7th Cir. 2014). The rise of the objector is an example of an innovation that makes adversary procedure more effective.

91. On *Brault v. Social Security Administration,* see note 75 above.

estimate of the number of jobs the applicant could perform from a statistical source that was not based on the same job categories and so could not yield an accurate estimate, but in fact yielded a gross overestimate.[92] Yet, rejecting the challenge by the applicant's lawyer to the vocational expert's statistics, the administrative law judge pointed to his testimony that he had "reduced" the numbers derived from the dubious statistical source to the number of "jobs . . . that I know exist."[93] How he had accomplished this legerdemain he did not explain intelligibly.[94] Again the applicant's lawyer objected. The administrative law judge, without bothering to respond to the objection, turned down the applicant's claim for benefits. The district court affirmed, and the court of appeals affirmed the district court, explaining:

> Assuming the ALJ had to consider Brault's objection to the VE's testimony, we are satisfied that he did so. There is no requirement that the ALJ discuss his specific analysis of it . . . Furthermore the proposition that the ALJ was *required* to inquire into Brault's objection, whether or not the ALJ discussed it on the record, is dubious . . . [But] assuming *arguendo* Brault had a right to have the ALJ consider his challenge to the VE, that is exactly what the ALJ did . . . In sum, Brault's attorney had a full opportunity to explain his objections in significant detail. Nothing more is required.[95]

Unwittingly the quoted passage acknowledges a dereliction of judicial duty. The applicant's lawyer had made a very damaging criticism of the vocational expert's estimate of the number of jobs in the econ-

92. A danger acknowledged in the *Brault* opinion. See 683 F.3d at 447 n. 4.
93. Id. at 447.
94. See the summary of his testimony in the Social Security Administration's brief, 2011 WL 5833316, pp. 9–10.
95. 683 F.3d at 448–451 (emphasis in original).

omy that the applicant could perform. A court has a duty to respond, not to every argument that a litigant makes, but to a powerful argument that if accepted requires judgment for the party making it. At the very least the court should have offered its own, however tentative, assessment of the argument, explaining why it thought the argument did or did not have sufficient merit to require a further hearing at the administrative level.

The quoted passage is also incoherent. The first sentence expresses doubt that the administrative law judge was required even to consider Brault's objection, serious though it was; and what sense can that make? Two sentences later the opinion states that it's "dubious" that the administrative law judge was "*required* to inquire into Brault's objection" (emphasis in original)—but in the last sentence in the quotation there is a strong suggestion that the administrative law judge *was* required to consider Brault's objection after all.

All that's clear is that the court thought it owed a high level of deference to the administrative law judge's determination. It noted that the standard of appellate review for agency determinations of fact is "substantial evidence," and called this a more deferential standard than "clearly erroneous,"[96] which is the standard governing appellate review of district court fact-findings. It relied for this proposition on a Supreme Court decision, but missed the part of the opinion in which the Court made clear that only a hair's breadth separates the two standards.[97] Because judges can no more discern a hair's breadth than they can an italicized period or a boldfaced space, there is no operational difference between "substantial evidence" and "clearly erroneous." As the court failed to understand, deference to an agency's determinations, as to a district court's, properly is something to be earned rather

96. Id. at 448.
97. *Dickinson v. Zurko*, 527 U.S. 150, 162–163 (1999).

than bestowed. The federal administrative agencies differ widely in competence. The Social Security Administration's Office of Disability Adjudication and Review nestles at the bottom with the Justice Department's Immigration Court and Board of Immigration Appeals,[98] in part (but only in part) because of these agencies' crushing caseloads. Federal agencies such as the National Labor Relations Board, the Federal Communications Commission, and the Environmental Protection Agency are greatly superior. It makes no sense for a reviewing court to bestow uniform deference on agencies of widely varying competence.

In fairness to the judges in the *Brault* case, they may have felt their hands tied by the doctrine of *Chevron, U.S.A., Inc. v. Natural Resources Defense Council, Inc.,*[99] which in its simplest form (it has generated numerous epicycles) tells judges to give a substantial measure of deference to formal agency interpretations of the statutes they administer.[100] The doctrine distinguishes among different levels of formality in agency decisions, but not among agencies, and so in principle, at least, the very weak federal agencies are entitled to the same deference as the very strong ones. That doesn't describe the actual behavior of

---

98. See, for example, Harold J. Krent and Scott B. Morris, "Inconsistency and Angst in District Court Resolution of Social Security Disability Appeals" (Chicago-Kent College of Law Research Paper, November 24, 2014), available on Social Science Research Network at http://papers.ssrn.com/sol3/papers.cfm?abstract_id=2530158; *Reflections on Judging,* note 31 above, 140–141; and opinions that I've written for my court in social security disability cases and immigration (especially asylum) cases, such as, regarding social security, the *Browning* and *Herrmann* cases cited in notes 74 and 75 above and, regarding immigration, *Lopez-Esparza v. Holder,* 770 F.3d 606 (7th Cir. 2014), and *Shu Han Liu v. Holder,* 718 F.3d 706 (7th Cir. 2013).

99. 467 U.S. 837 (1984).

100. See, for example, John F. Manning, "Chevron and Legislative History," 82 *George Washington Law Review* 1517 (2014).

most judges in reviewing agency decisions—which tends to be ad hoc and sometimes policy-driven—and doesn't make sense.[101] Furthermore, taken seriously it authorizes agency self-aggrandizement: the agency has only to interpret the statutes it administers as granting it the broadest possible powers, and many an agency has a strong incentive to interpret its statutes so—if it can get away with it by invoking the *Chevron* doctrine. The appeal of the doctrine to those judges (a minority) to whom it does appeal is that it gives judges an excuse not to spend time trying to understand the technical intricacies of administrative regulation.

A similarly questionable Supreme Court–made rule, but one that the Court has enforced with greater vigor than it has the *Chevron* doctrine, is that a lower court may not anticipate the Supreme Court's overruling of a decision by the Court, however obviously defunct that decision. The idea animating the rule is that a lower court that did that would be disrupting the Court's schedule, forcing it to decide a case out of turn, as it were, in order to preserve its precedent so rudely handled by the lower court. That doesn't make much sense. If the Supreme Court is happy to see the precedent discarded, it is spared work if a lower court declares the precedent deceased and the other lower

---

101. See, for example, Cass R. Sunstein and Adrian Vermeule, "Libertarian Administrative Law" (forthcoming in *University of Chicago Law Review*); William N. Eskridge and Lauren E. Baer, "The Continuum of Deference: Supreme Court Treatment of Agency Statutory Interpretations from Chevron to Hamdan," 96 *Georgetown Law Journal* 1083, 1090 (2008); Thomas J. Miles and Cass R. Sunstein, "Do Judges Make Regulatory Policy? An Empirical Investigation of *Chevron*," 73 *University of Chicago* 823 (2006); Emerson Tiller and Frank Cross, "Judicial Partisanship and Obedience to Legal Doctrine," 107 *Yale Law Journal* 2155 (1998); Richard Revesz, "Environmental Regulation, Ideology, and the D.C. Circuit," 83 *Virginia Law Review* 1717 (1993); cf. Thomas J. Miles and Cass R. Sunstein, "The Real World of Arbitrariness Review," 75 *University of Chicago Law Review* 761 (2008).

courts agree. And that is a likelier outcome than the Court's deciding that the lower court or courts are wrong and therefore deciding to hear and reverse a decision rejecting the Court's precedent. It is likelier because a lower court will not declare a Supreme Court decision defunct unless there is very little doubt that it is.

A good example of the process that the Court has mistakenly (in my view) condemned is found in *Browder v. Gayle*,[102] a decision by a three-judge district court that declared *Plessy v. Ferguson*[103] defunct. *Plessy* of course was the case in which the Supreme Court had upheld a state law requiring racial segregation of railroad transportation provided the services to the members of each race were, though separate, equal in quality. *Brown v. Board of Education* did not overrule *Plessy*, but held only that segregated public school education was inherently unequal. When *Browder*, a case involving a challenge to racial segregation of buses, was decided in 1956, the Supreme Court still had not addressed the issue of racial segregation in public transportation. Nevertheless the three-judge district court declared *Plessy* defunct. And that was that. The Supreme Court affirmed without bothering to write an opinion.

Decided just two years after *Brown*, the district court decision in *Browder* saved the Supreme Court from embarrassment because it is more difficult to describe "separate but equal" transportation accommodations as inherently unequal than it is to describe segregated schooling so. Of course the actual reason for segregation in both cases

---

102. 142 F. Supp. 707 (M.D. Ala. 1956). The Supreme Court affirmed the decision, but without discussion. Its opinion, *Gayle v. Browder*, 352 U.S. 903 (1956), reads in its entirety: "PER CURIAM. The motion to affirm is granted and the judgment is affirmed," citing *Brown v. Board of Education* and two other cases; those other cases stated merely that they were affirming the lower court decision per curiam.

103. 163 U.S. 537 (1896).

was to preserve white supremacy, but the Supreme Court had been careful to avoid that ground for its decision in *Brown,* fearing that its embrace might induce a violent reaction by white southerners. *Browder* could not have been decided by a lower court, thereby sparing the Supreme Court unwanted trouble, under the Court's current rule that a lower court may not anticipate the overruling of a decision by the Court, however old and stale.

10. Decision by formula—standards of appellate review revisited. I mentioned the insistence of the court in the *Brault* case that there's a difference between "substantial evidence" and "clearly erroneous" as standards of appellate review. I don't think there is one. Whether reviewing the decision of a district court or of a federal administrative agency, an appellate court will affirm if the decision under review seems clearly correct, or if the case is a toss-up—ties are affirmances—or if, as I suggested earlier in this chapter, the appellate court is willing to swallow its doubts in recognition of the greater knowledge of the district judge or the agency of the contested issues in the case.

Although there really isn't much more to say about standards of appellate review, courts will not leave well enough alone. They will say for example that "in passing on a motion for summary judgment, a court must indulge inferences in favor of the non-moving party, but it need not indulge all possible inferences."[104] I don't know what it means to "indulge" an inference. Is that like drawing an inference? But surely one can draw an inference in favor of the nonmoving party if the evidence supports such an inference. And what are the "possible inferences" that the court is not required to "indulge"?

In another opinion we read that "the position advanced by the dissent impermissibly indulges inferences unfavorable to the verdict."[105] But at least the court went on to explain that the "indul-

---

104. *Henn v. National Geographic Society,* 819 F.2d 824, 830 (7th Cir. 1987).
105. *United States v. Mangual-Corchado,* 139 F.3d 34, 39 n. 6 (1st Cir. 1998).

gence" was impermissible because the inference was unsound. But why not just say that and forget about "indulgence"? And does it really add anything to say that "specious inferences are not indulged"?[106] And what is one to make of this variant: "In reviewing [the defendant's] conviction, we are obligated to credit testimony and indulge inferences that benefit the prosecution. We therefore recount the facts in the light most favorable to the government."[107] How can there be an obligation to credit testimony, and indulge inferences, that favor the prosecution, without determining the credibility of the testimony and the accuracy of the inferences derived from it plus any nontestimonial evidence? And to "recount the facts in the light most favorable to the government" sounds like picking and choosing from the factual record, though doubtless this was not intended.

And how about this gem: "Only when the record contains no evidence, *regardless of how it is weighed,* from which the jury could find guilt beyond a reasonable doubt, may an appellate court overturn the verdict" (that is, a guilty verdict in a criminal case).[108] That was first said, as far as I can determine, forty-six years ago, but it has been repeated frequently since, most recently in December 2014, and to my knowledge has never been questioned.[109] Yet read literally it is nonsense—read literally it says that even if the evidence of guilt is greatly outweighed by evidence of innocence, the conviction must be affirmed. But how else can it be read? I have found no attempt to explain it. It is just repeated mindlessly from case to case.

---

106. *United States v. Jones,* 393 F.3d 107, 111 (2d Cir. 2004).
107. *United States v. Hatchett,* 245 F.3d 625, 627–628 (7th Cir. 2001).
108. *Brandom v. United States,* 431 F.2d 1391, 1400 (7th Cir. 1970) (emphasis added).
109. *United States v. Blitch,* 773 F.3d 837, 846 (7th Cir. 2014) (italicizing the phrase); *United States v. Torres-Chavez,* 744 F.3d 988, 993 (7th Cir. 2014). I am embarrassed to say that as far as I can determine the formula does not appear in opinions of any federal court other than mine, although it has never appeared in one of my opinions.

Or consider this: "If the [company's health] plan gives the administrator or fiduciary discretionary authority, then we apply an abuse of discretion standard. In applying the abuse of discretion standard, we analyze whether the plan administrator acted arbitrarily or capriciously."[110] What could this mean? What is an "abuse" of discretion—a mistake, or something much worse? It seems from the second sentence that an "abuse of discretion" is simply an arbitrary or capricious exercise of discretion. But what is the difference between "arbitrary" and "capricious"? Wouldn't it be a lot clearer to pose the question as whether the administrator had exceeded the limits of his discretionary authority? Why can't judges (or their law clerks) write clearly?

As I wrote in an opinion some years ago,

> We acknowledge that there are more verbal formulas for the scope of appellate review (plenary or de novo, clearly erroneous, abuse of discretion, substantial evidence, arbitrary and capricious, some evidence, reasonable basis, presumed correct, and maybe others) than there are distinctions actually capable of being drawn in the practice of appellate review. But even if, as we have sometimes heretically suggested, there are operationally only two degrees of review, plenary (that is, no deference given to the tribunal being reviewed) and deferential, *that* distinction at least is a feasible, intelligible, and important one.[111]

A great many opinions introduce the standard of review with the word "we," as in "we review the grant of summary judgment *de novo*"

---

110. *Salley v. E.I. DuPont de Nemours & Co.*, 966 F.2d 1011, 1014 (5th Cir. 1992) (citations omitted).

111. *United States v. Boyd*, 55 F.3d 239, 242 (7th Cir. 1995) (emphasis in original; citations omitted).

and "we review the dismissal on a statute of limitations defense *de novo*,"[112] or "we review the denial of a motion for summary judgment and the legal issues related to qualified immunity *de novo*,"[113] or "we review a district court's dismissal under Federal Rule of Civil Procedure 12(b)(6) *de novo*" and "we accept all well-pleaded facts as true and view all facts in the light most favorable to the plaintiff" but "we need not . . . accept the plaintiff's legal conclusions as true."[114] But who is the "we"? Is it the three judges on the panel? Their court? Or the federal judiciary as a whole? The "we" formula is just another example of what is all too common—careless judicial writing.

11. Informationally disabled judges. Frederick Schauer describes American courts as "informationally disabled."[115] Sections 6 through 10 of this chapter have been primarily concerned with judges' informational disabilities; Schauer's article should help one understand the magnitude of the problem. He points out that "as the world becomes more complex, and as sophisticated scientific, technical, and financial information becomes more central to litigation and to the judicial function, the systemic disabilities of the courts in obtaining the information they need become more apparent and increasingly more problematic."[116] These systemic disabilities are fivefold; in summary:

> The law of evidence excludes not only irrelevant facts, but many relevant ones that would otherwise be important; the adversary system bars the fact-finder from engaging in "persistent investigation" or initiating inquiries, leaving factfind-

112. *Memorylink Corp. v. Motorola Solutions, Inc.*, 773 F.3d 1266, 1270 (Fed. Cir. 2014).
113. *Williams v. City of Alexander*, 772 F.3d 1307, 1310 (8th Cir. 2014).
114. *Thompson v. City of Waco*, 764 F.3d 500, 502 (5th Cir. 2014).
115. Schauer, "Our Informationally Disabled Courts," *Daedalus*, Summer 2014, 105, 111.
116. Id., Abstract.

ing at the mercy of the variable talents and incentives of the competing parties; the reliance on witnesses produces a system in which actual firsthand knowledge on the part of the fact-finder is rare; the rules and traditions of the closed record make inquiry into matters outside the limited domain of accepted materials difficult; and the vagaries of case selection may encourage judicial policy-making to take place in the context of highly unrepresentative facts and events.[117]

As Schauer explains, the law of evidence and judicial fact-finding more broadly are rife with anachronisms. Many of these are self-inflicted by the judges and could be changed by them; Schauer mentions Justice Breyer and me as judges who are trying to do so. But most judges are reluctant to depart from the traditional ways—even though there rarely are significant reliance interests in adhering to traditional procedural rules as distinct from traditional substantive ones. When judges say as they often do that it is sometimes more important that the law be settled than that it be right, they are not talking about procedural rules.

It's difficult to think of a more serious affliction of judges than a weak sense of fact, reflected for example in an unrealistic conception of judges' and juries' abilities to extract truth from testimony and more broadly in excessive reliance on the adversary process to generate the factual information that judges need in order to decide cases intelligently, to the neglect of the vast informational resources found online and in nonlegal academic research. This by the way is one of the most important areas in which the law schools are failing to assist the judiciary, as we'll see in Chapter 4.

    12. Lack of curiosity. A number of the factors that I've been discuss-

---

117. Id. at 111.

ing, including formalism, passivity, complacency, and informational disability, reflect a lack of curiosity about the cases that come before judges for decision and the legal doctrines (many jejune) that the lawyers trot out in support of their positions. At the district court level a lack of curiosity follows naturally from the heavy caseload, which limits the amount of attention the judge can devote to a case and thus how deeply he can dig into it. Most appellate judges, at least in the federal system, including Supreme Court Justices, don't have heavy caseloads, or, more precisely, wouldn't have if they managed their time better. But the legal culture discourages appellate judges from straying from the trial record. Also, some judges like to think they're busy even when they're not, and so don't welcome a suggestion that they take a more active role in developing a record on which to base the decision of a case.

I came across a case recently that well illustrates judicial incuriosity. It concerns "supervised release," the federal parole substitute that I discuss at some length in Appendix C to this chapter. At sentencing, federal judges are permitted (sometimes required) to impose restrictions on the defendant's conduct to take effect upon his release from prison; these are called "conditions of supervised release." The defendant in *United States v. Wiltshire* had been convicted of illegal distribution of a prescription drug (Adderall, often used to treat narcolepsy or attention deficit disorder), and among the conditions of supervised release imposed on her were that she had to get her probation officer's permission to leave the federal judicial district (the Southern District of Ohio) in which she lived, and had to answer truthfully all questions put to her by the officer.[118] It turned out that she worked occasionally as an "exotic dancer" in Lexington, Kentucky, yet failed to mention this on a questionnaire that asked about employment, given her by

118. 772 F.3d 976 (2d Cir. 2014) (per curiam).

the probation officer. Also, Lexington is in a different federal judicial district from the Southern District of Ohio. As punishment for these two violations of supervised release, the district judge sentenced her to ninety days in jail and an additional two years of supervised release (on top of an original five years).

The Second Circuit's opinion affirming the district court is remarkable for what it does not tell the reader. It does not indicate where the defendant lived or how far her home was from Lexington, Kentucky (in fact she lived in Portsmouth, which is two hours by car northeast of Lexington), what if anything she'd been told the boundaries of her judicial district were, whether she was still doing exotic dancing in Lexington when asked how she was employed (she said no), and whether what appear to have been trivial violations (for there is no suggestion that her "exotic dancing" was more than normal nightclub entertainment) deserved punishment. The opinion evinces a lack of curiosity about facts suggestive of a miscarriage of justice, and would have been equally informative had it consisted of the single word "Affirmed." (I give another example of judicial incuriosity in Appendix B to this chapter, though that one appears to have been a product of ideological commitment.)

John Roberts famously remarked at his confirmation hearing for appointment as Chief Justice of the United States that the job of a Justice or any other judge is like that of a baseball umpire—calling balls and strikes, but not pitching or batting.[119] That's a bad analogy—

---

119. *Confirmation Hearing on the Nomination of John G. Roberts, Jr. to Be Chief Justice of the United States: Hearing before the Senate Committee on the Judiciary,* 109th Cong., Sen. Hearing 158, p. 56 (2005). The pattern of his voting as Chief Justice has been inconsistent with what he told the Senators it would be. See, for example, Emily Bazelon, "Marriage of Convenience: How Does the New Gay Rights Case before the Supreme Court Play into John Roberts's Long Game?" *New York Times Magazine,* February 1, 2015, 13.

as well as an endorsement of lack of curiosity—though questioned by none of the Senators at the hearing (a clue to the fatuity of confirmation hearings). Curiosity about baseball isn't a qualification for being an umpire; it may even be a distraction. The umpire has no responsibility for the quality of the game. His only job is to detect violations of various restrictions on the players' conduct that are imposed by league rules. This involves fact finding but not lawmaking. (Umpires have some flexibility in the interpretation of the rules, but not a great deal.) The position of a judge in the American legal system is different. His most important role is creative—fitting the law to novel activities, transactions, technologies, and institutions. A judge who lacks curiosity about such things—who is content with the bleached-out facts that the lawyers are likely to tender to him (especially in an appeal), who is indifferent to achieving a realistic understanding of a case, who accepts without question the existing doctrines and culture of the law—will not do a good job of keeping law up to date and in tune with a society undergoing dizzying change, which is our society.

Not that judges should be thought obligated to know everything about everything. They can't; cases can be bottomless pits. But a judge should always insist on understanding the situation that has given rise to the lawsuit that he is called upon to adjudicate. I would like to see a constant posing by judges of "why" questions—why, for example, against what background, for what reasons, did the parties to the lawsuit do the things that gave rise to it? I would like to see a critical interrogation of the legal rules urged as the key to resolving a case. Both types of inquiry often require going outside the record as the parties have framed it, and sometimes outside existing legal doctrine as well. I applaud judges, including appellate judges, who conduct "in-house" judicial fact-finding (recently dubbed "independent judicial research"). Not in-house fact-finding of the "adjudicative facts," which is to say what happened in the particular case before the judge; for such facts, unless they can be established with certainty without a hearing (that is, unless "judicial notice" can be taken of them), require evidentiary hearings to determine. I am thinking rather of background facts—facts that enable an understanding of transactions, businesses (lawful and otherwise), local cultures, belief systems, geography, and other contextual factors in a case, and also facts concerning such matters as the reliability of various types of evidence, such as survey evidence, eyewitness evidence, and DNA evidence—facts that are the domain not of lay testimony but of the natural and social sciences. Regrettably, independent judicial research continues to lag, encountering sharp criticism even as the social sciences mature and the natural sciences advance at a breakneck pace and the Internet becomes an ever vaster yet at the same time paradoxically more readily searchable body of information.[120] The linkage between lack of curiosity and refusal to conduct even elementary extrarecord research is illustrated by the recent D.C. Circuit case discussed in Appendix B.

An odd thing about the widespread disdain for such research is that judges are not criticized for having good memories and drawing from memory insights that enrich a judicial opinion and even guide decision. Yet what is the Internet but a giant memory supplement? Instead of searching one's brain for a name or an idea, one now can search the Internet, which is one's external brain—one is much more likely to find what one is searching for. In the not too distant future

---

120. See, for example, Allison Orr Larsen, "Confronting Supreme Court Fact Finding," 98 *Virginia Law Review* 1255 (2012); John Monahan and Laurens Walker, "Twenty-Five Years of *Social Science in Law*," 35 *Law and Human Behavior* 72 (2011). The risk of error must be acknowledged, however, especially when judges, "going outside the record," rely on amicus curiae briefs as sources of facts. See, for example, Allison Orr Larsen, "The Trouble with Amicus Facts," 100 *Virginia Law Review* 1757 (2014); Adam Liptak, "Seeking Facts, Justices Settle for What Briefs Tell Them," *New York Times,* September 2, 2014, A10.

the Internet will be inside our brains, but whether inside or outside it is a legitimate and indeed indispensable source of ideas and information that the judiciary badly needs.

Happily the ratio of citations in judicial opinions to nonlegal materials to citations to legal materials is growing. This may be attributable largely to the increased quantity of those materials and the increased number of law clerks, but another explanation, which has been suggested by Frederick Schauer and Virginia Wise—and resonates with the theme of this book—is "a perception by judges, even if not necessarily shared by their clerks, that the material now being produced by law reviews, especially the major national law reviews, is less useful to judges than the material produced by the same law reviews in the past."[121] As a result, the authors suggest, law may be losing its "informational autonomy," by which they mean the conception of law as a self-enclosed field of study and analysis, walled off from the social sciences and empirical inquiry (as distinguished from traditional legal fact-finding, focused on lay testimony given at a trial).[122] Those traditionalists who want to stay within the walls will have to take what comfort they can from St. Augustine's quip in the *Confessions* (Book 11, chapter 12) that (loosely translated) "God created hell for the inquisitive."

13. Lack of self-knowledge, is related to, and even undergirds, many of the other problems of judges. It figures in the stated belief of almost all judges that their judicial votes are uninfluenced by their priors (political ideology, religion, other sources of values including moral values, temperament, personal and professional experiences, ambition, culture, generation, family history, ethnic or racial background, gender,

---

121. Frederick Schauer and Virginia J. Wise, "Nonlegal Information and the Delegalization of Law," 29 *Journal of Legal Studies* 495, 507 n. 16 (2000).
122. Id. at 514–515.

age, education, intelligence, technical knowledge, cultural breadth, analytical ability, empathy, sympathy, energy, health). Actually the judge who thinks he isn't influenced by his priors—the judge who like King Lear "hath ever but slenderly known himself"—is more likely to be influenced by them than a more self-aware judge would be. He is likely to be excessively self-confident. His mind may be closing down. He should heed Oliver Cromwell's warning (which Learned Hand, a great judge not afflicted by excessive self-confidence, liked to repeat): "I beseech you, in the bowels of Christ, think it possible that you may be mistaken." Holmes put it even more succinctly in a passage I quoted earlier in this chapter: "Certitude is not the test of certainty."[123]

14. A loose attitude toward truth is distinct from secretiveness, lack of candor, and lack of self-knowledge, though related to those characteristics. It reflects in part the fact that all judges were once law students and that most had some, and often a great deal of, involvement in legal practice before they became judges. Litigation and negotiation are adversary activities and taught as such in law school. The object is to win a battle. How else to explain why a lawyer's discussions with his client are privileged? And though unlike his military counterpart the lawyer is not to lie, he is not required to believe even what he says in court, as that would undermine his effectiveness as the client's agent. The distinguished British judge Patrick Devlin once said that the lawyer's function is to say on behalf of his client what the client would say himself if learned in the law. In saying this Devlin was describing the lawyer as the client's "mouthpiece," to use a derogatory Americanism. The lawyer is an advocate, an agent; his commitment is to win for his client. He may be reluctant to say something he knows to be a lie—

---

123. See text at note 87 above.

though taken literally Devlin's description of the lawyer's function would permit and often require the lawyer to lie, since his client often would lie if he were representing himself in court. But a lawyer is allowed to state as truth what he doubts is true though does not know to be false. And if he becomes a judge or Justice he may have difficulty sloughing off habits engrained by the loose attitude toward truth that legal training and practice and the understanding of the lawyer's duty to a client beget.

Another bad habit is judicial self-flattery. Every profession likes to flatter itself. But none so blatantly as the legal profession, as when David Levi, who resigned his federal district judgeship to become Dean of Duke Law School (and he was a fine judge, and is a fine dean), said:

> Because of the training provided by our law schools, and by the experience of practice, we have a Bar of great skill and character, a Bar that has a tradition of democratic leadership that continues to inspire . . . There is no wall between the academy and the profession, or between the Bar and the judiciary. Because of our training, our experience, and our powerful legal culture, all of us are and should be ready to serve and assume new roles within the profession and within our democracy.[124]

I don't know what this passage means—I especially don't understand the reference to the Bar's having "a tradition of democratic leadership." The Bar has no leadership. But I know that the passage is intended to bathe bench and bar and the legal academy in a warm and

---

124. David F. Levi, "From Judge to Dean: Reflections on the Bench and the Academy," 70 *Louisiana Law Review* 913, 922 (2010).

flattering light. And I think I know that almost everything in the passage is false. Of course a dean must worry that candor about the profession could alienate lawyers and judges and by doing so impair the job opportunities of his law school's graduates.

More troublesome than the profession's self-praise is the tendency of judicial opinions to state what is conventional, or expected to appear in an opinion, yet what the judge who is either the actual or more likely the nominal author almost certainly does not believe. Consider some of the remarks in the plurality opinion in the Supreme Court's recent *McCutcheon* case, which, building on the *Citizens United* decision, further loosened, in the name of the free-speech clause of the First Amendment, the power of Congress to limit spending on political campaigns.[125] The opinion states that "Congress may target only a specific type of corruption—'*quid pro quo*' corruption"—that is, an *agreement* between donor and candidate that in exchange for the donation the candidate will support policies that will shower financial or other tangible benefits on the donor.[126] If there is no agreement, the *McCutcheon* opinion states, the First Amendment requires that the donation be allowed: "Constituents have the right to support candidates who share their views and concerns. Representatives are not to follow constituent orders, but can be expected to be cognizant of and responsive to those concerns. Such responsiveness is key to the very concept of self-governance through elected officials."[127]

Can so naïve a conception of the political process reflect the actual beliefs of a Supreme Court Justice? Probably not. Wealthy businessmen and large corporations make substantial political contribu-

125. *Citizens United v. Federal Election Commission*, 558 U.S. 310 (2010).
126. *McCutcheon v. Federal Election Commission*, 134 S. Ct. 1434, 1450 (2014) (plurality opinion).
127. Id. at 1462.

tions in the hope often fulfilled that by doing so they are buying the politician-recipient's support for policies that yield financial benefits to the donors. The legislator who does not honor the implicit deal is unlikely to receive similar donations in the future. If he honors the deal he isn't just being "responsive" to the political "views and concerns" of constituents; he is buying financial support from wealthy donors to enable him to win more votes from the electorate, paying for this support in currency consisting of votes for legislation valuable to his benefactors.

This is a form of corruption.[128] It is not criminal, but it is a proper object of regulation. There is no basis for thinking that the drafters and ratifiers of the free-speech clause of the First Amendment meant to place such misconduct beyond the power of government to regulate. In effect the Supreme Court has limited government regulation of corruption to the type of corruption that can be punished criminally.[129]

Eighteenth-century thinkers were not as narrow-minded as this. They believed that "corruption sets in when the electoral processes are perverted to favor the wealthy"—an exact description of the tendency that a decision like *McCutcheon* fosters.[130] (So much for conservatives' commitment to originalism.) To the extent that such a decision reflects a sincere belief by a majority of the Supreme Court Justices that limiting expenditures on influencing elections would curtail freedom of speech, those Justices should ponder a comment by

128. See Heather K. Gerken, "The Real Problem with *Citizens United:* Campaign Finance, Dark Money, and Shadow Parties," *Marquette Lawyer,* Summer 2014, 10.
129. See Zephyr Teachout, "Quid Pro Quo: The Supreme Court's Disastrous Definition of Corruption," *Democracy: A Journal of Ideas* 79 (Spring 2015).
130. Shelley Burtt, "Ideas of Corruption in Eighteenth-Century England," in *Private and Public Corruption* 101, 115 (William C. Heffernan and John Kleinig eds. 2004).

Isaiah Berlin in a talk he gave in 1996: "Freedoms," he said, "cannot be preserved if freedom to subvert them is permitted."[131] Freedom to deploy wealth, without limit, in pursuit of political gain (or financial gain from obtaining control of key politicians) hinders the expression of political choice by the vast majority of potential voters, who are unable to make substantial donations to political campaigns.

None of the opinions in the *McCutcheon* case refers to the economists' concept of an "efficiency wage," but it is apt. To pay an employee an efficiency wage is deliberately to overpay him, that is, to pay him more than the actual value of his work to his employer. The reason for such largesse is not generosity. It is to induce effort by and loyalty of the worker by the implicit threat that if his work is unsatisfactory and the employer therefore fires him he'll be unlikely to obtain an equivalent wage from another employer. Similarly, by donating generously to a legislator or legislative candidate the donor signals that if the recipient fails to reciprocate by voting for legislation beneficial to the donor, the generous donation will not be repeated. Nor is another donor likely to step into the breach—he'll be deterred by the legislator's demonstrated independence.

And finally it's not as if the term "freedom of speech" in the First Amendment has ever been taken literally. Burning the American flag is deemed "speech" and is "free" (it cannot be prohibited unless the flag is stolen or otherwise burned without the owner's consent or the fire would create a hazard), while numerous forms of actual speech are not "free," such as copyright infringement, threats, privileged communications, and defamation.

Another recent example of judicial pronouncements that cannot be thought to express a judge's or Justice's actual beliefs appears in the

131. Isaiah Berlin, "A Message to the 21st Century," *New York Review of Books,* October 23, 2014, 37.

Supreme Court's opinion in *McCullen v. Coakley.*[132] The decision invalidated a Massachusetts law requiring abortion protesters to stay at least thirty-five feet away from the entrance to abortion clinics. The core of the opinion can be found in two brief passages, which I've strung together:

> With respect to other means of communication, an individual confronted with an uncomfortable message can always turn the page, change the channel, or leave the Web site. Not so on public streets and sidewalks. There, a listener often encounters speech he might otherwise tune out . . . Petitioners wish to converse with their fellow citizens about an important subject on the public streets and sidewalks—sites that have hosted discussions about the issues of the day throughout history.[133]

Yet as the Justices must know, no one wants to be buttonholed on the sidewalk by bearers of "uncomfortable message[s]," who usually are nuts or fanatics. Nor is lecturing strangers on a sidewalk a means by which information and opinion are disseminated in today's America. Strangers don't meet on the sidewalk to discuss "the issues of the day." (Have any of the Justices ever done such a thing?) If you're assailed on the sidewalk by an "uncomfortable message," you don't stay to engage in a debate; you flee. The assertion that abortion protesters "wish to converse" with women outside an abortion clinic can't be taken seriously; we know they want to prevent the women from entering the clinic, by talking to them, yes, but also by showing them gruesome photos of aborted fetuses or calling down the wrath of God

132. 134 S. Ct. 2518 (2014).
133. Id. at 2529, 2541.

on them.[134] This is harassment of people who are in a very uncomfortable position; the last thing a woman about to have an abortion needs is to be screamed at by the godly.

The passage I quoted from the opinion is followed immediately by the statement: "Respondents assert undeniably significant interests in maintaining public safety on those same streets and sidewalks, as well as in preserving access to adjacent healthcare facilities."[135] But the relevant public interest is not the maintenance of public safety. Few abortion protesters are violent, and police will be present to protect persons who want to enter the clinic. The issue is the privacy, anxiety, and embarrassment of the clinic's patients—interests that local government might reasonably decide outweigh the negligible contribution that abortion protesters make to the marketplace in ideas and

134. The plaintiff in the *McCullen* case was a soft-spoken grandmother. But it took only two days after the Supreme Court's decision for the character of abortion protesters to be revealed. "For the first time in seven years, the Saturday morning antiabortion protest in front of Planned Parenthood on Commonwealth Avenue in the Back Bay pushed past the arcing yellow line that once marked protected territory: the 35-foot buffer zone. Activists chanted, prayed, and sang during a nonviolent six-hour protest that occasionally erupted into vitriol and shouting. 'Please don't kill your baby! You can celebrate a birthday next year!' protesters shouted at young women entering the clinic. They waved signs imploring passersby to say no to abortions, some depicting infants nestled serenely in their mothers' arms, another showing a bloody baby clutched by hands bearing the marks of stigmata. At its height, the protest drew about 70 people—three times more than the average Saturday morning crowd, typically the largest gathering of the week—a turnout inspired by Thursday's US Supreme Court ruling that struck down the Massachusetts law that since 2007 had kept them outside the yellow line." Evan Allen and Claire McNeille "Abortion Battle Spills Across Line at Boston Clinic: Territory No Longer Protected as Buffer Zone Erased," *Boston Globe,* June 29, 2014, www.bostonglobe.com/metro/2014/06/28/protesters -gather-planned-parenthood-clinic-first-saturday-after-supreme-court-ruling -against-buffer-zone/TkOlnXO5G6HSFlfZ9XB3NK/story.html.

135. 138 S. Ct. at 2541.

opinions. The right to speak is not a right to harass a captive audience. Or so I think; there is room for disagreement. But what I find difficult to believe is that any of the Justices actually believes that a thirty-five-foot buffer zone at the entrance of abortion clinics violates the First Amendment by preventing *productive* discourse on the sidewalks outside such clinics.

An opinion that states what the judge who signed it does not believe is hypocritical. But given that the legal profession is not strongly committed (if it is committed at all) to truthfulness, let alone to candor, one shouldn't be surprised to find an explicit endorsement of judicial hypocrisy in an opinion by Justice Scalia, which states: "I am not naïve (nor do I think our forbears were) as to be unaware that judges in a real sense 'make' law. But they make it *as judges make it,* which is to say *as though* they were 'finding' it—discerning what the law is, rather than decreeing what it is today *changed to,* or what it will *tomorrow* be."[136] Making is not finding or discerning.

Even more common than a judge saying something he doesn't believe is his saying something that has been said so many times in judicial opinions that for him to pause and ask himself or the lawyers

136. *James J. Beam Distilling Co. v. Georgia,* 501 U.S. 529, 549 (1991) (concurring opinion) (emphases in original). This is an ingenious adaptation of classic Jesuitical defensive casuistry: "If a Protestant persecutor asked a Catholic if a priest was hiding in his house, he could reply, 'non est hic', meaning, 'he is not here', or alternatively meaning, 'he is not eating here'. The Latin 'est' can bear both meanings. The Catholic meant that the person in hiding was not eating, but the searcher thought he meant that the person in hiding wasn't there. This was amphibology. Alternatively the Catholic could answer audibly, 'no', adding mentally, 'as far as persecutors should know'. The casuist justification for this was that the requirement to be completely transparent was overridden by the need to defend not only human life, but in the case of a priest hiding in a country run by persecuting Protestants the Catholic Faith itself." Roebuck Classes, "Casuistry," www .roebuckclasses.com/ethics/resources/idea/casuistry.htm.

whether it could possibly be true would seem an impertinence. An example is the stock phrase that statutory interpretation begins with the words of the statute to be interpreted, and ends there if the words are clear ("plain meaning").[137] This formula must with slight variation appear in thousands of opinions. But it is false. One always begins not with the words but with the name of the statute, and with some idea (often derived from the name, or if not then from the briefs in the case) of what the statute is about. These supply a context for interpretation; and context shapes meaning. (The limitations of "plain meaning" can be seen by asking oneself whether if an ordinance states "no vehicles in the park," the ban should be interpreted to include ambulances and police cars.) But the formula has been recited so often that it would seem impious to many judges to expel it from their judicial vocabulary.

That stock phrase illustrates a second function of what I am calling the loose judicial attitude toward truth—that of depicting the judge as a law follower rather than a law giver. If it's a statutory case and the relevant statutory language is clear, the tendency is to make that the end of the judicial inquiry, no matter if the "plain meaning" makes no practical sense and undoubtedly was unintended. Adopting the passive pose is, consciously or not, a political move. Judges stand in both a cooperative and an adversary relation to what they self-servingly call the "political branches" of the government, which in the federal system are of course Congress and the executive branch. All three branches are political in the sense of being power rivals. But only the judges deny that they are political (as by labeling the *other* branches "the political branches")—deny it even to the extent of re-

---

137. See, for example, *Hughes Aircraft Co. v. Jacobson*, 525 U.S. 432, 438 (1999): "As in any case of statutory construction, our analysis begins with 'the language of the statute.' And where the statutory language provides a clear answer, it ends there as well," quoting *Estate of Cowart v. Nicklos Drilling Co.*, 505 U.S. 469, 475 (1992).

fusing to acknowledge that statutory interpretation creates as well as discerns statutory meaning.[138] The judges wish to be seen as occupying a purely umpireal role. Some know better, some don't, but even those who know better think it a permissible means of self-defense against the other branches to disclaim any influence of ideological or other priors on judicial decisions: to pose as logicians, linguists, historians, and so forth rather than even as interstitial policymakers.

Some law professors either are deceived by the disclaimer or think it a "noble lie" that should be protected and even propagated. In the first camp I would put Brian Tamanaha, who attributes to judges "the attitude that rules will be faithfully applied unless, in the exceptional case, a compelling reason mandates departure. As long as most of the judges most of the time are more rule-bound than not, as is the case in the United States today, a rule of law system will exist."[139] The picture is of a legal system in which clear rules cover all possible cases and judges apply the rules unless to do so would produce a terrible or absurd result (the "exceptional case," the case in which "a compelling reason mandates departure" from the rules). Our legal system is not like that. Rules of law often are vague or ambiguous or inconsistent with one another, and often therefore cases arise that can't be said to be covered by any rule—the judge must make up a rule to cover it.

Tamanaha isn't actually beating the drum very loudly for what he calls the "rule of law." If most judges most of the time are rule-bound, this could just mean 51 percent of the judges each 51 percent of the time, implying an unimpressive percentage of 26 percent of cases governed by the rule of law. (Less, actually, since the most powerful judges, such as Supreme Court Justices, would be underrepresented in the 51

138. See William D. Popkin, *Statutes in Court: The History and Theory of Statutory Interpretation,* pt. 2 (1999).
139. Brian Z. Tamanaha, *Realistic Socio-Legal Theory: Pragmatism and a Social Theory of Law* 244 (1997).

percent.) Tamanaha acknowledges that judges "admit that they make law and that their values have an influence, and that there are gaps in the law, and that choices must be made; but they also insist that the law is often clear, and that in a large proportion of cases their decisions are determined by the law."[140] How large is large is the obvious question raised by this passage, but a more important question is the nature of the cases comprising the large proportion. Below the level of the Supreme Court most cases can be and are decided by a straightforward application of unchallengeable legal rules. But they are not the interesting or the important cases. Law is in constant flux, a flux marked or even created by "interesting" cases, in which the judges perforce exercise discretion often influenced by their priors.

I do not agree with Tamanaha's apparent implication that the decisions in those cases are therefore lawless. What judges do within their jurisdiction is—whether done badly or well, or openly or concealed—law. I think it inescapable, as I have argued elsewhere, that judges forced to decide cases in the "open area"—cases in which the orthodox guides to answering legal questions fail—will turn pragmatist.[141] They will try to understand the practical consequences of alternative possible rulings and pick the ruling that will have the "best" consequences consistent with either the understanding of best consequences by the legal and societal culture of the time, or that will suit the particular judge's personal preferences. The judges will still be doing law. A judge's inescapable duty is to decide the cases presented to him that are within his jurisdiction. Decide he must even if the orthodox legal materials do not tell him what the decision should be. Of course in a great many cases, indeed the majority of cases in all but the U.S. Supreme Court, the orthodox materials determine the result:

---

140. Id. at 229.

141. I have discussed this most thoroughly in my book *Law, Pragmatism, and Democracy* (2003).

the statute is unambiguous, the result dictated by binding precedent, the appellant's only good argument was forfeited, the appeal was untimely, or some other feature of the case doomed it. A judge who ignored these "formalist" features of the case would be irresponsible. The cases in the open area, however, though fewer, are more important, because the decisions in those cases often change the law; indeed, without an open area law would stagnate.

I disagree with Professor Tamanaha but his position is arguable. I cannot say the same for Professor Jeremy Waldron, who makes a number of questionable assertions about law and judging. He writes for example that "ordinary Americans" believe that "the judge will put his own views to one side and, when cases come before him, apply the rules embodied in statutes, precedents, and constitutional provisions."[142] But who are "ordinary Americans," what is the evidence of their belief about the judiciary, and has Waldron spoken to any of them recently? And what is the judge to do when the rules embodied in statutes, precedents, and constitutional provisions do not indicate how the case at hand should be decided?

He goes on to say that

> the formalist judge does not think he should legislate from the bench because he has not been elected or appointed for that purpose. No fair political procedure has consecrated his

---

142. My quotations are from Waldron's essay "Unfettered Judge Posner," *New York Review of Books,* March 20, 2014, p. 34 (emphasis in original). Criticisms of legal realism similar to Waldron's (and to me no more persuasive) are quite common. I refer the reader to Chad M. Oldfather, "Limitations (A Response to Judge Posner)," 51 *Dusquene Law Review* 67 (2013); Craig Green, "What Does Richard Posner Know about How Judges Think?" 98 *California Law Review* 625 (2010); Jeffrey S. Sutton, "A Review of Richard A. Posner, How Judges Think," 108 *Michigan Law Review* 859 (2010); David F. Levi, "Autocrat of the Armchair," 58 *Duke Law Journal* 1791 (2009); Michael J. Gerhardt, "How a Judge Thinks," 93 *Minnesota Law Review* 2185 (2009).

views about what would improve society over the views of his political opponents. (Even in jurisdictions where judges are elected, they are not elected to legislate.) Not only that, but the formalist judge believes that he ought to respect the work of those who *have* been elected as legislators and play his part in the process of legislative implementation.

But the "part" assigned to judges will often include, as I've suggested, completion and not merely implementation of legislation. And nowadays, given the role of big money and gerrymandering in the legislative process and the evidence of ideological influence in judicial decision making, how realistic is it to think that all legislation has genuine democratic legitimacy and that formalist judges are merely judges who, as Waldron asserts, "want to respect democratic processes?"

Some judges believe Waldon's credo (more pretend to believe it), but their judicial votes often *must* be driven by something else, simply because the orthodox materials of judicial decision making, whether statutory or constitutional texts, or regulations, or judge-made rules and principles, do not resolve all cases—yet all cases that are within a court's jurisdiction must, as I keep insisting, be decided.[143] This opens the door to political ideology and other unorthodox influences, which play a larger role in driving decisions the higher the court is. In the federal system the easiest cases—the ones that can be satisfactorily resolved by the orthodox methods—are decided definitively at the trial-court level; if there is an appeal, it is decided in perfunctory fashion. The cases that can't be resolved satisfactorily in that fashion require the appellate judges to go outside the orthodox judicial role—in fact cast the judges in a legislative role.

143. See, for example, the eclectic body of essays in *What's Law Got to Do with It? What Judges Do, Why They Do It, What's at Stake* (Charles Gardner Geyh ed. 2011).

Anyone who doubts the existence of a significant political element in judging should reflect on the growth of what Steven Teles in an interesting book calls the "conservative legal movement."[144] The movement began in the 1960s, grew rapidly in the 1970s, shot up in the early 1980s with the creation of the Federalist Society, and has continued growing with an assist from the formation of conservative public interest law firms. It is at once a political movement and a significant element in the outlook of many influential judges and Justices. If one were to speak of a "conservative movement" in medicine or physics, one would not be talking politics. Law is inescapably, pervasively, though far from completely, political.

One can imagine a judicial system that placed great value on judicial candor and self-awareness, but it is not our system. Imagine a case that is a toss-up, as many cases that reach the appellate courts are. The judge has to decide; he can't declare a draw. Total candor in such a case (assuming a degree of self-awareness) would require him to say something like what Oliver Wendell Holmes said in his dissent in the *Olmstead* case, the sort of thing that only Holmes could get away with. The issue was whether wiretapping was a "search" within the meaning of the Fourth Amendment. The Court held that it was not. Holmes dissented because the wiretap violated the law of the state in which it was conducted. He wrote:

> There is no body of precedents by which we are bound, and which confines us to logical deduction from established rules. Therefore we must consider the two objects of desire both of which we cannot have and make up our minds which to

144. Steven M. Teles, *The Rise of the Conservative Legal Movement: The Battle for Control of the Law* (2008). (I was once a member of the movement; see the index references to me at page 337 of his book.)

choose. It is desirable that criminals should be detected, and to that end that all available evidence should be used. It also is desirable that the government should not itself foster and pay for other crimes, when they are the means by which the evidence is to be obtained. If it pays its officers for having got evidence by crime I do not see why it may not as well pay them for getting it in the same way, and I can attach no importance to protestations of disapproval if it knowingly accepts and pays and announces that in future it will pay for the fruits. We have to choose, and for my part I think it a less evil that some criminals should escape than that the government should play an ignoble part.[145]

The last sentence is critical. I take it to be an acknowledgment that the case was a toss-up from a conventional legal-analytical standpoint, and so the judge had to choose sides on the basis of a weighing of considerations that were not derivative from any legal doctrine (the evil of some criminals escaping versus the evil of the government playing an ignoble part). That too is law. Casting one's judicial vote, as Holmes did in *Olmstead,* on the basis of a balancing of the consequences for society of reversing a lower court decision against the consequences of affirming is pragmatism, and is a frequent resort of American judges; Americans are famously pragmatic.

Judicial pragmatism at its narrowest sense would equate to cost-benefit analysis, but it is not exhausted by that or any other economic concept. The balancing done by judges faced with having to decide a case in what I've called the "open area" is often, as I remarked years ago in my fullest discussion of judicial psychology, inflected by "the

145. *Olmstead v. United States,* 277 U.S. 438, 470 (1928) (dissenting opinion).

personal, the emotional, and the intuitive."[146] It is not measurement, this "balancing," but what I have sometimes called in this book "moral intuition." Few judges are willing to acknowledge that it influences any of their decisions.[147] Many are unaware that it does.

15. The noble lie. I have been skirting the question whether the legal profession, including its judicial and academic branches, places a high value on truth. The answer is no. Since the basic training of lawyers is in a form of combat rather than in the ascertainment of truth, it's no surprise that "lawyers tend to have hyperpartisan dispositions."[148] Judges are political officials, though more (or maybe just differently) constrained than most politicians are; and we know from Max Weber's great essay "Politics as a Vocation"[149] that the morality of a politician is different from that of the ordinary person. Much of the constitutional jurisprudence of the Supreme Court is easier to understand in political terms than as the product of intellectual analysis, but the Justices are careful to disclaim any political dimension in their judging, as are other judges. Judges are also reluctant to criticize the bar, which

146. "The Mind of the Legislating Judge," in my book *How Judges Think* 93, 120 (2008).
147. For an interesting recent analysis (and defense) of the role of intuition in judging, see Linda L. Berger, "A Revised View of the Judicial Hunch" (University of Nevada, Las Vegas, William S. Boyd School of Law, Scholarly Works, Paper 808, Fall 2013), http://scholars.law.unlv.edu/facpub/808.
148. Jonathan Mermin, "Bad Arguments," 17 *Green Bag* 2d 435, 440 (2014).
149. *From Max Weber: Essays in Sociology* 77 (Hans H. Gerth and C. Wright Mills trans. 1946). See also my book *An Affair of State: The Investigation, Impeachment, and Trial of President Clinton,* ch. 4 ("Morality, Private and Public") (1999). And anent Dean Levi, note the remark in F. G. Bailey, *Humbuggery and Manipulation: The Art of Leadership* ix (1988): "Leaders everywhere are like deans, inescapably polluted by what they do, and, since leadership is by its very nature defiling, it follows that moral judgments are as appropriate in this regard as they are about foul weather."

they regard as a supportive constituency, and they are almost obsequious when discussing the legislative and executive branches. Academic lawyers pull their punches when they are discussing judges or practicing lawyers, reserving candor in their public writings for criticisms of each other.

Immanuel Kant distinguished sharply between truthfulness and candor. He thought it always wrong to lie, but did not think that there was any general duty of candor. If you encounter a friend walking a dog that you think very ugly, you are under no duty to tell him that you think his dog ugly, but Kant would say that you must not tell him that his dog is beautiful. But I think that judges should be candid (as well as truthful) about the grounds of their decisions, and likewise professors about what they believe to be the true grounds of a judicial decision.[150] Otherwise it may be impossible to evaluate a judge or predict his future decisions. There have been some notably candid judges—I mentioned Holmes and Robert Jackson earlier—but they have been few and far between. Most judges prefer the "noble lie."

The apogee of judicial candor may be Holmes's opinion for the Supreme Court in *Buck v. Bell,* a challenge based on the Fourteenth Amendment to a law of Virginia that authorized compulsory sterilization of "feebleminded" persons confined to state institutions for the mentally defective.[151] The plaintiff was believed to be the feebleminded daughter of a feebleminded woman and the mother of a feebleminded daughter. Holmes's opinion says almost nothing about the law—rather it is an eloquent paean to sterilizing mental defectives. The key passage is the following:

150. See David L. Schapiro, "In Defense of Judicial Candor," 100 *Harvard Law Review* 731 (1987). I discuss judicial candor further in Chapter 4, in relation to *Brown v. Board of Education.*
151. 274 U.S. 200 (1927).

We have seen more than once that the public welfare may call upon the best citizens for their lives. It would be strange if it could not call upon those who already sap the strength of the State for these lesser sacrifices, often not felt to be such by those concerned, in order to prevent our being swamped with incompetence. It is better for all the world if, instead of waiting to execute degenerate offspring for crime or to let them starve for their imbecility, society can prevent those who are manifestly unfit from continuing their kind. The principle that sustains compulsory vaccination is broad enough to cover cutting the Fallopian tubes. Three generations of imbeciles are enough.[152]

We know from Holmes's correspondence that he was an enthusiastic supporter of the eugenics movement, which worried that profligate breeding by persons of low IQ was endangering the prospects of the human race. That enthusiasm appears without disguise in *Buck v. Bell*. Really all that Holmes says in the opinion is that compulsory sterilization of persons with very low IQs is a very good thing. He offers this as a personal opinion without attempting to marshal evidence for it.

Buck v. Bell can fairly be described as a lawless opinion. But at least its distinguished author didn't try to pull the wool over our eyes. A great many judicial opinions are undoubtedly motivated by beliefs no less personal than Holmes's belief in eugenics. I referred in the Introduction to Bayesian decision making, which involves bringing to the decisional process a predisposition but modifying it by gathering evidence. In regard to judicial decision making, however, it is helpful to distinguish "motivated reasoning" from Bayesian decision making, the

152. Id. at 207.

former involving an emotional rather than a merely rational or experiential commitment to one's priors. The motivated reasoner resists modifying his priors on the basis of new evidence. As Keith Bybee points out, "Theories of motivated reasoning explain how judges may unfailingly and sincerely claim to be reasoning on the basis of legal principle, while at the same time scholars may continue to demonstrate that a significant portion of judicial decisions are driven by policy preferences. As a matter of individual psychology, there is no overt dissonance between legal principle and political preference to be resolved because judges seamlessly integrate both as they go about deciding different cases."[153]

But "political preference" is too limited a conception of the priors that influence judicial behavior; even "ideological preference" would be, as it would ignore elements of personality, and of personal, career, and family history and experiences, that also influence judicial behavior. Geoffrey Stone, a well-known and well-regarded professor at the University of Chicago Law School, several years ago published an article that provided statistical evidence that the then five Catholic Justices on the Supreme Court were influenced in some of their judicial votes by their Catholic beliefs.[154] Such candor on the part of professors at leading law schools is rare. They may not respect judges, but they don't want to alienate them. But the resulting conspiracy of silence embracing both the judiciary and the academy makes it difficult

153. Keith J. Bybee, "Paying Attention to What Judges Say: New Directions in the Study of Judicial Decision Making," 8 *Annual Review of Law and Social Science* 69, 75 (2012).
154. Geoffrey R. Stone, "Justice Sotomayor, Justice Scalia and Our Six Catholic Justices," "Huffpost Good News," *Huffington Post,* September 28, 2009, www .huffingtonpost.com/geoffrey-r-stone/justice-sotomayor-justice_b_271229.html. Despite the title of Stone's article, he did not discuss Sotomayor—the sixth Catholic—as she had been appointed to the Supreme Court only the month before.

for law professors to understand judges and to convey such understanding as they do have to students without a varnish of reticence. Stone's candor was praiseworthy.

All this said, there have to be limits to judicial (if not necessarily to academic) candor, albeit looser ones than at present. Judicial opinions should treat litigants, especially when they are individuals rather than institutions, and lawyers, politely, respectfully (though not uncritically), unless they misbehave egregiously. Judges should be respectful to legislators and other state and federal officials. But I do not agree with those members of the "noble lie" school who believe that the public would lose confidence in the courts if judges gave up the pretense of being mere umpires. I don't think many members of the public think about the courts. It is highly unlikely, for example, that people opposed to abortion shrug their shoulders and say to themselves: "I don't like the decision in *Roe v. Wade* but I am resigned to the fact that the law left the Justices with no choice." I especially don't see how such an attitude could be maintained in a system, which is our system, in which judicial dissents are public.

What would be harmful to the judiciary would be for the judges to say that "we're politicians just like the members of Congress." It would also be false. What judges should acknowledge and I think could do so without losing public respect is the role, which I've stressed throughout this chapter, of priors in judicial votes. One almost always has an initial leaning or "take" on a new issue while generally being open to modifying one's initial take as one learns more about the issue. There is no simple equation of priors to politics or ideology, though those are undoubtedly among most people's, including most judges', priors. Because of the different appointment criteria and procedures, different pressures, different goals, different constraints, and so on, judges don't behave the same as members of Congress, governors, and the like—they are much less political. I see no serious objection to giving up the absurd pretension that federal judges are bloodless human calculating machines. That of course is the formalist pretension.

We get a sense of a judge torn between caution and candor in Justice Alito's dissent in *United States v. Windsor*, the decision that invalidated the Defense of Marriage Act, which had denied federal marital benefits to married homosexual couples even if they had been married in a state that permitted same-sex marriage.[155] The Alito dissent makes a number of arguments against a federal right to same-sex marriage, but two in particular invite attention. The first is that "at present, no one—including social scientists, philosophers, and historians—can predict with any certainty what the long-term ramifications of widespread acceptance of same-sex marriage will be. And judges are certainly not equipped to make such an assessment."[156] This is a strange argument in the absence of any specification of the possible "ramifications" (by which Justice Alito seems to have meant simply consequences). For of a great many constitutional decisions it could be said that their possible consequences were unforeseeable, and anyway that if the consequences of a particular decision turned out to be untoward the decision could be reversed. The Justice does not say that the negative consequences of same-sex marriage are likely to outweigh the positive ones.

But at least the argument is secular, unlike the second argument in his opinion that I want to highlight: that "marriage is essentially the solemnizing of a comprehensive, exclusive, permanent union that is intrinsically ordered to producing new life, even if it does not always do so."[157] This is a religious argument, as is plain from the two works

155. 133 S. Ct. 2675 (2013).
156. Id. at 2716.
157. Id. at 2718. Note that "if" should be "though."

that Justice Alito cites in support of the proposition that I just quoted, both being Roman Catholic tracts by lay theologians.[158] The phrase "union . . . intrinsically ordered to producing new life" is more commonly rendered "all sexual acts are intrinsically ordered towards procreation, and . . . therefore it is objectively disordered to pursue a sexual act if you are intentionally seeking not to procreate," but that is a distinction without a difference.[159]

Justice Alito is well known to be a devout Roman Catholic, and so it is not surprising that he would find this kind of argument persuasive. Yet to make Roman Catholic doctrine constitutional doctrine creates acute tension with the prohibition in the First Amendment against Congress's establishing a religion. The Supreme Court is not Congress, but for the Court to make constitutional law conform to a set of explicitly religious doctrines would strike a theocratic note inconsistent with a democratic polity. Realism requires recognition that a judge's priors, which include religious beliefs, are apt to exert a gravitational pull on his judicial votes; yet most people would think that a judge should have sufficient self-awareness and self-control to resist the tug of inappropriate priors, including religious ones.

16. The limits of a generalist judiciary—and the help it isn't getting from the bar. As I noted earlier, most appellate judges in the United States are generalists; that is, they are judges of courts that have a generalized rather than a specialized jurisdiction. Of the thirteen federal courts of appeals, one is specialized (the U.S. Court of Appeals for the Federal Circuit, which has exclusive appellate jurisdiction over patent cases

158. See Sherif Girgis, Ryan T. Anderson, and Robert P. George, *What is Marriage? Man and Woman: A Defense* 23–28 (2012); John Finnis, "Marriage: A Basic and Exigent Good," 91 *The Monist* 388, 398 (2008).

159. Melinda Selmys, "Intimate Reflections on Homosexuality and Catholicism: Sexual Authenticity: Ordered to Procreation," November 11, 2013, http://sexualauthenticity.blogspot.com/2013/11/ordered-towards-procreation.html.

and a few other areas of federal law, but no other jurisdiction), and one is semispecialized—the U.S. Court of Appeals for the D.C. Circuit, which hears a disproportionate number of cases involving review of decisions by federal administrative agencies and has exclusive review jurisdiction over some of those decisions. The other eleven courts of appeals have a jurisdiction that embraces almost the entirety of federal law and by virtue of the diversity, bankruptcy, and supplemental jurisdictions much of state law as well.

Even generalist judges tend to know a fair amount about types of case that recur frequently in their courts, such as federal criminal cases, habeas corpus and prisoner civil rights cases, and employment discrimination cases. But because federal jurisdiction reaches far beyond these familiar types of case, many cases that federal judges hear are in areas of law that they encounter infrequently. Many cases even in familiar fields involve technical issues with which most judges are unfamiliar. Unless educated by the advocates in the case, therefore, or by his colleagues or his law clerks, the appellate judge is likely to fall back on hunch, intuition, or (encompassing these and other decision guides) background beliefs (that is, priors) derived from education, personal experience, and temperament.

One antidote is for the advocate to try to make the judges equally well informed about the subject matter of the case. I can assure the readers of this book that judges do not feel patronized, or condescended to, when a lawyer explains in words of one syllable some scientific, technological, or otherwise arcane feature of a case that is necessary to a full understanding of the issues. In all my years as an appellate judge none of my colleagues has ever complained in our postargument conferences that a lawyer was treating the judges as ignoramuses. The judges are happy to be educated by the lawyers in the intricacies of a case.

The problem of the underinformed judiciary is part of the explanation for the tendency of judges to fall back on stock phrases without critical reflection. I will give another example. Several years ago the Supreme Court announced the following formula for deciding whether to grant a preliminary injunction: "A plaintiff seeking a preliminary injunction must establish that he is likely to succeed on the merits, that he is likely to suffer irreparable harm in the absence of preliminary relief, that the balance of equities tips in his favor, and that an injunction is in the public interest."[160] If you reflect on this passage for a moment you'll see that it makes little sense. Could it really be true that the plaintiff must *always* establish as a prerequisite to obtaining a preliminary injunction that he is likely (and how likely?) to succeed on the merits? Suppose he has only a one-in-three chance of winning the case after a full adjudication, but will suffer great irreparable harm unless he obtains a preliminary injunction, while the defendant will suffer no harm at all by being temporarily prevented from doing whatever it is that the plaintiff is trying to prevent. Why refuse a preliminary injunction in such a case?

Suppose the plaintiff has shown both a likelihood of success in the full litigation and irreparable harm if the preliminary injunction is denied. The next question should be what irreparable harm the *defendant* would suffer if the preliminary injunction is *granted*. The Supreme Court in the passage I quoted did not take that step. Instead it instructed the trial court that after the plaintiff establishes likelihood of success plus irreparable harm the court must "balance [the] equities." What does that mean? What exactly are "equities" and what "equities" are involved in the decision whether to grant a preliminary injunction other than the strength of the plaintiff's case and the irreparable harm to the plaintiff from being denied preliminary relief and to the defendant from the grant of that relief to the plaintiff? Finally, where does the "public interest" enter the picture? One can understand the Supreme Court saying that the effect of preliminary re-

---

160. *Winter v. National Resources Defense Council, Inc.*, 555 U.S. 7, 20 (2008).

lief on third parties should be considered in deciding whether to grant such relief. Maybe that is what is meant by the "public interest." If so, why doesn't the Court say so?

If you're the advocate in a case in which a party is appealing from the grant or denial of a preliminary injunction, and you recite the Supreme Court's formula, you're not helping the appellate court at all. If you're the plaintiff's lawyer defending in the court of appeals the grant of the preliminary injunction, you need to explain that although you have a well-founded confidence of winning the case when it is tried, winning won't mean much without preliminary relief because the harm done to you by the delay in the completion of the litigation and the grant of a permanent injunction will make that final relief worth little. You should add that because the defendant eventually will (you hope) and should lose, he should not be given an undeserved interim win by being able to continue violating the law until the case is finally tried. You should conclude by stating that no innocent third party will be adversely affected by the grant of preliminary relief in your favor. Of course, you must be able to back up these claims with evidence or logic or common sense. But what isn't likely to work for you is a meaningless formula.[161]

17. Insufficient diversity. If Holmes was right, as I am convinced he

---

161. A simple mathematical formula, drawn from my book *Economic Analysis of Law* 776 (9th ed. 2014), may help some readers understand the approach suggested in the text for determining whether to grant a preliminary injunction: grant it if but only if $P(H_p) > (1 - P)H_d$, where P is the probability that the plaintiff will prevail in the full trial on the merits (and therefore $1 - P$ is the probability that the defendant will prevail), H_p is the irreparable harm that the plaintiff will suffer unless a preliminary injunction is granted to maintain the status quo pending the trial, and H_d the irreparable harm the defendant will suffer if the preliminary injunction is granted. (If the harm is not irreparable—if it can be cured by a remedy ordered at the end of trial, there is no reason to rush things and by doing so possibly incur additional error costs. It would be like rushing the con-

was, that the life of the law has been not logic but experience—the credo of legal realism—experience should be an important factor in the selection of federal judges. But it isn't, compared to race, sex, ethnicity, religion, and ideology (I noted in Chapter 1 that the first three of these characteristics have not produced meaningful diversity in the current Supreme Court.) None of the current Justices has an educational background, or has worked, in a scientific or technological field or even in a social science; none has ever held elective or high governmental office; none except Justice Breyer is steeped in the humanities (not even history, on which conservative judges place so much weight nowadays); none has business experience; and only one has substantial managerial experience—Justice Kagan, who after a responsible job in the White House was the dean of the Harvard Law School and then the Solicitor General of the United States. All the Justices are graduates of one of only three law schools: Harvard, Yale, and Columbia. Of the twenty-seven years that the Justices spent in law school, only one year was spent at Columbia (by Justice Ginsburg).

So it's an underdiversified Court. Most of the courts of appeals and district courts are likewise underdiversified, though none *so* underdiversified, *so* cloistered, *so* unrepresentative, as the Supreme Court.[162] This would be no problem were there really a "legal science" that like physics would enable persons of diverse political views and educational and vocational backgrounds to agree on key propositions.

---

struction of a house, at great additional cost, though the buyer had no wish to occupy it soon.) The formula can be rearranged in a way that may make it more intuitive for some readers: $P/(1 - P) > H_d/H_p$. In words, the preliminary injunction should be granted if but only if the ratio of the plaintiff's to the defendant's chances of winning exceeds the ratio of the defendant's to the plaintiff's irreparable harm.

162. As powerfully argued in Benjamin H. Barton, "An Empirical Study of Supreme Court Justice Pre-Appointment Experience," 64 *Florida Law Review* 1137 (2012).

But as there isn't, we need diversity in these respects to enrich deliberation in appellate panels.

It is true that the judiciary is politically diverse, but that is not because the appointing authorities favor political diversity—rather because the political composition of those authorities changes from election to election. That is not enough. Neither is diversity when understood as a response only to historic patterns of discrimination.

APPENDIX B

INCURIOUS ADJUDICATION: A CASE STUDY

In *Edwards v. District of Columbia,* owners and operators of a sightseeing company challenged, as a violation of the free-speech clause of the First Amendment, a regulation of the District of Columbia that required tour guides to pass a test of their "knowledge of buildings and points of general and historical interest" in the District, that is, in Washington.[163] The court held unanimously that the regulation was unconstitutional. The court's opinion is long and is full of the jargon of constitutional law—levels of scrutiny (rational basis review, strict scrutiny, intermediate scrutiny), narrow tailoring, facial and as-applied challenges, expressive speech, core political speech, content-based and content-neutral speech. But the decisional formula that the court settled on was straightforward: whether the regulation "burden[ed] substantially more speech than is necessary to further the government's legitimate interests."[164]

The court ruled that the regulation flunked this formula. It found no evidence that the health of Washington's tourism industry was

163. 755 F.3d 996 (D.C. Cir. 2014).
164. Id. at 1002.

threatened by ignorant tour guides, noted that most cities don't require the licensing of tour guides, and noted further that having to pass the test required by the Washington regulation would not prevent a tour guide from "call[ing] the White House the Washington Monument."[165] The court particularly emphasized the absence of evidence that "market forces are an inadequate defense to seedy, slothful tour guides."[166] It thought the tour guides' self-interest enough to achieve the objectives of the regulation—without regulation. The opinion rejects the legitimacy of government regulation in any situation in which the market can in principle do an adequate job of regulation, whatever the reality.

The implication, however, though unremarked by the court, is that requiring aspiring school teachers to pass a test in order to be licensed to teach in a public school is also unconstitutional. The judges should but may not have known that to be licensed to teach in a public or a private school in the District of Columbia requires passing a battery of tests that include (for most applicants) a "Content Knowledge exam in the applicable subject area."[167]

The court's opinion seems based entirely on hostility to regulation, as nothing else in it provides even a minimally plausible ground for the decision.[168] How can requiring a person to take a test to determine his fitness for a job impair freedom of speech? The person remains free to say what he wants, though not as a Washington tour guide, if he flunks the test. His situation is no different from that of an applicant for a teaching job who having flunked her licensing test

---

165. Id. at 1005.
166. Id. at 1006.
167. DCgov, Office of the State Superintendent of Education, "Teaching Licensure," http://osse.dc.gov/service/teacher-licensure.
168. That is, on libertarian ideology; as in the case of the *McCutcheon* and *McCullen* decisions discussed in the chapter, there is no plausible nonideological explanation for the decision.

cannot exercise her right of free speech at the front of a Washington schoolroom, or from the situation of a senatorial candidate who having lost the election cannot exercise his right of free speech on the Senate floor. And while a sightseeing company is in the speech business, the court acknowledged that it would not be in the company's financial self-interest to have incompetent tour guides. The court invoked the company's self-interest as a protection against tour guide incompetence, but not the corollary that screening tour guides for competence might be in the interest of the sightseeing industry and its customers.

The court's most serious mistake—a mistake indicative of that lack of curiosity that I suggested earlier is one of the besetting sins of the judiciary—was to ignore the social benefits of informed tour guides in Washington, D.C., and the economic realities of the capital's tour guide business. These considerations undercut the court's conclusion that the market is an adequate substitute for government regulation. Washington is the nation's capital and the site of an extraordinary array of buildings of profound historical interest and political significance. A visit to Washington can be a significant educational experience and promote responsible citizenship. But not if tour guides, who play a role in providing that experience to tourists, are uninformed about the sights that they point out (or maybe fail to point out) to the tourists whom they are shepherding. The court missed this point by treating Washington as being indistinguishable as a tourist mecca from any other American city.

The court's claim that an unregulated market can ensure that Washington tour guides are competent overlooks the distinctive character of a tourist market. Ripping off tourists is an international pastime. Not only is a tourist likely to be unfamiliar with prices, services, product quality, and other elements of a foreign market and thus unlikely to know when he is being cheated, but upon returning home he's unlikely to concern himself further with that market, as he plans never to return. The court was dreaming in supposing that "further incentivizing a quality consumer experience are the numerous consumer review websites, like Yelp and TripAdvisor, which provide consumers a forum to rate the quality of their experiences. One need only peruse such websites to sample the expressed outrage and contempt that would likely befall a less than scrupulous tour guide."[169] Hardly. For how many tourists will realize that they've been misinformed by their tour guide? And how many who do realize it will bother to post a complaint on the Web? Maybe none, in which event a person planning a sightseeing trip to Washington will not be warned off a tour company by checking the Internet before going. And if one or two disappointed tourists do post a warning? How many readers of Yelp or TripAdvisor or similar websites give much weight to negative comments? They are apt to know nothing about the people who post those comments, who may be sourpusses or fusspots or employees of competing companies. Moreover, since most people who are satisfied with a service do not post a comment (I have never done so, for example), a savvy reader of Yelp or TripAdvisor will assume that the true ratio of positive to negative experiences is higher than the ratio of posted positive to negative comments.

These advisory services come into their own when dealing with a local market, for example the local restaurant market. People have an incentive to post positive comments about restaurants they like, and negative comments about restaurants they don't like, because they are customers in that market. But once a person returns from Washington to his home in Wichita, the Washington tour guide market ceases to interest him, because he isn't planning another Washington tour. Lack of interest implies lack of frequent and meaningful comments on Yelp or equivalent websites.

The *Edwards* decision is nakedly ideological. The court's hostility

169. 755 F.3d at 1006–1007.

to government regulation is both palpable and uncritical.[170] Ideology can't be excluded as a factor in judicial decision making,[171] but it can be tempered if judges take pains to make sure they understand the case that has tickled their ideological funny bone. Had the court asked itself whether there was anything special about Washington that might justify the challenged regulation, or had examined similar licensing schemes in other cities (there are some), or had ruminated on the limitations of competition as a protection of tourists, or had noticed the oddity of regarding a test as a restriction of free speech, or had trawled the Web looking for complaints about ignorant tour guides in tourist-destination cities, it might have concluded that, grand as it would be to purify capitalism of government regulation, deeming the Washington regulation a violation of the Constitution would be a step too far.

We need more federal judges who are curious about their cases and determined to slake their curiosity. Take off the blinders, D.C. Circuit.

170. As emphasized in a law review comment on the case: "Recent Case: First Amendment—Freedom of Speech—D.C. Circuit Holds Unconstitutional District of Columbia's Tour Guide Licensing Regulation," 128 *Harvard Law Review* 777 (2014). For criticism of the antigovernment bias of the D.C. Circuit in general, see Cass R. Sunstein and Adrian Vermeule, "Libertarian Administrative Law" (forthcoming in *University of Chicago Law Review*).

171. Even at the trial court level. See for example Susan U. Philips, *Ideology in the Language of Judges: How Judges Practice Law, Politics, and Courtroom Control* (1998), discussing the "ideology in discourse"—the differences in how different judges express their views orally in dealing with litigants, lawyers, jurors, and witnesses in the courtroom.

APPENDIX C

THE TRAGEDY OF SUPERVISED RELEASE[172]

I've expressed my puzzlement at the frequent failure of federal judges to ask "why" questions. One might think that any time a judge encountered a proposition that seemed of dubious soundness he would pause and ask himself whether it actually was unsound, and if so whether nevertheless it was so well established that it had to be accepted as "law" binding on him. It is an aspect of a backward-looking legal culture committed to adversary procedure (the judge as umpire) to be reluctant to question established propositions even if they are neither sensible-seeming nor conclusively established.

There is no more striking an example of this blinkered view of familiar legal propositions than the judicial administration of "supervised release," which the Sentencing Reform Act of 1984 substituted for parole (to take effect in 1987).[173]

Parole is granted in the discretion of a parole board, which is an administrative agency rather than a judicial body, after a defendant begins serving his sentence. To be paroled is to be released from prison before the expiration of one's term, subject to restrictions on conduct between the release and when, if the prisoner hadn't been paroled, he would have been released upon the expiration of his prison sentence. The restrictions are intended to reduce the likelihood of his commit-

---

172. This appendix is based largely on a recent opinion of mine, *United States v. Thompson*, 777 F.3d 368 (7th Cir. 2015), deciding four appeals involving challenges to conditions of supervised release. A more recent decision by my court, *United States v. Kappes*, 782 F.3d 828 (7th Cir. 2015), amplifies the discussion in the *Thompson* opinion of supervised release.

173. See 18 U.S.C. § 3583 (2008). Parole is still available in some federal criminal cases, but too few to warrant discussion.

ting further crimes in the future. Supervised release, in contrast, consists of restrictions imposed by the judge at sentencing (called conditions or terms of supervised release) that are to take effect when the defendant is released from prison and to continue in force for a specified term of years (which can be life). Parole shortens prison time, substituting restrictions on the freed prisoner; supervised release instead imposes restrictions on the prisoner that take effect after he's released from prison upon completion of the prison term to which he was sentenced. So while parole mitigates punishment, supervised release augments it—most dramatically when the defendant, having been determined to have violated a condition or conditions of supervised release, is given, as punishment, a fresh term of imprisonment.[174]

Imposition of conditions of supervised release is required by statute in fewer than half the cases in which federal criminal defendants are sentenced to prison.[175] In the other half the sentencing judge has discretion as to whether or not to order it.[176] But almost always the judge will order it in those cases too—usually without explaining why.[177]

Apart from a handful of conditions required by the Sentencing Reform Act to be included in any order of supervised release ("mandatory" conditions, as they are called, some for all crimes, some for specific crimes such as sex offenses), the choice of conditions to im-

---

174. 18 U.S.C. § 3583(e)(3).

175. United States Sentencing Commission, *Federal Offenders Sentenced to Supervised Release* 3–4 (July 2010), www.ussc.gov/sites/default/files/pdf/training/annual-national-training-seminar/2012/2_Federal_Offenders_Sentenced_to_Supervised_Release.pdf.

176. See 18 U.S.C. § 3583(a).

177. United States Sentencing Commission, note 175 above, at 69–70; Michael P. Kenstowicz, "Imposing Discretionary Conditions of Supervised Release: Do Judges Follow the Law?" (forthcoming in *University of Chicago Law Review*, Summer 2015).

pose is in the discretion of the sentencing judge.[178] A number of conditions are recommended, however, including twenty-three discretionary conditions for probationers[179] (in essence, defendants paroled in lieu of being imprisoned at all), which have been made conditions of supervised release as well.[180] Adding confusion to complexity, the U.S. Sentencing Guidelines list eight mandatory conditions that do not overlap perfectly with the mandatory conditions in the statute, fifteen "standard" conditions recommended for all cases, and fifteen "special" and "additional" conditions recommended for particular types of case, for a total of thirty-eight.[181] And the judge can impose conditions of his own invention as well.

The problems with supervised release as it is designed and administered are multiple. One problem is that there are so many conditions required or suggested that judges tend just to list the conditions (generally more than twenty) that they're imposing, without explaining them or justifying their imposition. Sometimes the judge doesn't bother even to list them, but instead just says that he's imposing the "standard" or "normal" conditions of supervised release. That is surely improper.

Because conditions of supervised release do not take effect until the defendant completes his prison term and is released, defendants who are given long prison sentences often have little interest in contesting the conditions of supervised release. Criminals who court long sentences as a result of the crimes they decide to commit tend to have what economists call a "high discount rate." That is, they give little weight to future costs and benefits. Defendants or their lawyers may also worry that a successful challenge to a condition or conditions of

178. For "mandatory" conditions for sex offenses, see 18 U.S.C. § 3583(d).
179. 18 U.S.C. § 3563(b) (2008).
180. By § 3583(d).
181. See U.S.S.G. §§ 5D1.3(a), (c)–(e) (2009).

supervised release may induce the judge to impose a longer prison sentence, thinking that resistance to supervised release implies recidivist tendencies. And often a defendant is given no notice in advance of the sentencing hearing of the conditions of supervised release that the judge is thinking of imposing. That can make it difficult for his lawyer to marshal evidence, and prepare arguments, in opposition.

Many federal judges seem not even to realize that because the imposition of conditions of supervised release is part of the sentence, the judge is required by the Supreme Court's decision in *United States v. Booker*[182] to evaluate the propriety of any conditions of supervised release that he's thinking of imposing, by applying to them the list of factors that Congress requires federal judges to consider in sentencing. The factors include "the nature and circumstances of the offense and the history and characteristics of the defendant," "the need for the sentence imposed," and "the kinds of sentences available."[183] Furthermore "the court, at the time of sentencing, shall state in open court the reasons for its imposition of the particular sentence."[184] Any doubt that conditions of supervised release are a part of the sentence and subject therefore to these requirements is dispelled by another statutory provision: "The court, in determining whether to include a term of supervised release, and, if a term of supervised release is to be included, in determining the length of the term and the conditions of supervised release, shall consider the factors set forth in" eight enumerated subsections of section 3553(a).[185] From the fact that subsec-

---

182. 543 U.S. 220 (2005).
183. Listed in 18 U.S.C. § 3553(a) (2010).
184. 18 U.S.C. § 3553(c).
185. 18 U.S.C. § 3583(c). Subsection (a) of section 3553 lists the sentencing factors that the judges are to consider in determining the sentence to impose. See note 183 above.

tion 3553(a)(2)(A) is omitted from the enumeration, the court in *United States v. Murray* inferred "that the primary purpose of supervised release is to facilitate the reentry of offenders into their communities, rather than to inflict punishment."[186] (The subsection declares "the need for the sentence imposed to reflect the seriousness of the offense, to promote respect for the law, and to provide just punishment for the offense.") But rare is the sentencing judge who has noted this distinction.

The sheer number of conditions may induce haste in a sentencing judge's evaluation of the recommendations of the probation officer assigned to the case as to what conditions to impose. It is doubtless a factor in judges' frequent failure to mention *any* of the statutory sentencing factors or even any of the recommended conditions that they decide to include in the sentence. And because conditions of supervised release, though imposed at sentencing, do not become operational until the defendant is released, the judge has to guess at the time of sentencing what conditions are likely to make sense in what may be the distant future. Conditions that may seem sensible at sentencing may not be sensible years, maybe many years, later, when the defendant is finally released from prison. Although nonmandatory conditions of supervised release can be modified at any time, modification is a bother for the judge.[187] That is especially true when, as is common in cases involving very long sentences, it becomes the responsibility of the sentencing judge's successor because in the meantime the sentencing judge has retired or died, resigned, or been promoted; the successor will not be familiar with the defendant. Furthermore, although reducing recidivism is the main purpose of supervised release, it is difficult, often impossible, to predict whether a defendant is likely upon release to resume criminal activity.

Sentencing judges' *insouciance* about their statutory obligations in imposing conditions of supervised release is especially pronounced with regard to the standard conditions, in part it seems because of a form—AO-245B—issued by the Administrative Office of the U.S. Courts.[188] The form prints not only the mandatory conditions but also thirteen of the fifteen standard conditions, and by doing so seems to imply (or at least many judges seem to assume) that both the mandatory conditions and at least thirteen of the fifteen standard conditions should be imposed in the absence of reasons not to do so. Indeed one court was led to observe that the standard conditions "are almost uniformly imposed by the district courts and have become boilerplate"—and the court approved, describing the standard conditions as "'basic administrative requirement[s] essential to the functioning of the supervised release system.'"[189] They are indeed almost uniformly imposed, but most of them are substantive rather than administrative; I'll give examples later.

Another wrinkle is that because conditions of supervised release are imposed at sentencing, the conditions recommended to the judge at the sentencing hearing may be a product of negotiation between prosecution and defense. The defendant's lawyer may offer the prosecution a trade—more supervised release for a reduced prison term—and the prosecutor may agree. And when adversaries agree on the outcome of a legal proceeding the sentencing judge, habituated as American judges are to adversary procedure, may be reluctant to subject the agreement to critical scrutiny, even though the law is clear that the fact that prosecution and defense agree on a sentence does

---

188. See Kenstowicz, note 177 above.
189. *United States v. Truscello,* 168 F.3d 61, 63 (2d Cir. 1999). To similar effect see *United States v. Tulloch,* 380 F.3d 8, 13–14 (1st Cir. 2004).

not excuse the judge from having to determine its conformity to the statutory sentencing factors.[190]

An additional concern is that probation officers, upon whom many district judges rely heavily for recommendations as to what conditions of supervised release to impose, spend less time on supervision than on enforcement—that is, on investigating possible violations of conditions of supervised release and presenting the results of the investigations, when they indicate a likely violation, to the sentencing judge for a decision on whether to revoke supervised release and recommit the defendant to prison. This is a serious problem given the severe understaffing of the probation service and the reliance that most district judges place on recommendations of the probation officer assigned to a case.[191] A revocation of supervised release and recommittal to prison relieves the probation service of having to monitor the person during his term of imprisonment. A study finds that "on average, one-third of those individuals [that is, individuals on supervised release] will have their supervised release revoked, most as a result of technical violations, and receive, on average, a new prison sentence of 11 months."[192]

Not least, a number of the listed conditions, along with a number of conditions that judges invent, are, as we're about to see, hopelessly vague. The system of supervised release, now thirty years old, is overdue for an overhaul.

Given the problems that I have sketched, it is no surprise that the administration of supervised release by the district courts has not run smoothly. The four cases decided in the *Thompson* opinion illustrate some of the problems.

---

190. *Freeman v. United States,* 131 S. Ct. 2685, 2692 (2011).
191. Understaffing of the probation service is discussed in *United States v. Siegel,* 753 F.3d 705, 710 (7th Cir. 2014).
192. Christine S. Scott-Hayward, "Shadow Sentencing: The Imposition of Federal Supervised Release," 18 *Berkeley Journal of Criminal Law* 180, 182 (2013).

Defendant Thompson was twenty-three years old when he began an online relationship with a girl of fourteen. They exchanged nude pictures of themselves. When she was sixteen and he twenty-five she decided to run away from home. Thompson picked her up and drove her across state lines, and they had sex in a state in which the age of consent is sixteen and their sexual activity therefore legal under state law. Convicted in federal district court of possession of child pornography and of traveling in interstate commerce for the purpose of engaging in sexual conduct with a minor (in violation of federal laws that fix the age of consent as eighteen rather than sixteen), Thompson was sentenced to 210 months in prison.[193] Although this is a very long sentence, it was not challenged on appeal. The only challenge was to the conditions of supervised release.

Even with full credit for behaving himself in prison, Thompson will be forty-one when released, and it seems odd to be devising, so far in advance, restrictions to impose on him then; but that is how supervised release operates. What was beyond odd—what was unlawful—was that the judge imposed a lifetime of supervised release without any rational, articulated justification. The life term was especially gratuitous because, as the judge himself remarked, as a convicted sex offender Thompson will be subject after he is released to a lifetime of mandatory sex-offender reporting quite apart from supervised release. But sensible or not, the imposition of a lifetime term of supervised release was vitiated by the fact that in imposing it the judge was laboring under the misapprehension that, in his words, "a term of supervised release can be reduced but can't be extended." That's wrong; it can be extended.[194]

It's not that the judge thought that Thompson after being released

193. See, for example, 18 U.S.C. § 2423(a) (2013), for a federal law that fixes the age of consent at eighteen.
194. See 18 U.S.C. §§ 3583(e)(1)–(2); Fed. R. Crim. P. 32.1(c).

from prison would continue to be a menace to young girls until he died. It is rather, as the judge explained, that because the future cannot be predicted, any term of supervised release less than life would create a risk that Thompson would repeat his crime at an advanced age. But should that risk seem acute many years from now when Thompson completes his prison term, a finite term of supervised release imposed now can be extended then. Surprisingly, neither the government nor the defense pointed out the judge's error.

The judge committed other errors. One was his failure to include in the oral sentence a condition of supervised release requiring the defendant to receive treatment for drug addiction. Not because it's a mandatory condition or one that the judge would have been remiss in failing to impose, but rather because, though he intended to impose it, it appeared only in the written judgment, and the oral sentence, which omitted the drug addiction condition, controls.[195]

A more serious error was prohibiting Thompson from having "any contact with persons under the age of 18 unless in the presence of a responsible adult who is aware of the nature of the defendant's background and instant offense and who had been approved by the probation officer." This can't have been meant literally, since understood literally it would include males under eighteen as well as females, though there is no suggestion that Thompson is bisexual. Furthermore, even if males are excluded from the no-contact rule, "contact," being undefined, could be understood to mean being served by a waitress, paying a cashier, sitting next to a girl (a stranger) at a baseball game, replying to a girl asking directions, or being shown a friend's baby girl—or his own baby, for that matter.

The judge imposed a total of twenty-five nonmandatory conditions of supervised release on Thompson. Because all those conditions were part of Thompson's sentence, the judge was not permitted to

195. *United States v. Alburay,* 415 F.3d 782, 788 (7th Cir. 2005).

impose them without considering their conformity to the sentencing factors. There is no indication that he did so. He just checked boxes in a list of conditions. Some of the conditions seem appropriate or at least innocuous, but others are either inappropriate or vague. Among the inappropriate ones is that the "defendant shall support his or her dependents and meet other family responsibilities." Of course "or her" should not be in there; its inclusion suggests the rote nature of judicial imposition of conditions of supervised release. More important, the condition assumes arbitrarily that should Thompson ever acquire dependents he will have the resources necessary to support them despite being an ex-con subject to conditions of supervised release and state and local sex-offender restrictions and reporting requirements.

Among the vague conditions imposed by the judge is that "defendant shall refrain from excessive use of alcohol," with "excessive use" undefined, though it can readily be defined.[196] Approaching the absurd is a condition forbidding the defendant to "associate with any person convicted of a felony, unless granted permission to do so by the probation officer." A variant that is only a slight improvement, found in some cases, is that "the defendant shall not associate with any persons engaged in criminal activity, and shall not associate with any person convicted of a felony, unless granted permission to do so by the probation officer." Notice the absence of any requirement that the defendant know, believe, or even suspect that he is associating with a criminal or a felon. Most criminals try to conceal their criminal activity, and most persons with a felony conviction try to conceal the conviction. Many convicted felons, moreover, go straight after being convicted, and what is the danger of associating with them? And what exactly does "associate" mean? A sensible alternative to the language of the conditions I've just quoted would be: "The defendant shall not

196. *United States v. Siegel*, note 191 above, 753 F.3d at 715–716.

meet, communicate, or otherwise interact with a person whom he knows to be or has been engaged, or planning to engage, in criminal activity."

The government defended all the conditions of supervised release imposed by the judge on the ground that the defendant had not challenged them in time. The judge had sent a list of the conditions, with check marks next to the ones he was considering imposing, to the parties in advance of the sentencing hearing, and the government argues that this was the defendant's (more realistically, his lawyer's) last chance to oppose them. But because the judge gave no reasons for why he was considering imposing the particular conditions, it was difficult for the defendant's lawyer to develop a defense to them. The judge should either have told the parties in advance his reasons for thinking the conditions in question appropriate, so that they could develop arguments pro or con his leanings to present at the sentencing hearing, or have explained at the sentencing hearing what conditions he was inclined to impose and why and asked the defendant's lawyer whether he objected to any of them. If the lawyer had a reasonable need for more time to decide whether he had grounds for objecting to any of them, the judge could have adjourned the hearing for a reasonable time.

Either of the suggested approaches would be a "best practice," but as the case law now stands neither is a required practice except with regard to conditions not listed in the statute or the guidelines.[197] No advance notice is required for imposition of any of the listed conditions.[198]

The second defendant whose appeal was decided in the *Thompson* opinion, named Ortiz, pleaded guilty to four bank robberies and was sentenced to prison for 135 months. The judge imposed eighteen

---

197. *United States v. Bryant*, 754 F.3d 443, 446 (7th Cir. 2014).
198. Id. at 446–447; *United States v. McKissic*, 428 F.3d 719, 725–726 (7th Cir. 2005); *United States v. Shannon*, 743 F.3d 496, 499–500 (7th Cir. 2014).

conditions of supervised release, each to last for three years after Ortiz's release from prison. His appeal, like Thompson's, did not challenge the prison sentence but only the conditions of supervised release.

The presentence report, prepared by the probation officer assigned to the case, contained no suggested conditions of supervised
release. Nor had the prosecution suggested any. They were sprung on
the defendant at the sentencing hearing, and with amazing brevity.
The judge's entire discussion of the conditions he was imposing consisted of the following sentence: "The conditions of supervised release
will include the normal conditions, plus drug testing up to the maximum that's permitted, drug counseling and treatment at the direction
of the probation office, and mental health counseling and treatment at
the direction of the probation office, which may include taking necessary prescription medications." It's not clear what the judge meant
by "normal conditions," but the written judgment lists three mandatory conditions, fourteen standard conditions, and five additional
conditions. The judge gave no reasons for any of the conditions, even
though nineteen of them were optional.

The defendant's lawyer can't be faulted for having failed to object
to conditions that appeared out of the blue with no statement of reasons for imposing them. The government argued, much as in Thompson's case, that a defendant should anticipate the imposition of *all* the
conditions listed in the statute and the sentencing guidelines (that is,
not just the mandatory conditions but also the standard and special
and additional conditions) and be prepared to argue against all of
them. That's an unreasonable burden to impose on the defense. It's
equivalent to requiring the plaintiff in a civil case to contest in his
complaint all the possible affirmative defenses that the defendant
might plead in his answer. The prosecutor, the probation officer, or
the judge should indicate in advance of the sentencing hearing which

conditions are under serious consideration, so that the defense doesn't waste time tilting at what may prove to be windmills.

The conditions imposed are, as in Thompson's case, riddled with ambiguities. Apart from those I mentioned in discussing that case, they include requiring Ortiz to "follow the instructions of the probation officer" and "work regularly at a lawful occupation." What if, as an ex-con, Ortiz can't get regular work? The probation officer is authorized to excuse the defendant's failure to work regularly for any "acceptable reason," but there is no explanation of what is an acceptable reason. Another condition imposed on Ortiz is that "as directed by the probation officer, the defendant shall notify third parties of risks that may be occasioned by the defendant's criminal record or personal history or characteristics." Neither "personal history" nor "characteristics" is explained. The condition treats Ortiz like a leper. He might as well walk around in sandwich boards that say "I robbed banks; I might rob you! Be warned!"

He is also required to notify the probation officer of any "change in . . . employment." There's no indication whether this just means changing employers or also includes changing from one job to another for the same employer at the same workplace. He is forbidden to "frequent places where controlled substances are illegally sold, used, distributed, or administered," but there is no requirement that he know or have reason to know or even just suspect that such activities are taking place. Nor is he told how many trips constitute "frequent[ing]." And instead of forbidding him to use a controlled substance, the judge stated that he "shall have no use of controlled substance," a puzzling phrase. Ortiz is also required to pay restitution of more than thirteen thousand dollars "at a rate of at least 10% of new monthly income"—there is no explanation of what "new" is meant to signify. Nor did the district court specify a penalty should the defendant fail to pay the restitution ordered.

Ortiz's lawyer took particular issue with two standard conditions of supervised release that might be thought to impinge on constitutional rights: that "the defendant shall answer truthfully all inquiries by the probation officer" and that he "shall permit a probation officer to visit him or her [there is of course no "her" in the case] at any time at home or elsewhere and shall permit confiscation of any contraband observed in plain view of the probation officer." The first of these conditions essentially asks for a waiver of the right not to be forced to incriminate oneself, because it would require the defendant to answer "yes" if he were asked whether he had committed another crime and he had. The second condition would allow the probation officer to "visit" the defendant at 3:00 a.m. every day and look around for contraband, and also allow him to follow the defendant everywhere, looking for contraband. Both conditions, irrespective of possible constitutional problems, are too broad.[199]

To all these criticisms the government offered the same response: the defendant can always ask the probation officer what a condition means, and the officer will give him a sensible answer. This is some protection against unreasonable or ambiguous conditions, but not much. It is too much like telling a defendant he'll be on supervised release until the probation officer decides he's been on it long enough, or that if he isn't sure what is "excessive use of alcohol" he should ask the probation officer. As a practical matter the terms of supervised release would be determined not by a judge but by a probation officer. The law doesn't authorize that.[200] It's true that probation officers are employees of the federal judiciary, but so are law clerks and judges'

---

199. My court held in *United States v. Farmer*, 755 F.3d 849, 854–855 (7th Cir. 2014), that a search condition can't be imposed without an explanation of the reason the judge considers it necessary.

200. *United States v. Tejeda*, 476 F.3d 471, 473–476 (7th Cir. 2007).

secretaries, and they are not allowed to determine the sentences of convicted defendants.

In the third of the four cases decided in the *Thompson* opinion, the defendant, Bates, was sentenced to 188 months in prison for dealing in crack cocaine. No conditions of supervised release were mentioned in the presentence report. The judge sprang them on the parties in the sentencing hearing, imposing the usual thirteen standard conditions (though for eight years, rather than three as in Ortiz's case). He gave no reasons. All he said was: "The standard conditions are adopted by the Court." My criticisms of the handling of supervised release by the judge in Ortiz's case are equally applicable to Bates's case.

The defendant in the fourth case, Blount, challenged not only the conditions of supervised release but also the prison sentence (three hundred months, for running an extensive organization engaged in the sale of heroin), specifically the four-level enhancement in the defendant's base offense level by reason of his being "an organizer or leader of a criminal activity that involved five or more participants or was otherwise extensive."[201] The enhancement, and so the three-hundred-month sentence, were proper, but as in the other three cases the district judge's handling of supervised release was flawed. There was again no discussion of any of the section 3553(a) factors that the judge might have thought justified the duration and conditions of supervised release. His discussion of the conditions that he imposed is difficult even to understand. He listed eight conditions but said that the defendant "shall comply with the standard conditions that have been adopted by this court," and the written judgment lists the thirteen usual standard conditions—with all their ambiguities uncor-

201. U.S.S.G. § 3B1.1(a).

rected. The eight conditions he discussed are a mixture of mandatory and "additional" conditions.

Two of them are seriously questionable. One is that "if [the defendant is] unemployed after the first 60 days of supervision or if unemployed for 60 days after termination or layoff from employment, he shall perform at least 20 hours of community service work per week at the direction of and in the discretion of the Probation Office until gainfully employed." Taken literally this means that if at say age sixty-eight the defendant (who as we're about to see will still be in supervised release) is unemployed, he'll have to perform twenty hours of community service per week—indefinitely (till he dies?). Yet a guideline application note that the judge did not mention states that "community service generally should not be imposed in excess of 400 hours."[202] The government in its appeal brief stated that the judge's community-service condition "did not amount to the imposition of more than 400 hours of service." Wrong; the judge placed no limit on the amount of community service that the defendant could be ordered to do.

Another unsound condition imposed by the judge was that the defendant "obtain his GED within the first year of supervision." (The government's brief stated mistakenly that the judge had merely ordered the defendant to "seek" his GED.) The GED is a battery of five tests; if you pass, you get a General Education Development certificate roughly equivalent to a high school diploma (though try convincing a prospective employer of the equivalence). There is no assurance of passing the tests, let alone within a year. There is no method of "requiring" that a person pass the GED tests, unless cheating is permitted. This is an example of a palpably unsound condition of supervised release that could be repaired by changing a single word, and would

202. Application note to U.S.S.G. § 5F1.3 (1991).

have been years ago if anyone paid any attention to the conditions of supervised release, rather than imposing them blindly, by rote.[203] An added wrinkle is that the defendant was thirty-nine years old when sentenced; his prison sentence was 300 months (25 years), though good-time credit could reduce the sentence to 20 years. He will therefore be between fifty-nine and sixty-four years old when released. The judge imposed a ten-year term of supervised release on some though not all of the counts; on others it was three years. It is difficult to understand the need for a ten-year term of supervised release to take effect when the defendant is in or verging on his sixties. The probability of his reentering the heroin trade at that age is slight. Blount had, it's true, a long criminal record, but all stemming from dealing in heroin, a young man's game; he is likely to be burned out by the time he's released from prison. The imposition of a ten-year term of supervised release to take effect in twenty to twenty-five years does not make much sense; and while it can be modified at any time, a superior alternative would be to impose at the outset a nominal term, with the understanding (contrary to the error by the district judge in Thompson's case) that it can be extended, if that seems needful, on the eve of his completion of his prison sentence.

A number of decisions brush aside objections to the ambiguity of the many conditions of supervised release imposed by district judges.[204] But they do this by interpreting the conditions narrowly. In *United States v. Phillips,* for example, after noting that the district court

---

203. I'm mindful that both the employment and the GED conditions were upheld in *United States v. McKissic,* note 198 above, 428 F.3d at 724–725, but against objections different from those that I've just expressed.

204. See, for example, *United States v. Phillips,* 704 F.3d 754, 767–768 (9th Cir. 2012); *United States v. Zobel,* 696 F.3d 558, 574–575 (6th Cir. 2012); *United States v. Albertson,* 645 F.3d 191, 200–201 (3d Cir. 2011); *United States v. Mike,* 632 F.3d 686, 696–698 (10th Cir. 2011).

had imposed "a condition prohibiting Phillips from 'frequent[ing] places where controlled substances are illegally sold, used, distributed, or administered,'" a condition that Phillips contended on appeal was "'vague and overbroad,'" the Ninth Circuit held that the condition "prohibits Phillips from *knowingly* going to a specific place where drugs are illegally used or sold, but . . . does not prohibit him from . . . going to a given neighborhood simply because a person is selling drugs somewhere within that neighborhood."[205] But it's better for the district judge to specify required limitations in a condition of supervised release than to leave that to the appellate court.

The *Thompson* opinion reversed the supervised-release portion of the sentence in each of the four cases I've been discussing. If these cases are typical of how supervised release is being administered—and they are—the program is in serious trouble and requires to be re-thought from the ground up.[206]

In a fifth recent case (not consolidated with the four cases in the *Thompson* opinion), again there were no recommendations concerning conditions of supervised release from the probation service, the prosecution, or the defense.[207] The printed judgment imposes five mandatory conditions, thirteen standard conditions, and six additional conditions of which three duplicate the listed mandatory or standard conditions. The additional conditions that are not duplicates require

---

205. 704 F.3d 754, 767–768 (emphasis in original).
206. As powerfully argued in Scott-Hayward's article, cited in note 192 above. See also Fiona Doherty, "Indeterminate Sentencing Returns: The Invention of Supervised Release," 88 *New York University Law Review* 958, 1020 (2013): "The modern-day supervised release system is not grounded in any clear set of principles. Rather, it consists of a hodgepodge of amendments and procedures that were cobbled together by different actors over many years. I have not found any case or law review article that attempts to provide a coherent theory to explain the system as it currently exists."
207. *United States v. McMillian,* 777 F.3d 444, 450–452 (7th Cir. 2015).

the defendant to register with state and local authorities as a convicted sex offender, participate in a mental health assessment and treatment program for sex offenders, and provide his probation officer with access to financial information. That makes a total of twenty-one conditions of supervised release excluding the duplicates, all to go into effect when the defendant (sentenced to thirty years for a sex offense) is released from prison, when he will be about sixty years old.

At the sentencing hearing the judge imposed the standard conditions without naming any of them, without giving a reason for any of them, and without attempting to correct any of the numerous ambiguities in them. He recited several of the mandatory conditions, as well as the three nonduplicative additional conditions, but did not explain his failure to mention any of the other conditions that appear in the written judgment; he may have forgotten that all the components of a sentence (including therefore any conditions of supervised release imposed) must be stated in the oral sentence; those stated just in the written judgment are without effect.[208] The judge must also as I've emphasized give reasons for the conditions of supervised release that he imposes and consider the propriety of imposing them in light of the statutory sentencing factors. None of that was done either.

My discussion of these five cases has only scratched the surface of the problems that the design and administration of supervised release has created. The cases decided in the *Siegel* opinion contain a rich list of ambiguous or confused conditions imposed in those cases (and reversed by the decision). Here is a part of the opinion dealing with Siegel (one of two defendants discussed in the opinion), convicted of child sexual abuse including creation of child pornography:[209]

---

208. E.g., *United States v. Johnson,* 765 F.3d 702, 710–711 (7th Cir. 2014).
209. 753 F.3d at 712–714 (emphases in original).

The nudity condition was the only one discussed in any depth at the sentencing hearing. The presentence report had recommended the following wording: *"You shall neither possess nor have under your control any material, legal or illegal, that contains nudity or that depicts or alludes to sexual activity or depicts sexually arousing material."* Siegel's lawyer objected that this would forbid Siegel to read the Bible. He was right; the Bible contains allusions to sexual activity. The judge responded by changing the clause we've italicized to "text narratives concerning the sexual abuse of children, or internet chats exchanging ideas and experiences regarding the sexual abuse of children." He explained that by doing this he was providing "a laundry list of things that are specifically intended to address what [Siegel] did here, what he could reasonably be expected to consider doing in the future, and also the things based on this record that would suggest the things that might act as triggers for him."

The judge said enough to justify a nudity condition of some sort. But of what sort exactly? What about the Bible? It "contains nudity," unless "contains" only means "provides a visual depiction of"—but that would be a forced interpretation. The judge said that his revised nudity condition included "an element of common sense"; "I've been a judge for more than 30 years. To my knowledge, no one has ever been brought in front of this court . . . because they went to an art museum or read the Bible." No doubt. But that seems a reference to the exercise of discretion by probation officers, rather than a qualification of the "contains nudity" condition itself.

So that key condition remains a muddle, and for the additional reason that the judge did not explain why the condition should not be limited to visual depictions of nudity related or incidental to sexual urges or activities. Is "nudity" meant to include innocuous partial nudity, such as a photograph, in no respect prurient, of an adult wearing a bathing suit? So not only is "contains" vague, but "nudity" is overbroad, see *United States v. Simons*, 614 F.3d 475, 483–84 (8th Cir. 2010), and we suggest therefore that "contains nudity" be rephrased as "material that depicts nudity in a prurient or sexually arousing manner."

Several components of five of the nine conditions are troubling besides the nudity condition. The first is a prohibition of purchase, possession, or use of any "mood altering substances," a term neither defined nor self-evident. It could include coffee, cigarettes, sugar, and chocolate, among many others; yet these substances are not causal factors of recidivist behavior. At oral argument the government's lawyer suggested a much better definition, which would exclude coffee, cigarettes, sugar, and chocolate: "psychoactive substances that impair physical or mental functioning," including street, synthetic, or designer drugs, such as "bath salts" (a synthetic amphetamine-like product) and "potpourri" (also called "spice," a synthetic form of marijuana) some versions of which, when Siegel was sentenced, had only recently been designated controlled substances.

Conditions eight and nine require the defendant to "participate in a sex offender program as deemed necessary by the probation office," "submit to physiological testing, including polygraph testing, which may be part of a sex offender treatment program as directed by the . . . [probation] office," and participate in "psychiatric services and/or a program of mental health counseling/treatment as directed by the probation officer and . . . take any and all prescribed medications as directed by the probation officer."We have grouped these conditions because of their repetitiousness and lack of definition. If physiological testing *may* be rather than must be part of the required sex-offender treatment program, implying that it is not a mandatory part, why is it a free-standing requirement, imposed whether or not it is part of a sex-offender treatment program? What other function could it serve? Is it just a euphemism for giving the prisoner lie-detector tests?

And why are both psychiatric and mental health treatment, which differ mainly in that psychiatrists can prescribe drugs while psychologists generally cannot (and not all mental health counselors are even psychologists), specified as conditions of supervised release? It is unclear whether these are intended to be components of the sex-offender treatment program or separate from it, and if the latter why the defendant is to be subjected to separate psychiatric attention, since a sex-offender treatment program will have a significant psychiatric component. It's true that Siegel has been diagnosed with other psychological disorders besides pedophilia. But the judge did not indicate whether he believes that those disorders would be likely to cause Siegel to engage in criminal activity when he is released from prison many years from now unless he receives treatment then and perhaps for the rest of his life.

And why is a probation officer, rather than a physician or nurse or pharmacist, entrusted with directing *which* medications the defendant must take? And what is the force of "any and all" prescribed medications? And how can a judge have known on March 20, 2013, when the sentence was imposed, or the probation service, on January 31, 2013, when the presentence report was submitted, what if any psychiatric services the defendant would require when he was eventually released? By that time the medical and criminological understanding of recidivism and methods of minimizing it may have changed completely. But that is not a criticism that can be made of the sentencing judge. It is a flaw in the Sentencing Reform Act, which makes the conditions of supervised release a part of the sentence. One would think that they would be imposed after a court hearing held on the eve of the defendant's release from prison. The hearing would also serve as a reminder to the defendant that he is still under judicial supervision, even though his sentence was imposed a long time ago.

The opinion in *Siegel* recommended the following "best practices" regarding the imposition of conditions of supervised release:

1. Require the probation service to communicate its recommendations for conditions of supervised release to defense counsel at least two weeks before the sentencing hearing.

2. Make an *independent* judgment (as required in fact by 18 U.S.C. § 3553(a)) of the appropriateness of the recommended conditions—independent, that is, of agreement between prosecutor and defense counsel (and defendant) on the conditions, or of the failure of defense counsel to object to the conditions recommended by the probation service.

3. Determine appropriateness with reference to the *particular* conduct, character, etc., of the defendant, rather than on the basis of loose generalizations about the defendant's crime and criminal history, and where possible with reference also to the relevant criminological literature.

4. Make sure that each condition imposed is simply worded, bearing in mind that, with rare exceptions, neither the defendant nor the probation officer is a lawyer and that when released from prison the defendant will not have a lawyer to consult.

5. Require that on the eve of his release from prison, the defendant attend a brief hearing before the sentencing judge (or his successor) in order to be reminded of the conditions of supervised release. That would also be a proper occasion for the judge to consider whether to modify one or more of the conditions in light of any changed circumstances brought about by the defendant's experiences in prison.[210]

There is nothing esoteric about these recommendations. They are simple common sense.

One would think that by now the Sentencing Commission (which drafts the sentencing guidelines), the probation service, and the judges would have ironed the kinks out of the system. One might have expected the Supreme Court to have intervened. The persistence of the manifold serious kinks in the supervised-release program, undiminished, validates a major theme of this book, which is the passivity, the inertia, of the judiciary (five of the nine members of the Sentencing Commission are federal judges and the federal probation service is part of the federal judiciary). It's time we woke up.

Worse, though I use "kinks" to describe the system of supervised release as it is actually administered, these are not minor irregularities; they are violations of the federal criminal code. A careful recent empirical study at the University of Chicago Law School suggests that at least 90 percent of sentences imposing supervised release fail to com-

210. Id. at 716–717 (emphases in original).

ply with such basic statutory requirements as that the sentencing judge give reasons and specifically explain the consistency of the supervised-release provisions of the sentence with the statutory sentencing factors in section 3553(a).[211]

It is noteworthy and deplorable that there is so little academic attention to supervised release, despite its widespread and toxic effects on the lives of persons prosecuted for federal criminal violations.[212] Since the onset of supervised release in 1987 judges have imposed terms of supervised release on some one million convicted criminals; and at the end of 2010 there were 103,000 persons on supervised release—almost exactly half the number of federal prison inmates.[213]

211. Kenstowicz, note 177 above.
212. Besides the three articles cited in this appendix, there appears to be only a meager literature on supervised release—confined, moreover, to conditions of supervised release imposed on sex offenders. See Gabriel Gillett, "A World without Internet: A New Framework for Analyzing a Supervised Release Condition that Restricts Computer and Internet Access," 79 *Fordham Law Review* 217 (2010); Michael Smith, "Barely Legal: Vagueness and the Prohibition of Pornography as a Condition of Supervised Release," 84 *St. John's Law Review* 727 (2010); Paula Kei Biderman and Jon M. Sands, "A Prescribed Failure: The Lost Potential of Supervised Release," 6 *Federal Sentencing Reporter* 204 (1994); Harold B. Wooten, "Violation of Supervised Release: Erosion of a Promising Congressional Idea into Troubled Policy and Practice, 6 *Federal Sentencing Reporter* 183 (1994). Only two courts besides the Seventh Circuit appear to give consistently careful review to conditions of supervised release—see discussion and citations in John Rhodes and Daniel Donovan, "Branded by Life by the Modern Scarlet Letters: Do Convicted Sex Offenders Have Rights While on Parole, Probation, or Supervised Release?" *The Champion,* May 2014, 15—and the Seventh Circuit's activity in this area began quite recently. None of the articles cited in this footnote are by academics.
213. Doherty, note 206 above, at 1014.

3 | MANAGEMENT DEFICIENCIES

THE DEFICIENCIES of the federal judiciary discussed in this chapter are of a different character from the ones discussed in Chapter 2 because they're not problems of judicial reasoning or expression. They are deficiencies in the management of the various layers of the judiciary: the tiny staffs of the judges of the courts of appeals, the courts of appeals themselves (modest organizations), the Supreme Court (ditto), and the federal judiciary as a whole—a large organization. Each level requires management, and each has management problems. I begin with the lowest level.

1. Deficient management of judicial staff. Many judges lack elementary management skills and as a result have difficulty managing their staffs even though those staffs are very small: most federal appellate judges (including Supreme Court Justices) nowadays have four law clerks; some have three; some have five and therefore no secretary (because each judge has only five slots); and some (almost all of them being senior judges, most of whom do not take a full caseload) one or two law clerks.

One can't say with a straight face that judges' staffs are too large for judges to manage. I think the ratio of four (occasionally five) law clerks to one judge is too high, but not because it prevents a judge from managing his staff effectively—rather because it tempts him to delegate too much of his work to his eager staff.

Management skills are often not positively correlated with judicial ability. Henry Friendly had tense relations with most of his law clerks, intimidated them, neglected them, and got much less help from what was an outstanding sequence of clerks than he should have been able to get.[1] It didn't matter much, because he was brilliant, experienced, and lightning fast; but my impression is that a great many federal court of appeals judges do not manage their staffs well.

Most judges are heavily reliant on their clerks, including for the drafting of the judges' judicial opinions (the judges "own" the opinions issued under their name, even if they don't write them, or even edit them carefully). Indeed the vast majority of federal appellate judges (including Supreme Court Justices) delegate to their law clerks the drafting of at least the first drafts of their opinions.[2] A well-known statement of the regnant judicial attitude is that of Judge Patricia Wald: "Whether the judge writes the first draft for the clerks to critique and to flesh out, or the clerk writes the first draft for the judge to revise and to challenge is not dispositive of whether the judge is still in charge."[3] No one doubts that the judge is in charge; that's not the issue; the issue is who should be the opinion writer. I know for certain of only three federal court of appeals judges besides myself who write all their own first drafts. I imagine that there are a few others; and I know that there are judges who write at least some of their first drafts.

But for the most part even judges who are good writers prefer editing law clerks' opinion drafts to writing first drafts themselves. Judges of the lower federal courts, whether the courts of appeals or the district courts, may doubt that anyone is much interested in anything in their opinions except the bottom line (which side won). And

1. See David M. Dorsen, *Henry Friendly: Greatest Judge of His Era,* ch. 6 (2012). And see the brief summary in my Foreword to Dorsen's book. Id. at xii.

2. See, for example, Jonathan Matthew Cohen, *Inside Appellate Courts: The Impact of Court Organization on Judicial Decision Making in the United States Courts of Appeals* 112 (2002). For a typical example, see Daniel Mahoney, "Law Clerks for Better or for Worse?" 54 *Brooklyn Law Review* 321, 332–334 (1988).

3. Patricia M. Wald, "The Problem with the Courts: Black-Robed Bureaucracy, or Collegiality under Challenge?" 42 *Maryland Law Review* 766, 778 (1983).

they may think that opinions should be conventional rather than interesting and that law clerks are capable, with some editorial assistance by the judge, of writing competent conventional opinions—and that is true. There are judges who, like most Americans, disdain good writing and judges who feel they don't have time to write opinions.

Some judges edit their clerks' opinion drafts very heavily. A draft may pass back and forth between judge and law clerk and end up far from where it began—sometimes so far that it's little different from what it would have been had the judge written it from the start. Other judges do little editing and as a result the law clerk's first draft will be very close to the final, issued opinion. (That is known to happen not infrequently even in the Supreme Court.) And some assign the editing of the law clerk's draft to another of the judge's law clerks instead of doing the editing themselves. Sometimes although the drafting is the clerk's the judge has given the clerk detailed directions in advance with respect to the structure of the opinion. But perhaps the best analogy to the modern federal judge is a conceptual artist like Jeff Koons: he imagines the work of art but execution is delegated to a craftsman.

My practice is to write my opinion within a day or two after oral argument, while the case is still very fresh in my mind. One of my law clerks then conducts additional, deeper research, both factual and legal; checks the accuracy of the opinion; and makes stylistic and organizational suggestions. I am often led by the law clerk's work to revise my initial draft extensively, and the process may proceed for several or even many rounds before I am ready to circulate the opinion to the other judges on the panel.

The delegation of opinion writing to law clerks is a mistake unless the judge is a very poor writer or has a staggeringly heavy caseload, yet a mistake so deeply entrenched in the modern judicial culture that it won't be changed. One reason that such delegation is a mistake is that opinions drafted by law clerks lack authenticity—a judge's distinctive "voice," or personality, that would help lawyers and other judges understand "where the judge was coming from" and therefore how he or she would be likely to decide future cases. Judge Michael Boudin remarks that "law clerks may write well but—in speaking for another—they employ a safely formulaic mode usually learned in editing a law review."[4] Because most law clerks are inexperienced judicial opinion writers imbricated in the law-student culture of formalist legal analysis, slaves to the *Bluebook,* and somewhat intimidated by the often rather elderly person who is their judge and only boss, the opinions they write tend to be overlong, mechanical, weak on fact, and pedestrian. It's the judges who realize this who heavily edit their clerks' opinion drafts. One judge (not of my court) has told me that his published opinions have often been through twenty to twenty-five rounds of editing as he works to improve a law clerk's original draft. Interestingly, his opinions are very good (he tells me he's not a good writer but is a good editor—I'd say he's a producer of first-rate opinions), but the method of their creation strikes me as involving an inefficient use of both his and his clerks' time.

As inexperienced opinion writers eager to impress their judge, law clerks tend, at least late into what is usually just a one-year term as law clerk, to spend a great deal of time drafting each opinion (less if the clerk has been required to draft an elaborate bench memorandum before the case was argued that he can convert, though not without further work, into an opinion). That is time that if the judge wrote the opinion draft the clerk could be devoting to research both legal and factual (including extrarecord Internet research) and to helping the judge prepare for oral argument. Many judges are appointed from

4. Michael Boudin, "Judge Henry Friendly and the Craft of Judging," 159 *University of Pennsylvania Law Review* 1, 13 (2010).

managerial positions (so why are they so often such poor managers of their tiny judicial staffs? I have no idea) in law firms or government legal offices (usually a U.S. Attorney's office), and as a result haven't done much writing for a long time. What they don't realize is, as I keep saying, that if they wrote dozens of opinions a year they'd quickly become experienced writers. Practice doesn't make perfect but it makes better. Although many judges would need assistance to become good opinion writers, there are excellent books on how to write well and of course many books by great writers—and many opinions by great writing judges—from which new judges could learn to write at least as well as their law clerks, and as they accumulated experience to write faster than a fledgling clerk.[5] Law clerks excused from writing opinion drafts would have more time not only to do research (not, one hopes, limited to the orthodox sources of law), but also to criticize their judge's drafts and to edit them—for even good writers benefit from editing.

I am mindful of the argument that since judges are appointed by politicians (the President and the Senators) but law clerks by judges, intellectual ability plays a greater role in the selection of law clerks than in the selection of their bosses. And indeed it's not unusual for a law clerk to be smarter and harder working than his boss, especially if his judge is elderly. But it doesn't follow that law clerks would be better judges than their bosses. Aristotle pointed out that the young, be-

5. See, for example, Stephen J. Pyne, *Voice & Vision: A Guide to Writing History and Other Serious Nonfiction* (2009); Helen Sword, *Stylish Academic Writing* (2012). Neither book is concerned with writing judicial opinions—and that is one of their strengths! Judges have to learn to write like people. During the period of several months when I was awaiting my appointment to the Seventh Circuit I read widely in opinions by Holmes, Hand, and Jackson—all excellent writers—and that is a good way to train oneself how to write a good judicial opinion.

ing analytically sharp but inexperienced, rely on analysis rather than experience to make judgments and that the reverse is true of the old. The old are rich in experience, though their analytical abilities may have declined or been rendered obsolete by new analytical techniques that the judge is too set in his ways to master. But if experience is more important for sound judging than analysis, it makes sense for judges to be old and their assistants young. I think it *is* more important. Many of the cases that reach the appellate level of the federal judiciary, and those the most difficult and often the most important (because the decision in such cases will change or clarify the law), are toss-ups. The law may be vague or unsettled, the factual findings in the trial court scanty or of dubious accuracy, and arriving at a decision a matter of picking one's way through a trackless waste. Intuition honed by experience may be a surer guide to a reasonable decision than analytical power. Ordinarily the challenge to the judge is to come up with a sensible result, not to make an analytical breakthrough. There are many intelligent judicial opinions (of course many dumb ones too), but how many of the opinions of even the greatest judges are *intellectual* tours de force? All this is implicit in the emphasis I have placed on the indeterminacy of law, the fact that it is not a science or even a social science, that it is a kind of groping.

A further point is that writing happens to be more an experiential skill than an analytical one. Experienced writers are better than novices. Moreover, skill in writing is relatively impervious to the ravages of age—another reason judges have it backward in delegating the writing of their opinions to their young law clerks. But I must qualify this conclusion in an important respect. When the clerk writes the draft, the judge edits it or if not the judge then another of the judge's clerks; but when the judge writes the draft either no one edits it or the editor is a law clerk who is likely to be timid about rewriting his boss's draft. My solution is to purge law clerks of timidity. My law clerks call me by my first name and I treat them as my equals and insist that they treat me as their equal—as a colleague not a superior. Pursuant to a "no pussyfooting" edict that I have promulgated, they are required to be completely candid with me and I with them. In their editing role they have been known to wreak havoc on my first drafts. Often they force me to do a lot of rewriting. I never complain.

Editing is not a substitute for writing but it is an important aid to it—although the federal court of appeals judge went way overboard who called "silly" "the notion that the judge must be responsible for initially writing every word of the opinion"—who said, "If the judge insists on writing the first draft all the time, in many ways it is the easiest way to lose control of the opinion," and who added that he "always found" that he "didn't care who did the first draft."[6]

I don't doubt that law clerks, as recent law school graduates, are likely to be more au courant with recent legal scholarship than judges are; that is one of the things that make the clerks a vital component of the judiciary. But that's no reason to delegate opinion writing to them. They can impart their up-to-date knowledge to the judge in discussion and in editing his opinion drafts.

Two effects of the widespread delegation of opinion writing to law clerks at the Supreme Court level—effects that are also evidence of that delegation—are greater uniformity in opinion-writing style across Justices (that is, their opinions are stylistically more alike) but less uniformity in the opinion-writing style of a given Justice across time.[7] Most of the law clerks turn over every year, and there are likely to be stylistic differences between one year's law clerks and the next year's. But those differences must (to produce the effect just described)

---

6. Quoted in William Domnarski, *Federal Judges Revealed* 186 (2009).
7. Keith Carlson and Michael A. Livermore, "A Quantitative Analysis of Trends in Writing Style on the U.S. Supreme Court" (University of Virginia School of Law, Public Law and Legal Theory Research Paper Series 2015-3, January 2015).

be smaller than the differences in writing styles would be between two Justices if they wrote their own opinions, because as mature writers they would be more likely than young law clerks to have cultivated distinctive individual styles of writing.

A questionable though almost universal judicial management practice, which I've already mentioned and which is related to the delegation of opinion writing to law clerks, is requiring a law clerk to write a bench memorandum in advance of oral argument. The memorandum, aimed at helping the judge prepare for argument, will usually summarize the issues in the case and provide a recommendation, based largely on factual information and legal authorities furnished by the briefs, as to which party should prevail. If the case is assigned to the law clerk's judge, the bench memorandum will be convertible, though often only after considerable additional research and other effort, into an opinion draft. If the case is assigned to another judge, the effort that went into the bench memorandum may be wasted.

Preparation of bench memoranda is time-consuming and thus reduces the time that a law clerk has for doing legal, record, Internet, and other research for the case, though it may as I said reduce the amount of time the clerk has to devote to writing an opinion in the case. Unless the judge doesn't bother to read the briefs and lower court opinion, the bench memo may contribute rather little to his understanding of the case. My law clerks don't write bench memoranda, but they do as much preargument research as they have time for and we discuss the cases at length before oral argument.

Many a judge, having assigned each case to one of his or her law clerks, excludes the other clerks from any involvement in it. That's a mistake. I discuss each case with all my law clerks, both for my benefit and for theirs—the clerk experience is richer if each clerk is involved in discussion of every case rather than of just a third or fourth of all the cases (I have three law clerks, but most federal appellate judges have four). The judge benefits from having the views of several clerks rather than just one; law clerks are not fungible.

Still another common management mistake at the appellate-judge level is the addition to a judge's staff of externs—law students working part-time for the judge. (They are sometimes referred to as interns, but I prefer to call them externs because they work outside the law school.) Externs have not completed their legal education, work only part time, require more detailed guidance and supervision than law clerks, add to the administrative burden of the judge's office, and generally are able to make only a modest contribution to the judge's output. Often federal judges after experimenting with having externs decide they're more trouble than they're worth. I am speaking of appellate judges; the much heavier caseloads of district judges, and the fact that they have fewer law clerks, often creates an acute need for externs.

A combination of work-ethic problems and management problems explains—and undermines—the frequent complaints of judges (and academic observers) that they are overworked.[8] There are 179 authorized federal court of appeals judgeships, of which 169 are filled at this writing. There are also a number of senior judges. Most are semi-retired, yet in the aggregate senior judges handle about 15 percent of the federal appellate caseload, raising the full-time equivalent number of judges to 199 (169 ÷ .85). My court (the Seventh Circuit) has a full-time equivalent of almost twelve judges, which equates to four 3-judge panels. If each panel sits 30 days a year and hears 6 cases a day, it (and therefore each member of it) will hear 180 cases a year. Then four panels will hear a total of 720 cases a year, though each judge will be hearing only 180. Each will be responsible for the ma-

---

8. See, for example, William M. Richman and William L. Reynolds, *Injustice on Appeal: The United States Courts of Appeals in Crisis* (2012).

jority opinion in a third of all the cases he hears; so, since each judge hears 180 arguments, each judge will produce an opinion or an order (my court calls an "unpublished" opinion—judicial jargon for an opinion that, though in fact published, is accorded no significance as a precedent—an order) in 60 cases a year (this excludes concurring and dissenting opinions). That isn't enough opinion production to dispose of the court's entire caseload; but many cases, especially pro se cases, are disposed of without oral argument, and the judges' activity in those cases tends to be minimal.

My court has a relatively light caseload; in 2014 we heard oral argument in only 748 cases (close to the hypothetical 720 number in my numerical example). Courts of appeals that have heavier caseloads dispose of a higher fraction of their cases without oral argument than we do and therefore with less investment of judges' time per case. Of the 550 appeals argued to my court in 2014 that had been decided as of February 2, 2015, 458 had been decided in published opinions—83 percent. This is a much higher percentage than in the other courts of appeals.

There are more comprehensive statistics for the regional circuits (that is, excluding the court of appeals for the Federal Circuit, as its jurisdiction is nationwide), for the year ending September 20, 2013.[9]

9. United States Courts, Table S-3, "U.S. Courts of Appeals—Types of Opinions or Orders Filed in Cases Terminated on the Merits After Oral Hearing or Submission on Briefs During the 12-Month Period Ending September 30, 2013," www.uscourts.gov/uscourts/Statistics/JudicialBusiness/2013/tables/S03Sep13 .pdf. The statistics have now been updated to 2014. See Table S-12, www .uscourts.gov/uscourts/Statistics/JudicialBusiness/2014/appendices/B12Sep14 .pdf, but there are no significant changes from 2013, though I am pleased to note that in 2014 only the D.C. Circuit had a higher rate of published opinions than the Seventh Circuit, and that the number of the Seventh Circuit's signed published opinions (that is, excluding published per curiam opinions, which generally are less important) was 609, up from 570 in 2013.

The Seventh Circuit had the fourth lowest caseload; that year it terminated 1,702 cases on the merits (otherwise than by consolidation of cases), and issued published opinions (a total of 570) in a third of its cases. Only the D.C. and First Circuits have higher percentages of published opinions. The average for all twelve regional circuits is a surprisingly low 12 percent, reflecting the fact that the largest circuits have the lowest percentages of published opinions—the Ninth Circuit 8 percent, the Fifth Circuit 9 percent, the Fourth Circuit 6 percent, and the Eleventh Circuit also 6 percent. Yet all the circuits except the First and Eighth have a larger full-time-equivalent number of judges than the Seventh, and only the First has a smaller number. The Ninth has twenty-nine authorized court of appeals judgeships, the Fifth seventeen, the Fourth fifteen, and the Eleventh twelve.[10] The implication is that these courts (probably excepting the Eleventh, however, which has only one more authorized judgeship than the Seventh yet a considerably larger caseload) could be issuing more published opinions than they are, without experiencing workload strain. They have heavier caseloads but also more judges.

These figures convey only an approximate sense of the relative manpower of the different courts of appeals, because they exclude senior and visiting judges (both visiting judges from other circuits and visiting district judges from within the circuit). Senior judges in the aggregate carry a heavy caseload, and visiting judges should enable every circuit to increase its decisional capacity to a level at which it is not compelled to decide most of its appeals in unpublished opinions. I therefore find the workload argument for unpublished opinions unconvincing.

And here is a further bit of evidence. Table 3.1 displays the number of orally argued appeals that each of the regional courts of appeals

10. See 28 U.S.C. § 44(a).

Table 3.1. Merit Terminations after Oral Argument, Year Ending September 2013

Circuit	Total number of orally argued appeals decided	Total terminations on the merits	% of total merit terminations terminated after oral hearing
1st	259	997	26
2nd	958	3,399	28
3rd	225	2,845	8
4th	432	4,023	11
5th	796	4,789	17
6th	655	3,798	17
7th	644	1,868	34
8th	396	2,296	17
9th	1,512	7,582	20
10th	354	1,490	24
11th	450	4,196	11
D.C.	233	537	43
Total	6,914	37,820	18

decided in 2013, the total number of cases that each decided on the merits, and the percentage of those merit terminations that were made after oral argument.[11]

What is interesting is that setting aside the D.C. Circuit because of its very low number of appeals terminated on the merits (as distinct from termination by voluntary dismissal, or on procedural grounds unrelated to the merits of the case), we see that the Seventh Circuit, with its low number of terminations, has the highest percentage of cases decided on the merits after oral argument. Comparing columns 2 and 3, notice that the Ninth Circuit, with more than twice the number of judges as the Seventh Circuit, hears oral argument in only 20 percent of its cases terminated on the merits, compared to 34 per-

11. The source for the table is www.uscourts.gov/uscourts/Statistics/JudicialBusiness/2013/appendices/B01Sep13.pdf.

cent for the Seventh Circuit. True, the Ninth Circuit has a merits caseload about four times as great as the Seventh's, but it also has almost three times as many judges, so one would expect it to be able to hear oral argument in more than 20 percent of its merits cases.

Remarkably, the percentage of cases terminated on the merits after oral argument falls to 8 percent for the Third Circuit; and for the twelve regional circuits as a whole the average percentage is only 18. The very low percentages in the Third, Fourth, and Eleventh Circuits are puzzling.

Of course hearing a case argued and writing or editing a judicial opinion are not the only things court of appeals judges do. They must read and vote on opinions circulated by the other judges and field motions (for extensions of time, for permission to file an interlocutory appeal or an amicus curiae brief, for rehearing or rehearing en banc, and so forth). There are some other chores as well. Nevertheless the caseload should not be felt as crushing by a reasonably competent, at least moderately energetic, *well-organized* judge.

2. Lack of collegiality. Appellate courts are collegial bodies in the sense that their output requires a substantial degree of agreement among some or all the judges. It is important to the smooth, expeditious functioning of such an organization that the members get along with one another, implying civility, restraint, mutual respect, and willingness to compromise about inessentials.[12] Sometimes the members of an appellate court don't get along with each other—which is not actually a big surprise, when one bears in mind the resemblance of an appellate court to marriage in a culture of arranged marriage with no divorce; the judges can neither appoint their colleagues nor remove them.

---

12. See, for excellent discussions by excellent judges, Frank M. Coffin, *On Appeal: Courts, Lawyering, and Judging* 213–217 (1994); Harry T. Edwards, "The Effects of Collegiality on Judicial Decision Making," 151 *University of Pennsylvania Law Review* 1639 (2003).

Lack of collegiality may be expressed in snarky or even intemperate dissents and concurrences, in judges' nitpicking the opinions of colleagues even when agreeing with the analysis in those opinions, in slow voting on opinions circulated by the other judges, in rivalry, in professional jealousy, in unwillingness to compromise. An unfounded belief in the rightness of one's judicial ideas or methods (often, paradoxically, a belief that is a consequence of insecurity) can be a source of bitter disagreement with other judges. The result can be to multiply separate opinions, slow down the work of the court, and even drive judges to resign, or to retire prematurely. The Supreme Court in the 1940s was plagued by lack of collegiality as a result of the reciprocated hostility of Black and Douglas for Frankfurter and Jackson; at any given time several of the thirteen federal courts of appeals are quite likely to have a collegiality problem.[13] In one of the federal courts of appeals today the judges of opposing factions will not eat lunch together.

I repeat Oliver Cromwell's admonition to "think it possible that you may be mistaken." The judge who banishes all doubt from his opinions—who writes with an assurance that borders on cocksureness—not only gives a misleading impression of the law's certainty and the cogency of legal reasoning but also irritates the judges who disagree with him. The problem of feuding federal judges would be solved in a trice if the Chief Justice summoned them to his office in Washington and told them to stop behaving like children. His failure to have done that is a failure of judicial macromanagement; such failures are pervasive.

3. Deficient judicial macromanagement is caused by weakness in leadership and management skills at the court rather than the judge level. It

---

13. Marvin Schick, *Learned Hand's Court* (1970), vividly describes the feud between Second Circuit judges Charles E. Clark and Jerome Frank—both excellent judges—in the 1940s and 1950s.

is thus a problem that is or should be of particular concern to chief judges because they're selected solely on the basis of seniority, without any regard for their leadership or management skills or experience, and are given next to no training for their new role—all of which may explain why chief judges are not always able to maintain collegiality among the judges of their courts.[14] It is an especially challenging problem for the Chief Justice because he's the administrative head of the entire federal judicial system, yet at the same time a full-time judge, which limits the time he can devote to administration. It's an unsolved problem. For example, the Supreme Court is famously backward in utilizing technology,[15] as backhandedly conceded in the Chief Justice's latest year-end report, in which he tries to excuse his Court's backwardness by asserting that "federal judges are stewards of a judicial system that has served the Nation effectively for more than two centuries. Like other centuries-old institutions, courts may have practices that seem archaic and inefficient—and some are. But others rest on traditions that embody intangible wisdom."[16] I can't find the wisdom, tangible or intangible, in the archaic and inefficient practices that persist in the Supreme Court, such as the placement of a spittoon beside each Justice's seat in the courtroom. The lower federal courts are ahead of the Supreme Court in utilization of technology; there is no excuse for the Court's lagging behind them.

Weaknesses in federal judicial administration at the macro level

14. See Virginia A. Hettinger, Stefanie A. Lindquist, and Wendy L. Martinek, "The Role and Impact of Chief Judges on the United States Courts of Appeals," 24 *Justice System Journal* 91, 100, 102, 111 (2003). In my experience, judicial collegiality is mainly a function of personality.

15. See, for example, Adam Liptak, "High Court, in Big Leap, Plans to Put Filings Online," *New York Times,* January 1, 2015, A12.

16. "[Chief Justice's] 2014 Year-End Report on the Federal Judiciary," www.supremecourt.gov/publicinfo/year-end/2014year-endreport.pdf.

are manifested in inadequate provision of training for newly appointed judges and of continuing training for the already appointed;
in a wasteful proliferation of committees of the Federal Judicial Conference; in the lack of an intelligent policy regarding the ownership of
and public access to judicial papers (electronic as well as hard copy) of
Supreme Court Justices and other federal judges; and in a distorted
system of staff allocation: the judges with the heaviest caseloads—the
trial judges (district judges, bankruptcy judges, tax judges, and magistrate judges)—are allocated the smallest staff and the judges with the
lightest caseloads—the Justices of the Supreme Court—the largest.[17]
The management problems at the judge level that I discussed in
the preceding section of this chapter appear to receive little if any attention from the Chief Justice or from the judiciary's central staff,
consisting of the personnel of the Administrative Office of the U.S.
Courts and the Federal Judicial Center.

In one day recently the *New York Times* took two swipes at the
management of the federal judiciary. In one a professor at the University of Chicago upbraided the Supreme Court for its failure to publish
reasons for the orders that it issues, as distinct from decisions.[18] The
Court issues thousands of orders every year. Most are denials of certiorari, and a brief explanation of the reason for the denial would
provide helpful guidance to future litigants considering whether to
ask for cert. Obviously the Justices don't have time to write (or even
supervise the writing of by staff) thousands of orders, but they could
explain at least the denials based on grounds applicable to a large
number of cases. Sometimes there are written dissents from orders,

17. On the ownership of and access to judicial papers, see note 16, and accompanying text, in the Introduction.
18. William Baude, "The Supreme Court's Secret Decisions: Each Year, It Issues
Thousands of Rulings with No Transparency," *New York Times,* February 3, 2015,
A21.

but it is hard to infer from a dissent the majority's unstated ground for its order.

The other swipe was delivered by the *Times*'s Supreme Court correspondent, Adam Liptak, and is only obliquely aimed at the Court, more directly at the Chief Justice.[19] He points out that as noted in section 2 of this chapter, most opinions of the federal courts nowadays are designated "unpublished" but that this just means they're not to be given any precedential effect. They can be referred to in a subsequent opinion, just as law review articles can be quoted or cited in judicial opinions, for insights that bolster a subsequent decision. But the mere fact that an unpublished opinion had decided an issue that recurred is not a ground for resolving the issue the same way in a later case. In short, an unpublished opinion can have value, but it has no authority.

The justification for this caponized form of opinion is that the federal judicial caseload is so heavy that judges don't have time to write careful opinions in all cases, and a careless opinion should not bind the future. I'll suggest in the last section of this chapter that the judicial caseload is not that heavy; and anyway few judges write "their" opinions any more. But Liptak offers a different reason for the popularity of the unpublished opinion, though it supplements rather than displaces the work-ethic explanation. It is that judges designate certain opinions "unpublished" because a decision that lacks precedential force is less likely to be overturned either by rehearing en banc by the court in which the decision was rendered or by the Supreme Court on certiorari. He illustrates with a seventeen-page Fourth Circuit decision—hardly a casual knock-off that the court might have felt too carelessly written to warrant precedential signifi-

19. "Courts Write Decisions That Elude Long View: Refusing to Set Precedent by Declining Formal Publication," *New York Times*, February 3, 2015, A10.

cance.[20] Lack of precedential force reduces the effect and hence importance of the decision. The court in which the decision was rendered knows that it won't block an opposite result in an identical future case, and the Supreme Court knows that the decision may well be overruled at the circuit level.

An alternative would be to make all decisions precedential. The judges would have to work harder, but not much harder. Most precedential decisions are written by law clerks; and while the writing of nonprecendential opinions tends to be delegated to staff attorneys instead of to law clerks, most staff attorneys are fully competent and can be instructed to be extra careful when they write an opinion because any opinion they write will be deemed a precedent.[21] The principal problem with making all decisions precedential would be the increased time cost of Westlaw or Lexis or other electronic searches of judicial output.

Unpublished opinions are an issue that needs to be addressed by the Chief Justice, as it concerns the entire federal judiciary.

Another example of problematic judicial macromanagement is the statutory seven-year term for all chief judges of circuit and district courts. Seven years is too long (though, thank goodness, the term is nonrenewable). The learning curve of a chief judge is shallow, because the power and duties of the position are quite limited. More frequent turnover would produce a few more managerial improvements by involving more judges in management. It would also make judges happier, which would in turn encourage greater collegiality. They would

---

20. *Plumley v. Austin,* 565 Fed. App'x 175 (4th Cir. April 7, 2014). Liptak calls it a "40-page" decision. He must be referring to the opinion as issued by the court; it is only seventeen pages in the Westlaw version that I am citing; still, that is a substantial opinion.

21. The depressed condition of the law-firm job market has helped to make the job of a federal staff attorney a coveted one.

be happier because being a chief judge confers a certain prestige even though appointment is as I said based solely on seniority, and also because the chief judge is the presiding and assigning judge in all cases in which he or she participates.[22] A five-year term for chief judges would certainly be adequate; three years might be optimal.

Examples of poor administration at the court of appeals level include an excessively high ratio of nonprecendential to precedential judicial opinions and the use of screening panels of judges to determine which cases shall be orally argued and which not, a process that takes significant judicial time, reduces the number of argued cases and so the amount of information that enters into the decisional process, and can create needless friction among judges. With regard to the first point, deciding whether an opinion shall be citable as precedent consumes time but more important falsely assumes that the precedential significance of a judicial opinion can be reliably determined when the opinion is issued. It is only later, maybe years later, that the opinion may turn out to guide the decision of a new case.

My court avoids the need for screening panels by making oral argument the default rule in all cases in which both sides are represented by counsel. If the opposing lawyers jointly ask us to waive oral argument we'll usually oblige them, but such requests are rare. Our circuit executive (the circuit's senior civil servant) allots the time for argument, depending usually on the complexity of the case, but the

22. Upon the office of the chief judge becoming vacant, whichever judge in active service—as distinct from a "senior judge" (see section 7 of this chapter, below) who has taken the first steps toward retirement and has fewer obligations than the active judges—has the most seniority but is not yet sixty five years old becomes chief judge automatically unless he declines the position, as some judges do. Upon reaching age seventy the chief judge must relinquish his post even if he hasn't served the full seven-year term because he was sixty-four when appointed. On the limited influence that most chief judges have on their colleagues, see Hettinger et al., note 14 above, at 100, 102, 111.

presiding judge can alter the allotted time. Pro se cases are referred to staff attorneys (who remember are law clerks hired by the court rather than by individual judges); the staff attorneys make recommendations to the judges for the disposition of the cases that they, the staff attorneys, handle. If the appeal has significant merit, the court often will appoint a lawyer to brief and argue the case for the appellant as an amicus curiae.

In fairness to the other circuits, my court has a lighter than average caseload; most of the courts of appeals could not make oral argument the default rule in all its counseled cases because it would consume too much of the judges' time. Nevertheless I consider insidious the growing practice (in force in the Fifth, Sixth, and Ninth Circuits —maybe others, but those three I know employ the practice), defended on grounds of workload pressure, of preassigning (usually by the presiding judge, sometimes by the chief judge) each case to one judge of the panel designated to hear it. The preassigned judge is responsible for distributing a bench memo—invariably written by one of his law clerks rather than by him—to the other judges before oral argument. This practice saves some judge (and law clerk) time, but can make a three-judge panel effectively a panel of one.

My sense is that circuit chief judges could do more than most of them are doing in regard to court management. A number of judges take a very long time to issue their judicial opinions. This is generally a result of poor staff management. Chief judges should be able to assist such judges to manage their staffs better. A retreat at which the judges would exchange information and suggestions concerning staff management might be useful.[23] Chief judges can and sometimes do help nudge into retirement district and circuit judges of their circuit who have reached their sell-by date as a result of the infirmities of age. And

23. As suggested in Wald, note 3 above, at 785.

they can and sometimes do play a constructive role in defusing conflicts between judges and, in general, improving collegiality and esprit de corps in their court.

The greatest obstacle to good management by chief judges, an obstacle probably insurmountable, is that like kings in hereditary monarchies chief judges are not chosen. They inherit the position, like an eldest son; for the appointment goes to the active judge (that is, a judge who has not taken senior status—see footnote 15 above) who is the "oldest" in judge years. It is an accident if the appointee happens to have management skills. Yet for the chief judge to be elected by the other judges of his court, as is done in some judicial systems, would be a mistake; it would lead to politicking and bitterness. Appointment by the President would lead to politicking too, and the appointments would often reflect a President's political preferences; and so with appointment by the Chief Justice of the United States. I don't have a solution to this problem.

The absence of a limit on the term of the Chief Justice is particularly problematic, as it is well known that CEOs, university presidents, and other high-level bosses tend after a long time in office to become ineffective—they accumulate enemies, are slow to adapt to change, and lose energy, interest, patience, and commitment. That is an argument for rotating the Chief Justiceship among the members of the Supreme Court every five years or so, as suggested to me by Geoffrey Stone. But it would probably require amending Article III, as it could not be presumed that after five years a Chief Justice is no longer meeting the standard of "good Behaviour."

A judicial macromanagement problem that as far as I know has received no attention from either the circuit chief judges or the Chief Justice is departures from randomization of circuit panel assignments. Except in the case of rehearings en banc, appeals in the federal courts of appeals are heard by panels of three judges picked (I had thought) at random. In my court, for example, a computer program assigns the judges randomly and also ensures that over a two-year period each judge will sit the same number of times with each other judge (except those senior judges who take a substantially reduced caseload). A recent article, however, employing sophisticated statistical methods, identifies four circuits—D.C., Second, Eighth, and Ninth—in which assignments are not random, but indeed appear to produce an ideological slant.[24]

Suppose a chief judge of a court of appeals is conservative, and likewise roughly half the other judges (the article uses, as proxies for conservative and liberal, whether the judge was appointed by a Republican or a Democratic President). Suppose the chief judge wants to maximize the number of conservative panel decisions. He would not want panels to be composed of three conservatives, because only two votes are required in order to decide a case heard by three judges, and so a third conservative vote would be wasted. Likewise he would want panels with a liberal majority to consist of three liberals, thus wasting a liberal vote. Hence one would expect in such a circuit that panels consisting of three conservative judges would be underrepresented and panels consisting of three liberal judges overrepresented and likewise panels in which two of the judges were conservative.

The authors of the article find, as illustrated below by comparing one of the random with one of the nonrandomizing courts, an apparent ideological skew in the latter courts:[25]

24. Adam S. Chilton and Marin K. Levy, "Challenging the Randomness of Panel Assignment in the Federal Courts of Appeals" (December 17, 2014), http://scholarship.law.duke.edu/cgi/viewcontent.cgi?article=6074&context=faculty_scholarship.

25. Id. at 46. Comparison between the other panels yields broadly similar results. See id. at 45–46.

Seventh Circuit:

0	Republicans	2	4
1	Republicans	63	65
2	Republicans	277	273
3	Republicans	267	268

Ninth Circuit:

0	Republicans	505	442
1	Republicans	900	999
2	Republicans	720	705
3	Republicans	176	155

The first column of numbers indicates the number of judges appointed by Republican Presidents on the actual panels in the court, and the second column the number of such judges there would be on the court's panels if panel assignments were indeed random. In the Seventh Circuit, which the authors found did not make nonrandom assignments, the numbers are almost identical (the numbers in the first row are too small for the 100 percent difference between them to be significant). In the Ninth Circuit, one of the courts that the authors found makes nonrandom assignments, there is an excess of panels on which there are no Republicans (hence no wasted Republican votes), a dearth of Republicans on panels with two Democrats (panels on which a Republican vote would be wasted), and an overrepresentation of panels with two Republicans, as expected if Republicans are favored in the panel assignments. The fact that there are more panels with three Republicans, which is nonoptimal from a Republican standpoint, is anomalous; but those are the fewest panels.

As the authors acknowledge, additional study of the nonrandomization that they find in almost a third of the courts of appeals (4/13) is needed—in particular, research is required on who is responsible in each of those courts for nonrandomization and what are the effects on the law.

Were there no ideological factors in judicial voting, nonrandomization would not be problematic—on the contrary, it would be desirable. Court of appeals judges vary widely in knowledge of specific areas of law and specific analytical and empirical techniques, and so one can imagine a system in which a judge's assignment to a panel would be based on the chief judge's assessment of the judge's competence to hear and vote on the cases to be argued on a particular day. The insistence on randomization evinces awareness that, as I emphasize throughout this book, there indeed are ideological influences in court of appeals' decision making (reluctant as the judiciary is to acknowledge this) and that those influences might impart an ideological bias to nonrandom assignment of judges to panels.

This is not to say that the departures from randomization that the authors of the article find *are* motivated by ideology. Some or all of them may be the unintended consequences of such ideologically innocent policies as wanting no more than one senior judge to sit on any panel, wanting some balance on all panels and therefore requiring that not all members of a panel have been appointed by a President of the same political party, or wanting to give junior judges an occasional opportunity to preside. But whatever the motivation, the ideological skew that appears to be created in some circuits is disturbing, and one would think would warrant the attention of the administrators of the federal judiciary, but is not, as far as I know, receiving any.

The nonrandomization problem is related to another problem of judicial management, which is the opacity of management at the court of appeals level.[26] Judges of a court of appeals are apt to know little about the management practices (such as use of screening panels, policy on whether to treat opinions as precedential, use of staff attorneys—and how panel assignments are made) of other courts of ap-

---

26. See Marin K. Levy, "The Mechanics of Federal Appeals: Uniformity and Case Management in the Circuit Courts," 61 *Duke Law Journal* 315 (2011).

peals. One would have thought that such information would be centrally collected (by the Administrative Office of the U.S. Courts or the Federal Judicial Center) and distributed to all court of appeals judges, and that the AO or FJC would derive a set of "best management practices" to recommend or at least disseminate to all the courts of appeals. That these things are not done is a testament to the weakness of what I am calling federal judicial macromanagement.

I hinted earlier that the Supreme Court itself does not appear to be terribly well managed. I have long been puzzled by the interval now of about five years between the issuance of a Supreme Court decision and its publication in *U.S. Reports,* the official edition of the Court's decisions. If there are discrepancies between the copy of the case in *U.S. Reports* and copies in other judicial reporters, such as the *Supreme Court Reporter,* the copy in *U.S. Reports* governs. What has only recently become widely known (it was news to me) is that during this long interval the Justices will sometimes make substantive changes in an opinion with little in the way of public notice.[27] Future litigants may have the rug pulled out from under them by such changes, though apparently that happens very rarely.

Besides the inexplicable interval between initial issuance and final, authoritative product, Supreme Court opinions tend to be of inordinate length, and the Court's insistence that all its opinions be issued by the last day of the term results in a bunching of opinions and creates the impression that Supreme Court Justices are unwilling to work during the summer or perhaps want to reduce the number of days on which their cases are discussed, often critically, in the media.[28]

There are two types of bunching, both bad. One, call it pure

27. See Adam Liptak, "Final Word on U.S. Law Isn't: Supreme Court Keeps Editing," *New York Times,* May 25, 2014, A1.
28. See Lee Epstein, William M. Landes, and Richard A Posner, "The Best for Last: The Timing of U.S. Supreme Court Decisions," 64 *Duke Law Journal* 101 (2015).

bunching, is that whenever the case was argued, if it's decided at the end of the term it means the Justices were also working on other cases, and this crowding should reduce quality. The other type, call it temporal bunching, hypothesizes that the shorter the interval between argument and end-of-term decision, the worse written an opinion is likely to be.

The end-of-term deadline goes back I believe to the late 1930s, when Chief Justice Hughes imposed it in order to counter complaints that the Justices were too elderly to complete their work in timely fashion. Three-quarters of a century later it's time to abandon the rule. The Court hears cases through about mid-April and ends the term at the end of June, thus allowing only about two and a half months for the nine Justices to hash out an opinion or more likely a series of opinions (majority, concurring, dissenting) in each case argued in April, whereas the deadline for deciding a case argued at the beginning of October is nine months. That makes no sense. When you have a court with nine members all eager to be involved in the important cases, quality will suffer with an arbitrary tight deadline. The Court could fix the deadline for all decisions at September 1, or have a sliding schedule of deadlines that would give the Court the same amount of time for deciding cases whenever the cases happened to be argued.

The problems of the Supreme Court that I've just been describing are not problems of the courts of appeals. In my court, and I assume the other courts of appeals, occasionally a substantive change will be made by court order shortly after the issuance of an opinion but never, so far as I am aware, after the opinion has been published in the bound volumes of the *Federal Reporter, 3d series;* and that will be within a few months after the opinion is issued. Our opinions are on average shorter than the Supreme Court's and there is no deadline for issuance. The judges can take their time checking an opinion for errors before rather than after issuing it. The Supreme Court's artificial end-of-term deadline for issuing its opinions amplifies the risk of error.

It might seem that the Court's opinions would *have* to be longer than the courts of appeals' opinions because the Supreme Court deals with the more difficult and momentous cases. But the Court rarely agrees to decide more than one or two issues presented by the cases it hears. And the fact that it's the final stop for a case means that the opinion could be more summary and less larded with citations to precedents than a court of appeals' opinion. Could be, but isn't. The Court's opinions tend to be verbose, in part perhaps because the ratio of law clerks to opinions is so high and in part perhaps to convey an impression of scholarship, rigor, and thoroughness in order to confound critics who argue that the Court is too political in its decision making.

The Court's management problems stem in large part from the substantial ideological component in its decision making. For that makes politicization of the appointment process inevitable, and the result is that there are few outstanding appointments even though when there's a vacancy the President has a pool of a million lawyers to choose from. Between the appointment of Oliver Wendell Holmes in 1902 and the death of Robert Jackson in 1954 there was always at least one great Supreme Court Justice: sometimes more than one (Brandeis and Holmes, Brandeis and Cardozo—who replaced Holmes—and Hughes). But since 1954? Competent, influential Justices, galore, but great? Maybe it's too early to tell.

The last Chief Justice who assumed the position with a rich background of experience in leadership and management was Charles Evans Hughes—his c.v. included former law professor, law firm partner, Governor of New York, Associate Justice of the U.S. Supreme Court, Presidential candidate, Secretary of State, and member of the Court of International Justice. But he retired as Chief Justice in 1941, three-quarters of a century ago. William Howard Taft—the twenty-seventh

President of the United States—was the only other Chief Justice with a preappointment c.v. comparable to Hughes'. Presidents seem no longer to consider management experience or leadership ability in picking a Chief Justice.

But here is the remarkable thing about the Supreme Court—a testament to poor management, and to the politicization of the appointments process. When I think back to the 1960s, when I was a clerk to a Supreme Court Justice for one year (the 1962 term) and later (1965–1967) an assistant to the Solicitor General, I am struck by the poverty of the Court's resources then compared to what they are now—yet by a sense that its much greater resources at present have not improved it. Each Justice now has four law clerks; in the 1962 term each had just two (except the Chief Justice, who had a third law clerk to process the pro se petitions for certiorari). And rarely these days is a clerk hired who has not clerked for a federal court of appeals judge; often the clerk will have had several years of professional experience before he becomes a Supreme Court clerk. The clerks in the early 1960s were often hired directly from law school (as I was, for example). The clerks were good—some were excellent—but the average quality was inferior to what it is today; the job was less coveted, there was no signing bonus, and the Justices tended to be more casual about the appointments process, often delegating the appointment to a law professor, a personal friend, or a professional acquaintance, without interviewing the clerk candidate or even receiving an application. There was of course no electronic research back then. There also was no cert. pool; no organized Supreme Court bar; and, dramatically unlike today, the Justices asked very few questions at the oral arguments—and this despite the fact that the standard amount of time allotted for argument to each side was forty-five minutes rather than the current thirty minutes. And yet, despite everything, the Court heard twice as many cases as it does now. Probably the Justices also worked harder in those days, since the celebrity culture had not yet embraced them. Indeed, with the exception of Douglas, they were wallflowers. (Black like Douglas had charisma, but did not cut a public figure.)

The members of the Court back then, in order of appointment, were Black, Douglas, Clark, Warren, Harlan, Stewart, Brennan, Goldberg, and White. There were some dim bulbs, but Black, Douglas, and White were extremely smart (though Douglas was irresponsible), and Harlan, Stewart, and Brennan were thoroughly competent. The professional backgrounds of the Justices were far more diverse than those of any of the current Justices. Black had been a successful trial lawyer and influential Senator; Douglas a prominent "realist" law professor at Yale and head of the Securities and Exchange Commission; Warren a three-term governor of California, his first term being during World War II. Clark had been U.S. Attorney General in the Truman Administration; Brennan had had a distinguished career as a private practitioner, as a military administrator during World War II, and as a state trial judge and state supreme court justice in New Jersey at a time when the Jersey judiciary, under the leadership of Chief Justice Arthur Vanderberg, was outstanding; Goldberg had been Secretary of Labor in the Kennedy Administration, and White Deputy Attorney General in that Administration. There was greater educational diversity as well. Two Justices had graduated from Harvard, two from Yale, and two from Columbia, and one each from the University of Texas, the University of Alabama, and Berkeley. In contrast, all the present Justices attended law school at either Harvard or Yale, though Ginsburg spent a year at (and graduated from) Columbia.

The 1962 term was the term in which Whittaker and Frankfurter were replaced by White and Goldberg, consolidating the "Warren Court," which persisted with only one change in membership (the replacement of Goldberg by Fortas in 1965, which was not an ideological change) until Warren's retirement in 1969 and his replacement by Warren Burger. The Warren Court went overboard in a number of areas, but most of its landmark decisions, dealing with such issues as reapportionment, the right to counsel, the application of the Fourth Amendment to the states, the *Miranda* warnings, and sexual rights have survived to this day. It seems unlikely that the current Court will have a comparable legacy, despite what might appear to be its vastly greater resources and vastly superior working conditions.

I believe that the average quality of the Justices back then was slightly higher than that of the current Justices, that the current Justices are overstaffed, talk too much at oral argument, and devote excessive time to extrajudicial activities, but that what made the earlier Court better despite its meager resources by current standards was mainly the diversity in the Justices' professional backgrounds. Today, judged by educational and professional backgrounds, and despite pronounced ideological differences, the Justices are peas in a pod.

4. Managing the federal judicial system as a whole. I touched on this issue in the preceding section of this chapter but it needs to be considered at greater length. The federal judiciary is decentralized; the thirteen circuits have a good deal of autonomy, as do the federal judicial districts within them. Nevertheless the judiciary is formally a hierarchical organization presided over by the Chief Justice of the United States. He sits atop a bureaucracy that consists mainly of the Administrative Office of the U.S. Courts and the Federal Judicial Center, a training and research organization that because of its quasi-academic character I defer discussion of to Chapter 6. There is also a quasi-legislative body over which the Chief Justice presides: the Judicial Conference of the United States, consisting of the chief judge of, and one district judge from, each of the thirteen circuits. The Judicial Conference is assisted in turn by numerous committees consisting of federal judges, with staff assistance supplied by the Administrative Office.

The absence of management skills and experience in Chief Justice Hughes' successors shows, for example, in the weaknesses of the

Federal Judicial Center (the Chief Justice is the chairman *ex officio* of the Center's board of directors), which I discuss in Chapter 6, and in the cumbersome committee structure of the Judicial Conference. There are too many committees, they are too large, and too many of the members lack relevant expertise in their committee's work. It shows also in recent Chief Justices' seeming lack of interest in the rest of the federal judiciary. (Chief Justice Burger was an exception.)[29] For example, at any moment there are poor collegial relations in several of the courts of appeals (see section 2 above), and mainly though not only in those courts, judges who are unconscionably slow in turning out opinions. These are problems that a Chief Justice could readily solve in face-to-face conversation with the judges who cause such problems. (Federal judges kowtow to the Chief Justice whatever their personal opinion of him.) But I don't believe such conversations occur. One has the impression that modern Chief Justices are interested only in the Supreme Court and think it a sufficient discharge of their duties to the rest of the federal judiciary to ask Congress from time to time to give federal judges a raise. The Chief Justice appoints a Justice for each circuit to be that circuit's Circuit Justice, but as far as I know Circuit Justices usually play only a nominal role in their assigned circuit.

5. *Work ethic.* Some federal judges do not work very hard, and for reasons unrelated to age or infirmity. It's not so much that they don't put in the hours; it's that they tend to treat the job as a civil service sinecure and duck the intellectual challenges that face a federal judge. The "they" I am talking about are fortunately a minority of federal judges; most work hard and many very hard (even too hard). But

---

29. See Edward A. Tamm and Paul C. Reardon, "The Office of Chief Justice: Warren E. Burger and the Administration of Justice," in *Judges on Judging: Views from the Bench* 113 (David M. O'Brien ed. 1997).

whether in academia, in civil services, or in the judiciary, secure lifetime tenure is bound to create a deficiency in work ethic for some of the tenure holders. The combination of secure lifetime tenure with uniform salaries within each tier of the federal judiciary and with ability to delegate a great deal of judicial work to eager young staff creates a recipe for a judge to take it easy while appearing to the outside world (even to his colleagues) to be fully engaged. Court of appeals judges may be more vulnerable to this temptation than legislators and high-ranking executive branch officials, because they don't have to play an active role in public. They can choose to ask no questions at oral arguments (notoriously the practice of Justice Thomas) and thereby avoid being exposed as unprepared or over the hill. Trial judges can't hide as easily because they have to make oral rulings in the course of trials. Still, it's difficult to imagine alternatives to life tenure that wouldn't encourage early retirement (when you're still a desirable hire, but won't be for long even when you'll want to continue working after your judicial career ends) and consequent preoccupation with private-sector jobs, a preoccupation likely to distract and maybe even bias a judge.

6. *Foot dragging.* A common consequence of a weak judicial work ethic is the indifference of some judges to expedition in the disposition of their cases. A case can languish for years at the district court level for lack of strict supervision by the judge presiding over the case, while at the court of appeals level there are judges who will sometimes (even often) allow a year or more to elapse between the argument of a case and the issuance of their opinion deciding it. Some judges are slow or inefficient or simply incapable of managing even a moderate caseload. But others seem not even to realize that there are costs to the litigants, and to the legal system as a whole, of protracted delay in deciding cases. Decisions disseminate valuable information to litigants, potential litigants, and other judges. The later

the decision and thus its dissemination, the less value the decision produces.

7. Overstaying their welcome. Not being subject to compulsory retirement, and able to delegate much of their work to staff, federal judges sometimes fail to retire even when old age and its related ills have greatly impaired their judicial performance. To be blunt, there is a problem of judicial senility and it is growing with the general increase in the longevity of the American population. The problem is alleviated though not solved by the ingenious institution of the "senior" judgeship, a managerial coup for the federal judiciary, requiring qualification of my criticisms of federal judicial management. Because it is so difficult to force federal judges to retire, a carrot has been substituted for a stick. Upon reaching age sixty-five with at least fifteen years as an Article III judge, or age seventy with at least ten years, a judge can either retire at full pay or, also without a reduction in pay, continue as a "senior judge," essentially hearing as many or as few cases as he wants. Semiretirement at full pay is an attractive option and most of the eligible judges exercise it, though often not until a few years after they reach the eligibility date. There are certain limitations on senior judges, however, of which the one most pertinent to the work-ethic problem is that the chief judge of the circuit can deny a senior judge the right to hear cases (in effect forcing him to retire, though at full pay). The judge can, however, appeal the denial to the circuit's judicial conference, which consists of a subset of the active as distinct from the senior judges, usually drawn from both the court of appeals and the district courts of the circuit but with a preponderance of the former.

The chief judge of one of the circuits once toyed with the idea of requiring every senior judge to take a mental test administered by a leading hospital; if he flunked, he would be forbidden to continue hearing cases (of course his pay would not be diminished). The idea was dropped, for several reasons of which the most potent was that it would discourage judges from taking senior status. A chief judge has no authority to deprive an active judge of his right to hear cases; and so by remaining an active judge (as a judge can elect to do regardless of his age), a judge eligible for senior status would escape having to take the mental test. Discouraging judges from taking senior status thus would actually exacerbate the problem of judicial senility.[30]

8. Excessive travel by judges. Except for the D.C. and Federal Circuits, each circuit covers a multistate territory. The offices of many federal court of appeals judges, and of many lawyers who practice in federal circuit courts, are hundreds of miles from the courthouse or courthouses in which the court of appeals hears argument. The result is that many lawyers and judges waste a good deal of time (in the case of the lawyers their clients' money, in the case of the judges federal taxpayers' money) in traveling to and from court. This waste could easily be avoided by permitting distant lawyers and judges to participate in oral argument by video. Videoconferencing techniques have advanced to a point at which participation in a conference (including a judges' postargument conference), or in an appellate argument, by video is a perfectly good substitute for physical presence and a big time- and money-saver. Some federal courts (and many more federal agencies) have at last begun to implement this approach.[31]

30. Remember that there is at present no way to force an Article III judge to retire because of disability except impeachment (see text in Chapter 1 of this book at footnote 3), but if a judge is certified to be disabled an additional judge can be appointed to his court beyond the number otherwise authorized by statute. 28 U.S.C. § 372(b). Congress would be reluctant to impeach a judge because of disability, as impeachment carries the connotation of punishment, and senility is a misfortune rather than a crime.

31. See Center for Legal & Court Technology, "Best Practices for Using Video Teleconferencing for Hearings and Related Proceedings" (Draft Report to the Administrative Conference of the United States, October 8, 2014), www.acus.gov/sites/default/files/documents/Draft_Best%20Practices%20Video%20Hearings_10-09-14_1.pdf.

9. Are federal judges overworked? In a word, no. This may be my biggest heresy. The "crushing" workload of federal judges is a given in judicial and academic circles. Has not Justice Alito described the "crushing" workload of federal court of appeals judges as one of the greatest problems of the federal judiciary?[32] Federal caseloads have indeed increased a good deal since the 1950s, and while the number of federal judges has also increased, the average number of appeals heard by a federal court of appeals judge has increased more than fourfold, from 73 appeals to 329.[33] Judges and law professors alike argue that the result has been excessive though unavoidable delegation of judicial work to staff (law clerks and staff attorneys, primarily), a sharp decline in the percentage of appeals in which oral argument is allowed, a precipitate decline in the number of judicial opinions accorded precedential effect ("published" versus "unpublished opinions," discussed earlier in this chapter), and a damaging shrinkage in the amount of time that judges can devote to research, reflection, and discussion with colleagues. The overall result, these critics contend, is a reduction in the quality of justice meted out by the federal courts. A variety of cures is suggested, such as substantially increasing the number of federal judges and the size and quality of staff.[34]

The problem appears to be exaggerated; in part through utilization of senior and visiting judges, the busiest federal courts of appeals should be able to handle their caseload without undue delay or strain. And certainly the last thing the federal judiciary needs is

32. Marin K. Levy, "Judging Justice on Appeal" (review of William M. Richman and William L. Reynolds, *Injustice on Appeal: The United States Courts of Appeals in Crisis* [2012]), 123 *Yale Law Journal* 2386, 2388 (2014).

33. Id. at 2388 and n. 4.

34. The entire subject is thoroughly reviewed in Professor Levy's review, note 32 above.

more judges and more staff, to complicate the management of an institution that is poorly managed. Federal appellate judges, including Supreme Court Justices, do not have crushing workloads, because those courts that have heavy caseloads delegate more of the work on the cases to staff than courts with lighter caseloads do, or (though not the Supreme Court) rely more heavily on visiting judges.

One reason the workload is perceived as "crushing" by some (perhaps many) judges is that many federal judges want to do a lot of things besides hear and decide cases. They want to travel, judge moot courts, be lionized by their local bar association, serve on committees of the Judicial Conference of the United States or of their local judicial conference or of their court. Supreme Court Justices are celebrities with many opportunities to preen and prance. Chief judges often take a reduced caseload. Some court of appeals judges have to travel a distance to the city in which their court sits, owing to the unwillingness of most of the courts to allow judges to participate in oral argument, postargument conferences, and court meetings by video. Some spend a lot of time recruiting, managing, socializing with, and occasionally tormenting their law clerks. Some nitpick their colleagues' opinion drafts. Some are procrastinators.

Not much can be done about these drains, at worst frivolous, on judicial time, but I also don't see any evidence that the performance of the federal judiciary as a whole has deteriorated since the 1950s. I think the average quality of judges is actually higher now than it was then and that most of them work somewhat harder than their predecessors—including on their strictly judicial work.

10. Congressional intervention? Senator Grassley of Iowa has since 2009 been trying to persuade Congress to create an Inspector General for the federal judiciary, who would be appointed by the Chief Justice after consultation with congressional leaders; and the proposal may be gathering momentum.[35] The role envisaged for such an official by Senator Grassley is that of a "watchdog" concerned with judicial misconduct, but one could easily imagine the job description being changed to general manager of the judiciary—a role most Chief Justices are reluctant to play.

35. National Constitution Center, *Constitution Daily: Smart Conversation from the National Constitution Center,* Lyle Denniston, "Constitution Check: Do the Supreme Court and Other Federal Courts Need a Watchdog?" May 28, 2015, http://blog.constitutioncenter.org/2015/05/constitution-check-do-the-supreme-court-and-other-federal-courts-need-a-watchdog/.

II | THE ACADEMY TO THE RESCUE?

4 | THE CONTRIBUTION OF SCHOLARSHIP

I HAVE DISCUSSED the deficiencies of the judiciary at such length in Part One in an effort to convince readers who are or aspiring to be law school professors that the judicial system really needs help; how much it will get, in light of the current culture and structure of the legal academy, is an open question. I know that judicial psychology, behavior, and management can't be the principal foci of the law schools. It is no accident that Part Two of this book, which this chapter kicks off, is much shorter than Part One. The academy can't solve anywhere near all the problems that beset the federal judiciary. But given the importance of the federal judiciary to the functioning of the American legal system, the judiciary as an institution (as distinguished from its legal-doctrinal output) should be receiving a good deal more attention from the academy than it is.

So this part of the book is devoted to constructive suggestions aimed at law schools and law professors, beginning in this chapter with thoughts on how legal scholarship might better contribute to the improvement of the judiciary and moving in the following two chapters to changes in the law school curriculum and in the structure and methods of continuing judicial education that might contribute to that improvement.

Now it might seem that there is no need for such a chapter—that all that I need to say is that law professors should attack the problems of the judiciary that I flagged in Chapters 2 and 3. But attack how?

That is not obvious; the last part of this chapter will suggest a novel mode of attack—namely collaborative research between law professors and judges. Some other novel responses to the problems flagged in the earlier chapters will also be discussed.

I begin, however, by addressing the objection that the academy is already doing all that can or needs to be done in this domain by criticizing (occasionally praising) specific legal doctrines and judicial decisions, albeit with disproportionate emphasis on the Supreme Court. The Justices are less likely than other judges to pay attention to scholarly—to any—criticisms, believing that no one not a Supreme Court Justice could understand the Court, or that the Court's critics are motivated by envy or political disagreement, or that to accept criticism would signal weakness and impair the Court's prestige and with it its power. Nevertheless there have been periods in which academic thinking has influenced the Court (think of the impact of economic analysis on the Court's antitrust jurisprudence beginning in the 1960s), or at least has furnished it with politically charged fighting words ("originalism" and "textualism," for example), though there is suspicion that the Justices choose to adopt only those scholarly suggestions that confirm their priors.

But this is not one of those periods. The abstract character of "constitutional theory" as practiced in the modern academy has diminished its impact. And because the Supreme Court decisions that attract the most scholarly commentary are also the most political, and academics are more outspoken than they used to be (for ours is not a decorous era), the scholarly commentary has a large political element as well. The liberal law professors face off against the conservative ones, paralleling the split in the Court itself. Constitutional scholars form a kind of shadow Supreme Court, albeit one largely ignored by the real one.

The problem is less that the Court receives disproportionate attention from academics (though it does) than that it receives attention of the wrong kind. The focus is on particular decisions rather than on the Court's structure, method, character, and personnel or on the administration (or lack thereof) of the entire federal judiciary by the Chief Justice. Those systemic or institutional issues are neglected by the academy, yet they are areas of acute need and ones in which the Court could be expected to be more responsive to academic proposals, because the issues are not highly charged politically. No doubt many of the Court's institutional deficiencies are inherent in the concept of a supreme court, especially a supreme *constitutional* court, as our Supreme Court largely is (weighting number of cases by their impact on the legal system and the larger society), and in the nature of the American political system. For example it's an unavoidable consequence of caseload pressures that the Justices have to select the cases they'll decide—the Court can't decide ten thousand cases a year, which is the approximate annual number of petitions for certiorari filed. But whether they are going about the process of selection in the right way—whether their screening machinery, very heavily reliant on law clerks, is optimal—is a promising subject for academic research.

The Supreme Court's high visibility and the unavoidably discretionary character of most of its decisions (and not only in constitutional cases) cause the Justices to deny emphatically the ideological element in their judicial votes. The validity of the denial is an important issue and requires additional academic attention. Academics of the legal realism movement of the 1920s and 1930s, and of the critical legal studies movement that flourished in the 1970s, insisted that ideology played a central role in judicial decisions at all levels. They— the "crits" especially—exaggerated when they generalized their criticisms to all courts—exaggerated to a point at which they were seen as a residue of 1960s-style infantile leftism. Eventually they became a laughing-stock, imploded, and vanished with few traces.[1] But legal realism, acknowledged or not, outlived the legal-realism movement, and political scientists became influential students of the ideological element in judicial decisions—an element that many of today's legal academics continue to downplay. I'm surprised that the very liberal law professor David Cole should say that "it's much more likely that the Justices are guided by their best understandings of the law, filtered by their basic legal perspectives, rather than by short-term partisan or political interests."[2] It's a confused statement. What is "the law" that the Justices are assumed to be offering their best understandings of? The Constitution? Most of the constitutional provisions that get dragged into litigation that reaches the Supreme Court provide no guidance on how to decide today's constitutional cases. And how are "best understandings" of the law "filtered" by a judge's "basic legal perspectives," and what does that phrase mean? Notice too the awkward antithesis of "best understandings of the law" and "short-term partisan or political interests," which leaves open the possibility that the Justices' "best understandings" are actually their long-term partisan or political interests—and how is a judicial decision less partisan or political if it is guided by long-term rather than short-term political preferences? Or does Cole think (maybe he does) that "best un-

---

1. "Another of my professors [at Harvard Law School], the radical Duncan Kennedy, who was so prominent and respected among law professors that he was called the 'Pope' of the 'Critical Legal Studies' movement, advocated rotating the law professors and the janitors into each others' jobs. (The janitors liked the idea of being paid like law professors, but had no interest in teaching law, and thought Kennedy's idea was flaky)." Hans Bader, "What Left-Wing Law Professors Really Think about You, and the Role of Lawyers," *Competitive Enterprise Institute,* April 3, 2012, https://cei.org/blog/what-left-wing-law-professors-really-think-about-you-and-role-lawyers.

2. Cole, "The Anti-Court Court," *New York Review of Books,* August 14, 2014, 10, 12.

derstandings" of the law are statesmanlike political forecasts? And finally what are his sources?

Cole is right to point out that conservative Justices don't *always* vote conservatively or liberal ones *always* liberally. But that doesn't mean that ideology is absent from, as distinct from occasionally muted in, Supreme Court decision making. A Justice might occasionally vote contrary to his ideological views in order to be able to argue with at least minimum plausibility that he or she is not an ideologue, as Justice Scalia has argued by pointing to his votes in the flag-burning cases.[3] Or a Justice might vote in some cases contrary to his ideological preferences because his other priors overrode ideology in those cases. One can be influenced by ideology without being an ideologue through and through, and one can also be an ideologue through and through yet not conform to any of the reigning ideologies; one can be an Ayn Rand libertarian, a Scientologist, an anarcho-capitalist, a socialist, an isolationist.

Cole's apparent denial of the ideological element in Supreme Court decisions is surprising but not atypical. Criticism of the Court by academics tends to be muted, whether out of respect for the Court's place in the judicial hierarchy, belief in the Court's indispensability and concern for its vulnerability to political attack, or fear that the Justices will not hire as law clerks students of the Justices' critics. There is an argument for a shift of academic emphasis to the lower courts. Lower court judges are more likely to be responsive to academic criticisms and suggestions, if properly focused and packaged (to be intelligible to judges) than the grandees of the Supreme Court—

---

3. Antonin Scalia and Bryan A. Garner, *Reading Law: The Interpretation of Legal Texts* 17 (2012). The example is an odd one. The notion that burning the American flag is a form of free speech within the *original* meaning of the Constitution seems preposterous, hence inconsistent with the "originalist" approach to constitutional interpretation that Justice Scalia advocates and claims to follow.

and academics don't have to tiptoe as lightly in criticizing lower court judges.

As for academic attention to individual judges as distinct from courts, Justices receive significant though often rather muted critique. Academic research into the workings of the lower federal courts focuses less on individual judges than on doctrines and decisions, and that is a shame because it is important that the legal profession understand those judges. They are the judges with whom law school graduates who become litigators will have much more frequent contact than they do (all but a tiny handful) with the Supreme Court.

I thus would like to see a shift in academic emphasis from critique of particular decisions and doctrines to critique of particular judges, and of judging, below the level of the Supreme Court. But it needs to be *systemic* critique. The federal judiciary is a system, with many moving parts. Not many scholars are interested in it as a system. One of those moving parts, as we saw in Appendix C to Chapter 2, is supervised release, a subsystem of federal criminal law that is administered by district judges with limited oversight by the courts of appeals and the Supreme Court—so limited as to constitute inexcusable neglect of a malfunctioning system now entering its second quarter-century that has inflicted gratuitous hardship on a large number of criminal defendants with few benefits to society to show for it. Yet it has received very little academic attention. For example, a forty-four-page empirical article on the sentencing guidelines by a pair of distinguished law professors does not mention supervised release.[4]

That article has a further relevance to this chapter: it illustrates the proclivity of law professors to propose reforms that are unrealistic. The authors (repeating a proposal they had made in an earlier article) want

---

4. Max M. Schanzenbach and Emerson H. Tiller, "Reviewing the Sentencing Guidelines: Judicial Politics, Empirical Evidence, and Reform," 75 *University of Chicago Law Review* 715 (2008).

court of appeals panels that review criminal sentences to be politically diverse and thus to contain at least one judge appointed by a Republican President and at least one appointed by a Democratic President.[5] The obvious objections are that equalizing caseload across a court's judges would be impossible unless the number of judges appointed by each type of President was identical, that liberal judges are sometimes appointed by Republican Presidents and conservative judges sometimes appointed by Democratic ones (or their political ideology shifts over what may be a long tenure as a judge), and that judges often are conservative in some areas of law and liberal in others. A more subtle objection, pointed out by Judge Patricia Wald, is that the proposal if adopted would make judges more partisan. The member of the panel who had been appointed a judge by a Democratic President (say), the other two members of the panel having been appointed by Republican Presidents, would be more likely to think of himself as the designated Democratic representative on the panel, expected therefore to uphold Democratic Party values.[6] Otherwise what would be the point of requiring what the proponents themselves call a "split partisan arrangement"?[7]

There have been influential academic contributions to law at the system level. An example is the uniform codes, notably but not only the Uniform Commercial Code. Not all such contributions have been successful; in my opinion at least, the academic reshaping of conflict of laws, though it has had an enormous influence on state law, has made conflict of laws doctrine far more complex than it was or that it should be, in part by replacing the common law principles with vague multifactor tests. The huge academic literature on statutory and constitutional interpretation seems to me another bust. And there

5. Id. at 745–747.
6. Patricia M. Wald, "A Response to Tiller and Cross," 99 *Columbia Law Review* 235, 255 (1999).
7. Schanzenbach and Tiller, note 4 above, at 746.

have been excellent bodies of academic research, such as research on jury comprehension (some cited in Chapter 2), that seem somehow not to be able to penetrate the judicial consciousness. My abiding sense is that system-level legal academic research has dwindled except in fields that economic analysis can reshape. I can't think of a better subject for systemic academic legal research than supervised release— except possibly judicial management.

With regard to understanding and evaluating individual judges as distinct from the judicial system and its subsystems, it is natural to look to biography. But biographies of lower court judges are few and far between because biographies take so long to research and write and because the interest of the public in such judges is slight. I am told that David Dorsen's superb biography (mentioned in previous chapters of this book) of Henry Friendly, a genuinely great judge of the modern era, has had only modest sales.[8] A feasible alternative is the critical study of a judge, such as my short book on Cardozo (versus Andrew Kaufman's massive tome, thorough, accurate, and authoritative though it is—744 pages to my 156 pages).[9] Such books, which dispense with most biographical detail (and so might be regarded as the distant descendants of Plutarch's *Lives*), are remarkably, and lamentably, rare, and likewise article-length versions. Indeed, academic critique of lower court judges is close to nonexistent, and though there are more judges and more law professors today than in the past it may even be declining.[10]

8. David M. Dorsen, *Henry Friendly: Greatest Judge of His Era* (2012).
9. See Richard A. Posner, *Cardozo: A Study in Reputation* (1990); Andrew L. Kaufman, *Cardozo* (1998). Of course Cardozo served on the Supreme Court, but the longer and more creative part of his judicial career was spent on the New York Court of Appeals.
10. An excellent though dated critical study of federal lower court judges is Marvin Schick, *Learned Hand's Court* (1970).

Also rare is critique, at once individual and systemic, of the structure of judicial opinions (as distinct from their content)—of elements such as length (inordinate) and style (lame, colorless, jargon-ridden, smothered in nonobvious abbreviations,[11] neglectful that the goal of writing should be "simplification to the language of natural speech"[12]), factual accuracy, breadth and imaginativeness of research, the weight that a court of appeals gives to a trial court's or administrative agency's opinion, the give and take of oral argument (how reflected in the opinion), judges' reliance on lawyers' briefs, timeliness in deciding cases, the candor of judicial opinions (to what extent do they reflect the judges' actual thinking?), the embrace or rejection of jar-

---

11. The *Bluebook* is a major villain here, prescribing endless nonobvious abbreviations, as if there were an acute paper shortage in the United States. (Try this one on for size—*Bluebook* abbreviations of words beginning with *s*:

School[s]	Sch.
Science	Sci.
Secretary	Sec'y
Securit[y, ies]	Sec.
Service	Serv.
Shareholder	S'holder
Social	Soc.
Society	Soc'y
South[ern]	S.
Southwest[ern]	Sw.
Steamship[s]	S.S.
Street	St.
Subcommittee	Subcomm.
Surety	Sur.
System[s]	Sys.

No word or name should ever be abbreviated in a judicial opinion if a nontrivial fraction of the intended audience for the opinion would not understand the abbreviation—and might as a result not even know who the parties to a cited opinion were.

12. T. S. Eliot, "Poetry and Drama," in *Selected Prose of T. S. Eliot* 132, 147 (Frank Kermode ed. 1975).

gon (are opinions written to be understood by nonlawyers and why or why not?), the adequacy of the real-world context in which the opinion situates the case (and, closely related, an opinion's reliance on reliable data and responsible scholarship, nonlegal as well as legal), an opinion's brevity and clarity, its rhetorical effectiveness, its authenticity, culture, and "voice," its fidelity to the trial record, and finally the length of time between the assignment of the preparation of the majority opinion to a member of the panel that heard the case (the assignment usually is made right after oral argument) and the issuance of the decision.

Judicial opinions are the principal output of appellate judges. And as I keep saying, the opinions are on average not well written at all. There is plenty of good advice to be found in books and articles about how to write a good judicial opinion, but the advice is not heeded. The reason may be that the authors of such books and articles, though competent (none more so than Bryan Garner, for example), are not prominent academics (Garner is not an academic at all). They do not speak with authority. And maybe they speak at too great length to hold the judges' attention.

The cause may be hopeless; neither the judges nor the law clerks may wish to break the traditional mold. But it would be helpful I think if some prominent academic would boil down the principles of good judicial opinion writing to its barest bones, perhaps as follows:

Good judicial opinion writing requires:

1. No jargon.
2. No footnotes.
3. Forget citation form—just make sure every citation will enable the reader to find the cited item.
4. Delete every superfluous word. Make sure that every word, every sentence, *everything* in the opinion does useful work.

5. Use adverbs and adjectives sparingly.

6. Avoid section headings (sectioning an opinion is bound to lengthen it unnecessarily).

7. Be grammatical, but not fussy (do not, on pain of expulsion from the legal profession, ever look at the *Chicago Manual of Style*). Do not, for example, fuss about grammarians' "rules" for placement of commas; place commas where they will help the reader understand what you're saying.

8. Brevity is the soul of wit, all right, but be sure you don't leave out of the opinion anything the reader may need in order to understand what the case is about and why you are deciding it as you are. It's remarkable how many judicial opinions are simultaneously overlong and incomplete.

9. Be candid as well as truthful. Tell the reader the real reason for the outcome.

No doubt these rules are easier to state than to follow. Many judges are appointed from managerial positions (so why are they so often such poor managers of their tiny judicial staffs? I have no idea) in law firms or government legal offices (usually a U.S. Attorney's office), and as a result haven't done much writing, or even editing, for a long time. What they don't realize is, as I keep saying, that if they wrote dozens of opinions a year they'd quickly become experienced writers. The extensive academic literature on how to write a good judicial opinion has had negligible effects on opinion writing; maybe what is needed instead is emphasis on fine judicial opinions as models for the current generation of judges.

What ought to be an attainable goal for legal academics, though it will strike many law professors as pedestrian, is to persuade bar and bench to banish superfluous terms, especially when misleading, from briefs and judicial opinions. I'll offer one candidate for extinction:

"willfulness." My court has said, for example, that "an OSHA violation is willful if it is committed with intentional disregard of, or plain
indifference to, the requirements of the statute," and other courts have
used similar formulas.[13] The first alternative corresponds to the tort
concept of recklessness: you know there's a danger, you could prevent
it, but you do nothing. (In contrast, negligence requires only that there
be a danger of which a reasonable person would be aware, not that the
particular defendant, who may not be a reasonable person, have been
aware of it.) But OSHA based its determination that the defendant's
violation had been willful on the second formula—"plain indifference"—and it's unclear what it means. Our opinion said that "ignoring obvious violations of OSHA safety standards amounts to 'plain
indifference,'" but that sounds like either negligence (if "ignore" can
just mean "doesn't notice") or recklessness (the violation was obvious
to you, but you decided to do nothing about it) and therefore duplicates the first formula.[14]

The underlying problem is that "willfulness," despite its ubiq-
uity in judicial opinions, has no standard definition. Often bracketed
with "wanton" or "malicious," willfulness can equate to recklessness
(ignoring known risk) or denote a heightened form of negligence
(carelessness) falling short, however, of recklessness.[15] We have perfectly good terms for each of the gradations of culpability denoted by
"willfulness": negligence, gross negligence, recklessness. Why lump together disparate degrees of culpability under one word?

What this example illustrates is the pervasive and unhealthy legal
habit of treating as interchangeable or largely so terms of uncertain

13. *Lakeland Enterprises of Rhinelander, Inc. v. Chao,* 402 F.3d 739, 747 (7th Cir. 2005).
14. Id. at 747–748.
15. See, e.g., *Nightingale Home Healthcare, Inc. v. Anodyne Therapy, LLC,* 626 F.3d 958
(7th Cir. 2010); *Fagocki v. Algonquin/Lake-In-The-Hills Fire Protection District,* 496
F.3d 623 (7th Cir. 2007); *Wassell v. Adams,* 856 F.2d 849, 853–854 (7th Cir. 1989).

meaning, such as "willful," "wanton," "reckless," "deliberately indifferent," "plainly indifferent," "intentionally disregarding," or, in regard to standards of review, "clearly erroneous," "substantial evidence," "arbitrary and capricious," "abuse of discretion," "plain error." The academy should be able to help judges prune the lush, overgrown judicial vocabulary. Simplification should be the battle cry of the academic legal profession. Unfortunately many academics prefer complexification, which makes them seem smarter.

Also welcome from the academy would be more analysis of the process of selection of federal judges; judicial culture, organization, and management; the training or rather lack of training of federal judges; judicial compensation; the effect of age on judicial competence; and the fitness of law professors to be appointed to federal judgeships. And that is just a partial list. There is a great deal that legal scholars can do to improve the judiciary.

Political scientists and, latterly, economists have written a lot about federal judges, though again with a heavy concentration on the Supreme Court Justices. The focus generally is on the average characteristics of judges rather than on the characteristics, sometimes idiosyncratic, of individual judges.[16] Cognitive quirks that judges share with other human thinkers, such as hindsight bias (the instinctive belief that what has happened was certain to happen), have received attention.[17] But other priors that predispose judges to resolve issues in

---

16. See, for example, Lee Epstein, William M. Landes, and Richard A. Posner, *The Behavior of Federal Judges: A Theoretical and Empirical Study of Rational Choice* (2013), and the extensive bibliography of earlier social-scientific studies of the judiciary in Chapter 2 of that book.

17. See, for example, Chris Guthrie, Jeffrey J. Rachlinski, and Andrew J. Wistrich, "Blinking on the Bench: How Judges Decide Cases," 93 *Cornell Law Review* 1 (2007). I criticized aspects of this article in my book *Reflections on Judging* 312–313 (2013).

particular ways before considering the evidence and the arguments, and may turn out to have a decisive impact on their decision, deserve additional attention.

Academic neglect of the issues I've listed puzzles me. There are eighteen thousand law professors. Can they all be wanting to write just about legal doctrines? Can the makers of the doctrines hold no interest for professors, unless they are especially colorful or controversial Supreme Court Justices? (And even those attract little frank and insightful commentary from the academy.)

The reader who recalls my criticisms of the judiciary in Chapters 2 and 3 and is familiar as well with the emphases found in current legal scholarship will be struck by the disconnect between the problems and the proffered academic solutions. The problems of the modern judiciary that I think most serious receive little attention from the academy (an important exception, however, is the mess that is the administration of patent law), whether the problem is overcommitment to adversary procedure, incompetent adjudication of social security disability and immigration cases, the disgrace that is the administration of supervised release in criminal cases, the mismanagement of judges' staffs, the dearth of judicial training, the misunderstanding of statutory "interpretation," the increasing technological complexity of federal cases, or the suspicion of "independent judicial research."

Karl Llewellyn attempted the kind of structural critique that I am suggesting in *The Common Law Tradition: Deciding Appeals* (1960), and with considerable success, although the length, style, age, and errant organization of the book deter most readers. (Though Llewellyn was brilliant, his writing style resembled that of the Dr. Seuss books.) More recently William D. Popkin undertook a similar critique in his book *Evolution of the Judicial Opinion: Institutional and Individual Styles* (2007), which likewise has failed to receive the attention it deserves, though it has none of the structural and stylistic weaknesses of

Llewellyn's book. The approach of those two books is similar to what I've attempted in chapters of several books of mine, cited earlier in this book, including *How Judges Think, Law and Literature,* and *Reflections on Judging,* and to my articulation of a realist approach in Chapter 2. I don't think any of these books have had much impact on judges or their law clerks or on appellate advocates.

One thing that has dated Llewellyn's book is that it discusses only state courts, and few legal scholars nowadays are interested in those courts. For that matter, relatively few legal scholars nowadays seem interested in any court other than the Supreme Court. If they teach and write about fields of federal law not wholly dominated by the Court—and there are many such—they discuss specific opinions but not institutions, personnel, culture, opinion style, and so forth. An exception is the U.S. Court of Appeals for the Federal Circuit; its exclusive jurisdiction of patent appeals has made it, and not just patent doctrine, a magnet to professors of patent law—a most distinguished legal academic field.

The methodology of academic legal research needs to be updated. The academy is not exploiting to the full the opportunities opened up by modern statistics and the computer for analyzing the judiciary empirically, substituting rich and solid data for hunch and bias. The Administrative Office of the U.S. Courts publishes detailed statistics (of which I offered a glimmer in the preceding chapter) on the federal courts. Additional such statistics are either available from other sources or can readily be found or created by use of technologically advanced methods of data collection and analysis now widely available, cheap, and easy to use.[18] The large variance in the output (as measured by

---

18. A rich but somewhat neglected source well worth noting is the Judge Information Center in Syracuse University's Transactional Records Access Clearinghouse (TRAC), http://tracfed.syr.edu/judges/interp/.

number of judicial decisions, for example) of individual judges can now readily be tracked and analyzed, explained and assessed; and likewise the variance in the impact of different judges on the law (as proxied for example by citations, in cases or books or articles or the Internet, to their judicial opinions), as well as in the average time that it takes a particular judge to issue a judicial opinion in a case and the average number of opinions that he or she issues per year.[19] These measures can be aggregated to the circuit level and the aggregations used to evaluate and compare the performances of the thirteen federal courts of appeals. Similar evaluations and comparisons can be made at the district court level. (The Transactional Records Access Clearinghouse at Syracuse University is a vast repository of data about federal courts and agencies, with particular emphasis on the district courts.)[20] There already is an academic literature on these subjects, to which law professors like Mitu Gulati and Corey Yung, and social scientists such as Lee Epstein and William Landes, have contributed. But there is need for more.

The problems of judicial management that I discuss in Chapter 3 have been almost entirely ignored by law professors despite a rich body of organization theory on which law professors interested in judicial management could draw.[21] There is, it is true, an extensive literature on law clerks and their relation to their judges; and manage-

---

19. See, for example, Stephen J. Choi and G. Mitu Gulati, "Choosing the Next Supreme Court Justice: An Empirical Ranking of Judicial Performance," 78 *Southern California Law Review* 23 (2004).

20. See, for example, TRAC REPORTS, Judge Information Center, "As Workloads Rise in Federal Courts, Judge Counts Remain Flat," October 14, 2014, http://trac.syr.edu/tracreports/judge/364/; note 18 above.

21. An excellent place to start is John Roberts, *The Modern Firm: Organizational Design for Performance and Growth* (2004). This John Roberts is not the Chief Justice. He is a professor at the Stanford business school. Jonathan Matthew Cohen's *Inside Appellate Courts: The Impact of Court Organization on Judicial Decision Making in the United States Courts of Appeals* (2002) is, as far as I know, the only systematic

ment of law clerks is the principal managerial activity in the judiciary. But this literature is largely the product of judges and former law clerks; it is anecdotal, to a significant degree self-serving, and does not bring to bear organization theory or other sources of principles of good management.[22]

Despite the endless fascination that the Supreme Court holds for law professors, even its management problems attract little academic attention. Little is not nothing; the Court's refusal to allow its oral arguments to be televised, its light caseload, and the bunching of decisions at the end of the Court's term receive some attention. But most law professors who write or teach about the Supreme Court are preoccupied with issues of judicial philosophy. It's an unhealthy preoccupation. The Justices are not "philosophical." They do not engage with abstruse issues of "meaning." They do not read H. L. A. Hart or Ronald Dworkin, or the flights of fancy of such current constitutional gurus as Laurence Tribe and Akhil Amar.[23] The age of the Constitution (including key amendments beginning with the Bill of Rights) and the vagueness of many of its key provisions leave the Justices pretty much at large, which is where they want to be left, undisturbed by pesky academics. To avoid accusations of "activism" a Justice may subscribe publicly to a political philosophy, an approach, a methodology—whatever—designed, consciously or not, to clothe his or her judicial votes in a garb of neutrality, objectivity, and intellectual

application of organization theory to a court system, namely the federal courts of appeals.

22. See, for example, Cohen, preceding note; Frank M. Coffin, *On Appeal: Courts, Lawyering, and Judging* 213–217 (1994); Daniel Mahoney, "Law Clerks: For Better or for Worse," 54 *Brooklyn Law Review* 321 (1988); John Bilyeu Oakley and Robert S. Thompson, *Law Clerks and the Judicial Process: Perceptions of the Qualities and Functions of Law Clerks in American Courts* (1980); Norman Dorsen, "Law Clerks in Appellate Courts in the United States," 26 *Modern Law Review* 265 (1963).

23. See, for example, Tribe, *The Invisible Constitution* (2008); Amar, *America's Unwritten Constitution: The Precedents and Principles We Live By* (2012).

rigor. Invariably it is a philosophy, approach, or the like, that is loose enough to leave an ample residue for the exercise of discretion guided by the Justice's ideological and other priors.

The fundamental problem of academic commentary on the judiciary today is that academics are not judges and judges are not academics and that the gulf between these two branches of the legal profession has widened to a point at which academics (not all of course, and not always) write for each other on the issues that happen to interest the academic community and judges rightly feel that they're not part of the academics' intended audience. I noted the gulf and some of the causes of it in the Introduction, one being what Judge Edwards has called the "abstract" character of current legal scholarship. Using Professor Fallon as my whipping boy I criticized the opacity of "advanced" legal scholarship to judges, who do not have facility with the jargon that legal scholars far removed from the practice of law tend to employ. And obviously the denser the prose, the shorter a book or article should be if it is to hold the attention of a reader who will have to struggle to understand it.

The opacity of so much current academic writing is thus exacerbated by the inordinate length of faculty-authored articles in law reviews, which remain the major publication venues for law professors. The November 2014 issue of the *Harvard Law Review* contains four articles by law professors, totaling 190 pages. One, labeled "Foreword," is eighty-four pages long. The others, labeled "Comments," average thirty-five pages. They are doubtless called "Comments" because they are shorter than the law review editors' conception of an article. The four pieces aggregate about 89,300 words—if one ignores the fact that almost all the pages have footnotes, which are set in smaller type. The total number of words, including the words in the footnotes, in the four pieces must be close to a hundred thousand. All four pieces are longer than they need be, and the sum is book length.

Also, much academic writing misperceives what judges need in the way of academic analysis, as I can illustrate with a recent article by law professor Elizabeth Porter on visual images (mainly photos, including Google aerial photos, diagrams, maps, and very occasionally a video link) in judicial opinions.[24] I have been using such images (all but the video link) in my judicial opinions for many years, and welcome the article, which notes the utility of images in the judicial process. But at ninety-five pages the article is too long to hold a judge's attention. Worse, the article does what many, maybe most, academic literature about the judicial process does, and that is propose new rules to limit judicial discretion. The assumption seems to be that judges are likely to run amok unless cabined very tightly. There is indeed a problem of willful judges. But the greater problem, as I tried to show in Chapter 2, is judicial passivity—the judge conceiving his role as just that of an umpire. Professor Porter thinks that visual images have a role to play in litigation, which is certainly true, but she doesn't want *judges* to be picking images from the Web. She wants the federal rules of procedure or evidence amended to forbid that. No independent judicial research for her.[25] Uncritical about the adversary process, she wants the images to be selected by the lawyers. She seems not to realize how reluctant lawyers are to make visual images a part of their advocacy. I have twice said in opinions that lawyers seem to think that a word is worth a thousand pictures. That's an exaggeration, obviously, but the blunt fact is that a great many lawyers cannot be trusted to make an adequate record, and as a result the adversary process is less reliable than Professor Porter assumes it to be.

She distrusts judges more than lawyers, as in the discussion that

---

24. Elizabeth G. Porter, "Taking Images Seriously," 114 *Columbia Law Review* 1687 (2014). See also Elizabeth G. Thornburg, "The Lure of the Internet and the Limits on Judicial Fact Research," *Litigation,* vol. 38, no. 4, p. 41 (2012).
25. On independent judicial research, see Chapter 2, section 11, of this book.

leads off her article of an image in one of my opinions—a photograph of one of my law clerks wearing a steelworker's outfit.[26] The issue in the case, a labor-management dispute, was whether the outfit was "work clothes" (in which event the employer prevailed, as we held) or "personal protective equipment" (in which event the workers would have won). It seemed to me that a photograph, although not conclusive, would be helpful evidence. The appellate record contained one of the outfits; it fitted one of my law clerks; and I suggested that one of the other clerks take a picture of the one wearing the outfit. He did so and I included it in my opinion. Professor Porter is *very* suspicious. She says the photo "appears to have been conceived of, staged, created, curated (assuming there were multiple photos taken and only one was selected), and edited by someone in Judge Posner's chambers," and that "instead of standing amid the sparks and flames of a steelworks, Judge Posner's model leans against what appears to be a (flameproof?) chambers door. What is presented in the Seventh Circuit's opinion as a neutral depiction of evidence—a complete picture—is in fact a purposefully crafted visual argument, subtly but persuasively advancing Judge Posner's interpretation of the Fair Labor Standards Act."[27]

Her imagination has run away with her. The idea of the photo was mine, but there was no staging, curating, multiple photos (as far as I know), editing, flameproof door, or "purposefully crafted visual argument," and no opportunity to photograph, instead of my law clerk, a steelworker "standing amid the sparks and flames of a steelworks."

26. *Sandifer v. U.S. Steel Corp.*, 678 F.3d 590, 593 (7th Cir. 2012), affirmed, 134 S. Ct. 870 (2014).

27. Porter, note 24 above, at 1690. She also seems to think that I or a law clerk forbade the photographed clerk "wearing the leggings and wristlets also in contention, or perhaps the respirator" (Id.). Those items, so far as I am aware, weren't in the appellate record.

One might have expected Porter to check with me before accusing me in print of falsifying the record; she did not.

The new rules she wants to see adopted for regulating visual images in litigation would include interpretive canons, like the canons of statutory interpretation (she refers to "law's rich and detailed traditions for interpreting ambiguous text"[28]—would they were rich and not merely detailed!) but used to determine the meaning of any visual images that might appear in a case.[29] Lawyers and judges are drowning in rules. Yet academics keep urging more rules to fence in judges and prosecutors.

The conservatism (methodological, not political) that is so marked and, if my analysis in Chapter 2 is sound, so regrettable a feature of the legal culture is illustrated in Porter's article when she expresses concern that "routine use of images will erode established structures of legal decisionmaking, particularly including the allocation of power between judge and jury, and between appellate courts and trial courts."[30] Indeed so. If two witnesses give conflicting testimony, and a videotape of the incident they're testifying about makes clear which witness is telling the truth, the role of the trier of fact, be it a judge or a jury, is diminished; the videotape eliminates a factual issue. That is an example of technical progress "erod[ing] established structures of legal decisionmaking." To which I say: so much the worse for the "established structures." Trial by ordeal was once an established structure of adjudication too, yet is not missed. A time will come when juries are not missed either, at least in complex civil cases.

Much academic legal writing is ostensibly directed to judges, such as the Porter article, but doesn't reach them because it's written with-

28. Id. at 1687.
29. See id. at 1775–1782.
30. Id. at 1766; see also id. at 1767.

out a good understanding of judges or for that matter of the needs of the legal system, and because the actually intended audience is other academics rather than judges. If Porter were interested in judges, you'd think she would have asked me why and how I included in my opinion a photo of a law clerk garbed as a steelworker. Instead of urging judges to be more timid, rule-bound, cautious, and deferential to the bar, academics should be trying to persuade judges to broaden their intellectual horizons, to innovate, to understand the breadth of their discretion and exercise it imaginatively.

I'm not aware that any judge shares Professor Porter's dismay at my use of photography in the *Sandifer* opinion, but some of my own judicial colleagues were distressed by a photographic foray in another of my opinions, *Mitchell v. JCG Industries, Inc.*[31] This was another labor case, like *Sandifer.* The main issue was the length of the lunch break for workers in a poultry processing plant. It was nominally a half hour, but the plaintiff workers argued that since they had to spend up to a quarter of an hour doffing and then (at the end of the lunch break) donning their protective clothing (poultry processing is a very messy business, and the workers were not allowed to wear their protective clothing while eating), it wasn't a bona fide lunch break and therefore they were entitled to be paid for that half hour. The defendant argued that it took only two to three minutes to doff and don the protective clothing. The district judge had not tried to resolve the question.

My colleagues and I on the appellate panel did not think an evidentiary hearing was the way to resolve it. Some of the workers would testify that the doffing and donning consumed ten to fifteen minutes, but others, aligned with the defendant (for the union was on the defendant's side), would testify that it took only two to three minutes. If asked to demonstrate how much time it took by doffing and don-

31. 745 F.3d 837 (7th Cir. 2014).

ning in the courtroom, the plaintiffs would dawdle while the company doubtless would find a few speed demons among the workers aligned with the company and the union. The limitations of the trial process as a method of finding certain types of fact have to be recognized. How would a judge or a jury decide who was telling the truth?

We tried something different. My law clerks and I began by identifying the protective clothing (all of which is worn over the worker's street clothes) used by the defendant's employees and buying it (at my expense) from the supplier. Upon arrival of the clothing my three law clerks donned and doffed it as they would do if they were workers at the defendant's plant. Their endeavors were videotaped by my secretary. The videotape automatically recorded the time consumed in donning and doffing and also enabled verification that the "workers" were neither rushing nor dawdling. The videotape revealed that the average doffing time is 15 seconds and the average donning time 95 seconds. The total, 110 seconds, is less than two minutes, even though the "actors" had never worked in a poultry processing plant and were therefore inexperienced donners/doffers of the items in question. The panel was unanimous that this was compelling evidence in favor of the defendant, but some judges not on the panel thought the issue should have been left to a jury to decide. The panel disagreed because the videotaped evidence, though unconventional, made clear that no reasonable jury could find that workers at the defendant's plant spend half their lunch break taking off and putting on a lab coat, an apron, a hairnet, plastic sleeves, earplugs, and gloves (the items that comprised the protective clothing). A factual allegation that no reasonable jury would accept can't create a triable issue of fact.

Though there was disagreement among judges in the poultry case, there was no misunderstanding as to what each judge thought. Professor Porter's problem regarding the steelworkers case was that she didn't understand the what and the why of the judges' action. If academics are to provide informed critique of judges, they have to understand judges. Some academics make an effort, more or less successful, to do so, though the effort sometime fails because of judges' secretiveness (or even deceptiveness). But what is far more common is for an academic article to suggest a change in legal doctrine without evincing recognition that the suggested change will come about only if judges decide to adopt it, and therefore that the feasibility of the suggestion (and hence whether there's any point in making it) requires an understanding of judges.

A good deal of academic legal writing seems intended less to alter the legal system than to demonstrate the ingenuity of the author.[32] This may be the inevitable consequence of the increased size and intellectuality of law school faculties. And much of the academic writing that does seem seriously concerned with changing the legal system is too impractical, too otherworldly (an example being the ambitious article by Bijal Shah that I discussed in the Introduction), to have any chance of succeeding—the authors seeming not to realize which reforms of the legal system are both needed and feasible, what kind and level of analysis, including empirical analysis, are necessary to lay a solid foundation for a proposed reform, and how to justify reform to those (whether judges or others) empowered to implement it. And once again a big stumbling block to the endeavor when success depends on judicial support or implementation is that academic lawyers tend not to have a good understanding of judges' capabilities and intentions.

Maybe law professors interested in legal reform that would require acceptance or implementation by the federal judiciary should, operating under the auspices of the American Law Institute or the

---

32. That's my sense of Amar's book *America's Unwritten Constitution: The Precedents and Principles We Live By,* note 23 above, which I discuss critically in my book *Reflections on Judging,* note 17 above, at 219–233.

Federal Judicial Center, ask selected federal judges for suggestions of promising areas for academic study of such reform.

Law schools may argue that high-flying interdisciplinary scholarship, whatever the authors' intent or the intelligibility of such scholarship to the judiciary, may lead to breakthroughs in the understanding and improvement of the legal system. And it may—yet a considerable literature documents the difficulty of and frequent failures in putting academic ideas into practice in a variety of fields, and why should law be an exception?[33] Academic scholarship, if it is to influence judges, needs to be aimed at judges—that is, written with knowledge of judges' interests, needs, and comprehension.

The academic-authored amicus curiae brief is one vehicle for exerting academic influence on the judiciary; it has proved effective in patent law.[34] In contrast, and well illustrating the gulf between the professoriate and the judiciary, the amicus briefs filed by a number of Harvard and Yale law professors in *Rumsfeld v. Forum for Academic & Institutional Rights, Inc. (FAIR)*[35]—the decision that upheld the Solomon Amendment, a federal statute that penalizes universities that forbid access to military recruiters—was embarrassingly inept.[36]

Another possibility worth considering is to launch a law journal

---

33. See, for example, Walter D. Valdivia, "University Start-Ups: Critical for Improving Technological Transfer" (Center for Technology Innovation at Brookings, November 2013); Russell E. Glasgow and Karen M. Emmons, "How Can We Increase Translation of Research into Practice? Types of Evidence Needed," 28 *Annual Review of Public Health* 413 (2007); David Gann, "Putting Academic Ideas into Practice: Technological Progress and the Absorptive Capacity of Construction Organizations," 19 *Construction Management and Economics* 321 (2001). Valdivia, above, at 8, states that "over the last 20 years, on average, 87% [of university technology-transfer offices] did not break even."

34. Colleen V. Chien, "Patent Amicus Briefs: What the Courts' Friends Can Teach Us about the Patent System," 1:2 *UC Irvine Law Review* 398 (2011).

35. 547 U.S. 47 (2006).

36. See my book *How Judges Think* 221–229 (2008).

whose only mission would be to translate academic research into feasible legal reform that was within judicial authority to implement.

Although pessimistic about the contribution that the modern academy, increasingly distant as it is from the judiciary, can or will make to improving the judiciary, I hold out a hope that there may be room for fruitful *collaboration* between judges and law professors on studies of the judiciary. Books and articles coauthored by judges and law professors or other lawyers are very rare, though I've mentioned several times the book on judicial behavior that I recently coauthored with a political scientist (Lee Epstein) and an economist (William Landes), both of whom teach in a law school, as indeed do I, though my teaching is strictly part-time. I am engaged at present in two other collaborative academic studies with nonjudges. One, in which my collaborator is a law professor (Mitu Gulati), is a study of how federal court of appeals judges manage their staffs.[37] The other, in which I am collaborating with a different law professor (Abbe Gluck), is a study of judges' approaches to statutory interpretation. Both studies are based on interviews of dozens of federal court of appeals judges, and the hope that animates the studies is that the results will help judges improve both their staff management and their approach to statutory interpretation, both being areas in which many judges are deficient— as some will even admit.

The studies (the second unfinished) have yeilded insights that suggest paths to improvement. Regarding judicial management, we find little systematic thinking and very little in the way of published

---

37. "The Management of Staff by Federal Court of Appeals Judges," April 5, 2015, http://papers.ssrn.com/sol3/papers.cfm?abstract_id=2590179. Although there is already a considerable academic literature on law clerks, it is less focused on management issues than our study is. See, for example, *Symposium: Judicial Assistants or Junior Judges: The Hiring, Utilization, and Influence of Law Clerks*, 98 Marquette Law Review 1 (2014).

guidance to newly appointed federal judges on how best to select and direct staff. These are surprising gaps in judicial training. Because judicial staff management is not a focus of what little training the Federal Judicial Center offers to newly appointed court of appeals judges, there is little that the new judge (unless he had been a law clerk) can do to inform himself about how to organize and supervise his staff besides asking other judges for suggestions. It is no surprise, therefore, that we find that in the absence of guidance judges tend to experiment with different ways of selecting and using law clerks and other staff, often altering their management style as a result of their experimentation. Trial and error is time-consuming and inefficient. I do not sense much progress toward solution of the problems of judicial staff management that I discussed in Chapter 3.

Given the large role of judicial staff in the operation of the judiciary, one would think judicial staff management a fertile area for academic research. It isn't, and one reason is that it is difficult to conduct such research because of the secretiveness of judges and their tendency to mistrust, as outsiders, law professors who want to study them. The reason that the collaborative studies that I've mentioned are based on interviews of judges is that it is very difficult otherwise to learn what goes on in a federal judge's office. There is no documentary record, and the law clerks and secretaries who work for judges are very unlikely to be forthcoming about the management of the judge's office. (The judge may well have sworn them to secrecy about anything that goes on in his office.) So the feasibility of research on judicial staff management depends on judges' willingness to be interviewed. Although some judges are reluctant to grant interviews, a judge collaborator in an interview study usually can overcome that reluctance, because judges tend to trust each other and will therefore accept the collaborating judge's assurances of the bona fides of the study and that the interviewees' anonymity will be protected. There is a certain clubbiness about the federal judiciary. I recall that when I was appointed, a judge of another federal court of appeals, whom I knew, wrote me a brief congratulatory note saying "welcome to the club." But there is also a certain loneliness about the job. (Introverts don't feel it, but we're not all introverts.) There is less extensive human contact than in legal practice or teaching. District judges work in isolation from each other, and even court of appeals judges, though they hear and decide cases together, often have their offices in different cities, and even if their offices are in the same building they often prefer to communicate by email or otherwise in writing rather than in person. Moreover, because of the panel system of appellate judging, a given judge may, depending on the size of his court, sit only infrequently with each of the other judges.

Most judges therefore welcome being interviewed—at least by, or under the auspices of, another judge. (Many of the interviews were conducted by my collaborators rather than by me, but I had made the initial approach to most of the judges, and all were made aware that I was part of the study.)

My other collaborative study, that of how judges interpret statutes (or how they think they interpret statutes), is, though also based on interviews with a number of federal court of appeals judges, of a different character from the study of staff management. Issues of statutory interpretation are briefed in cases in which those issues arise and are discussed at length in federal appellate opinions, especially opinions of the Supreme Court. There is, as I mentioned in Chapter 2, a vast scholarly literature on statutory interpretation, and most federal judges have at least a nodding acquaintance with some of that literature. Experienced federal court of appeals judges whom my coauthor and I have interviewed have a quite good, and fairly uniform, understanding of the various techniques of statutory interpretation, though an understanding more often produced by experience and intuition than by familiarity with the academic literature. Where the judges mainly differ from each other is in their sense of the proper division of responsibilities between court and legislature. Some (call them "purposivists" or, the older term, "loose constructionists") think that when a statutory provision that is to be construed is ambiguous (two or more meanings are equally plausible from a linguistic standpoint) or vague (it is unclear what the possible meanings are), the judge should adopt the interpretation that advances the statutory purpose, so far as it can be discerned.

But it is important for the judge to bear in mind that compromise with opposing legislators is common and can blunt a statute's purpose, and that the blunted purpose is the true purpose that should therefore guide the judge in interpreting the statute. Subject to that important qualification the purposivist approach gives the court a legitimate helping role with respect to the legislature—a role based on recognition that because of carelessness or haste or limitations of foresight the expression of legislative purpose may be blurred. My own view—interpretation as completion, argued in Chapter 2—is a version of purposivism, substituting the judge's purpose for the often inscrutable or even nonexistent purpose of the enacting legislature.

Other judges (call them "textualists" or, the older term, "strict constructionists") take the opposite view. They believe that a judge's job is not to improve a statute, not to clean up after the legislature, but merely to enforce the meaning either clearly stated in the statute or discernible by use of various linguistic conventions or substantive policies (such as the "rule of lenity," which means construing vague criminal statutes in favor of the criminal defendant, a policy rooted in such principles as that there are no common law crimes, as there would be in effect if judges extended criminal statutes beyond their literal meaning). In part this approach is based on a desire to reduce judicial power relative to legislative, in part (amounting to the same thing) on a desire to maintain what the judges who follow this approach consider the proper balance of powers between the judiciary and the legislature, and in part to give legislators an incentive to draft statutes more carefully, both to facilitate accurate statutory interpretation by courts and to provide better notice to persons potentially subject to the statute. But notice the paradox that by insisting, perhaps unrealistically, that if the legislature wants statutory interpretation to advance the legislature's purpose in enacting a statute it must make its intention clear, the textualist judge encumbers the legislative process, thereby reducing the legislature's power. Textualism can in fact hamstring the legislative process. And that may be the aim, whether or not conscious. For textualists usually are conservatives who want to limit the power of the federal government.

There is greater delicacy in questioning judges about their thought processes in a sensitive area of their jurisdiction than in asking them how they manage their staffs. The role of the judge collaborator in a sensitive study is not only to reassure the judge–interviewees that it is a legitimate academic project and not an exposé, but also to help design the format for the interview in point of length and wording and particular questions that judges are likely to understand and be comfortable with.

Since I have done considerable academic writing throughout my judicial (which followed my full-time academic) career, I may be thought a freakish example of a judicial collaborator in an academic study. But I think my judicial experience is a considerable asset in the two studies I've been describing. It enables me both to allay suspicions of the bona fides of such studies and, because I know the judiciary from the inside, to suggest questions designed to elicit candid and thoughtful answers.

If cats were articulate they would be valuable collaborators in research on feline behavior, and likewise judges, being articulate, can participate helpfully in collaborative research on judicial behavior. And not only in studies based on interviews of judges. Most of my academic writing in recent years has focused on judicial behavior, and some of it has been collaborative—and the collaborators are academics, not other judges. In that collaborative research, as in the two current collaborative studies that I have mentioned, my judicial experience had been a major part of my contribution.

I suspect that until I began a few paragraphs ago discussing collaborative scholarship between law professors and judges, this has been the book's least persuasive chapter. Telling academics that their research priorities are awry is unlikely to strike a responsive chord; they are likely to be committed to those priorities. But the suggestion that they experiment with a slightly different style of scholarship, one involving collaboration with some of the people whose work they analyze and comment on—like an anthropologist collaborating with the natives whom he or she studies—may resonate with some law professors as a research method that could yield new insights into the legal system. And that system is after all what law professors study, and what the judges form an important, an influential, and, to a degree, an insightful component of. I am not too optimistic, however, because of what has become the ingrained tendency of law school faculties to seek out, attract, and reward "theoretical" scholars, for example of constitutional law, at the expense of practical ones, such as (in that same field) the late David P. Currie.[38]

But commentary on—critique of—judges is only a part of what

---

38. See Currie, *The Constitution in the Supreme Court: The First Hundred Years, 1789–1888* (1985); *The Constitution in the Supreme Court: The Second Century, 1888–1986* (1990).

the judiciary needs from academic scholarship. Because of the frequent inability of the adversary system to produce reliable knowledge of facts essential to sound judicial decisions, judges should be relying more than they do on facts established to a reasonable degree of certainty by science, including the social sciences, and technology, including statistical tools for marshaling and analyzing evidence. Judges are influenced by facts but have difficulty with modern methods for finding them. This is surely an area where the academy can be helpful to the judiciary by publishing articles and books that take the judge-reader step by step through the intricacies of advanced modern methods of obtaining and evaluating evidence.

There is such a literature but it is not written with judges in mind, or if it is the authors seemingly make no effort to write with sufficient brevity, clarity, and simplicity to hold the attention of—to educate—the judge reader. One mustn't be fooled by the increased frequency of references in judicial opinions to social-scientific and other technical materials. It can't be inferred from such references that judges are actually using science to determine or influence their decisions. Remember that almost all federal judicial opinions are written by law clerks, with more or less editing of their drafts by their judge, and that an opinion written by a law clerk is essentially a brief in support of the judge's vote. The clerk may insert empirical findings based on scientific or social-scientific research into the opinion to provide "support" for the conclusion, but the conclusion, which usually is the judge's, is rarely generated by such findings.

Reference to such findings often indeed is window dressing. A famous example is the "doll tests" conducted by psychologists Kenneth and Mamie Clark and cited though not discussed in *Brown v. Board of Education*.[39] The tests found that black children preferred white to black dolls. The rhetorical challenge in *Brown* as the Justices

---

39. 347 U.S. 483, 494 n. 11 (1954). See American Psychological Association, "Segre-

saw it was, as I intimated in my brief discussion of the case in Chapter 2, to invalidate public school segregation without insulting white southerners, lest denunciation of southern bigotry foment unrest and defiance in the South (which in fact occurred, despite the Court's rhetorical strategy). So the opinion says nothing about the motive of the southern white establishment in segregating schools, but instead cites empirical evidence (not limited to the Clarks' study) of the bad effects of segregation on black children. It is unlikely that the studies actually played a causal role in the decision, but they may have been essential to its being unanimous.

This raises once again the issue of judicial candor, which I discussed briefly in section 15 of Chapter 2. If I am right about the thinking behind the reference in *Brown* to the doll tests, does this commit me to Guido Calabresi's claim that "the Supreme Court must occasionally lie"?[40] I don't think so. The Court did not *lie* in citing the doll tests as evidence that black children were harmed by public school segregation—more broadly by the system of apartheid of which that segregation was a significant component. It's rather that the Court could have said more in justification of invalidating public school segregation. Doubtless a majority of the Justices wanted to do so, but decided it would be best to avoid, so far as possible (it proved not to be possible), inflaming southern whites by adopting a ground of decision that would have implied the invalidation of segregation of parks and drinking fountains, and invalidation too of the antimiscegenation laws. So dismantlement of the system of apartheid that would remain after the public schools were desegregated was left for the future. And so there was a lack of candor. But as I noted in Chapter 2

---

gation Ruled Unequal, and Therefore Unconstitutional," July 2007, www.apa.org/research/action/segregation.aspx, discussing the Clarks' extensive research (not limited to the doll study) on the effects of racial segregation on black children.

40. Calabresi, *A Common Law for the Age of Statutes* 179 (1982).

there is no general duty of candor. Judges shouldn't lie, *pace* Calabresi, but they need to balance the public interest in candor on the part of public officials against competing interests, as the Justices did in *Brown*.

An important implication of the Court's reference to the doll tests was that systematic empirical evidence can be a source of judicial knowledge. But for such evidence to play that role, rather than to serve merely as rhetorical decor in judicial opinions, judges must distinguish carefully among the different types: published academic or otherwise professional studies; testimony or reports by expert witnesses hired by the parties; evidence presented by neutral experts pursuant to Federal Rule of Evidence 706 (a very underutilized power, as I noted in Chapter 2); empirical data in amicus curiae briefs, often briefs by allies of one side of the case or the other, often unreliable. The reliability of data submitted to judges, including by their own law clerks, varies greatly and so requires careful screening by the judges, if necessary with the aid of neutral experts appointed by them.

Authors of empirical studies aimed at judges and law clerks need to understand the limitations of their audience's understanding. They have to be able to explain the methodology and conclusions of a study in words of one syllable, or in easily understood tables or graphs. They have to be able to show that empirical research can establish facts, often more reliably than testimony by lay witnesses (including the parties themselves, who often have a strong incentive to lie) and other conventional law-court evidence. They have to realize that they bear a heavy burden if the facts they establish by the methods of social science clash with the judges' priors. And they must be alert to the fact that expert witnesses, unless they are neutrals appointed by the judge, have a financial incentive to shape their testimony so that it will provide the maximum possible support for the positions of their clients.

I mentioned in Chapter 2 that judges are beginning to exploit the rich resources of the Internet to supplement the facts developed by the ordinary processes of litigation. I cannot think of a form of academic research that would be more useful to the judiciary today than research that would guide the judges to reliable websites and away from unreliable ones. It is unfortunately no paradox that it is a type of research unlikely to have the slightest attraction to law professors.

A brief recapitulation of the book up to this point may help readers work their way through the rest of it. Chapter 1 dealt with the stubbornest problems of the federal judiciary. Since they are so stubborn, the legal professoriate probably shouldn't spend much time worrying about them—though that may not stop them from doing so, because the feasibility of proposed reforms is not high on the professorial agenda. Chapters 2 and 3 enumerated twenty-six deficiencies of the federal judiciary that can be, if not solved, at least alleviated to a significant extent. Every one of those deserves scholarly attention—though not necessarily and certainly not exclusively from law professors. Scholarship dealing with judges and the judicial process is also produced by economists, political scientists, sociologists, psychologists, historians, and philosophers, employed elsewhere in universities. But little of this large scholarly literature gives the judiciary the kind of help it most needs. Partly this is because of the academic obsession with the Supreme Court, the judicial organ least responsive to the academy. Partly it is because of judges' secretiveness. Partly it is because rewards (status, prestige, not necessarily money) in academic law go to doctrinalists and theoreticians who write for each other on a plane of discourse inaccessible or unhelpful to judges, as distinct from institutionalists interested in judicial systems and their personnel. What judges need—better staff management and court-level management, better communicative skills, better process, better grasp of technology, greater realism about facts, about interpretation, about the limitations of doctrine and tradition—is not what many academics want to provide, or, perhaps, can provide.

I wish finally to emphasize that it would go far to bridge the gap between the academy and the judiciary if only law professors could decide to write for a broad audience and not just for each other. A radical step in this direction, but one long overdue, is for faculty to wrest control of law reviews from the students, enamored as law students are of length, detail, jargon, and format, provincial as they are in their conception of the value of different types of legal scholarship, and ignorant as they are of the potential audience for such scholarship—a potential audience that includes judges, as the current audience of the student-run law reviews for the most part does not.

5 | THE LAW SCHOOL CURRICULUM

IN THIS CHAPTER I consider how law schools might modify their curriculum beginning in the student's first year—the future judge's initiation into law except for the occasional student who may have been a paralegal for a time before entering law school—in order to impart a keener understanding of judges. In the next chapter I consider how law schools might provide better continuing judicial education—education not of law students but of judges.

The first year of law school, usually so different from the student's previous educational experiences, is bound to make a lasting, indeed a lifelong, impression. The first-year program at most law schools is demanding, though less than it used to be; current tuition levels tend to induce law schools to treat students more as customers than as plebes. I felt changed after my first year (1959–1960) as a student at the Harvard Law School—I felt that I had become more intelligent. The basic training was in learning how to extract holdings from judicial opinions in common law fields and how to apply those holdings to novel factual situations—in other words how to determine the scope and meaning of a legal doctrine. The courses were very difficult because the legal vocabulary was unfamiliar; the professors asked incessant, difficult questions, usually cold calling; the casebooks had very little explanatory material; and we were told not to waste our time reading secondary materials—and most of us were docile and so obeyed. That first year of Harvard Law School was active learning at its best.

We learned to be careful and imaginative readers; we learned that American law is malleable and relatedly that notions of public policy,

and sheer common sense, were legitimate and important considerations in interpreting and applying legal doctrines. There were no references to systematic bodies of thought outside law, however, and statutes were rarely encountered and the Constitution never. The canvas
broadened in the second and third years. But the courses in those
years had much less impact on me, in part because the school tended
to stack its best teachers in the first year, in part because a certain
freshness had worn off, and in part because I devoted most of my time
in my second and third years to the law review, which I found more
interesting than most of the second- and third-year courses. But as I
think back on those years I realize that another factor was that the
common law really is the most commonsensical, intelligible, politically neutral body of American law, compared to which most of constitutional law, and most statutory law, are a muddle.

I don't think the professors who taught the first-year courses
when I was a student (or indeed any of the professors) were formalists,
in the sense of believing that the meaning and scope of a legal rule or
doctrine could be determined without consideration of the real-
world consequences of applying it in a given case. But I wouldn't call
them legal realists either, for they were highly respectful of doctrine.
Law students are natural formalists—a point I'll return to—and I
think my fellow students and I acquired from our courses an essentially formalist conception of law. The jargon of law was welcome—
even the complexity of legal-citation form. The *Bluebook* was in force
then, as it had been since the late 1920s, and though considerably
shorter than the current version was already far too long—more than
a hundred pages—and like its successors nonsensically complex.[1] But

---

1. My law clerks' handbook tells the clerks not to use the *Bluebook* or any other
citation-form manual, but instead to follow the handbook's very brief instructions on citation form (2 pages, compared to the *Bluebook*'s 511 pages). Although
I receive my share of criticism as a judge, I don't think I've ever been criticized

it helped make us students feel in possession of a technical vocabulary that was the gateway to a rigorous analytical logic—feel that each of us was therefore a budding expert, a real professional, like a physician. We had left childish things (as we thought them to be) behind, such as our undergraduate majors (English for me), and had embarked on a serious, demanding, intellectually rigorous career. Yet I was never able to master the *Bluebook* completely, and toward the end of my first year on the law review was excoriated by the law review's treasurer (as the managing editor was called) for doing a citecheck riddled with blue-booking errors.

That was more than half a century ago and legal education has changed a good deal since, especially at the elite law schools. It is less narrow, in part because of higher faculty-student ratios and correspondingly more varied course offerings, but in larger part because of the growing influence of the social sciences on law and the greater representation in the faculties of the elite law schools of professors who have significant competence in a field other than law. The enormous growth in statutory and constitutional law in the last half-century has resulted in curricular change, notably in the tendency to include constitutional law in the first year. There is also under way a movement to make a course in statutory interpretation mandatory in the first year. (In my student days courses in statutory interpretation were unknown, at least at Harvard, though one encountered issues of statutory interpretation in such courses as tax and securities law.) In addition the average quality of law students at the elite schools has increased, enabling a more intellectually challenging curriculum to be offered. In my time as a law student the professors had, unlike today, tended to identify more closely with the legal profession than with the university professoriate. They thus were far less interdisciplinary

---

for errors in citation form. The legal profession's obsession with citation form is beyond absurd.

than their current-day successors are; most weren't interdisciplinary at all. And although most professors, like most judges, were realists (and a great many law professors still are, whatever they say), "legal realism" as a rallying cry or formal designation of a judicial approach had faded.

Students emerge from law school today about as formalist as their predecessors of a half-century ago, possibly even more so because of the law schools' greater emphasis on legal theory, which supplies tools that the inventors and suppliers claim can assure correct decisions without any taint of ideology or any need to choose among competing factual claims. I mentioned the movement to make statutory interpretation a mandatory course. As I understand it, considerable emphasis in such courses is placed on the canons. This is perverse, if my criticism of the canons in Chapter 2 has merit. Other than the small number of substantive canons, such as the rule of lenity or the rule of constitutional avoidance—avoid deciding on constitutional grounds a case that can be decided on nonconstitutional grounds—the canons are at best window dressing, at worst the emperor's new clothes in Hans Christian Andersen's tale of that name. They are not valid instruments for guiding statutory interpretation.

I actually doubt the need for any course on statutory interpretation. Interpretation is a natural human activity; it doesn't require instruction. What would be useful would be a course on Congress, or the legislative process more generally. The more realistic a judge's or law clerk's or litigating lawyer's understanding of how legislation is produced—the relative role of the legislators, their staffs, executive branch officials, and lobbyists, and of the procedures employed by Congress to enact legislation—the better equipped the judge or his law clerks will be to "legislate" in the interstices left open by the legislative process, when the judge is confronted with an interpretive question.

If the professor teaches the canons, even while telling the students that the canons (with the exception of the handful of substantive ones) are window dressing, the lesson the students will take from the course and seek to apply as law clerks or litigators is to dress statutory opinions in canons, much as the sharpies in *The Emperor's New Clothes* dressed the emperor in luxurious nonexistent clothing.

Another curricular error is the continued emphasis in legal-writing courses on the *Bluebook,* which has swollen from obese to grotesque size and by reason of its length and complexity has spawned auxiliary book-length treatments of citation form, such as Harvard's *Blackbook,* which annotates and extends the *Bluebook* in an effort to cope with its gaps and contradictions, the result of its great length and its authors' outsized ambitions. There are alternatives to the *Bluebook,* some simpler, but they have not caught on. In part this reflects the intellectual conservatism of the legal profession, which students find comforting. But in part the *Bluebook*'s very complexity is an attraction. Modern students want the same things their predecessors wanted—a good job upon graduation, of course, but also to be the members of a real profession (a guild, even a mystery), "profession" implying eso-teric knowledge, a specialized vocabulary, and a technique for gener-ating objectively correct answers to even the most difficult questions that arise in one's professional field.

The consequence is a student legal culture that exists at some re-move from that inhabited by the faculty. The professors don't give a straw for the *Bluebook* or care how "professional" the law really is; and many of them emphasize to the students the limitations of doctrine as an explanation of judicial outcomes, and the role of policy in those outcomes. But the reaction of many students is that the professors are trying to hide the ball from them. The students are hungry for the doctrine, the jargon. They resist the intellectual approach of a faculty oriented to the social sciences. Few are interested in becoming legal intellectuals. They want to become successful legal professionals. Some think that faculty make what is simple seem difficult in order to chal-lenge the students, and the students don't like that, because they don't want to be challenged; they want to be fed technique.[2] As one law professor has explained to me in a private note, "students are natural formalists because formalism is an intellectual crutch and they are in an unfamiliar environment. So they are like aspiring poets who learn, say, the sonnet form and then follow it slavishly without realizing poetry advances by breaking old forms. But this is not something that can be changed through instruction."

Even realist professors often convey their realist insights in a manner that promotes formalism. In discussing a judicial opinion the professor may explain to the class that the judge probably arrived at his or her decision by considering the likely consequences of deciding the case one way or another, but didn't say so and instead wrapped the decision in a formalist mantle—a judicial opinion that pretended that the decision had been merely an application of "law," with no addition from realist insights. But the students' takeaway is not that judges are deficient in candor but that what is difficult and important and professional in law is not deriving a decision from a realistic appraisal of the situation revealed in the litigation (for that's just common sense); it is making the decision seem the unalloyed product of formalist analysis. The student surmises that the judge's (and law clerk's) most challenging duty is thus to *conceal* the true nature of judicial decision making, and that it is the lawyer's duty to abet the judge in such obfuscation—to help him encode his decisions in opinions that make the decisions seem compelled by legal logic.

2. Or as Justice Alito is reported to have said, "Law Profs inculcate students with [the] idea that law is a lot more indeterminate than it is" (*Josh Blackman's Blog,* "Highlights from Justice Alito's 2014 Federalist Society Gala," http://joshblackman .com/blog/2014/11/14/highlights-from-justice-alitos-2014-federalist-society -gala/). (I believe that the quotation is Blackman's paraphrase of what he heard Alito say, rather than Alito's exact language.) The opposite would be nearer the truth.

Many law school faculty members are former law clerks and one might expect their firsthand familiarity with the judiciary to influence their teaching. There is some influence but not I think a great deal. Some of these ex–law clerk professors learned little about the judges they clerked for, because some judges are quite reserved with their clerks. And law clerks who pierce the veil, whether because of their own acuity or because of their judge's candor, may as law professors be reluctant to share their insights regarding judges with law students. They may worry that they would be breaching confidences (remember that almost all judges swear their law clerks to eternal secrecy about the clerkship experience), impairing their students' clerkship opportunities by arousing the enmity of judges, and breeding premature cynicism in the students about the judicial process. The last point deserves emphasis. Students might wonder why they were being made to study innumerable legal technicalities (and whether they should spend much time studying them), if told that to a great extent the rules, doctrines, and methods they study actually mask what drives judicial decisions. Cynicism about "the law" would handicap the students, because to be effective lawyers they have to learn how to talk the talk and walk the walk, even if the talk and the walk really aren't what drive judicial decisions, or at least the difficult and important ones. Lawyers have to internalize the conventional methods of legal analysis and decision making while at the same time seeing through or around them.

Still, it's surprising that even in courses on constitutional law, if one may judge from a leading constitutional law casebook that is 1,671 pages long and focuses almost exclusively on the Supreme Court, no attention is paid to the role of priors, such as ideological priors, in constitutional law decisions.[3] And this despite the existence

---

3. Geoffrey R. Stone et al., *Constitutional Law* (7th ed. 2013).

of a vast literature on ideological factors in judicial decisions especially (though not only) in constitutional cases at the Supreme Court level—a literature to which Professor Stone, the principal author of the casebook I just mentioned, has made important contributions.[4]

A recent article of his makes a persuasive showing that Justices' votes in important constitutional cases are determined by their political preferences rather than by politically neutral interpretive methodologies.[5] And yet he argues in that article that the liberal Justices are more in tune than the conservative ones with the values of the eighteenth-century framers of the Constitution. It's most unlikely that this supposed concordance of views exists or if it does that it's what makes liberal Justices liberal. Professor Stone is a distinguished liberal academic and my guess is that it's liberalism, rather than his theory of concordance, that explains his claim that the liberal Justices are less political than their conservative colleagues—which just goes to show the inescapability of a thinker's priors.

Some part-time professors, and a few full-time ones, are current or former judges. Yet from what I understand they are with rare exceptions as guarded concerning the nature of the judicial process—as formalist, as traditional—as law professors who have no judicial background. For remember that judges are secretive. Professors who are current or former judges, and the far larger number who are former law clerks, are inhibited from presenting a realistic picture of judicial behavior by a sense of loyalty to the judiciary, while the professors who have no former or present links to the judiciary have no insider knowledge of that behavior to impart—and indeed, because judges

---

4. See, for example, *The Oxford Handbook of Law and Politics* (Keith E. Whittington et al. eds. 2008), another massive tome (815 pages); the contributors are mainly law professors and political scientists.

5. Geoffrey R. Stone, "The Behavior of Supreme Court Justices When Their Behavior Counts the Most: An Informal Study," 97 *Judicature* 82 (2013).

are secretive, may know little about them even though there is an extensive literature on judicial behavior. For these professors the default position is to assume that judges are much like law students, in the sense that both the judges and the students are trying to do the same thing—fit legal doctrine, formalist fashion, to every new case.

Law professors are not uncritical of the judiciary, though often they mute their criticism and many are reluctant publicly to attribute impure motives to judges. But typically, as I suggested in the Introduction, the professors criticize decisions in particular cases rather than the judges who participated in the decisions, or the methodology of judicial decision making revealed by the decisions, unless a particular methodology of which the professor may disapprove is identified with a particular Supreme Court Justice, such as Scalia or Kennedy. There is a difference between teaching about doctrines and decisions and teaching about judges, and between criticizing analyses and conclusions and criticizing judicial mindsets. How often does the law professor ask himself or his students: Why is that judicial opinion written in the way it is? Are there statements in it that the judge almost certainly does not believe? Is the tone of the opinion right? Is it too long or too short? Why are there so many citations? Is the opinion analytical or rhetorical? Why did it take so long from the date of the appeal for the opinion to be issued? Why does the opinion stray so far from the trial record, or from the briefs, or from the trial court's decision? Does the opinion reflect too much, or perhaps too little, extrarecord research (failing to Google the parties' names, for example)? Is it candid? Truthful? And to whom is it addressed? Is it the opinion of an "auditioner" (a judge angling for a promotion)?

One might expect these questions (essentially the questions I raised in Chapter 2) to be raised in casebooks, which remain the principal text materials in most law school courses. But one would be disappointed; and their absence reinforces the impression that apart from the often considerable social-scientific component of case analysis in today's law school classroom, the emphasis in legal education remains on conventional legal-doctrinal analysis of opinions reproduced in casebooks and heavily edited by the casebook editors, with the brunt of the deletions falling on the facts. The editors would call this inevitable given the limitations (driven mainly by cost) on the length of casebooks. It is not inevitable; all that's needed to keep a casebook's length within desired limits is to reduce the number of opinions published in it. A law student can't get a real feel for the appellate process (appellate opinions vastly outnumber trial-court opinions in casebooks) without knowing how the appellate court treated the facts—which facts it found important and why, how faithful the factual narrative in the opinion is to the record in the trial court, how detailed the factual analysis in the opinion is, and how persuasive its legal analysis is in relation to the facts. Casebook editing denatures judicial opinions.

But there's a deeper problem with casebooks than their length, their editing, and their price ($229 for the latest edition of the Stone et al. constitutional law casebook—I think that's tops, but there are plenty of other casebooks that cost more than $200 or nearly $200, though used copies can usually be bought at a lower price). Casebooks are an anachronism. It would be better as well as incredibly cheaper (in fact costless) for the teacher simply to hand out to the students a list of the cases that he wanted them to read, together perhaps with a list of questions that he wanted them to ruminate about before class. They would read the cases online, unedited, on Westlaw, free of charge—they could if they liked read the briefs in a case also, as well as key cases cited in, and citing, the opinion, for all that material is cited at the Westlaw website for the case. If students wanted background or other supplemental reading material relating to the case, they would use Westlaw or Google to find it. And they would think about the questions the teacher had asked them to think about. The monetary cost of their virtual "casebook" would be zero. And they would be encountering cases and commentary in a more realistic setting, with a fuller background—encountering them in the identical way in which practicing lawyers, law clerks, judges, and law professors encounter them.

The first modern casebook, Langdell's *Selection of Cases on the Law of Contracts*, was published in 1871. That's almost a century and a half ago. Casebooks have become longer and have become distended by inclusion of interstitial material, including problems posed by the casebook authors. Indeed they have become massive (the Stone casebook weighs five pounds) and correspondingly expensive. The composition of them is drudgery. They are print dinosaurs. They exemplify the stodginess of important aspects of the American legal system. (While I'm at it, I should say that I see little need for print versions of treatises or law reviews, either, provided the online versions are readily accessible, free or at least very cheap, and can be downloaded.) Casebooks should be abolished.

Largely because of the curriculum and the attitudes that law students bring to law school, a formalist student culture flourishes in the law school environment without effective faculty opposition or correction. I became acutely aware of this when some years ago I taught, two years running, a course on judicial opinion writing at the University of Chicago Law School. Many of the school's students upon graduation obtain clerkships, mainly in the federal courts of appeals, and most of the clerks will be writing opinions. So I thought such a course would provide helpful preparation for the future clerks. What I found to my surprise was that the students' conception of a good opinion differed strikingly from my own and, I am pretty sure, from that of most of the faculty. The great judicial writers, like Holmes, Hand, Cardozo, and Jackson, left the students cold. Those judges' informal style, their air of general culture, the paucity of citations, their candor, and the brevity of most of their opinions struck the students as indicating an absence of rigor, of a requisite technical vocabulary, a god-like impersonality, a reassuring density of citations, an obsessive recitation of doctrine—marked the opinions, in short, as amateurish. I recall a student describing an opinion that I admired as "brazen."[6] I was appalled.

Recently I taught a somewhat similar course on judicial opinion writing, but my methods were different and my rapport with the

6. In Chapter 9, "Judicial Opinions as Literature," of my book *Law and Literature* (3d ed. 2009), pp. 371–372, I contrasted the "impure" style of opinion writing of the greats with the "pure" style of the pedestrian modern opinion writer, usually a law clerk. I said that

> judicial opinions in the pure style tend to be long for what they have to say, solemn, and predictable in the sense of conforming closely to professional expectations about the structure and style of a judicial opinion . . . The pure opinion uses technical legal terms without translation into everyday English, quotes heavily from previous judicial opinions, includes much unnecessary detail concerning names, dates, and places, complies scrupulously with whatever are the current conventions of citation form, avoids any note of levity, . . . conceals the author's personality, prefers ready-made formulations to novelties, and bows to the current norms of political correctness . . . at whatever cost in stilted diction. The familiarity of the pure style makes it invisible to its practitioners and the intended audience of lawyers. But it is not a plain or transparent style. Its artificiality is revealed by a comparison with the prose of a nonlawyer dealing with a similar issue. Impure stylists like to pretend that what they are doing when they write a judicial opinion is explaining to a hypothetical audience of lay persons why the case is being decided in the way that it is. These judges eschew what has been aptly termed the "rhetoric of inevitability." They prefer the bolder approach . . . of trying to persuade without using stylistic devices intended to overawe. They write as it were for the ear rather than for the eye and avoid long quotations from previous decisions so that they can speak with their own tongue—make it new, make it fresh . . . They like to be candid and not pretend to know more than they do or to speak with greater con-

students much better. I began by giving them a set of citations to recent federal court of appeals opinions selected largely at random, and assigning cases in the set to randomly selected students and asking each student to rewrite the opinion assigned to him or her and in doing so try to cut the length of the opinion at least in half, along with eschewing footnotes and the use of citation-form guides and (so far as possible) of legal jargon. The students' rewrites turned out to be consistently superior to the originals, especially in point of brevity. The assignment succeeded in inducing the students to focus on what is important in an opinion and to realize how much is unimportant.

I then asked them to read some old opinions that I admire, written by the great judges (and I *mean* written—not just edited), and to tell the class and me which they liked best and why, and how they thought opinions have changed in the last century and why.

The culminating and most difficult and important assignment that I gave the students was to draft opinions in recently argued, and not yet decided, federal court of appeals cases. Through Bloomberg Law the students at the University of Chicago Law School have free online access to the briefs and records in federal court of appeals cases, and also in all but two circuits to recordings of the oral arguments in the cases. (For reasons I don't understand, the Second and Eleventh Circuits do not record their oral arguments, or if they do record them

---

fidence than they feel. They eschew unnecessary details, however impressive the piling on of them might be, and shun clichés. They imitate the movement of thought—unfriendly critics call their style "stream of consciousness." The judicial impurists, as Robert Penn Warren said of the modernist poets, "have tried, within the limits of their gifts, to remain faithful to the complexities of the problems with which they are dealing . . . They have refused to take the easy statement as solution."

they don't make the recordings available to the public, as do the other eleven federal courts of appeals.) I assigned cases that had been argued sufficiently recently to make it unlikely that they would be decided before the students finished the assignment. The students were thus in approximately the same position in regard to writing the assigned opinions as real judges and the judges' law clerks are, except that the judge may have benefited from discussing the case with his or her law clerks before oral argument or from reading a bench memorandum drafted by one of the clerks. Nevertheless the assignment gave the students a taste of what it's like to be a judge who writes his or her own opinions or, what is far more common, a law clerk who drafts opinions for his judge. And students in the class who do not become law clerks or who go into appellate practice after clerking will have the advantage of an insider's feel for the judicial process.

The opinions that the students wrote (the original opinions, as distinct from revisions of official opinions) were surprisingly close, and sometimes superior, in quality to the average federal court of appeals opinion, even though the student had to do all the work himself—there was no one to citecheck, proofread, or edit his draft, as there would be in a judge's office—and a student has even less legal experience than a law clerk.

Naturally there were some flaws in a number of the students' opinions (both their revised and their original opinions): grammatical errors, a failure adequately to introduce the case (to tee it up, so to speak, by indicating at the outset the source of federal jurisdiction, who the parties are, what the main issue is, and the procedural posture of the case), a failure to explore anomalies in a case, and a propensity uncritically to quote or repeat a judicial proposition that is mistaken, meaningless, or unintelligible. I attribute these flaws not to the students but to the judiciary and the law school faculty, because the flaws are ones found in many judicial opinions and not remarked by the law professors, and also to traces of the student culture that I had observed when I taught the similar course, many years ago, that I mentioned. I'll give a few examples of the flaws.

A quotation in one student's opinion, taken from *United States v. Maryea,* states that to prove the defendant's participation in a conspiracy "the evidence must show that: (1) a conspiracy existed; (2) the defendant had knowledge of the conspiracy; and (3) the defendant knowingly and voluntarily participated in the conspiracy."[7] Points (1) and (2) are superfluous, since (3) presupposes that there was a conspiracy that the defendant knew about and voluntarily joined. And "knowingly" in (3) is superfluous because the defendant could not have joined the conspiracy voluntarily without knowing that he was joining a conspiracy. But because the quoted rule appears in a published judicial opinion, the student may have felt that it would be an impertinence to challenge or ignore it.

Unsurprisingly, common errors of grammar or usage abound in the students' opinions as they do in official opinions, such as "the allegations he pled" rather than "the allegations he pleaded"—pleading, not supplication. Or "alternate" for "alternative," or "data" as a singular rather than a plural noun, or a sentence beginning with "Here" when it is perfectly clear that the author is discussing the case that is the subject of the opinion rather than some other case.

I came across occasional unintelligible clauses, phrases, and sentences in the opinions written by my students. In one the reader is told that certain persons "were not subject to systematic cancellation of their accounts at the hands of letters from Huntington's headquarters"—what could "at the hands of letters" mean? And what does the following sentence mean: "their privacy has been co-opted by some-

7. 704 F.3d 55, 73 (1st Cir. 2013).

one who had no right to do so"? And what is the antecedent of "granted" in the sentence "To establish Article III standing to sue, the plaintiffs must allege that they have experienced an injury likely caused by [the defendant's] conduct which will if granted avert, mitigate, or compensate them for that injury"?

When a jury having delivered its verdict has just been discharged and leaves the courtroom, the judge may realize that he discharged the jury prematurely, and he may want to recall the jury, and the question arises whether he is authorized to do so. One of the student opinions notes correctly that courts give different answers. Some courts hold that once the jurors have left the courtroom, the judge cannot recall them even if they're still in the courthouse and have not had any contact with any of the lawyers, litigants, witnesses, or court personnel. Other courts hold that recall is permissible if, as one court put it, "the jurors did not disperse and interact with any individuals, ideas, or coverage of the proceeding" after their discharge even though they had left the courtroom.[8] The student opinion (which quoted the passage from the opinion that I just quoted) terms the first approach "a bright-line rule" and the second "a totality-of-the-circumstances standard." But the second approach makes only one circumstance pertinent: whether there was any postdischarge discussion, with or among the jurors, of the case. There is no "totality of circumstances" (another bit of legal jargon that we could live happily without).

Normally a new rule of criminal procedure is not given retroactive effect, and so a person languishing in prison because convicted under the old rule cannot invoke the new one as a basis for obtaining postconviction relief. But there are two exceptions, stated as follows in one of the student opinions: "rules that implicate the fundamental

8. *United States v. Figueroa*, 638 F.3d 69, 73 (3d Cir. 2012).

nature of the criminal justice system and 'without which the likelihood of an accurate conviction is seriously diminished,'" quoting *Teague v. Lane.*[9] I understand the second clause but not the first. If under the old rule the likelihood of an accurate conviction was "seriously diminished," that would seem a sufficient reason to apply the new rule retroactively. I cannot see what is added by saying that the new rule also must "implicate the fundamental nature of the criminal justice system." The term "to implicate" usually means to be involved in, as where one is accused of being implicated in a crime (the most common usage of "implicated"). What does it mean to say that a new rule is involved in the fundamental nature of the criminal justice system—and by the way what is that "fundamental nature"?

Sometimes a student's opinion reveals a puzzling fact without solving the puzzle, thus leaving the reader puzzled. For example, an opinion in a case in which the plaintiff was seeking postconviction relief on the ground of his lawyer's failure to assert a critical right of the plaintiff in the criminal proceeding mentions in passing that the plaintiff had been sentenced in that case to thirty years in prison for stealing a $200 television set. There has to have been more than so trivial a theft to produce such a long sentence in a federal case. (The judge did suspend twenty of the thirty years, but even ten years is much too severe a sentence for such a theft.) The length of the sentence was irrelevant to the postconviction case, yet a reader would like to be reassured that he isn't witnessing a grotesque miscarriage of justice.

The opinion also contains another common but meaningless phrase introducing a sentence—"As such, defendants are entitled to confront forensic analysts at trial." The writer used "As such" to mean "Therefore"—a confusing usage. The opinion also contains the fol-

9. 488 U.S. 288, 313 (1989).

lowing obscure clause: "The adversarial trial process . . . requires at a minimum, that evidence proffered against a criminal defendant is challenged and verified." In this sentence "is" should be "be," but more important there is no requirement that a defendant "challenge" all the evidence introduced by the prosecution.

If an appellant argues for reversal on the basis of an alleged error that he failed to challenge in the trial court, ordinarily he can prevail only by showing that the error was "plain." So what is a plain error? One of the student opinions described it as follows: "For a defendant to prevail under plain error review, he must show 'that an error occurred,' 'that the error was clear or obvious,' that it affected his substantial rights, and that it seriously impaired the 'fairness or integrity' of the proceedings," quoting *United States v. Delgado-Marrero*.[10] The student's characterization of the test adopted in that case is not quite accurate, but probably is superior. What the opinion states at the cited page is that

the plain-error standard requires an initial showing of three elements: (1) that an error occurred; (2) that the error was clear or obvious; and (3) that the error affected substantial rights or the outcome of the case. Even if those requirements are satisfied, however, we have the discretion to affirm the ruling if "the error does not distort the fairness or integrity of the lower court proceedings in some extreme way." This multi-factor analysis makes the road to success under the plain error standard rather steep; hence, reversal constitutes a remedy that is granted sparingly.

What a mishmash! (1) is superfluous because the commission of the error by the trial court is a given. In (2) it's unclear what the dif-

10. 744 F.3d 167, 184 (1st Cir. 2014).

ference between "clear" and "obvious" is. As for (3), "substantial" rights is vague but, more important, if the error affected the outcome of the case, that would seem a sufficient reason for reversal. Why the court should go on to consider whether the error had distorted the "fairness or integrity of the lower court proceedings in some extreme way" is another unsolved mystery, because, again, if the error was clear (or obvious) and changed the outcome, that should be enough to compel reversal. And what makes the determination of whether distorting the fairness or integrity of the lower court proceeding should be a reversible error "discretionary" with the appellate court? The student opinion sheared off some of the weird features of the judicial test but was infected by others.

The faults that I've been pointing out are not to be blamed on the students, but on legal education. With the deterioration of the literary culture in America and the decline in the frequency of written communication, it is inevitable that many highly promising students when admitted to law school will not write well; and since it is important for lawyers to be able to write well, the law schools should be teaching students how to do that, rather than teaching them how to *Bluebook*. Law schools should also be teaching their students to avoid headings and footnotes, to be brief, and so forth, but even more important to be critical of assertions, some of which border on the nonsensical or even cross the line from sense to nonsense, that mar many judicial opinions.

I co-taught the course in judicial opinion writing that I've been describing with a highly successful appellate practitioner—Robert Hochman, whom I mentioned in the Introduction to this book—so that the students could learn how practitioners seek to shape a judicial opinion in briefing and arguing an appeal and how they interpret and apply opinions.

Nowhere is the formalist student culture against which the law schools should be fighting more pernicious than in the selection and

editing of law review articles. The vast majority of law reviews continue to be managed and staffed entirely by law students. These student editors favor long articles, which mirror the verbosity endemic
to the legal profession including its judicial branch. They love footnotes—the more there are and the longer they are, the better. They
push authors to increase the number of citations and footnotes—one
student-edited law journal requires student article submissions to have
a minimum of 125 footnotes. That's sick. The student editors are also
of course obsessed with citation form, including de-italicization of
italic periods. And because they lack confidence in their ability to understand and evaluate complex, innovative, or social-scientific articles,
they favor conventional doctrinal articles. They do publish, though
often with trepidation, articles that break the formalist mold, but in
doing so they sometimes experience difficulty with quality control.

I have come to believe that students should not be allowed to
manage law reviews—to staff them is fine, but management should be
a faculty responsibility. There are a growing number of faculty-edited
journals, but I don't want to see them replace the traditional law reviews; I want to see the reviews changed from being managed by
students to just being staffed by them. The students can both ease the
editing burden on the faculty and learn much about legal analysis and
expression from the writing and editing that they do for the law review, without having to be in charge.

The students' devotion to formalism is harmful to the judiciary,
because it's usually the best students—the same best students—who
go from being law review editors to federal judicial law clerks, hauling
with them the student culture that I have described, augmented by
their law review experience, into the judge's "chambers" (another of
the archaic terms that the profession refuses to shake off). After that
they become practicing lawyers and carry the culture now firmly
lodged in their brains into their practice—as they are expected by

their superiors to do, because their superiors were law students once and imbibed the student culture that I have described and, more important, because they think it's what judges expect and desire. And when eventually a few of these fledgling lawyers metamorphose into judges, they are likely to believe that they are expected in their new role to adhere to the traditional culture.

As practitioners they would, one might think, gradually have wised up to the realities of law and realized the limitations of legal formalism. One might think. But my experience over the past thirty-four years of reading briefs and hearing oral arguments (I've heard almost seven thousand) is that the vast majority of appellate lawyers remain immersed in the culture of formalism that they imbibed in law school. Their advocacy is for example obsessed with precedent, even though a case actually ruled by precedent is unlikely to be appealed. The main significance of precedential opinions in nonfrivolous appeals, as I explained in Chapter 2, is to provide a framework for analysis—to exclude certain arguments and identify relevant policies—rather than to determine the decision in the case. For these purposes there is no need to cite many cases. Only the unhealthy obsession with precedent causes brief writers to lard their briefs with superfluous citations. A good rule would be to limit to twenty the number of case citations that can appear in an opening brief, and to ten the number that can appear in a reply brief.

The obsession with precedent, constituting a giant distraction, unsurprisingly coexists with what is frequently a casual attitude toward facts. Lawyers will cite what they consider the most helpful facts that they can find in the trial-court record, but often the record will be missing facts that are important to the judges. Often these are facts easily found by a Google search, but most lawyers haven't discovered the Internet's value as a mode of research into facts relating to the law. Moreover, few lawyers have a good sense of what judges are interested in, and at the same time may fail to realize that unless lawyers give the judges the information the judges need, some judges will conduct independent research in an effort to obtain the information and by doing so may catch the lawyers unawares. For the lawyers were taught in law schools that ours is an adversary system—a system in which the factual contentions and supporting evidence are presented by the lawyers and the judicial role is umpireal. Umpires just police compliance with rules; they are not permitted to decide which team should win. Most judges, however, want to produce what they consider sensible decisions. Often that is the only possible aspiration because the formal legal materials—the cases, statutory provisions, doctrinal intricacies, and so on—can be inapt or baffling. If the lawyers have not tried to make their position seem sensible rather than just the logical entailment of a legal doctrine, the judges may search outside the briefs and record for guidance. As yet few judges do so but that will change as a new generation of judges comes online.

I place much of the blame for the inability of so many of the lawyers who argue cases in my court to educate and inform my colleagues and me on the headlock that adversary procedure has on the American legal profession. The profession prizes our adversary system of law, so different from the inquisitorial legal systems of so many countries outside the Anglo-American legal sphere. It prizes our system because it is our system and creates greater demand and more lucrative opportunities for litigators than inquisitorial systems do, and because it caters to American dislike of government by greatly reducing the number of judges and other court personnel. Inquisitorial systems employ many more judges, because the judges are responsible for creating the record on which the decision of a case is based. The adversary system focuses lawyers on whacking each other forensically rather than on creating a balanced and complete and accurate record. I've often witnessed the unedifying spectacle of both opposing lawyers in a case arguing that the meaning they ascribe to a statutory provision at issue is the "plain meaning" and should therefore govern, though it is hardly likely that the same sentence or phrase can "plainly" be read in opposite ways. Lawyer adversaries don't want to help the court; they want to bash their opponents. Bashing an opponent is one way of persuading a judge, but it is a bad way and fortunately often fails. It amounts to saying: my case may be crappy, but my opponent's is crappier. That's not the most effective form of legal rhetoric.

Complicating the relationship between the academy and the judiciary is the increased complexity of cases and legal materials (the evolution of the *Bluebook* is a parody of that growth). Legal complexity has grown and also of course factual complexity, importantly including scientific and technological complexity but also the increased complexity of financial and other commercial instruments and practices.[11] But it is *legal* complexity that commands most of the attention of faculty and students. That is a mistake, because judges can't decide their most important cases without radical simplification of "the law." If you doubt that, you have only to read Professor Fallon's recent paper on legal interpretation.[12] The paper is a learned and detailed canvas of theories of statutory and constitutional interpretation. But on the last page, noting "that there can be multiple linguistically and legally plausible referents for claims of legal meaning—including semantic or literal meaning, contextual or pragmatic meaning (in its distinguishable variations), speaker's intended meaning, reasonable

11. The growth of these complexities is the central theme of my book *Reflections on Judging* (2013).
12. Richard H. Fallon, Jr., "The Meaning of Legal 'Meaning' and Its Implications for Theories of Legal Interpretation" (Harvard Law School, October 2014, unpublished). Recall my discussion in the Introduction of a similar article by Professor Fallon.

meaning, and interpreted meaning," and after "a careful examination of textualism, legislative intentionalism, purposivism, originalism, and leading forms of non-originalism," Fallon concludes that "none [of the theories of interpretation] possesses the resources to determine a consistent, uniquely correct referent for claims of legal meaning without reliance on relatively ad hoc normative judgments."[13] To which a judge is likely to react by saying to himself, "Thanks, but no thanks, Professor Fallon."

Fallon is a distinguished scholar. He is not a tease, an agent provocateur, who wants law students to think about such questions as "what is wrong with torturing a prisoner when he consents to it to shorten his sentence?" or "is it permissible to carve up one person to use his organs—his two kidneys, his two lungs, and his heart—to save five?"[14] He does not write books called *The Invisible Constitution* (illustrated!— it makes one think of those boldfaced spaces that I discussed in Chapter 2) or *America's Unwritten Constitution: The Precedents and Principles We Live By*.[15] But what he should be saying is that theories of legal interpretation are a useless muddle, and what law schools should be teaching their students is to eschew legal complexity (and while they're at it burn the *Bluebook*) and learn to cope with factual complexity and make the unraveling of that complexity the centerpiece of their advocacy as lawyers.

In fairness to lawyers, their timidity about breaking with tradition is based in part at least on fear of getting ahead of the judges, who are accustomed to heavy emphasis on doctrine in briefs and oral argument and may regard departures from custom with suspicion. Feeling dependent on the lawyers' briefs and arguments and on doctrine-saturated, jargon-rich, *Bluebook*-marinated law clerks recently gradu-

---

13. Id. at 56.

14. Leo Katz, *Why the Law Is So Perverse* 15, 128 (2011). See also id. at 40–42, 77–78.

15. These are books by Laurence Tribe and Akhil Amar—both very prominent professors of constitutional law—respectively.

ated from law school, judges publish opinions larded with citations to precedents yet barren of facts not found in the record, or even facts that are in the record but were not mentioned by the district court. It's natural for the lawyer to conform his brief and argument to what he thinks the judges expect. He doesn't want to file an unconventional brief and then lose the case and have to explain the loss to his client. ("I tried something different; it didn't work; sorry.") For the modern lawyer inhabits a legal culture in which competition is attaining Darwinian intensity—a culture in which a corporate general counsel may deliberately overpay a law firm representing the corporation in litigation so that if the corporation loses the case the general counsel can explain to his angry CEO that it was not for want of trying.

I am put in mind of an incident from the 1970s, when IBM, then at the acme of its greatness, was under siege from government and private antitrust enforcers. After Nicholas Katzenbach, IBM's general counsel, explained to the company's outside lawyers how determined IBM was to defeat the trustbusters at any cost, one of the lawyers asked him whether that meant that the sky was the limit so far as legal expense was concerned. To which Katzenbach replied: "There is no limit."

The competitive pressures besetting the legal profession help explain why law schools are reluctant to train students in unconventional methods of legal advocacy. A failed experiment in litigation tactics is difficult to justify to the client. For the same reason the now greatly curtailed on-the-job training that fledgling lawyers receive from their employers tends also to be highly conventional. Assistant U.S. Attorneys may be the only lawyers who still get first-rate on-the-job training—in every district of my circuit the ablest litigation "firm" is the office of the U.S. Attorney for the district. The reason is partly that being an Assistant U.S. Attorney is a highly coveted job, for which competition is intense because it provides more opportunities for young lawyers actually to conduct trials (as well as to argue appeals) than associates in private law firms are given, and because each U.S. Attorney's office provides extensive training of its new lawyers—something that private law firms, owing to the increasingly competitive culture of the modern American legal profession, can no longer afford.

The training programs in the U.S. Attorneys' offices fill gaps in legal education without breaking out of the conventional model of legal advocacy. Many a federal judge has had a prior stint as a U.S. Attorney or an Assistant U.S. Attorney, understands the realities of litigation better than most lawyers, yet remains conventional in outlook and upon becoming a judge is likely to undergo reimmersion in the old culture. That is natural because it is the culture of the law clerks and therefore permeates the opinions that the clerks draft for the judge and that his colleagues' clerks draft for their judges. The new judge will find himself paddling in formalist waters and will find it easier to remain there than to seek dry land and become a legal realist and by doing so invite criticism for being "result oriented," a maverick, a fossil remnant of the legal realism of the 1920s and 1930s.

So the law schools must shoulder part of the blame for our excessively formalist legal culture. What can they do to atone? I suggest four reforms: changes in the teaching of substantive legal courses; changes in the curriculum broadly understood as the entire law school educational program including continuing judicial education (the subject of the next chapter) when undertaken by a law school; changes in faculty composition; and changes in the faculty's relation to the traditionally student-run moot courts and law reviews.

The conventional courses should be taught with less emphasis on doctrine and other foci of a formalist legal education and more on the realities of the legal process, such as how the actual legislative drafting process differs (dramatically) from what most judges and lawyers believe (or assume) it to be, and what this implies for sound statutory interpretation.[16] It's also important to understand cases in their full factual contexts rather than as etiolated sketches convenient for doctrinal analysis, and how judges' actual reactions to cases differ from the orthodox concept of judicial behavior.

Clinical education deserves emphasis not merely as a supplement to conventional law courses but also as a substitute for some of them. Civil procedure and evidence are important courses but should not be taught, as they almost always are, out of a casebook. For they are fields inseparable from trial (and pretrial) practice, intelligible only in the context of practice, lifeless in books. The federal rules of civil and criminal procedure and of evidence can be understood only in the trial and pretrial settings in which they are invoked. For several years in the early 1990s I taught a combination of evidence and trial advocacy in a mock-trial format, using the brilliantly realistic case files created by the National Institute for Trial Advocacy for such use. I considered the course a success though some students thought it slighted legal doctrine. I'm convinced that it's the way evidence should always be taught, and procedure too.

I recall having appointed one of the students to be the judge in the first mock trial in the course, and though he did a good job the students were insistent that I be the judge in the remaining mock trials, and I yielded to their importuning. I shouldn't have. The Institute's case files are as I said realistic and so student judges would get a sense of what it feels like to be a real judge. Only a few students could have had this experience in the course because the course was too short to accommodate more than three or four trials, but those students could have been asked to discuss their experiences as (mock) judges with the entire class. It would have been an eye opener. Of course few of the students would ever become judges—there are very few judges, especially federal judges, relative to the size of the legal profession.

16. See the Gluck-Bressman articles cited in Chapter 2, note 27, of this book.

(That is why it would be quixotic to think we could give up the adversary system, flawed as it is: it would require an enormous increase in the number of judges.)[17] But to be a really effective trial or appellate lawyer one has to know how judges think. Impersonation can be education. The student judge would learn among other things that judges do not think like professors.

The evidence course that I have been describing is not the usual clinical fare.[18] It was "mock clinical" or "quasi-clinical." The usual clinical course has law students, under faculty supervision, providing legal services to indigents. In effect the students are practicing law. That gives them a head start on law firm practice, and is welcomed by law firms as preparing first-year associates to engage in productive practice from the get-go. But it's unlikely to do more to foster student understanding of judges than practice itself does. If the lawyers who appear before me both in appeals and, when I am volunteering to handle cases in district court, in trials (or pretrial phases of cases that may or may not go to trial) are representative, lawyers don't learn a great deal about judges from appearing before them. They learn something, of course, but more about the attitudes of particular judges (toward criminal defendants, for example) than about what makes judges tick, what the basic mindset of a judge is.

17. See my book *Law and Legal Theory in the UK and USA* 27–30 (1996). The ratio of lawyers to judges is *much* lower in an inquisitorial than in an adversarial legal system. For example, it is 6.86 to 1 in Germany and 2.86 to 1 in Switzerland, compared to 54.59 to 1 in the United States and 57.05 to 1 in the United Kingdom. Id. at 27 tab. 1.1. Another problem with the inquisitorial system is that it is bureaucratized: judges lack independence because their careers (location, promotion, and the like) are controlled by their judicial or ministerial superiors.

18. For a good brief discussion of the growth and character of clinical legal education, see Marc Rotenberg, Ginger McCall, and Julia Horwitz, "The Open Government Clinic: Teaching the Basics of Lawyering," 48 *Indiana Law Review* 149, 176–183 (2014).

A further problem is that many, perhaps most, clinical law professors do not receive tenure, are not expected to publish, and do not do much teaching in the conventional sense—their time is consumed with assisting and advising students on how to provide legal assistance to the clinic's clients.[19] These characteristics set the clinical faculty apart from the regular faculty. I would like to see the clinical professors do more teaching because, as I've suggested, fields like civil and criminal procedure, evidence, and trial advocacy are practical; doctrine in such fields is for the most part simple, secondary, and often ignored by both the lawyers and the judge.

Good judges, and therefore good lawyers, are interested in the facts of cases in a broad sense of "fact," and not just in legal doctrine. Law students who have no technical background should be required to take courses, not necessarily in the law school but either elsewhere in the university or online (the domain of the "MOOCs"—massive open online courses), that will help them understand the full factual contexts of complicated modern lawsuits. It will also help them help judges understand the importance to sensible judicial decision making of fully understanding context.

I have in mind courses in finance, accounting, business management, computer science (including coding, Web design, and "Big Data" tools), statistics as a tool of empirical research, economics, psychology, political science, medicine and biology, fingerprint and DNA evidence, electronic surveillance, and the patent system (the union of law and technology). It is important that law students be permitted to take college as well as graduate school courses in these areas, because they may not have an adequate educational background to take

---

19. See generally, William P. Quigley, "Introducing Clinical Law Teaching for the New Clinical Law Professor: A View from the First Floor," 28 *Akron Law Review* 463 (1995).

graduate-level courses in technical fields and because they may not need to have a deep knowledge of any of these fields in order to practice law governing disputes arising from them.

Law students who enter law school with a background in technical, scientific, or social-scientific fields have a growing representation in law school student bodies and should, if as a result of their concentration on such fields they have little acquaintance with the humanities—philosophy, literature, history, the arts—be required to take courses in them as part of their law school education. Such courses will improve their ability to interpret complicated texts, to write clearly and gracefully, and to bring historical and, where relevant, philosophical insights to bear on legal issues. The culture of the humanities has enriched the legal process—it shines through the opinions of the great judges, such as Holmes, Brandeis, and Cardozo, and, though its light has dimmed, it can continue to enrich the judicial system.

One needs to distinguish between knowledge on the one hand and communication or expression on the other. It is one thing to be knowledgeable, whether about law, sciences, humanities, or all these domains, and another to be able to communicate to an audience of lawyers and laypersons insights gleaned from this knowledge and assimilated to the judge's understanding. Too many judicial opinions are flat, jargon-ridden, uncandid, hypertechnical, overlong. Judges (or, as a second-best substitute, their law clerks) need familiarity with the humanities but they also need the expressive skills that such familiarity can, with proper training, bring, as well as at least a minimum comfort level with science, technology, and the insights and research techniques of the social sciences.

Time is limited, selection and abbreviation therefore unavoidable. But the law student who achieves some proficiency in all three cultures—law, humanities, and science (including the social sciences) and technology—and learns how to communicate the insights of those fields to nonspecialists, will be acquiring foundations for a distinguished judicial career should luck and desire eventually make him or her a judge.[20]

I would also like to see law schools offer courses on the judiciary. The seeds have been planted. The political scientist Lee Epstein, the economist William Landes, and I teach a workshop on judicial behavior at the University of Chicago Law School. Political scientists have been the pioneers in the study of judicial behavior, though they have tended to emphasize the political element in judging to the exclusion of the other elements. Economists and economics-minded lawyers have contributed to the study of judicial behavior as well. They have emphasized the incentives and constraints of judges viewed as self-interested employees who thus, like other workers, have a "utility function"—a schedule of weighted preferences.[21] But these economically minded lawyers have had to adjust their model of employee behavior to reflect the fact that unlike the situation of most employees, financial incentives play little role in aspirations for a judicial career. Most though not all federal judges could make more, often much more, money as practicing lawyers, and some as businessmen.

Issues of incentives and constraints in the judicial career are approached by social scientists not only theoretically, or through case studies and anecdotes, but also statistically, as by correlating the ideological slant of a judge's decisions with the politics of the President who appointed him and of the Senators who voted to confirm him.

20. See, for example, Penn Law, Center for Technology, Innovation and Competition, "Law and Technology at Penn, 2012–2013," www.law.upenn.edu/live/files/2625-ctic-201213-report; www.law.upenn.edu/academics/crossdisciplinary/jd-engineering/. The University of Pennsylvania now offers joint degrees in law and engineering and in law and computing and information technology.

21. See, for example, my long-ago article "What Do Judges and Justices Maximize? (The Same Thing Everybody Else Does)," 3 *Supreme Court Economic Review* 1 (1993).

These are valuable things to study and learn. They are the subject of the recent book on judicial behavior by Lee Epstein, William Landes, and me that I've cited and are the sort of thing on which our workshop on judicial behavior concentrates.[22] Yet the workshop is not considered central to the educational mission of the law school. Indeed it is notably peripheral, attracting mainly foreign graduate students. That the study of the judiciary should not engage the interest of students and faculty at a leading law school is, if one thinks about it, passing strange.

The law school offers a short, highly compressed (thirteen hours spread over only three days), highly realistic course on the Supreme Court taught by Lee Epstein, the political scientist whom I just mentioned, and Adam Liptak, the *New York Times*'s Supreme Court correspondent. Their approaches are complementary, reflecting the differences in their professions. Their teaching tools include tables and graphs and audiovisual aids, which this year included videos of the Bork and Sotomayor Senate confirmation proceedings. Dennis Hutchinson, a law professor with a very deep knowledge of the Court, and I in a guinea-pig role as an appellate judge having therefore some feel for how Supreme Court Justices approach their jobs (both Hutchinson and I are former Supreme Court law clerks—he having worked for two Justices, White and Douglas, and I for Brennan) sit in on the course, participating as junior faculty. Despite its brevity and its focus on process and personality rather than on doctrine, the course gives students a better sense of the judicial process than the traditional constitutional law and other doctrinal courses give. (One student said it was the best course she had taken at the law school.)

Both that course and the judicial behavior workshop that I mentioned have a social-scientific orientation, but are brought down to

---

22. Lee Epstein, William M. Landes, and Richard A. Posner, *The Behavior of Federal Judges: A Theoretical and Empirical Study of Rational Choice* (2013).

earth by their focus on how judges act rather than on what they (often their law clerks rather than they) say in their opinions. Psychology, sociology, economics, organization theory, and related fields are important to getting behind the mask and understanding the actual behavior of judges. They are an aid to understanding that old-school law professors, though closer to the practice of law than most present-day law professors, didn't have. They are underutilized but even if fully utilized would not be enough to impart to students an adequate understanding of judicial behavior. And so a further possibility worth considering would be to offer a course that provided not only a social-scientific understanding of the judiciary but also an "acquaintance" with actual judges through first-rate biographies (for example of Cardozo by Andrew Kaufman, Byron White by Dennis Hutchinson, and Henry Friendly by David Dorsen), through formal and informal extrajudicial writings of judges (Friendly's essay "Reactions of a Lawyer-Newly-Become-Judge"[23] exemplifies the former, and Holmes's extensive correspondence is a treasure trove of informal extrajudicial writing by our greatest judge), and through published interviews of judges[24] and studies of different types or styles of judging.[25]

Professor Stone, whom I mentioned earlier in this chapter, has

23. In Henry J. Friendly, *Benchmarks* 1 (1967). See, for other articles by judges, *Judges on Judging: Views from the Bench* (David M. O'Brien ed., 4th ed. 2013).

24. See, for example, William Domnarski, *Federal Judges Revealed*, ch. 8 and p. 186 (2009).

25. See Corey Rayburn Yung, "A Typology of Judging Styles," 107 *Northwestern University Law Review* 1757 (2013). The most elaborate study of types and styles of judging, one long predating the social-scientific approach of Yung and most other current scholars, is Karl N. Llewellyn's 565-page treatise *The Common Law Tradition: Deciding Appeals* (1960), which I mentioned in Chapter 4. It articulates a legal-realist approach to adjudication that I find congenial, though it is dated and excessively long and its style is off-putting and it doesn't discuss federal courts. It is well summarized in William Twining, *Karl Llewellyn and the Realist Movement*, ch. 10 (1973).

since 1973 taught a seminar on constitutional decision making, in which (according to the course description)

> students enrolled in the seminar will work as "courts" consisting of five "Justices" each. During each of the first eight weeks of the quarter, each court will be assigned two hypothetical cases raising issues under the Equal Protection Clause of the Fourteenth Amendment. All cases must be decided with opinion (concurring and dissenting opinions are permitted/encouraged). The decisions may be premised on the "legislative history" of the Equal Protection Clause (materials on that history will be provided) and on any doctrines, theories, or precedents created by the "Justices" themselves. The "Justices" may not rely, however, on any *actual* decisions of the United States Supreme Court. The seminar is designed to give students some insight into the problems a Justice confronts in collaborating with colleagues, interpreting an ambiguous constitutional provision, and then living with the doctrines and precedents he or she creates. Enrollment will be limited to three courts. Since the members of each court must work together closely under rigid time constraints, students must sign up as five-person courts. This seminar will not have regularly–scheduled classes (except for an introductory meeting), but you should not underestimate the time demands. It is a very demanding seminar. If more than three courts sign up, I will select the participating courts by lot.

The average "court" in the seminar produces more than three hundred single-spaced pages of opinions, and Professor Stone gives the students detailed feedback each week. My only criticism is that I would like to see the seminar include court of appeals as well as Supreme Court cases, because lawyers have far more to do with those courts than with the Supreme Court.

Chief Judge Diane Wood of my court teaches a seminar, aimed mainly at students who are going to be judicial law clerks, that focuses on issues important to courts but unlikely to receive much attention in the standard law school classes. That is very worthwhile, as is Professor Arthur Hellman's suggestion that the standard law school course on the federal courts be humanized by focusing on how judges and lawyers use the tactical opportunities that the rules of jurisdiction and procedure create and not just on the rules themselves.[26] This would complement the mock-clinical courses on evidence and procedure that I have suggested. Legal rules are usually not rigid; they are malleable and bend to circumstance. There is a sense in which legal rules are made to be broken.

A variant of these suggestions for teaching about judicial behavior is, as some law schools are doing, inviting judges to the law school to give talks to students, or to meet informally with them, or both. The University of Chicago Law School has what it calls the Edward H. Levi Distinguished Jurists Program. New York University Law School has an Institute of Judicial Administration (which, among other things, co-sponsors with the Federal Judicial Center a New Appellate Judges Seminar). The University of Pennsylvania Law School has a Visiting Jurist Program, and Vanderbilt University Law School offers a Mid-Career Seminar for U.S. District Judges. And this is not an exhaustive list.[27]

The programs differ but the University of Chicago's probably is typical. It is described as a program in which federal district and court of appeals judges

---

26. Arthur Hellman, "Another Voice for the 'Dialogue': Federal Courts as a Litigation Course," 53 *Saint Louis University Law Journal* 761 (2009).
27. See, for example, Colloquium on Courts and the Legal Process (Columbia Law School), www.law.columbia.edu/faculty/workshops/courts-legal-process.

offer students and faculty up-close insights into their decision-making processes. During the visits [in the program's first year, 2013], each judge gave a lunch talk to the Law School community, participated in a *Sidebar: Conversations with the Bench* workshop featuring candid discussions of faculty scholarship and its utility for the work that judges do, and met with faculty members for dinner. The program was started to "bring the best judges in the country to campus so they can interact with students and faculty," said Professor Lior Strahilevitz, who organized the series . . . "Judges reinforce, supplement, and challenge what students get in the classroom, and the judges get to speak to some of the best soon-to-be lawyers in the country. We've learned a great deal from the judges this year, and we hope they have learned from us as well." The program will continue next year. Joshua Ackerman, '13, called the program "fantastic," and said that "these are probably the best lunch talks we've had. It demystifies the experience of interacting with a judge, and helps students to get comfortable asking questions in front of them." Esther Lifshitz, '14, agreed. "It's always exciting for law students to get a better understanding of their ultimate bosses, the people they're going to have to answer to as lawyers."[28]

These programs have value in acquainting law students with judges at first hand rather than just with the judges' judicial opinions (cropped) in casebooks. But not many judges will "open up" to law students (many will not open up to their own law clerks, or to their colleagues for that matter). Notice that the blurb about the visiting-

28. "Visiting Jurists Program Offers Inside View of Being a Judge," May 29, 2013, www.law.uchicago.edu/news/visiting-jurists-program-offers-inside-view-being -judge.

judges program doesn't say *what* the students and professors learned from the judges. From speaking to faculty who have attended these sessions I infer that some of the judges do provide insights into the challenges of being a federal judge, thus affording valuable but limited glimpses of judicial behavior.

As for those judges who teach part time, some of whom were law professors before becoming judges, generally their teaching doesn't differ much from that of full-time faculty. From this one can infer that it is more important for law students to learn about judges than to learn legal doctrine from them. The University of Chicago Law School is missing an opportunity for informal instruction in the realities of adjudication: three judges of the Seventh Circuit (Frank Easterbrook, Diane Wood, and I) are part-time faculty members at the law school but are used as teachers rather than as guinea pigs, although Wood's seminar and my course on judicial writing give students a glimpse of the judicial mentality.

More important than bringing judges to the campus to be displayed or to teach is for law professors to impart to the students a more realistic understanding of what makes judges tick than students are likely to obtain from casebooks. That is important not just for students who aspire to be law clerks, or eventually judges. Lawyers who practice before courts need to know how judges think; and law students who intend to practice before courts can gain insight into how judges think by writing judicial opinions as classwork.[29] Such insight

29. "One of the most important things law schools could do to train students to better appreciate judging [is] actually asking them to draft judicial opinions. Law schools are rife with classes that call upon students to criticize judges, but few if any classes are devoted to instructing students in the art of writing judicial opinions or working together on a collegial court. Granted, such training might be premature, but it might be a good start for lawyers to begin to understand the thought processes of judges and the challenges of deciding cases, forging majorities in contentious cases, and crafting judicial opinions." Michael J. Gerhardt, "How a Judge Thinks," 93 *Minnesota Law Review* 2185, 2202–2203 (2009).

would make them more effective brief writers and oral advocates, because they would have a better feel for the audience (the judges). And because they would be more effective they would enhance judicial performance.

Opinion writing (including the writing of bench memoranda, a task of most judicial law clerks and often in effect a first draft of a judge's opinion), and brief writing, should be major components of a three-year legal writing program that all students are required to take rather than an optional occasional course. I suppose that law students still need to learn to write legal memoranda, though they are a diminishing part of the work of first-year associates in law firms. But that should not be the exclusive focus of a writing program limited to the first year of law school; nor should the writing program be limited to the first year. Professor Anne Mullins has reminded me that the legal writing course required for all first year-students is usually the only writing course that law students take, and she points out that the first year of law school may be too early for students to learn effective brief writing, to which I would add: or effective opinion writing. Apart from the writing course, student writing in law school courses is confined to writing exam answers, which are not graded on writing skill. Students on law review write articles (very short articles called case comments, or somewhat longer articles called notes), but they are not evaluated by faculty.

Law students need instruction in how to *write,* as distinct from instruction in learning to write a particular kind of document. It is remarkable how badly the modern law student, modern law clerk, modern lawyer, and modern judge write. One reason is that good writing is not much valued in modern America (the electronic revolution is partly to blame), not much taught in college—not much taught in high school or earlier, for that matter. Another reason is that law students, abetted by their legal-writing instructors, think that legal documents (contracts, statutes, pleadings, briefs, opinions, and so forth) must be written in an artificial "professional" style—which is false. Such documents should be written in standard English, with an absolute minimum of legal jargon.

Legal documents need to be recognized as rhetorical endeavors—endeavors to persuade an audience. In rhetorical composition, sensitivity to audience is almost everything. Ever since Aristotle's treatise on rhetoric it's been understood that effective rhetoric depends on understanding the needs, desires, and comprehension of the intended audience. Because the audience of an appellate lawyer consists of judges, effective rhetoric at the appellate level requires understanding of judges. To that understanding the law schools contribute rather little, because they don't think in Aristotelian terms. The first year of law school focuses the students on learning the basics of legal vocabulary, doctrine, and analysis rather than on learning what judges need or want in a lawyer's brief and therefore how to argue effectively to a judge, as distinct from how to argue effectively to the teacher of the legal-writing course. So one thing worth adding to first-year and also second- and third-year law courses is brief *reading:* the students should be assigned both good and bad briefs to read. The briefs filed in the Supreme Court, for example, are often better written, reasoned, organized, and persuasive than the Court's opinions.

There is need for a third-year course in legal writing, or better yet for a series of legal writing courses embracing all three years of law school. And the better that new lawyers understand how to write to and for judges, the better off the judges are; for most law clerks are new lawyers.

I was surprised to learn recently how numerous and ambitious are the legal writing programs offered by some law schools.[30] The fo-

30. See Association of Legal Writing Directors (ALWD), Legal Writing Institute, *Report of the Annual Legal Writing Survey* (2013), www.alwd.org/wp-content/uploads/2013/08/2013-Survey-Report-final.pdf.

cus is on writing (not reading) briefs and other legal documents, and some programs even teach judicial opinion writing.[31] Yet when I think of the briefs I've read over the past thirty-four years, including briefs in almost seven thousand orally argued cases, I have to say that the average brief is mediocre. Of course I don't know what the average brief would be like were there no legal writing programs. But it's apparent that the programs are failing to turn out highly skilled brief writers. Consistent with my earlier remarks about the U.S. Attorneys' offices, the best brief writers tend to be the attorneys in those offices—by virtue of the training they get on the job.

The first-year writing course at many law schools is one of the culprits in the inadequacy of brief writing. The course is likely to teach students either the "IRAC" system of legal writing or the "CRAC" system. IRAC stands for "Issue, Rule, Application, Conclusion," CRAC for "Conclusion, Rule, Application, Conclusion." Either or both are taught as proper sequences for a legal memorandum, brief, and opinion. CRAC is the more absurd, because two conclusions are one too many, and because starting an opinion by announcing the result creates the appearance that the case was decided and only then was the search on for reasons that could be given for the decision. IRAC is bad enough, however. It is mechanical, unimaginative, and downplays facts.

There is more that is wrong with the typical first-year required writing course. Invariably the students are told not to use contractions, so that their memos will be properly stuffy. Worse, they are taught that legal argument is a specialized discourse, that its jargon must be embraced, that students must master the *Bluebook* (I wish I knew why), that brevity is not a virtue or repetition and footnotes and jargon vices. At some law schools students are required to *Bluebook* their legal-writing memos even if the school's journals and moot

31. See id. at 12, 24–30.

court program do not use it. And students may be penalized if their memos include italicized periods (recall this preposterous formalism from Chapter 2). All this is stupid and wrong and contributes to the disappointing quality of briefs and opinions. I would like someone to tell me what possible societal value mastery of the *Bluebook* could have.

The preoccupation of legal instruction with picayune formalities feeds the misimpression that law is a technical discipline, a misimpression capsulized in the widespread belief that the function of law schools is to teach students how to "think like a lawyer." The consequence is to sideline considerations of equity, politics, feasibility, ethics, humanity, and sheer factuality, considerations that Holmes summarized in his famous aphorism that the life of the law has not been logic, but experience.[32]

The notion of law as a technical discipline deflects whatever impulse might otherwise be felt to provide law students with models of good writing. After all, no one worries whether scientists are good or bad writers. But law, though it ought to draw more on science and technology than it does (for we live in the twenty-first century, not in the eighteenth century), is not a science; it is a humanity. Good writing is important to law, for clarification and stimulation. There are a handful of judges, most of them dead (but so what?), who write (or wrote) well: Holmes, Learned Hand, Cardozo, and Robert Jackson are, in my opinion, the best among the dead. Among the living, not so many: Michael Boudin of the First Circuit, Alex Kozinski of the Ninth Circuit, and Frank Easterbrook of my court come first to my mind, but there are many others (especially on my court!). And the quality of a person's writing is apt to be to a significant extent a func-

---

32. For cogent criticism of the law schools' overemphasis on "thinking like a lawyer," see Elizabeth Mertz, *The Language of Law School: Learning to "Think Like a Lawyer"* (2007).

tion of what he reads, whether inside or outside his field. Law students should be, but are not, deliberately exposed not only to the best legal writing—including, in Holmes's case for example, scholarly writing and correspondence—but also to models of good writing in any field, a huge body of literature that includes Lincoln's addresses, almost anything written by George Orwell (including his indispensable essay "Politics and the English Language"), Saul Bellow, Philip Roth, William Empson, and C. S. Lewis. (And that's just for starters.)

Coming back to briefs: a further though only partial explanation for their disappointing quality is that briefs of private attorneys are often written as much with clients in mind as with judges in mind, in order to demonstrate the lawyer's commitment to, and indeed identification with, the client. Lawyers have two audiences—judges and clients—and have to play to both of them. And so briefs often boil over with anger, indignation, righteousness, exaggeration, and downright falsehood, in these respects faithfully mirroring the emotions and deceptions of the client. About these tendencies there is little that legal writing programs can do. But the result is that the average brief isn't very helpful to a good judge, and the adversary system is weakened. Law schools should be able to do more to combat at least some of the deficiencies, so harmful to the judiciary, of adversary procedure than they are doing.

Brief writing is a major part of moot court competition, which many law students participate in. But moot court programs are run by students rather than by faculty, though usually there's a faculty advisor. Although there is no dearth of books and articles that seek to improve brief writing, the focus is on better writing in the sense of writing that is clearer, more concise, more punchy, and the like.[33] That's fine,

---

33. See Bryan A. Garner, *The Winning Brief: 100 Tips for Persuasive Briefing in Trial and Appellate Courts* (3d ed. 2014); Starla J. Williams and Iva J. Ferrell, "No At-

but instruction in rhetoric is largely ignored, with the result that the sense of an audience, which I stressed a few pages back, goes missing. Effective brief writing and oral argument depend on the advocate's knowing and conveying the information about the case, the law, the parties, and so forth that the *judges* want and need, for they are the principal audience. But good briefing and arguing depend as well on a knowledge of rhetoric—specifically knowledge of the three "appeals of argument" that Aristotle identified. They are the logical appeal (use of logic and evidence to convince), the ethical appeal (establishing the speaker/writer as trustworthy and knowledgeable), and the emotional appeal (which at its best is a persuasive appeal to what in the introduction I called "moral intuition)."

There need be no tension between instructing law students in the principles of rhetoric and ensuring that they master at least the rudiments of technical knowledge (by which I mean the language of science and technology, not the language of an imagined technical field called "law")—another essential element of a worthwhile modern legal education. An example will illustrate.[34] Suppose your client is accused of a crime, and his DNA is found at the crime scene. And suppose the probability that it isn't his DNA but that of another person is only 1 in 100,000. This may seem damning evidence—"the probability that this match has occurred by chance is 1 in 100,000."[35] But it isn't really, if the crime occurred in a city with a population of, say, two million; for then one would expect that twenty persons in the city would have DNA that matched the defendant's; and now the

---

Risk Law Student Left Behind: The Convergence of Academic Support Pedagogy and Experiential Education," 2014, http://papers.ssrn.com/sol3/papers .cfm?abstract_id=2384589.

34. The example is drawn from Gerd Gigerenzer, "How I Got Started: Teaching Physicians and Judges Risk Literacy," 28 *Applied Cognitive Psychology* 612, 613 (2014).

35. Id.

probability that the DNA found at the crime scene is not his is not 1 in 100,000 but 1 in 20. If you are his lawyer, you'd better understand this and be able to explain it to a jury—and likewise if you are the judge in the case, or on the panel hearing an appeal.

The efficacy of moot court competition as a method of educating future lawyers in briefing and arguing cases is undermined by four tendencies: the tendency to pick a constitutional case (constitutional law is the least disciplined, least professional, most emotional, most politicized area of American law, and receives disproportionate attention in law schools); the tendency to use an invented case rather than a real one; the tendency, if a real case is used, to omit the trial record; and the tendency to discourage extrarecord research. The result of these tendencies is to make moot court competition much less realistic, relative to real cases, than it has to be. I am told that at some law schools the moot court board lays down strict rules, requiring for example that the briefs contain headings and subheadings—a bad rule, for reasons discussed in Chapter 2.

It's also a mistake to choose as judges of moot courts law professors, actual judges, or lawyers. Moot court judges should be students, and should write opinions deciding the cases they judge. That will help them to prepare for clerkships, legal practice, and for some of them an eventual judgeship. Generally moot court judges do not decide the case, but instead decide which student-lawyer team did the best job, whether in briefing or arguing. But that would not be an appropriate role for a student judge, because, apart from the question of competence, it would reduce the realism of the student's experience as a judge. Judges decide cases; they do not grade the lawyers (except that they will occasionally criticize a lawyer who has done an especially bad job). The student-judges should decide the case on the merits; faculty should decide which team did a better job of advocacy.

And likewise faculty, not students, should administer the moot court programs (just as they should manage the law reviews), with the students who join the moot court as an extracurricular activity serving as staff. To place the administration of such programs in the hands of students is equivalent to having the first-year civil procedure course taught by third-year law students.

So the student-managed law reviews and the student-managed moot courts should be phased out, along with casebooks, although the law reviews and the moot courts, unlike the casebooks, should remain a part of legal education.

The question of redesigning the law school curriculum to give students a greater insight into the actual as distinct from an imagined or idealized judicial process can't be separated from the question of the staffing of law schools—specifically, whether law schools are over-invested in the hiring of refugees from other disciplines. It is becoming commonplace, as the reader will recall from the Introduction, for law schools to hire as tenure-track faculty men and women who enrolled in law school after extensive graduate work in another field, such as history, economics, political science, electrical engineering, philosophy, or psychology. Having started their legal career late they don't want to defer their entry into their academic career further by practicing law. The result is that when they become members of a law school faculty they may be apt to think of themselves as historians, economists, political scientists, and so on, who apply knowledge acquired from their first academic love to law. They have valuable insights to impart to law students, but the students also need practical instruction. Where are they to get it? Increasingly from adjuncts, which is to say practitioners who teach part-time. Because they teach part-time and are not academics, they tend to teach whatever is their practice specialty, and it is often very narrow. Which is fine. Often their courses are deservedly very popular. But the result of this dual-track system of legal education is a buffet rather than a program.

In between the high-academic faculty and the adjuncts are the clinical professors, who are practical and who as I said earlier could and should be utilized to teach courses like procedure and evidence, and not just trial practice, negotiation, and other courses seen as peripheral to the educational program of a law school. They are part of the solution to the curricular deficiencies that I've been discussing. But the clinical faculty tends to be rather isolated from what I am calling the high-academic faculty, and to lack influence. If a law school were to take my suggestions about teaching procedure and evidence (and perhaps other subjects) as mock-clinical courses, and take away the administration of moot court programs from the students, and take over the management of the law reviews (law students would still staff them, but would not make article or book-review or note or case-comment selections), and try to convey to students a realistic understanding of judicial behavior, the balance between the practical and the theoretical in law teaching would shift in favor of the practical. The judiciary and the legal profession would be better for the shift.

The academy will resist the changes that I am suggesting because faculties in hiring reproduce themselves, and because so far as better teaching about judges is concerned, law professors really aren't very interested in judges, who strike them as remote, aloof, masked, unintellectual, limited. As I noted in the last chapter, few law professors are interested in the role, important as it is, of judges in mediating between academic proposals for doctrinal change and the proposals becoming law. And law students are likely to welcome only such changes in legal education as would improve the lawyer job market, about which many students even in elite law schools are anxious today because of the growth of outsourcing of legal services to foreign countries and to lowly paid contract attorneys, the growing substitution of computers for lawyers in the performance of lawyer tasks such as research and pretrial discovery, and tighter client control of lawyers. Students are unlikely to think that learning more about judges will help them in the job market. What they know for sure is that landing a good job after graduation requires good grades. So they work very hard for them (though slacking off as soon as they secure a job for when they graduate). That requires concentration on exam preparation, and the focus of most law school exams is on legal doctrine and its application to imaginary facts. The message is that the understanding of legal doctrine is the key to success in law school. But it is not the key to understanding judges, especially appellate judges, whose dockets are crowded with cases that are appealed only because doctrine doesn't dictate the outcome.

If neither law professors nor law students are interested in judges—if the judiciary (always excepting the Supreme Court, which exercises a malign fascination for a significant swatch of law professors) is a mere backdrop to legal scholarship and teaching—this chapter may seem an essay in futility. But the outlook is not quite so bleak. The professors at least recognize that the lawyers they are producing will benefit from understanding judges, even if the lawyers plan to be transactional lawyers rather than litigators. For in negotiating a deal a lawyer knows that it may become a subject of litigation, and so it behooves him to negotiate for provisions that will make litigation less likely, and a loss if there is litigation *much* less likely.

It should be possible and would be highly desirable for a law school's faculty (more realistically, the dean in collaboration with a faculty committee) to decide what every student should know about judges by the time of graduation and how they should acquire that knowledge—by what combination of classroom and clinical courses, field trips (to courts and judges' offices), reading assignments, moot courts, and ad hoc lectures. All the students would benefit, though especially those headed for a clerkship and/or for a career in litigation. The judiciary would benefit. And the faculty who participated in the program would by teaching about judges learn more about them, and this would help bridge the chasm that yawns between the academy and the judiciary.

Having decided what students should know about the judiciary by the time they graduate, including what they should know in order to be effective trial and appellate litigators, a law school could proceed to revamp its curriculum, and its faculty-appointment criteria, to equip the students with the requisite knowledge. The revision need not be radical, but it would include making civil procedure and evidence clinical courses, vesting management of the law school's journals and moot court program in faculty, creating a mandatory three-year legal-writing program taught by regular faculty and focused on the writing of briefs and judicial opinions, adding to the faculty some lawyers with substantial practical experience, and banning references to the *Bluebook,* IRAC, and CRAC.

6 | CONTINUING JUDICIAL EDUCATION

STUDENTS OF FOREIGN legal systems, such as the French system, find it remarkable that there is no degree or training requirement to become a judge in the United States; most foreign systems require that a judge have extensive preappointment judicial training.[1] It's been suggested that our law schools should offer a graduate program that would prepare lawyers to become judges.[2] That suggestion (made more than a decade ago) has not, to my knowledge, been taken up as yet by any law school, I assume because obtaining a judgeship is so chancy that the expense of obtaining the degree would often be wasted, making it a very risky investment. Inquisitorial legal systems, such as that of France and most other countries outside the Anglo-American sphere, have a much higher ratio of judges to practicing lawyers than adversarial systems do. Judges usually are appointed shortly after completion of their legal education and upon appointment begin a long climb up the judicial hierarchy. It is possible therefore for law students in those legal systems to plan for a judicial career.

A more realistic possibility in our system is for law schools to offer programs of continuing judicial education focused on the defi-

---

1. See, for example, Peter Bozzo, "The Jurisprudence of 'As Though': Democratic Dialogue and the Signed Supreme Court Opinion," 26 *Yale Journal of Law & the Humanities* 269, 279–281 (2014), and references cited there.
2. Marc T. Amy, "Judiciary School: A Proposal for a Pre-Judicial LL.M. Degree," 52 *Journal of Legal Education* 130 (2002). Duke Law School offers a program leading to a Master of Judicial Studies degree, but it is for existing rather than prospective judges. See Duke Law, Center for Judicial Studies, *Curriculum,* http://law .duke.edu/judicialstudies/degree/.

ciencies discussed in Part One of this book. That is the subject of this chapter.

One needs to distinguish between a course or seminar for judges that deals with a particular field of law, such as antitrust or securities regulation, and a course or seminar that by dealing with the judicial role and process can improve judicial performance more broadly. The former is the most common form of continuing judicial education. But it is not optimal. The jurisdiction of the federal courts is vast and not even limited to federal law, since issues of state law and increasingly of foreign law figure in many federal cases. Not only is it infeasible for the law schools to try to educate judges about the substantive law that they may have to apply in cases before them; it is unnecessary. Between the briefs of the parties and the research of the law clerks and the legal materials that reach the judges by these routes, judges should be able to learn enough about the legal doctrines applicable to their cases to apply the doctrines competently.

This observation does not contradict the claim by Professor Bator that "judges should be enormously sensitive to the fact that, in an important sense, they never really know what they are doing . . . Litigation is an episodic and pathological event. Judges cannot know in any systematic or deep way whether the pathology is aberrant or pervasive, isolated or systemic. Correcting the pathology can affect a large body of practice that may be entirely successful and acceptable and that of course is unknown to the judge because it does not generate litigation. Changing a rule here may have unanticipated effects over there."[3] The reason that most judges much of the time do not know what they (here I should say what "we") are doing is not, however,

3. Paul M. Bator, "The Judicial Universe of Judge Richard Posner," 52 *University of Chicago Law Review* 1146, 1165 (1985). For amplification of Bator's criticism, see James L. Robertson, "Variations on a Theme by Posner: Facing the Factual Component of the Reliability Imperative in the Process of Adjudication," 84 *Mississippi Law Journal* 471 (2015).

ignorance of legal doctrine; it is ignorance of nonlegal phenomena that relate importantly to the application of legal doctrine—phenomena such as the reliability of eyewitness testimony, the subject of a vast and persuasive debunking literature unknown to many judges.[4]

One great need of continuing judicial education is educating judges in areas of the natural and social sciences that they have to be comfortable with in order to apply legal doctrine competently.[5] I would prefer, for example, to attend a seminar on sentencing than one on criminal RICO or some other body of substantive criminal law. Sentencing is an important part of every federal district judge's job, and the review of sentences has become an important part of the job of federal appellate judges. The federal sentencing guidelines, promulgated by the United States Sentencing Commission, can help trial judges (and appellate judges as well, when they review sentences) to make intelligent or at least defensible sentencing decisions, as can advice from the federal probation service. The judges are not bound by these aids, however. They have a largely freewheeling discretion to impose sentences that are above or below the sentencing range determined by the guidelines.[6] In fact no longer are they *allowed* to impose

4. See, for example, Roy S. Malpass et al., "The Need for Expert Psychological Testimony on Eyewitness Identification," in *Expert Testimony on the Psychology of Eyewitness Identification* 3, 11 (Brian L. Cutler ed. 2009); Saul M. Kassin et al., "On the 'General Acceptance' of Eyewitness Testimony Research: A New Survey of the Experts," 56 *American Psychologist* 405 (2001). And recall the discussion in Chapter 2 of Federal Rule of Evidence 804.

5. George Mason's Economic Institute for Judges is the pioneer of this form of continuing judicial education. See George Mason University School of Law, Law & Economics Center, "Mason Judicial Education Program," www .masonlec.org/programs/mason-judicial-education-program.

6. See, for example, Kevin Clancy et al., "Sentence Decisionmaking: The Logic of Sentence Decisions and the Extent and Sources of Sentence Disparity," 72 *Journal of Criminal Law and Criminology* 524 (1981). A sentence must of course be within the *statutory* sentencing range, but federal statutory sentencing ranges usually are quite wide.

a sentence, even if it is within the applicable guidelines sentencing range, without first applying a set of statutory sentencing factors to the particular crime and particular criminal.[7] Nor are they allowed merely to rubber stamp the sentencing recommendations of the probation service.

So the sentencing decision is ultimately the judge's, but what do judges know about the right sentence to impose on particular criminals who have committed particular crimes? Very little, as I said in Chapter 2. Yet there is a rich literature on criminology[8] and extensive empirical evidence relating to such relevant issues as recidivism (for example as a function of the defendant's age and background and the nature of his crime).[9] The literature has provided inputs into the federal sentencing guidelines and has influenced the advice that the federal probation service gives to sentencing judges.[10] But the judges need what few of them have—a firsthand acquaintance with the aca-

---

7. See 18 U.S.C. § 3553(a). Recall the discussion of the statutory sentencing factors in Appendix C to Chapter 2.

8. See discussion and references in Richard A. Posner, *Reflections on Judging* 68–71 (2013).

9. See, for example, Francis T. Cullen, Cheryl Lero Jonson, and Daniel S. Nagin, "Prisons Do Not Reduce Recidivism: The High Cost of Ignoring Science," 91 *Prison Journal* 48S (2011); Cassia Spohn and David Holleran, "The Effect of Imprisonment on Recidivism Rates of Felony Offenders: A Focus on Drug Offenders," 40 *Criminology* 329 (2002); Kevin Clancy et al., note 6 above; R. Karl Hanson and Monique T. Bussière, "Predicting Relapse: A Meta-Analysis of Sexual Offender Recidivism Studies," 66 *Journal of Consulting and Clinical Psychology* 348 (1998); Julye Myner et al., "Variables Related to Recidivism among Juvenile Offenders," 42 *International Journal of Offender Therapy and Comparative Criminology* 65 (1998); Paul Gendreau, Tracy Little, and Claire Goggin, "A Meta-Analysis of the Predictors of Adult Offender Recidivism: What Works!" 34 *Criminology* 575 (1996).

10. A single exception is the part of federal sentencing that consists of imposition of conditions of supervised release, which as noted, again in Appendix C to Chapter 2, has received little academic attention.

demic literature. This is a gap that continuing judicial education programs offered by law schools to judges could begin to fill.

Recidivism is central to understanding and dealing with criminal punishment. Although it is conventional to distinguish between deterrence and rehabilitation as objects of punishment, as a practical matter the distinction is between deterring a person from committing future crimes by punishing him for a crime he has committed ("specific deterrence") and deterring others by the prospect that they will be punished if they commit crimes ("general deterrence"). If a criminal decides to go straight after being released from prison, what he does as long as he doesn't commit further crimes is the only "rehabilitation" that the criminal justice system seeks, though it is possible that educational programs in the prison, or conduct requirements imposed on him after release from prison, will help him obtain lawful employment and thus make it easier for him to resist resumption of his criminal career. For giving up his lawful employment to return to a life of crime would impose a cost on him—what economists call an "opportunity cost"—consisting of the forgone income from lawful employment.

The analytical problem concerning recidivism—a grave problem, because of the centrality of recidivism to the evaluation of the effects of punishment—is that statistics of recidivism distinguish only between those persons who are caught committing crimes after release from prison and those who are not; an unknown fraction of those who are not caught may be criminals who manage to commit further crimes after their release without being detected and prosecuted. Could those criminals be identified and counted, we might discover that punishment had much less deterrent effect than we thought.

This problem, though serious, by no means renders the literature on recidivism useless to judges involved with sentencing. Persons punished in different ways (for example, probation versus imprisonment) for the same crimes may be detected recidivating at different rates, and if so it would be a reasonable inference that the pattern probably would be similar if the observer had access to the number of crimes committed postpunishment but not detected.[11]

There is more that law schools could do to train judges. It could train them in managing their staffs, in conducting Internet research, in writing judicial opinions that are candid, readable, and concise, in understanding how the legislative process actually works, even in getting along with colleagues. An especially promising area for continuing judicial education is the psychology of decision making. Judges, like most people, tend not to know themselves very well. Some judges harbor unrealistic, self-serving notions of their motivations and of the accuracy of their decisions. This kind of self-flattery is not special to judges; most people think better of themselves than they should, just as most people are more optimistic than it is realistic for them to be. These traits contributed to survival in the harsh conditions of early humanity, became genetically encoded, and so continue to influence human behavior.

In the case of the judge the dominant form of self-deception is the belief that his or her sole motivation is to apply the law to the facts, with no addition of personal or political views, and that the law is knowable and known to the judge and the facts are knowable as well because judge and jury can and do determine them accurately. Many judges do not recognize the high degree of uncertainty in American law and that it is a major driver of litigation and especially of appeals. Some don't realize that their decision making is likely to be influenced by beliefs of which they may be unaware, by temperament and upbringing, by education and personal experiences, by their career before becoming a judge, and by ambition and work ethic. Some

11. See the Spohn and Holleran article cited in note 9 above.

judges believe that what they don't know is not knowledge relevant to their judicial work. Some don't know how little they know (and would be offended by what Professor Bator had to say on that score), or how cognitive deficiencies that they share with other decision makers can distort their findings. Many a judge exaggerates the extent to which he can retain control over his judicial decision making while delegating opinion drafting to his law clerks. A course in the psychology of values, preferences, and personality, focusing on judicial self-deception—bound to be a humbling and eye-opening experience for many of the judge students—would be of value to the judiciary and the nation. And it's a course that *judges* need; it's not enough if many years earlier they were exposed to such ideas (which they may not have been) as law students.

In a nutshell, the need is for continuing judicial education in process rather than in substance, in judging rather than in doctrine. Law schools can provide that education as long as they have a clear sense of the judges' needs and which of those needs law schools can fulfill.

The most ambitious program of continuing judicial education that I know of is the Master of Judicial Studies program at Duke Law School.[12] But there are other academic programs in continuing judicial education that, like Duke's program, focus on process rather than on doctrine. For example, the Institute of Judicial Administration at New York University Law School offers a five-day seminar for newly appointed appellate judges, emphasizing the editing of judicial opinions—a realistic emphasis, given that most judicial opinions are drafted by law clerks rather than by judges and then edited by the judges sometimes after editing by another of the judge's law clerks.

Five days may seem too short, but one thing I learned from the University of Chicago Law School's thirteen-hour seminar on the

---

12. See note 2 above.

Supreme Court mentioned in the preceding chapter is how much can be packed into two and a half days of instruction, provided that a "day" means more than two hours. Short, intensive courses are optimal for judges, not only because they don't have (or at least don't think they have) much time for continuing education but also because a seminar of such intensity, leaving no time for an afternoon of golfing, separates the serious judge students from the boondogglers.

The potential for continuing judicial education is, one must admit, limited. A law school can't run a judge boot camp. It doesn't want to anger judges by harping on their limitations. And because law professors are unlikely to know how to train judges in judicial management of staff, or in the organization of federal courts (or of the entire federal judiciary), or in how to avoid spats with one's judicial colleagues, programs covering these important issues would have to be interdisciplinary, and staffed accordingly. Staff would have to include professors of management and of psychology, drawn from other departments of the university.

There is a danger that even if well-grounded in the literature on management and human relations and well taught by experts, continuing judicial education in such matters would have little credibility with judges—they would consider these to be matters about which academics know nothing. But there would be at least one exception: judges who acquired from a psychologically sophisticated continuing education course in self-knowledge a more accurate understanding of the true springs of judicial decision making would be less likely to have spats with other judges. They would learn that having a strong conviction about the proper outcome of a dispute is no evidence that one is "right" and anyone who disagrees with you is "wrong": a case may fall in the open area, where uncertainty dominates and a provably "correct" outcome is unattainable.

A difficult question is whether and to what extent continuing judicial education should include criticism of established legal doctrine, the sort of criticism presented in Chapter 2 of this book—criticism of legal formalism, of conventional techniques of statutory interpretation, of excessive (as it seems to me) reliance of judges on adversary procedure, of questionable rules of evidence, and so forth. And why stop there? There is much else to criticize in established doctrine. Take the rule of harmless error as applied in criminal cases. Since prosecutors can't appeal an acquittal, invariably the issue of harmless error is whether an error committed by the trial judge should be a ground for reversal or ignored as harmless. Harmless in this context means that it would not have swayed a reasonable jury. But not all juries are reasonable. Prosecutors may (I suspect do) sometimes find it in their interest, in cases in which they worry that the jury may unreasonably acquit, to commit deliberate errors that would not sway a reasonable jury but that they hope will sway the unreasonable jury in the case at hand. If this tactic works and the jury convicts, the prosecutor is home free because the error was "harmless" in the special sense that the word bears, and so will not result in a reversal on appeal. Yet such deliberate errors could be thought to subvert trial by jury.

Or consider the principle that ignorance of the law is no defense to criminal guilt. Canonical as that defense is, it is fully convincing only when the criminal act is immoral, so that a person should know it's wrong even if he doesn't know the penalty for it, and when in addition the penalty is rationally related to the gravity of the crime, so that the defendant who knows that he's doing wrong will not or should not be shocked by the penalty. When either condition is missing, the defense seems fictional—yet judges rarely acknowledge this, as if to say, "We know the defendant couldn't have had any hint of the legal consequences of his act, but we don't care because everyone is charged with knowledge of the law." Yet a person can't be convicted for violating a secret law, a law that was never published, and what is the difference between that case and one in which it is certain that the defendant could not have known anything about the law that fixed the punishment for his act—the law would be intelligible only to a lawyer and the defendant is not a lawyer—and the punishment happens to be unforeseeably severe? The law should require some intuitive connection between the crime and the punishment, so that a person who is thinking of committing a crime has at least a general idea of the magnitude of punishment that he faces if he commits the crime and is apprehended.

The problem of the intelligibility of the penal consequences of committing a crime has grown since the promulgation of the federal sentencing guidelines, which are so intricate and complex as to baffle many judges and lawyers and to be utterly opaque to most potential criminals. Nevertheless most courts extend the principle that ignorance of the law is no defense to the failure of a criminal defendant to have read and understood the guidelines before committing his criminal act.[13] Yet how many criminals or would-be criminals read and study the Guidelines Manual?

The problem of adequate notice of punishments would be alleviated if prosecutors tried to educate the public—more precisely the segments of the public from which particular criminal populations (drug dealers, Ponzi schemers, counterfeiters, and so on) are drawn—about the punishments that criminals of various kinds face. Especially when, as in the case of drug crimes, the states and the federal government punish the same crimes but most of the prosecutions are by the states, and as the punishments meted out by the states tend to be much less severe than the federal punishments, potential criminals

13. See, for example, *United States v. Fletcher,* 763 F.3d 711, 717 (7th Cir. 2014), and cases cited there.

may be ignorant of the risk they face should they be prosecuted federally. (The probability of such punishment may be small, but the expected cost of punishment to the criminal—the cost of the punishment discounted by the probability of its imposition—may be great.) The Justice Department does nothing as far as I know to try to remedy the knowledge gap. Maybe if challenged on the point it would reply: To publicize the severe punishments for committing federal crimes would be like warning schools of fish to avoid being caught in fishermen's nets. The argument against such reasoning is that proper notice of punishments for serious federal crimes could have a significant deterrent effect at low cost to the government. We want to deter crime but not fishing.

The Supreme Court held in *Lambert v. California* that the concept of due process of law places limits on the principle that ignorance of the law is no defense.[14] The question is whether the limits should be enlarged and the scope of the principle therefore contracted.

Now are these the types of issue, along with the much longer list of troublesome issues of federal judicial practice discussed in Part One, that should be foci of continuing judicial education? Should federal judges, new or experienced, be exposed to, perhaps immersed in, criticisms of established practices of the federal judiciary? The doctrine of harmless error and the rule that ignorance of the law is no defense are so well established as to be unquestioned; should these sleeping dogs therefore be left in peace? I think not, because (to recur to the opening of the Introduction to this book) I want a judge's moral intuition to play a significant role in his or her decisions, and this implies a willingness to question, and to chip away at, legal doctrines that have either outlived their usefulness entirely or need to be modified, subject always to recognition of the importance of reliance interests and the

14. 355 U.S. 225 (1957).

hierarchical character of the judiciary, which limits innovation by lower court judges.

I will surprise many readers by my next suggestion: that a promising subject for continuing judicial education is how to conduct a jury trial. I anticipate two objections: that surely judges know how to conduct jury trials because trial judges conduct so many of them, and that members of law faculties are unlikely to have a feel for jury trials. Both objections are or should be groundless. Consistent with the fact that judges tend not to be good managers, they tend not to think a great deal about how best to manage a jury trial, a complex proceeding that requires good management to have a fighting chance of yielding a just result. At this writing, the legal profession is busy celebrating the eight hundredth anniversary of Magna Carta, incorrectly believed by many members of the profession to have created trial by jury in England. Actually trial by jury was already established; the significance of Magna Carta—a power play by the barons to increase their power relative to the king's—was that it required that the jury be composed of peers of the accused, and thus that barons be tried by barons, not by the king or by judges appointed by him.

Still, Magna Carta is celebrated as a major step on the road to the modern jury, and since judges and other lawyers are constantly looking backward, the age of Magna Carta creates an aura. That's unfortunate because it contributes to exaggerating the jury's qualities and forestalls the necessary reforms of trials involving complex technical or financial issues that few jurors are familiar with. A jury's competence to decide such issues can't be taken for granted. A complex patent or antitrust or finance case tried to a jury requires the judge to take on a more exacting managerial role than when a jury trial deals with issues within the day-to-day experience of the average juror. The judge overseeing such a trial should give jury instructions (and at intervals during the trial, to help the jury understand what's going on before it deliberates, and not just at the end) that contain no legal or technical jargon (including such silly anachronisms as telling the jury that determination of the facts is within the "province" of the jury, a phrase that appears in almost all jury instructions). The judge should appoint a neutral expert witness, normally a professor with experience in teaching beginners. He should allow jurors not only to take notes and to submit written instructions to him but also to ask questions of the lawyers or witnesses out loud, so that the jurors will feel they're active participants in the trial and not just mute observers until they retire to deliberate. The judge should limit the documents submitted to the jury, should explain to the jurors the grounds on which he rejects or sustains objections to questions to witnesses, and should give reasons to jurors for why they are not permitted to do their own Internet research. (They may have difficulty determining the accuracy of an online posting and integrating what they learn online with the evidence presented in the courtroom.) A judge should *always* give reasons to jurors for his rulings, so that they don't feel that they're being treated like children ("do this because I tell you to do this, kid").

The law schools have a potential teaching role here. But to fulfill it they will need to alter the composition of the faculty. They need both academic experts on trial by jury (of which there aren't many) and experienced trial lawyers or former (or present) trial judges, or appellate judges with trial experience.

My discussion of continuing judicial education would be incomplete without mention of the Federal Judicial Center, an agency of the federal judiciary that engages in both research and judicial training. It is not a school. The Center's director and board members rarely have an academic or other research background; of the nine current members of the board (including the director), one is a former adjunct professor at a law school but none of the others has any academic background other than as a student.[15] This governance structure—a good example of deficient macromanagement of the federal judiciary—limits the Center's utility. The Center is additionally handicapped by having very limited resources. And because it's an arm of the federal judiciary it has to tiptoe around the judiciary's deficiencies; those cannot be its focus, though they are what need focusing on. Many judges are sensitive creatures, proud but often insecure and on both accounts resentful of criticism. As a result of the constraints imposed by its being embedded in the judiciary, the Judicial Center is cautious to a degree that renders much of its instructional output rather pedestrian.[16] Whether for financial or other reasons the Center does not reach out very effectively to the judges it is supposed to be helping. It issues pertinent research yet does not disseminate it to the judges except upon request. I don't understand why it doesn't email all its research studies to all federal judges.

What the Center has and the law schools cannot match is its credibility with federal judges, acquired by virtue of being an arm of the federal judiciary. I do not understand therefore why the Center conducts so little judicial training of court of appeals judges (other than in the form of lectures or workshops on substantive topics, which

15. See "Federal Judicial Center," http://en.wikipedia.org/wiki/Federal_Judicial _Center#Board_of_the_Center. The Chief Justice is the chairman *ex officio* of the Federal Judicial Center. Chief Justice Roberts is not a former academic and I doubt takes much interest in the Center.

16. See, for example, Federal Judicial Center, "Judicial Writing Manual: A Pocket Guide for Judges" (2d ed. 2013), www.fjc.gov/public/pdf.nsf/lookup/judicial -writing-manual-2d-fjc-2013.pdf/$file/judicial-writing-manual-2d-fjc-2013.pdf.

as I explained earlier are not very useful forms of judicial training) unless it is lack of resources or a concern that the judges would feel condescended to or even humiliated if required or even invited to undergo any but the briefest, lightest training.[17] Still, little is not none; there is a week-long orientation program for newly appointed federal judges and a second week a year later for the district, magistrate, and bankruptcy judges among the appointees.[18] Supreme Court Justices are of course too proud to subject themselves to *any* training for their job, though many come to it ill prepared and face a steep learning curve. This is an aspect of the Court's monarchical air, which the Justices may believe increases its prestige and power and which is fostered by the fawning deference that many lower court judges (the judges of the "inferior" federal courts) accord to the Justices.

Persuading judges to write their own judicial opinions rather than work from law clerks' drafts may well be a lost cause. But there might be some value in the Federal Judicial Center's at least trying to explain to new judges the costs of the present system of clerk-written, judge-edited judicial opinions.

The biggest obstacles to effective continuing judicial education programs—and I don't know how to overcome them—are the heterogeneity of federal judges in point of knowledge and the fact that they can't (as a practical matter) be compelled to attend continuing judicial education classes. The effect of such a combination could be that the judges who most needed such programs would not enroll in them and that the programs would not be geared to the judges who needed continuing legal education the most.

I mustn't overlook, as a potentially important form of continuing

17. See Federal Judicial Center, "Federal Judicial Center Annual Report 2013," www.fjc.gov/public/pdf.nsf/lookup/AnnRep13.pdf/$file/AnnRep13.pdf.
18. Id. at 5.

judicial education, judicial self-education. Physicians take for granted that they have to keep up to date with developments in their field of specialization. Practicing lawyers too, if only because the bar authorities now require them to undergo a modicum of continuing legal education annually. Judges and law professors are under no compulsion to self-educate—to keep themselves abreast of new developments relating to their areas of professional responsibility. But judges could at least be encouraged to enroll in MOOCs, which are a kind of hybrid of self- and organized education. They could even be given sabbaticals, as judges of some state courts are given; that would encourage continuing judicial self-education.[19]

For completeness I note that halfway between continuing judicial education offered by the academy or the quasi-academic Federal Judicial Center and judicial self-education are learning programs that bring judges and practicing lawyers together. An exemplary sponsor of such programs is the Sedona Conference, which focuses on antitrust law, complex litigation, and intellectual property rights, offering

> dialogue-based, mini-sabbaticals for the nation's leading jurists, lawyers, and experts that allow them to examine cutting edge issues of law and policy. They feature a faculty of approximately fifteen judges, lawyers and experts, and are limited to 45 additional participants, to ensure an intimate environment for meaningful dialogue. The conferences serve as incubators to identify "tipping points" in the law that may benefit from the creation of a Working Group for in-depth focus. When appropriate, a Working Group is formed that in-

---

19. As proposed in Ira P. Robbins, *Judicial Sabbaticals* (1987). I am not aware that this suggestion has been taken up by any of the federal courts.

cludes as many viewpoints and areas of expertise as possible to develop best practices, guidelines, or principles that may be of practical and immediate benefit to the bench and bar, and all other participants in the legal system.[20]

Federal judges will never achieve omniscience. But avoidable ignorance of what they (that is, we) need to know in order to do a competent job is inexcusable.

APPENDIX D

LIST OF JUDICIARY'S PROBLEMS AND POSSIBLE ACADEMIC SOLUTIONS

With my discussion of the judiciary's problems (as I see them) and the possible academic solutions to them now complete, it may help readers for me to put before them a list of all the problems and of all my suggested academic solutions, arrayed by chapter but without elaboration. The list of solutions is much shorter than the list of problems, being truncated by the fact that law professors have no power to alter judicial behavior directly—no legislative power as it were. They can conduct research, and engage in advocacy, designed to bring about changes in that behavior. But the only changes they're actually empowered to make are changes internal to the academy, such as faculty

---

20. The Sedona Conference, "Frequently Asked Questions," https://thesedona conference.org/faq. For example, the Conference's Working Group on Patent Damages and Remedies has produced a very useful Commentary on Patent Damages and Remedies (June 2014 Public Comment Version).

hiring, choice of research projects, and curriculum design. So these are the only changes that I list under solutions—though many of the problems I list could easily be solved by changes of behavior by the judges themselves, without, as it were, academic intervention.

I offer no opinion on the gravity or extent of the problems listed or on the likelihood that the academic solutions I've suggested will be adopted, whether in the near or the remote future.

Chapter 1. Judicial Problems
Uneven quality of judicial appointments
Excessive delay in filling judicial vacancies
Poor statutory draftsmanship by Congress and other legislative
    bodies
The indeterminacy of much American law
The Senate's role in judicial appointments
Politicization of judicial appointments
Emphasis on the wrong kinds of diversity in judicial appointments
Secure lifetime tenure
Expansion of judicial staff
Salary differentials among the three tiers of Article III judges
Absence of cost of living adjustment of judicial salaries
Wasteful use of building space by judiciary

Chapter 2. Judicial Problems
Legal formalism
Originalism, textualism, interpretive naïveté, use of dictionaries in
    interpretation, canons of construction, and methods of statu-
    tory and constitutional interpretation generally
Misunderstanding of the nature of interpretation and its role in law
The rearview mirror syndrome (closely related to formalism)
    standpattism

Exaggerated reliance on precedent

Refusal to acknowledge and confront the role of priors in judicial decision making

Neglect, misunderstanding, and disparagement of legal realism, and of the role of moral intuition in judicial decision making

Politicization of constitutional law

Idealization of the judiciary and of Congress; denial that judges have a legislative role other than in common law cases

The *Bluebook* and other citation-format manuals

Multifactor tests

Judicial word fetishism; legal jargon

Judicial opinion writing

Overcommitment to adversary process

Weak sense of fact, of context; reluctance to conduct independent judicial research, especially online

Failure to keep abreast of scientific and technological advances

Umpireal conception of judging; judicial passivity

Excessive delegation to staff

Excessive appellate deference to findings by trial judges and administrative law judges

Chevron doctrine

Lack of trial experience (appellate judges)

Complacency; overconfidence; self-flattery

Deficiency of curiosity

Reluctance to change, to keep abreast of new knowledge

Commitment to anachronistic rules of evidence and stale formulas governing scope of appellate review

Uncritical approval of class action settlements

Reluctance of judges to appoint their own expert witnesses

Judges' deficiencies of curiosity, self-knowledge, and candor

Judges' loose attitude toward truth, and lack of candor

Unrealistic conception of jurors' capabilities
Neglect of criminology in sentencing
Careless attitude toward conditions of supervised release
Insufficient judicial diversity of the right sort

Chapter 3. Judicial Problems
Inadequate training of new judges, both appellate and trial
Judges' deficient management of their staffs (consisting mainly of
 law clerks)
Delegation of opinion writing to law clerks
Lack of collegiality
Management problems at the court of appeals level, such as the
 excessively long term of chief judges and use of screening
 panels
Technological backwardness and other managerial problems of the
 Supreme Court
Work-ethic problems
Foot-dragging
Judges who overstay their welcome
Excessive travel; reluctance to allow judges and lawyers to substi-
 tute videoconferencing for in-person appearance in court

Chapter 4. Possible Academic Solutions: Academic Scholarship
Redirect focus of academic scholarship from legal doctrines and
 particular decisions to systemic and institutional issues
Conduct detailed analyses of Supreme Court's structure, operating
 methods (including case selection), and personnel
Pay greater attention to problems of judicial management in
 general
Evaluate the administration of the federal judiciary by the Chief
 Justice

Pay greater attention to problems of judicial management in general, utilizing modern organization theory to analyze the structure, operation, and management of today's federal judiciary, including such practices as departures from randomization of panel assignments in courts of appeals

Deemphasize the study of Supreme Court decisions relative to decisions of the lower federal courts

Pay renewed attention to the actual and the desirable place of legal realism in modern federal judicial decision making

Conduct scientifically grounded research into the role of ideological and other priors in judging

Avoid abstruse issues of judicial philosophy, and deemphasize abstract legal theory

Seek a realistic understanding of judges

Conduct critical studies of judges (as distinct from biographies)

Shift emphasis from studies of judicial outcomes and doctrines to studies of judicial opinion structures and style, the conduct of trials and oral argument, and delay at different levels of the judiciary

Make greater use of modern empirical methods (statistical, and the like) to study judicial behavior

Shift emphasis (to a degree) from abstract to practical scholarly analysis of the federal judiciary

Write academic articles that are shorter and simpler, and therefore more accessible to judges

In the case of articles reporting the results of empirical research, provide full and clear and jargon-free explanations of the research techniques and results

Conduct candid, realistic, data-rich research on the judiciary itself

Collaborate with judges in authoring books and articles about the judiciary

Hire more faculty who have practical legal experience, relative to theoreticians

Provide guidance to judges about which commonly used law-related or data-related websites are reliable and which not

Take over the management of law reviews and the administration of moot court programs from students

Chapter 5. Possible Academic Solutions: Curricular Change

Teach against the dominant law student subculture, which is formalist; be candid and realistic about the judiciary

Teach that law clerks should not try to encode the judge's decisions in opinions designed to make the decisions seem the products of formalist analysis

Teach students what the teacher knows about judicial behavior, whether from having been a law clerk or from having studied the literature on judicial behavior, including biographical literature

Teach about judges, and not just particular decisions—about the person and not just about the doctrine (judges are not computers—yet)

Include in the curriculum a full-fledged course in judicial behavior

When teaching judicial opinion writing, don't stop with an opinion's doctrinal adequacy; teach also about its rhetorical quality, its candor, truthfulness, and the quality of the research, both factual and legal, reflected in the opinion

Teach not (or at least not just) from casebooks, which edit opinions too severely, especially their facts, but also from unedited opinions, thus enabling the student to assess the fit between the facts of a case and the outcome

Indeed, work toward the abolition of casebooks—which have become costly, dispensable dinosaurs. Let the students be told which cases to read. They can read them online, where they will also find the briefs that were filed in the cases

Deemphasize instruction in legal doctrine relative to instruction in complex financial and technological products and techniques that give rise to litigation

Refer students to MOOCs to fill in gaps in their knowledge

Emphasize the essential simplicity of law, concealed by lawyers' delight in jargon and doctrinal complexity

Substitute for conventional courses in fields like civil procedure and evidence clinical-style courses that use case materials prepared by the Institute of Trial Advocacy to simulate the trial process realistically

Make sure that students graduate from law school familiar with the natural and social sciences and the humanities, having a realistic understanding of the judiciary and with the legal profession more broadly, and able to write clearly and simply

Forbid student use of and references to citation-format manuals

Revamp the legal-writing program so that it extends over three years, deemphasize legal memoranda, and add instruction in judicial opinion writing, not only to help students who will be law clerks but also to help all students who will be litigators, because learning to write judicial opinions will help them understand and interpret real judicial opinions

Use real cases for moot court (but no constitutional cases) with full records and with students as the judges as well as the advocates

Have faculty make a collective decision about what students should know about judges (for example, about the role of priors or moral intuition in judicial decisions) by the time they graduate, and design the curriculum to provide them with the requisite knowledge

Chapter 6. Possible Academic Solutions: Continuing Judicial Education

Provide continuing judicial education to judges that is focused not on substantive law but on process, such as evaluation of the reliability of evidence, sentencing (and hence criminology), the psychology of decision making under uncertainty with emphasis on the role of unconscious priors, and the use of computer technology in legal, factual, and Internet research

Educate judges about writing style, grammar, and judicial history

Educate judges about modern management theory and practice, as every judge has a staff to manage and chief judges have larger management responsibilities

Train judges in how to manage a complex jury trial

Staff courses for judges with a combination of law professors and professors from other parts of the university, such as the psychology and computer science departments, the history and literature departments, and the business school

Acquaint judges with learning programs that bring judges and practical lawyers together, such as programs of the Sedona Conference

Package continuing judicial education in short but intensive courses, such as three-day, seven-hours-a-day, courses; permit participation by videoconferencing for judges who can't spare the time for travel

Place academics on the Federal Judicial Center's board of directors

Partner with the Center to provide increased training of newly appointed federal judges

Encourage judicial self-education, utilizing MOOCs

CONCLUSION

Everything is to be viewed as
Though for the first time

—SAUL BELLOW, *There Is Simply Too Much to Think About*

THE LIST OF PROBLEMS of the federal judiciary that I have discussed in this book is long, and sheer inertia is likely to retard solutions, perhaps indefinitely. (To the structural deformations discussed in Chapter 1 there are at present no feasible solutions.) There is overcommitment to adversary procedure (the judge as umpire, resistance therefore to conducting independent judicial research or appointing his own, neutral expert witnesses) as a means of determining facts, and—a related point—antiquated rules of evidence that retard utilization of online research in legal proceedings. It bears reminding that the adversary system is not enthroned in the Constitution and is riddled with exceptions, such as Rule 706 of the Federal Rules of Evidence, which authorizes federal judges to appoint expert witnesses; Rule 42(b) of the Federal Rules of Appellate Procedure, which allows a federal court of appeals to refuse to dismiss an appeal though both parties to it have stipulated to a dismissal; the judicial authority to reject a class action settlement, discussed in Chapter 2; and the rise, albeit criticized, of "independent judicial research" (that is, research conducted by the judge rather than by the parties).[1]

There is also the difficulty that judges and juries have in coping with scientific and social-scientific evidence. And there is what seems to me a deep misunderstanding of what statutory "interpretation" really is. (I would be inclined to call it statutory "completion" or "plugging holes in statutes.") There is the shambles that is criminal sentencing. There is the deeply flawed administration of patent law by the U.S. Court of Appeals for the Federal Circuit, and the deeply flawed administrative adjudication of immigration cases and of claims for social security disability benefits. And these are just a few examples of the deficiencies discussed in Chapter 2. There are also the serious managerial problems discussed in Chapter 3.

And underlying all these and the other problems of the federal judiciary that I have discussed in this book is what I have called the legal culture, reflecting the standpattism, the backward-looking focus, that is endemic to the judiciary. It is captured in the current Chief Justice's statement, which I quoted in Chapter 3 from his latest year-end report on the Supreme Court, that "practices [of the Court] that seem archaic and inefficient" may turn out to "rest on traditions that embody intangible wisdom." (Does that include the spittoons behind the Court's bench?)

The past is fixed. And so if the past is to be our guide, we are entitled to a certain complacency. In fairness I must note that the Chief Justice's report does recognize the need for some changes in how the Supreme Court operates. But the wiser the traditions (an ineffable wisdom, for the traditions are "intangible"), the less warranted is en-

---

1. For an example of a federal court of appeals refusing to dismiss an appeal though both parties stipulated to a dismissal, see *Alvarado v. Corporate Cleaning Services, Inc.*, 782 F.3d 365 (7th Cir. 2015).

thusiasm for change. We see this resistance in the Chief Justice's earlier year-end reports, for example the 2013 report, in which he said that

> through over two hundred years of committed effort, our federal court system has become a model for justice through-out the world. I know this first-hand from my conversations with foreign judges and judicial administrators, who visit our courts to gain insights, share ideas, and improve their own systems. Foreign jurists—especially those from emerging de-mocracies who best understand the debilitating effects of in-justice—uniformly admire the efficiency, fairness, and trans-parency of United States courts. They want to know the secret of our success. They are not surprised when I com-mend the intelligence and integrity of our federal judges, whose selfless commitment to public service is the core of our justice system.[2]

Or the 2010 report, where he said: "Thanks to the genius of those who framed our Constitution, and those who have maintained faith with its words and ideals over the past two centuries, the American people have a Supreme Court and a national judicial system that are the model for justice throughout the world. But that is no reason for complacency."[3] Certainly not a *reason* for complacency (when is there ever a "reason" for complacency?), but such self-congratulatory lan-guage (which I must say I find rather sickening) bespeaks and breeds complacency. The judiciary needs to be reminded that "the instinct to return to the modesty of thinking dominant in the past is a purely

2. "2013 Year-End Report on the Federal Judiciary," December 2013, www .supremecourt.gov/publicinfo/year-end/2013year-endreport.pdf.
3. "2010 Year-End Report on the Federal Judiciary," December 2010, www .supremecourt.gov/publicinfo/year-end/2010year-endreport.pdf.

modern one. In that case, the conservative disposition is embattled by nature. While it desires to make use of all worthy inheritance, *it actually invents what it inherits."*[4]

Complacency feeds the stale legal culture that I have been complaining about throughout this book—the lawyer/judge tendency to venerate tradition and resist change. Here's a trivial but I think illuminating example. In the collaborative study of judges' management of their staffs (consisting mainly of law clerks) that I mention in Chapter 4, we asked each judge whether his law clerks called him by his first name or instead called him "judge." Not only did 95 percent of the judges we interviewed answer "judge," but a number of them expressed shock at the thought that any judge would permit a law clerk to call him by his first name, let alone tell the law clerk to do so. I would find this reaction incomprehensible were it not for what I am calling the stale legal culture. It is obvious, to me anyway, that law clerks should call their judge by his first name, as my law clerks have been doing since my appointment as a judge in 1981. That encourages the clerks to be candid (I further encourage candor by my "no pussyfooting" rule—if a clerk thinks I'm wrong about something, which I often am, he is to say so forthrightly rather than beating about the bush), to think of themselves as colleagues rather than as subordinates, to feel they're full-fledged members of the team, to feel closer to the judge, to enjoy the job more while working harder. I can't see any downside.

Fifty years ago a law clerk's calling his judge by the judge's first name would have been unthinkable—would have been thought *lèse-majesté*. A culture of formality pervaded high-class professional employment. But nowadays in most large businesses the junior-most ex-

---

4. Elizabeth Stoker Bruenig, "Francis Agonistes: The Pope Is Engaged in a Struggle to Bring the Church into the Modern Age. And American Conservatives Are Fighting Him Every Step of the Way," *New Republic,* March–April 2015, 24, 30 (emphasis added).

ecutives are on a first-name basis with the senior-most, including the CEO, and for a good reason:

> Using first names to address colleagues, clients, and bosses at work is good for both young and old, junior staffers and senior executives alike. For junior employees, it levels the playing field; for senior or 'seasoned' managers, it implies accessibility . . . Knowing I had the backing of senior management to address clients by their first names helped with some of the fear I had of working with people much older (and presumably a lot smarter) than myself. That first name basis set the tone for future interactions and communicated to the lofty CEOs that we, the junior bankers, were in fact valued and had real contributions to make to the conversation.[5]

The point is that the first-name policy is good management—in most any organization, including a judge's office. That something wasn't done fifty years ago is an absurd reason for refusing to do it now. Judges have difficulty understanding that times change. It's been more than a century since Supreme Court Justices spat into the spittoons located next to their chairs behind the bench, but the spittoons are still there, apparently still used—as wastebaskets. Maybe they have some historical interest but if so one would expect them to be exhibited rather than hidden.

Given the tendency of the judiciary to remain stuck in the past, it seems almost a miracle that there have been salutary changes in the law, and in its administration by judges, in the last half-century. And

---

5. Jodi Glickman, "What's in a (First) Name" (Harvard Business Review, Career Planning, November 1, 2011), https://hbr.org/2011/11/the-power-of-a-first-name.html. One of my recent law clerks had been a junior executive at Intel. He told me that he and everyone else at Intel addressed the founder of the company, Andrew Grove, as "Andy."

there have been many, including more careful screening of judicial candidates, less racial and sexual discrimination in judicial selection, abler staff, greater receptivity to scientific (including social-scientific, especially economic and psychological) and technological insights, a number of procedural improvements, and, thanks to computerization and the Internet, far more accurate legal research. But there have been fewer salutary changes than there would have been had judges embraced Ezra Pound's motto: "Make it new!" Or, more modestly, if judges were comfortable with asking, about every practice, norm, habit, of their profession: "Why?"

Speaking of being stuck in the past, I invite the reader's attention to the Supreme Court's jurisprudence of electronic surveillance. Such surveillance has become extremely common, and various surveillance techniques have been challenged, sometimes successfully, as violations of the Fourth Amendment unless conducted pursuant to a search warrant. The decisions are precedents, and courts dealing with current challenges to electronic surveillance struggle to fit the precedents to those challenges as well as to the Fourth Amendment, the ground of the precedents. The precedents, however, turn out to be of no help to the appraisal of current challenges, because rapid advances in the technology of surveillance, together with increased concern about terrorism, cybercrime, and cyberharassment, have rendered the precedents obsolete. Nothing can be gained by recourse to the language and background of the Fourth Amendment itself, not only because of the yawning gap between eighteenth- and twenty-first-century surveillance techniques but also because the Fourth Amendment is so sparse. All it says is that searches and seizures must be "reasonable" and that search warrants must satisfy certain requirements, mainly that they be based on probable cause to believe the search will turn up contraband or other evidence of crime and that they describe in detail what is to be searched and seized. There is no hint that a warrant is ever *required* for a search or seizure. Nothing in the meager text of the amendment provides any guidance to judges or legislators on where to strike the balance between privacy and property rights on the one hand and national security and crime prevention on the other hand. If ever there was a case for a forward-looking rather than backward-looking judiciary, it is the regulation of electronic surveillance.

Beneath the standpattism that I keep criticizing may lie, I have to admit, a deep, though not fatal, inadequacy in law itself. A recent paper contrasts law with economics and quotes me as remarking that law "has no theoretical core or empirical methodology,"[6] while, as the author of the paper explains, economics consists of "a theoretical core (microeconomic theory and macroeconomic theory) and an empirical methodology (econometrics [statistics applied to empirical economic questions])."[7] The contrast is real but should not be exaggerated. As a distinguished economist acknowledged recently, economics is not "a true science. This accusation is a little gratuitous, since hardly anyone ever believed it . . . I have long been distressed by the high correlation between economists' political views and their allegedly objective research findings . . . [A critic points out that] 'experimentation and empirical proof in economics rarely rise to the standards of true science.' Guilty as charged."[8] Still, the theoretical component of law is especially meager and lawyers therefore "often have to make persuasive arguments in situations characterized by irreducible factual

6. Richard A. Posner, *Catastrophe: Risk and Response* 202 (2004), quoted in Elliott Ash, "Scholarly Agreement in Law and Economics" 3 (Department of Economics, Columbia University, no date). The complete quotation from my book is: "A striking feature of law that is largely invisible to its practitioners and to most outsiders as well is that it has (except perhaps where it has embraced the economic approach) no theoretical core or empirical methodology."
7. These are Ash's words, not mine.
8. Alan S. Blinder, "What's the Matter with Economics?" *New York Review of Books,* December 18, 2014, 55, 57.

uncertainty . . . A lawyer is . . . expected to make a decisive argument for his client (as an attorney), his ruling (as a judge), his policy recommendation (as an analyst), or his statement about the world (as a scholar). An integral component of the training of law students is to make them comfortable in making persuasive and decisive arguments under conditions of uncertainty."[9] The author's criticisms of legal scholarship culminate in his remarking that "the system of scholarly publication in legal academia rests on ersatz foundations."[10]

Other professions, such as medicine, engineering, accounting, many types of business, and the military professions, rest on a scientific or quasi-scientific base, which gives a profession a measure of solidity, objectivity, accuracy, and reliability. But law, like literary criticism with which it is sometimes compared, and politics, which it resembles (while resenting the comparison), and moral philosophy (which could be thought a branch of politics), does not have solid foundations. It is ultimately a collection of rules and procedures, highly malleable, often antiquated, often contestable, often internally conflicted, for managing social conflict—a set of aging, blunt tools.

The specific problems of the federal judiciary that I've discussed in this book may (or at least some of them may) eventually go away by themselves as society changes. They can't all be solved by any feasible measures available today, but most of them can at least be ameliorated. I've limited my attention largely to problems that should be within the capacity of the law schools to ameliorate. I'd like to see the legal academy become more helpful to the judiciary because the judiciary needs help and the academy should be able to provide it— should think it its duty to help and a boon to its students.

I anticipate criticism for saying that the judiciary needs help, and

9. Ash, note 6 above, at 6.
10. Id. at 21.

even for suggesting that it is the author of many of its problems. Am I betraying my class, fouling my own nest? Should not judges close ranks, forming a phalanx against the judiciary's critics? The impulse to do so is natural, but it also reflects an exaggerated belief in the judiciary's role in society and an exaggerated concern for its fragility, as when a plurality opinion of the Supreme Court in *Planned Parenthood of Pennsylvania v. Casey,* in refusing to overrule *Roe v. Wade,* warned that

> liberty finds no refuge in a jurisprudence of doubt . . . Like the character of an individual, the legitimacy of the Court must be earned over time. So, indeed, must be the character of a Nation of people who aspire to live according to the rule of law. Their belief in themselves as such a people is not readily separable from their understanding of the Court invested with the authority to decide their constitutional cases and speak before all others for their constitutional ideals. If the Court's legitimacy should be undermined, then, so would the country be in its very ability to see itself through its constitutional ideals.[11]

The implication of this inflated pronunciamento is that the law-abiding "character" of the American population, and therefore compliance with law, would be impaired if the "people" questioned the Supreme Court's "legitimacy" because the Court had embraced a "jurisprudence of doubt," which seems to mean frequent overruling of its precedents. The Supreme Court has overruled many of its decisions. Why should *Roe v. Wade* be thought sacrosanct, even by persons who do not think that abortion should be forbidden? (In fact the Supreme

11. 505 U.S. 833, 844, 868 (1992).

Court has been chipping away at that decision for years, beginning with the *Casey* decision.)

A further implication of the quoted passage is that any criticism of the Supreme Court (and by extension the rest of the judiciary) is dangerous—and better a noble lie than a lawless population. So what is important is not that the Court be right but that it be perceived as right so that its "legitimacy" is not questioned. This is pretentious nonsense. The judiciary is not so fragile that criticism of its decisions, even when it implies criticism of the judges who render the decisions or the system that produces the judges, will endanger the rule of law. Criticism is good for institutions. As William Blake said in *The Marriage of Heaven and Hell,* "Damn braces: Bless relaxes." Judges, like other officials, can be too full of themselves.

I have tried to make constructive suggestions for improving the contribution that the academy can make to the quality of the judiciary. I anticipate the criticism that I have misdiagnosed the problem—that I have missed the fact that judges are impervious to most of what the academy might offer them because their incentives preclude receptivity to what law professors have to offer. For example, many judges want to appear to be formalists because they think the judiciary will be less likely to be challenged by other branches of government if those branches think that judges really are umpires and not part-time legislators in effect though not in name. (But is anyone in public office actually fooled by this pretense?) They also want to minimize criticism by the losing parties in litigation by posing as agents rather than principals—"the law made me do it." They want to project an aura of certainty, even of infallibility, admitting no doubt about the correctness of their every vote (of course this is difficult to do when an appellate panel is not unanimous), just as baseball umpires want to be thought always to call balls and strikes correctly. Like the oracle at Delphi, to whom Blackstone famously compared the English common law judges, judges want to express themselves in an idiom at once mysterious and authoritative, evocative of infallibility. They also want to keep doing what they've been doing. Most judges are not young, and the older one gets, the more resistant to change one is likely to become.

These are tendencies at once psychological and prudential. But at least in the case of the federal judiciary I don't think it's correct to attribute the tendencies to incentives. Federal judges have secure tenure. It's only at Senate confirmation hearings that the judge (which is to say the judge candidate) needs to genuflect to legislators. After confirmation he or she can be a free spirit. Judges who are excessively formalistic (for certainly formalism in the sense of respecting statutory text, well-settled legal doctrines, and binding precedents is a vital element of the judicial process, and indeed suffices to decide most cases correctly—just not the important ones, the ones that change or advance the law), who get entangled in briar patches of jargon, who lack a realistic understanding of the commercial or other activities out of which their cases arise, who lack curiosity and self-knowledge, who are neither empathetic nor hardheaded, or who confuse certitude with certainty, are making unforced errors. Nothing but habit is causing them to behave in such ways. But the secure tenure that would enable them to break the mold without fear of retribution also protects them from retribution for refusing to change, for planing the same old groove indifferent to a changed social environment.

Much is wanting in the formation, the education, of judges. The law schools are doing little to fill the empty space. They should do more. They *can* do more. But I am not optimistic that they *will* do more. Like other university faculties, law faculties are self-replicating, like amoebas. University departments enjoy a good deal of autonomy.

Faculty members are free to and inclined to vote for faculty candidates who are like themselves, and the university administration rarely vetoes their choices. Theoreticians hire theoreticians, and most legal theoreticians, who nowadays dominate the elite law schools or at the very least exert a strong influence on them, are not much interested in judges, from whom they feel remote. Increasingly dominated by constitutional theorists, by legal theorists more generally, by social-scientific theorists, law school faculties gaze upon the everyday activities of judges and lawyers from a great height. If one thinks back to the problems of the judiciary that I discussed at such length in Part One of this book and to the discussion in Part Two of what little the academy is doing to help the judiciary or even what it *could* do to help the judiciary, one will be struck by the disjunction between what I think the problems of the judiciary are and what academic lawyers are interested in researching and writing about, and by the unlikelihood that the academics will want to substitute my menu for theirs.

Faculty at lower-tier law schools tend to produce journeyman legal scholarship that has utility for judges, law clerks, practicing lawyers, and law students. Top-tier law schools tend to produce esoteric scholarship, illustrated by Professor Fallon's articles that I have cited in earlier chapters, that with a few exceptions is beyond the ken of anyone who is not himself a faculty member at a top-tier law school.

I'm not confident that even the journeyman scholarship is having much impact. The standard method of assessing the impact of scholarship on the judiciary—the frequency of citations in judicial opinions to such scholarship—is largely worthless, because it doesn't distinguish between scholarship that influences a judicial opinion and scholarship that merely ornaments it, inserted by law clerks in an effort to create an aura of scholarship. What is required in research on the academic influence on judicial output is to trace a causal relation between an academic book or article and a judicial doctrine or decision, the kind of thing done in such areas as economic analysis of law and in some other areas as well, as explained in a highly informative article by Judge Kozinski.[12] But the aggregate amount of such constructive scholarship, relative to areas of need in the judiciary, is small and even shrinking.

Pressure for change that may go some distance toward ameliorating the problems of the judiciary discussed in this book is, however, coming from the outside—from the law firms, which hire most law school graduates and therefore are vital to law schools. The economics of legal practice have changed. One reaction to the deep economic downturn that began with the financial collapse of September 2008 was an effort by corporations to economize on their legal expenses. And one economy was to refuse to pay high fees for the work of very junior law firm associates—neophytes many of whom, clients felt, lacked the training needed to do useful work. Law firms in the halcyon days before the financial collapse and ensuing severe recession "had no expectation that associates would arrive knowing how to do more complex tasks."[13] Yet even then practitioners had "complained about the 'inability of recent law school graduates to handle basic legal matters.'"[14] But the complaints have intensified. Now "firms will

12. Alex Kozinski, "The Fourth Annual Frankel Lecture: The Relevance of Legal Scholarship to the Judiciary and Legal Community: Who Gives a Hoot about Legal Scholarship?" 37 *Houston Law Review* 295 (2000). For a contrary view, see Adam Liptak, "When Rendering Decisions, Judges Are Finding Law Reviews Irrelevant," *New York Times,* March 19, 2007, A8.

13. Daniel Thies, "Rethinking Legal Education in Hard Times: The Recession, Practical Legal Education, and the New Job Market," 59 *Journal of Legal Education* 598, 602 (2010).

14. Neil J. Dilloff, "Law School Training: Bridging the Gap Between Legal Education and the Practice of Law," 24 *Stanford Law & Policy Review* 425, 428 (2013).

covet the associate who can come up with the correct answer in a timely and cost-effective manner."[15] One response of law firms has been to reduce the number of associates whom they hire. This has placed pressure on the law schools to provide more practical instruction to their students, so that newly hired associates at law firms will be more productive and therefore recent law school graduates will be more in demand and better remunerated. The law firms want to off-load to the law schools some of the training they used to provide to their new associates but can no longer charge to their clients. The firms do not, as far as I am aware, exert pressure directly on the law schools. They don't have to. Without practical training. fresh law school graduates have difficulty landing decent law jobs, and the result is bound to be—already is—fewer law school applicants and a downward spiral in law school finances. For example, Washington & Lee law school dropped from twenty-sixth to forty-third place in the 2014 *U.S. News & World Report* law school rankings as a result of the fact that only 56.9 percent of the school's graduates in 2012 were able to land full-time jobs requiring a law degree. Such a low rate is likely to lead to a reduction in the number and quality of applicants in the next round of applications.[16]

The American economy has revived after years in the doldrums, but the law firms' economic problems persist. This is in part because corporate clients have learned that they can squeeze law firm billing harder than they had thought possible, in part because improvements

---

15. Neil J. Dilloff, "The Changing Cultures and Economics of Large Law Firm Practice and Their Impact on Legal Education," 70 *Maryland Law Review* 341, 354 (2011).

16. See Elie Mystal, "Washington & Lee Tries to Calm Fears of Entering Students," *Above the Law,* March 13, 2014, www.abovethelaw.com/2014/03/washington -lee-tries-to-calm-fears-of-entering-students/.

in technological aids to legal research and document search[17] are reducing law firm staffing needs, and in part because of increased opportunities (facilitated in part by technological advances) to outsource legal work to low-paid lawyers in Third World countries, notably India.[18]

And so we read in a recent report of a task force of the American Bar Association that

> the calls for more attention to skills training, experiential learning, and the development of practice-related competencies have been heard and many law schools have expanded practice-preparation opportunities for students. Yet, there is need to do much more. The balance between doctrinal instruction and focused preparation for the delivery of legal services needs to shift still further toward developing the competencies and professionalism required of people who will deliver services to clients.[19]

The pressure on law schools to do more practical training of the students so that from the outset of their employment they'll do work that clients are willing to pay for has led the schools to hire more clinical professors and offer more clinical courses—courses that seek to equip students to do useful work for a law firm from day one of

17. See, for example, Richard Susskind, *The End of Lawyers? Rethinking the Nature of Legal Services* 66, 69, 99 (2008).
18. See, for example, Carlo D'Angelo, "Overseas Legal Outsourcing and the American Legal Profession: Friend or 'Flattener'?" 14 *Texas Wesleyan Law Review* 167, 168 (2007).
19. American Bar Association, Task Force on the Future of Legal Education, "Report and Recommendations" 3 (January 2014).

their employment. The more a law school faculty becomes seeded with clinical professors, the more the nonclinical faculty comes under pressure to provide more practical instruction, and the more "high" theory in law schools ("high" more in the sense of helium-filled balloons and deep drafts of a marijuana cigarette than high theory in the natural and social sciences) is shunted aside as an unaffordable luxury and replaced by courses that focus on the shortcomings of the American legal system—including its judicial branch. And the better able the law firms are to fill the hole in their balance sheets.

Gradually, legal education is becoming more practical. And because judges are practical rather than theoretical—doers rather than dreamers—the gap between the academy and the judiciary should narrow. But probably not by a great deal. For the focus of practical instruction in law school is bound to remain not on judicial behavior but on understanding the tasks that junior associates in law firms are asked to do. Those tasks mainly involve legal research and analyzing documents produced in pretrial discovery. The junior associate does not argue cases in court, though he may sometimes be in court as an observer or amanuensis. The behavior of judges will not be a focus of his attention, and so will not be a focus of his education in law school. But the change in legal education that I've been describing would, by tilting the composition of law school faculties more toward the practical, create a greater faculty interest in judges. And that would be a step forward. It would enable law schools to narrow the gap that has been the subject of this book.

May I end on a light note without being accused of traducing the judiciary to which I belong?

Very near the end of Lewis Carroll's *Alice's Adventures in Wonderland* occurs the chaotic trial of the Knave of Hearts, accused of having stolen the Queen's tarts. Alice, a little girl, is present as a witness. The trial isn't going well.

"Let the jury consider their verdict," the King said, for about the twentieth time that day.

"No, no!" said the Queen. "Sentence first—verdict afterwards."

"Stuff and nonsense!" said Alice loudly. "The idea of having the sentence first!"

"Hold your tongue!" said the Queen, turning purple.

"I won't" said Alice.

"Off with her head!" the Queen shouted at the top of her voice. Nobody moved.

"Who cares for you?" said Alice, (she had grown to her full size by this time.) "You're nothing but a pack of cards!"

At this the whole pack rose up into the air, and came flying down upon her: she gave a little scream, half of fright and half of anger, and tried to beat them off, and found herself lying on the bank, with her head in the lap of her sister, who was gently brushing away some dead leaves that had fluttered down from the trees upon her face.

This book is my Alice moment.

EPILOGUE

A cat may look at a king.[1]

THIS BOOK, up to and including the Conclusion, was completed in April of 2015 and soon was in page proofs. But I had reserved the right to update the book to the end of June or beginning of July, when the Supreme Court's 2014 Term would end (it ended on July 1). For reasons not fully understood, the Court tends to bunch the issuance of its most important decisions in the last few days of the term, before breaking for its long summer recess.[2] I thought it likely that some of those late-decided cases would cast light on issues discussed in this book; and I was right.

I am going to discuss three of these decisions—*King v. Burwell*,[3] which rejected a challenge to a key provision of the Affordable Care

1. A medieval proverb that means that humble people are entitled to express their opinions about supposedly "superior" people. I shall be making some critical remarks in this Epilogue, as I have elsewhere in this book, about my judicial superiors—Supreme Court Justices. Of course, the superior person may not be receptive to feline criticism. And thus in response to a criticism of mine, Justice Scalia once remarked: "'He's a court of appeals judge, isn't he?' Scalia, 76, said of Posner. 'He doesn't sit in judgment of my opinions as far as I'm concerned.'" David Lat, "Benchslap of the Day—Justice Scalia Pulls Rank on Judge Posner," *Above the Law*, July 30, 2012, http://abovethelaw.com/2012/07/benchslap-of-the-day-justice-scalia-pulls-rank-on-judge-posner/.
2. See Lee Epstein, William M. Landes, and Richard A. Posner, "The Best for Last: The Timing of U.S. Supreme Court Decisions," 64 *Duke Law Journal* 101 (2015).
3. Docket No. 14-114, June 25, 2015.

Act; *Obergefell v. Hodges,*[4] which held that there is a constitutional right to same-sex marriage; and, least important of the three, *Kimble v. Marvel Entertainment, LLC,* a patent case[5]—and close with a brief discussion of an issue related to the principal issue in that case, namely stare decisis as illustrative of the judiciary's reverence for the past. For my purposes in this book, I am less interested in the outcomes of any of these cases than in the analytical moves by the Justices (and in the last case I discuss, by lower court judges as well), particularly in the dissenting opinions in the first two cases, which reflect persistent weaknesses in how judges, even at the highest level, grope their way to conclusions.

King v. Burwell. Rarely can one be certain about what moves a judge to vote as he or she did in a particular case—that's one of the themes of this book—and especially if the judge is the Chief Justice of the United States and the case has momentous practical significance, as was true of *King v. Burwell;* a literal reading of the Affordable Care Act, advocated by Scalia in his dissent, would have deprived more than six million persons of health benefits to which the Act entitled them.

The use of terms like "Warren Court" or "Rehnquist Court" or "Roberts Court" reflects the tendency to make the Chief Justice the Court's personification. Had *King* been decided against the government's defense of the Affordable Care Act, it would have been thought, depending on one's politics, a success or a failure of the Roberts Court, whichever way the Chief Justice voted. Had he voted against the government and been the deciding vote (maybe if he had voted against it Justice Kennedy would have joined him, delivering victory to King), he would have been vilified—possibly by Republicans as

---

4. Docket No. 14-556, June 26, 2015.
5. Docket No. 13-729, June 22, 2015.

well as by Democrats. A Chief Justice thus has a greater *personal* interest in how he votes than the other Justices.

A great deal of legal doctrine is, as I have emphasized throughout this book, spongy, creating a wide field for the exercise of judicial discretion. The interpretation of statutes, discussed in Chapter 2, is an important example. Interpretation is a natural human act, but it is intuitive, and trying to bound it by rules, though a natural ambition of lawyers and judges, has always failed. A question of statutory interpretation that gets as far as an appellate court is generally a question that the legislature did not anticipate when it enacted the statute. The judicial role in such a case is not interpretation but, as I stressed in that earlier chapter, completion. And that is the character of the Chief Justice's opinion in *King v. Burwell.* The sheer length of the Affordable Care Act—2,700 pages (the longest statute I've ever heard of)—made it inevitable that there would be mistakes and omissions. The mistake in the *King* case—the statutory text authorizes the provision of federal tax subsidies (which help low- and moderate-income people obtain health insurance) by health-insurance exchanges "established by the States" but does not mention such provision by federal exchanges in states that don't establish their own exchanges—was threatening the health benefits of millions. No reason could be imagined for Congress's having wanted to produce that result. Pragmatic, common-sense completion of defective statutory language concerning "exchanges" was both a sensible approach and a way of avoiding public anger likely to be directed at the Supreme Court—primarily at the Chief Justice—and secondarily at Republicans—ferocious enemies of the Act—and at Congress too if it proved unable to patch up the Act should the Court have refused to do so—and both houses of Congress are controlled by the Republicans.

Three Justices dissented, in an intemperate opinion by Justice Scalia that can be summed up in four words: *fiat justitia, ruat coelum,* a

Latin expression understood to mean in law-speak "do justice even if the consequence is that the heavens fall." In other words, sever legal analysis from consequences however great. It is a ridiculous proposition. Legal doctrine should always be shaped with careful regard for consequences—that is the essential tenet of the most persuasive version of pragmatism—especially when doctrine is flexible, as in the case of statutory interpretation, which as we've seen earlier in this book cannot be cabined by rules.

It's true, as Scalia points out, that Congress can amend the statute to eliminate any untoward consequences of a literal interpretation. But that suggestion indicates naïveté about the legislative process. The Affordable Care Act was passed by a Democratic Congress; by the time *King v. Burwell* was argued in the Supreme Court the Congress was controlled by Republicans, in whose interest it would *not* be to amend the Act to make it conform better to the views of the enacting Congress. Casual suggestions that if Congress made a mistake, let it correct it and that will teach it to be more careful the next time, are thus irresponsible.

Justice Scalia may not be fully committed to the extreme position that he took in *King v. Burwell*. John Campbell, in an unpublished comment, notes the inconsistency between Justice Scalia's dissent in *King* and his majority opinion in *AT&T Mobility IIC v. Concepcion,* where he said, quoting an earlier case, that "a federal statute's saving clause 'cannot in reason be construed as [allowing] a common law right, the continued existence of which would be absolutely inconsistent with the provisions of the act. In other words, *the [federal] act cannot be held to destroy itself.'"* [6] But in his dissent in *King* he said that the Affordable Care Act had destroyed itself.

Obergefell v. Hodges. It was no surprise, from a legal-doctrinal ap-

6. 131 S. Ct. 1740, 1747 (2011) (emphasis added).

proach, that the Supreme Court held there to be a constitutional right to same-sex marriage; only the closeness of the vote (5-4) was a surprise. The case of same-sex marriage can't be distinguished from that of interracial marriage, which is to say the case of *Loving v. Virginia*, the Supreme Court decision that in 1967 invalidated state laws forbidding such marriage.[7] There was, as an economist would say, a "demand" (though rather limited) for such marriage and it was difficult, to say the least, to understand why such marriages should be prohibited. In fact the only "ground" for the prohibition was bigotry—the racism endemic in the South. The hostility, also centered in the South, to homosexual marriage is of the same character. No more than biracial marriage does homosexual marriage harm people who don't have or want to enter into such a marriage. The prohibition of homosexual marriage harms a nontrivial number of Americans because other Americans disapprove of such marriage though unaffected by it. That was precisely the situation of interracial marriage in the South before the Supreme Court stepped in.

John Stuart Mill in *On Liberty* had drawn an important distinction between what he called "self-regarding acts" and "other-regarding acts." The former involve doing things to yourself that don't harm other people, though they may be self-destructive. The latter involve doing things that do harm other people. He thought that government had no business with the former (and hence—his example—the English had no business concerning themselves with polygamy in Utah merely because they hated it). Unless it can be shown that homosexual marriage harms people who are not homosexual (or who are homosexual but don't want to marry)—and it hasn't been shown—there is no compelling reason for state intervention, and specifically for

7. 388 U.S. 1 (1967).

banning homosexual marriage. The dissenters in *Obergefell* missed this rather obvious point.

I go further than Mill. I call gratuitous interference in other people's lives bigotry. The fact that it is often religiously motivated does not make it less offensive. The United States is not a theocracy, and religious disapproval of harmless practices is not a proper basis for prohibiting them, especially if the practices are highly valued by their practitioners. Homosexual couples and the children (mostly heterosexual) whom they adopt (or one may have given birth to and the other adopted) derive substantial benefits, both economic and psychological, from marriage.[8] Efforts to deny them those benefits by forbidding same-sex marriage confer no offsetting social benefits—in fact no offsetting benefits at all beyond gratifying feelings of hostility toward homosexuals, feelings that feed such assertions as that heterosexual marriage is "degraded" by allowing homosexual couples to annex the word marriage to their cohabitation.

Justice Kennedy's majority opinion invalidating state laws against homosexual marriage is convincing, though I would have preferred to see it longer on facts and shorter on quotations from Supreme Court decisions.[9] Obsession with precedent to the neglect of facts is a besetting sin of federal adjudication, incomprehensibly so in the case of the Supreme Court since its decisions can't be appealed to a higher court and its high ratio of staff to caseload would enable it to dig deeply into the practical consequences of deciding a case one way or the other.

The four dissents in *Obergefell* are notably weak. On the first page of the Chief Justice's dissent we read that "marriage 'has existed for

8. See *Baskin v. Bogan,* 766 F.3d 648, 662–664 (7th Cir. 2014).

9. As in the *Baskin* opinion, cited in the previous footnote. The majority opinion in *Obergefell* does mention some of the benefits of same-sex marriage to children adopted by homosexuals, but not all and not in any detail.

millennia and across civilizations,'" and "for all those millennia, across all those civilizations, 'marriage' referred to only one relationship: the union of a man and a woman." That's nonsense; polygamy—the union of one man with more than one woman (sometimes with hundreds of women)—has long been common in many civilizations (let's not forget Utah) and remains so in much of the vast Muslim world. (Nor is polyandry unknown, though very rare.) But later in his opinion the Chief Justice has an awakening, remembers polygamy, and suggests that if homosexual marriage is allowed, so perhaps must polygamy. He fails to mention that polygamy imposes real costs, primarily on men, by reducing the ratio of marriageable women to unmarried men. Imagine a society of a million men and a million women, but the 10,000 wealthiest men have a total of 300,000 wives. That leaves 990,000 men to compete for only 700,000 unmarried women.

The Chief Justice criticizes the majority opinion for "order[ing] the transformation of a social institution that has formed the basis of human society for millennia, for the Kalahari Bushmen and the Han Chinese, the Carthaginians and the Aztecs. Just who do we think we are?" What a curious collection! The Han Chinese are the dominant ethnic group in China. The Carthaginians and the Aztecs are of course extinct. And there are only about 80,000 Kalahari Bushmen left; they seem likely to become extinct too. Few Americans would want to model our social institutions on those of the Bushmen, the Carthaginians, or the Aztecs.

Ah, the millennia! Ah, the wisdom of the ages! How arrogant it would be (the Chief Justice implies) to think we knew more about marriage than the Aztecs—we who don't even know how to cut a person's heart out of his chest while he's still alive, a maneuver the Aztecs were experts at.

Ancestor worship is a besetting sin of the legal profession. This is the eight hundredth anniversary of Magna Carta, a document with no relevance to our legal system yet the legal profession is salivating over it; the Aztec Empire fell to the Spanish on August 13, 1521; Carthage was destroyed in 146 B.C. The Bushmen are hanging on by a thread; Han Chinese are plentiful, but we don't want to model our social institutions on China's.

The only distinction the Chief Justice makes between the *Loving* case and the same-sex marriage case is to declare that *Loving* did not alter "the core structure of marriage as the union between a man and a woman." But the states that forbade interracial marriage considered the prohibition to be part of the core structure of marriage. For they considered part of the core to be that whites should marry just whites and blacks marry just blacks. They were resolute against racial mixing whether in buses, schools, or the marriage bed.

The Chief Justice worried in his dissent in *Obergefell* that the majority opinion had mounted "assaults on the character of fair-minded people" who oppose same-sex marriage, by remarking that they impose "'d[i]gnitary wounds' upon their gay and lesbian neighbors.'" But of course they do, even if innocently, because a married couple doesn't like being told that its marriage, though legal, is sinful. That isn't to say that people should be forbidden to oppose same-sex marriage; it is merely to remark one of the costs of that opposition, and one of the reasons to doubt that it should be permitted to express itself in a law forbidding such marriage.

And finally the Chief Justice's opinion is heartless. There is of course a long history of persecution of homosexuals, a history punctuated by such names, doubtless known to the Chief Justice, as Oscar Wilde, Pyotr Ilyich Tchaikovsky, and Alan Turing. Until quite recently many American homosexuals took great pains to conceal their homosexuality in order to avoid discrimination. Many homosexuals value marriage just as heterosexuals do. They want their adopted children to have the psychological and financial advantages of legitimacy. They are hurt by the discrimination that the dissenting Justices condone. Prohibiting homosexual marriage *is* discrimination. I would like to see Chief Justice Roberts try to defend the right of states to prevent hundreds of thousands of children from having married parents.

Nowhere does he state in his opinion that homosexual marriage harms heterosexuals, or the nation at large. He does not echo the suspicions of Jerry Falwell and Pat Robertson that the 9/11 terrorist attacks on the United States may have been divine punishment for homosexuality. If same-sex marriage does no harm, as the Chief Justice implicitly concedes, yet we know that banning such marriage harms a great many homosexual adults and the children, most of them heterosexual, adopted by homosexual couples, and the ban is of course a governmental act subject therefore to scrutiny under the equal protection clause of the Fourteenth Amendment, his dissent is ungrounded.

I wonder by the way whether he or the other dissenters thought at all about the muddle that would have ensued had the Court held that states have the right to forbid homosexual marriage. What would have happened to married homosexuals in states in which the lower federal courts had held that there is a right to homosexual marriage, and many homosexual couples had taken the opportunity to get married? If those states were permitted to reinstate their prohibitions, would the existing homosexual marriages have been grandfathered, creating a favored and a disfavored class of homosexuals? How would the status of children have been affected? Would states have been free to refuse to recognize homosexual marriages made in states that had recognized such marriages?

Justice Scalia's dissent (rich in characteristic Scalian rage and hyperbole and outright insult of his colleagues, as when he writes that "what really astounds is the hubris reflected in today's judicial Putsch" and terms the majority opinion "couched in a style that is as pretentious as its content is egotistic" and contains "silly extravagances, of thought and expression") is actually quite similar to the Chief Justice's calmer dissent. Both Justices come close to implying that violations of the Fourteenth Amendment are not justiciable. For Scalia says: "We have no basis for striking down a practice that is not expressly prohibited by the Fourteenth Amendment's text, and that bears the endorsement of a long tradition of open, widespread, and unchallenged use dating back to the Amendment's ratification." That is an exact description of segregated public school education in the South until its invalidation in *Brown v. Board of Education,* a decision that the logic of the Roberts and Scalia dissents would require them to repudiate.

Justice Thomas's dissent, though refreshingly civil after Scalia's, is hard to take seriously. He says for example that "as a philosophical matter, liberty is only freedom from governmental action, not an entitlement to governmental benefits. And as a constitutional matter, it is likely even narrower than that, encompassing only freedom from physical restraint and imprisonment." That means that slavery would (but for the Thirteenth Amendment) be constitutionally secure, unless government was the slaves' owner. He remarks, very near the end of his opinion, that "slaves did not lose their dignity (any more than they lost their humanity) because the government allowed them to be enslaved . . . The government cannot bestow dignity, and it cannot take it away. The majority's musings are thus deeply misguided, but at least those musings can have no effect on the dignity of the persons the majority demeans." In other words, the majority opinion, by conferring a right to homosexual marriage, "demeans" the opponents of such marriage, but leaves them with their dignity. The implication is that the beneficiaries of the opinion obtain no dignity from it, any more than blacks did from being freed from slavery, because government cannot confer dignity. I find this chain of reasoning weird.

Justice Alito's dissent ascribes to the states that want to forbid homosexual marriage the desire "to encourage potentially procreative conduct to take place within a lasting unit that has long been thought to provide the best atmosphere for raising children. They thus argue that there are reasonable secular grounds for restricting marriage to opposite-sex couples."That can't be right. States that forbid homosexual marriage do not do so in an effort to encourage homosexuals to marry persons of the opposite sex and thereby procreate.The nation is not suffering from a shortage of children. Sterile people are not forbidden to marry, though by definition they do not procreate. Indeed laws forbidding incestuous marriages will often make an exception for first cousins too old to procreate.There is no greater reason to forbid homosexual marriage, which is actually good for children by making the children adopted by homosexual couples (and there are a great many such children) better off emotionally and financially. But Justice Alito, I take it, would not object that some states *permit* aged first cousins to marry because they are sterile, and *forbid* homosexual marriages because such marriages are sterile.

Justice Alito says that states that want to prohibit homosexual marriage "worry that by officially abandoning the older understanding, they may contribute to marriage's further decay." This doesn't make sense.Why would heterosexuals marry less often and procreate less often just because homosexuals also marry, and raise adopted children who were it not for adoption would languish in foster homes?

Justice Alito adds that "today's decision usurps the constitutional right of the people to decide whether to keep or alter the traditional understanding of marriage." But why should the people who control a state be entitled to deny the right of some of their fellow citizens to marry, without any reason? Why is it any of their business? Justice Alito has no answer.

He deplores the fact that "a bare majority of Justices can invent a new right and impose that right on the rest of the country." Would he then have been content had the vote in the Supreme Court in favor of same-sex marriage been 6-3 rather than 5-4? Obviously not. And isn't the history of constitutional law the history of Supreme Court

Justices, often by a narrow vote, inventing new rights and imposing them on the rest of the country? Wasn't the right of blacks to attend integrated public schools a new right? The right to an abortion? To use contraceptives? "One man one vote"? The First Amendment rights of corporations, established in a 5-4 decision (with Alito one of the five)?[10] In fact isn't what we call constitutional law a body of judge-made law only loosely tethered to the constitutional text?[11] Isn't it true that when society changes, the meaning of the Constitution may change even though the words are unchanged?[12] *Brown v. Board of*

10. *Citizens United v. Federal Election Commission*, 558 U.S. 310 (2010).
11. See David A. Strauss, "Does the Constitution Mean What It Says?" (University of Chicago Law School, May 2015).
12. See Eric J. Segall, "A Century Lost: The End of the Originalism Debate," 15 *Constitutional Commentary* 411 (1998); Lawrence Lessig, "Fidelity and Constraint," 65 *Fordham Law Review* 1365 (1997). An example from earlier in this book is how the meaning of "inferior" has changed from "lower," as in the "inferior Courts" that Article III of the Constitution authorized Congress to create, to "worse," the modern usage, the change reflecting the decline of a culture strongly influenced by eighteenth-century English notions of hierarchy and aristocracy. The idea of a frozen Constitution (the idea dramatized by Justice Scalia's claim, noted in Chapter 2 of this book, that flogging would be a constitutional form of punishment today because it was in the eighteenth century) was strongly opposed by Thomas Jefferson, one of the most influential of the founders of the nation. In his letter to Samuel Kercheval, June 12, 1816, Jefferson said:

> Some men look at constitutions with sanctimonious reverence, and deem them like the arc of the covenant, too sacred to be touched. They ascribe to the men of the preceding age a wisdom more than human, and suppose what they did to be beyond amendment. I knew that age well; I belonged to it, and labored with it. It deserved well of its country. It was very like the present, but without the experience of the present; and forty years of experience in government is worth a century of book-reading; and this they would say themselves, were they to rise from the dead. I am certainly not an advocate for frequent and untried changes in laws and constitutions. I think moderate imperfections had better be borne with; because, when once known, we

Education was possible only because American attitudes toward race had changed, and *Obergefell* was possible only because American attitudes toward homosexuality have changed.

Remarkably, none of the four dissents actually presents a reason for forbidding same-sex marriage. That is what makes the issue identical to the issue in the *Loving* case of whether states should continue to be allowed to forbid interracial marriage. In both cases there is palpable harm to a group long discriminated against, and no harm to other people—at least no tangible harm; obviously people who fear divine retribution for allowing homosexuals to marry each other, or less dramatically who simply dislike homosexuality or, if not homosexuality as such, homosexual marriage, consider themselves harmed. Such people, however, correspond to the people who opposed *Loving* because they didn't like interracial marriage.

Religious grounds for discrimination may seem special. (It may, incidentally, be no accident that the four dissenters in *Obergefell* are the four most orthodox Roman Catholics on the Court.) But no one thinks a state should be allowed to ban a religion, even if a large majority of the state's voters despise the religion on religious grounds—even the Church of Satan is left in peace—or to ban a belief system, such as atheism, that rejects religion. By the same token, until *Obergefell*, it would not have been thought that demonstrably harmful prac-

---

accommodate ourselves to them, and find practical means of correcting their ill effects. But I know also, that laws and institutions must go hand in hand with the progress of the human mind. As that becomes more developed, more enlightened, as new discoveries are made, new truths disclosed, and manners and opinions change with the change of circumstances, institutions must advance also, and keep pace with the times. We might as well require a man to wear still the coat which fitted him when a boy, as civilized society to remain ever under the regimen of their barbarous ancestors. http://teachingamericanhistory.org/library/document/letter-to-samuel-kercheval/

tices were immune to regulation if based on religion. The implication of such a position would be that, if a state made adultery a capital offense, citing *Leviticus*, the government would be helpless to intervene.

Kimble v. Marvel Entertainment, LLC. In contrast to *King* and *Obergefell*, a bad decision. A half-century ago, in a case called *Brulotte v. Thys*, the Supreme Court had held that a patentee cannot make a contract with a licensee of the patent that requires the licensee to pay royalties to the patentee after the patent expires.[13] The Court thought that enforcement of such a contract would extend the patent monopoly beyond the statutory term (usually twenty years). That doesn't make any sense. When the patent expires, anyone can make the patented product or process without compensating the patentee. The licensee who had agreed to pay postexpiration royalties is not by paying those royalties compensating the patentee for being allowed to make the patented product or process—he is paying the deferred portion of the fee as partial compensation for his license to use the patented item before the patent expired. Such deferral may benefit the licensee by spreading the costs of the license, and may benefit the patentee by attracting licensees who would find the costs excessive if all those costs were squeezed into the patent period. As explained in a decision by my court:

> After the patent expires, anyone can make the patented process or product without being guilty of patent infringement. The patent can no longer be used to exclude anybody from such production. Expiration thus accomplishes what it is supposed to accomplish. For a licensee in accordance with a provision in the license agreement to go on paying royalties after the patent expires does not extend the duration of the patent either technically or practically, because, as this case demon-

13. 379 U.S. 29 (1964).

strates, if the licensee agrees to continue paying royalties after the patent expires the royalty rate will be lower. The duration of the patent fixes the limit of the patentee's power to extract royalties; it is a detail whether he extracts them at a higher rate over a shorter period of time or a lower rate over a longer period of time.[14]

The opinion pointed out (as did Justice Alito's dissent in *Kimble*) that it would be one thing if "*Brulotte* had been based on a interpretation of the patent clause of the Constitution, or of the patent statute or any other statute; but it seems rather to have been a free-floating product of a misplaced fear of monopoly . . . that was not even tied to one of the antitrust statutes."[15]

Justice Kagan's majority opinion in *Kimble* is a veritable paean to stare decisis, which means adhering to precedent. When a half-century-old precedent is demonstrably erroneous, and has not generated substantial reliance interests, and doesn't even have a constitutional or statutory pedigree but is purely judge-created, the refusal to overrule it is mere antiquarianism—the judge's head screwed on backward. I am confident that Justice Kagan does not believe that the Supreme Court is infallible, that it can look a half-century ahead, or more, and determine whether the decision it renders today will fit the conditions of that future period, and that that was a feat that the Court had performed in *Brulotte v. Thys*. But I can't think of an alternative basis for the *Kimble* decision. It's a decision that well illustrates one of my central concerns in this book—the backward-looking tendency of legal thinkers, especially judges.

The majority opinion in *Kimble,* with its reverential attitude toward stare decisis, put me in mind of a recent case (not yet decided

14. *Scheiber v. Dolby Laboratories, Inc.,* 293 F.3d 1014, 1017 (7th Cir. 2002).
15. Id. at 1018.

when this epilogue was written) involving a parallel issue, one connected with the problem of poorly articulated legal doctrines that has preoccupied me in this book.

It has to do with the familiar legal term "frivolous." Familiar as it is, it has no fixed meaning. Sometimes it denotes a case in which it is apparent just from reading the plaintiff's complaint that there is no need to await the defendant's answer or motion to dismiss, or await the conduct of discovery or legal research, to determine that the case is going nowhere—that there's zero possibility of the court's having authority to provide relief to the plaintiff.[16] Such a suit will often be said not to invoke the jurisdiction of a federal court; "if it is clear beyond any reasonable doubt that a case doesn't belong in federal court, the parties cannot by agreeing to litigate it there authorize the federal courts to decide it."[17]

In contrast, a complaint that makes a claim that if true would provide a basis on which a federal court could grant the plaintiff monetary or other relief, but is later shown (normally by a motion to dismiss or other action taken by the defendant) to have no merit, nevertheless successfully invokes federal jurisdiction and so if it is dismissed the dismissal is on the merits.[18] The *Carr* decision cited in note

16. *Reed v. Columbia St. Mary's Hospital,* 782 F.3d 331, 336 (7th Cir. 2015); *Ricketts v. Midwest National Bank,* 874 F.2d 1177, 1180–1182 (7th Cir. 1989); *Crowley Cutlery Co. v. United States,* 849 F.2d 273, 276–277 (7th Cir. 1988); *Association of American Physicians & Surgeons v. Sebelius,* 746 F.3d 468, 473 (D.C. Cir. 2014); *ACS Recovery Services, Inc. v. Griffin,* 723 F.3d 518, 523 (5th Cir. 2013); *In re Stock Exchanges Options Trading Antitrust Litigation,* 317 F.3d 134, 150 (2d Cir. 2003).

17. *Carr v. Tillery,* 591 F.3d 909, 917 (7th Cir. 2010).

18. *Steel Co. v. Citizens for a Better Environment,* 523 U.S. 83, 89 (1998); *LaSalle National Trust, N.A. v. ECM Motor Co.,* 76 F.3d 140, 143–144 (7th Cir. 1996); *Holloway v. Pagan River Dockside Seafood, Inc.,* 669 F.3d 448, 452 (4th Cir. 2012); *Blue Cross & Blue Shield of Alabama v. Sanders,* 138 F.3d 1347, 1353–1354 (11th Cir. 1998).

17 pointed to a "presumption . . . that the dismissal of even a very weak case should be on the merits rather than because it was too weak even to engage federal jurisdiction. (Hence our use [in that case] of the term 'utterly frivolous.') Otherwise courts would spend too much time distinguishing degrees of weakness. And there is a certain perversity in a jurisdictional dismissal; it permits the plaintiff to refile his case, albeit (as we noted) not on the ground on which the dismissal was based."[19]

But the insertion of the adverb—"utterly" before "frivolous"—in the passage just quoted was unfortunate. It suggested that maybe if the plaintiff's claim, though frivolous, was not utterly so, the case could be decided on the merits. Later my court questioned the wisdom of "distinguishing so finely among degrees of substantive weakness"—how indeed would one distinguish "frivolous" from "utterly frivolous"?[20] Worse, the courts have not been content with just one variant of "frivolous." They have taken to substituting "insubstantial" for "frivolous" and then to distinguishing among degrees of "insubstantiality"; so we are treated to imagined distinctions between "insubstantial" and "wholly insubstantial," between "so utterly frivolous" and "so insubstantial," between "plainly insubstantial" and "not substantial enough" versus "sufficiently substantial," and also between "essentially fictitious and "obviously without merit" and between "frivolous" and "insubstantial" (though they seem to be used as synonyms).[21]

This explosion of redundant verbiage can be traced back to *Bell v.*

19. 591 F.3d at 917 (citations omitted).

20. *McCoy v. Iberdrola Renewables, Inc.*, 769 F.3d 535, 537 (7th Cir. 2014).

21. *Bovee v. Broom*, 732 F.3d 743, 744 (7th Cir. 2013); *Ricketts v. Midwest National Bank*, above, note 16, 874 F.2d at 1180, 1182, 1185; *Crowley Cutlery Co. v. United States*, above, note 16, 849 F.2d at 278; *Association of American Physicians & Surgeons v. Sebelius, supra; Arena v. Graybar Electric Co.*, 669 F.3d 214, 222 (5th Cir. 2012); *Karnak Educational Trust v. Bowen*, 821 F.2d 1517, 1520 (11th Cir. 1987).

Hood,[22] and perhaps farther (but I haven't tried), and was enlarged and emphatically endorsed in *Hagans v. Lavine*[23] as having "cogent legal significance." The Court took the opportunity to add to the list of synonyms for "frivolous" the following terms: "obviously frivolous," "so attenuated and unsubstantial as to be absolutely devoid of merit," "no longer open to discussion," and the federal "question may be plainly unsubstantial, either because it is 'obviously without merit' or because 'its unsoundness so clearly results from the previous decisions of this court as to foreclose the subject and leave no room for the inference that the question sought to be raised can be the subject of controversy,'" or the question may be "essentially fictitious" or "prior decisions inescapably render the claims frivolous," and so on.[24] The lower courts, eager echoers, have joined the bandwagon.[25]

The bare word "frivolous" should be enough to denote a complaint that on its face does not invoke federal jurisdiction. "Utterly frivolous" is redundant. As for "wholly insubstantial," "too insubstantial," "not substantial enough," and all the rest, these are confusing substitutes for "frivolous" that imply misleadingly that a merely "insubstantial" (as opposed to "too insubstantial" or "not substantial enough" or "wholly insubstantial") claim might suffice to invoke federal jurisdiction—in other words that there is a sliding scale of substantiality at some point on which a claim is actionable. No one has explained how

---

22. 327 U.S. 678, 682–683 (1946).

23. 415 U.S. 528, 537 (1974).

24. Id. at 536–537.

25. See *Morrison v. YTB International, Inc.*, 649 F.3d 533, 536 (7th Cir. 2011); *Gammon v. GC Services Ltd.*, 27 F.3d 1254, 1256 (7th Cir. 1994); *Davis v. U.S. Sentencing Commission*, 716 F.3d 660, 666–667 (D.C. Cir. 2013); *Harris v. Blue Cross/Blue Shield of Alabama, Inc.*, 951 F.2d 325, 327 (11th Cir. 1992); *Molina-Crespo v. Califano*, 583 F.2d 572, 573–574 (1st Cir. 1978).

that point is to be determined. It remains indeterminate, a source of needless uncertainty.

So here is a further illustration of the inveterate tendency of lawyers and judges to multiply the verbal formulas used to express legal doctrines. The tendency should be resisted. Law is complicated enough without fuzzy standards and needless redundancy. That is a major theme of this book.

And mightn't it be better to chuck "frivolous" from the legal lexicon—a word that in modern American English means "skittish," "flighty," "giddy," "silly," "foolish," "superficial," "shallow," "irresponsible," "thoughtless," "featherbrained," "empty-headed," "pea-brained," "birdbrained," "vacuous," and "vapid," and say rather that a complaint that fails to invoke federal jurisdiction is to be dismissed for want of jurisdiction, while a complaint that invokes federal jurisdiction but pleads itself out of court (for example by making a claim expressly rejected in a Supreme Court decision) should be dismissed by the district court on the merits without awaiting a pleading from the defendant? (One might call such a decision "groundless," and the other kind "nonjusticiable.") Isn't it high time, therefore, that the Supreme Court reexamined its forty-one-year-old decision in *Hagans*?[26]

So I would like in closing to propose, as an academic contribution to reforming judicial reasoning, a third-year legal course picking apart *King, Obergefell, Kimble,* and *Hagans.*

I have been, to recur to the epigraph at the beginning of this epilogue, a busy cat looking (critically) at a bunch of kings. That is a risky stance

---

26. Some further work would be needed, however, because the word "frivolous" sometimes appears in federal statutes as a synonym for what I am calling "groundless," rather than as a directive to refuse to assume federal jurisdiction. See, for example, 27 U.S.C. § 6702; 42 U.S.C. § 1915.

but I take refuge in the following statement by a distinguished English literary critic: "The only way to escape misrepresentation is never to commit oneself to any critical judgment that makes an impact—that is, never to *say* anything. I still, however think that the best way to promote profitable discussion is to be as clear as possible with oneself about what one sees and judges, to try and establish the essential discriminations in the given field of interest, and to state them as clearly as one can (for disagreement, if necessary)."[27]

27. F. R. Leavis, *The Great Tradition: George Eliot, Henry James, Joseph Conrad* 1 (1962) (emphasis in original).

INDEX